Street's Cruising Guide to the Eastern Caribbean

Martinique to Trinidad

In the beginning was the word and the word came from Street. In the first of his **nine** guides to the Eastern Caribbean Don Street chartered the rocks and shoals, sent cruisers to the local bakeries, introduced them to the islands characters and thereby helped to make the world of bareboat chartering possible. Since 1964 all other guide authors have followed in Street's and Iolaire's wake, avoiding the rocks and shoals Street and Iolaire discovered.
Patience Wales—Editor, Sail magazine.

If you want a quiet anchorage buy the other guides, circle in red in Street's Guides the anchorages not described in the other guides. Visit them, and if you do not have a deserted anchorage, you will at least have a quiet one.
Dick Johnson, Former Editor Yachting World.

Experience counts, and no Caribbean cruising guide author has more than Don Street. Don arrived in the Caribbean in 1956, wrote his first guide in 1964, and both Don and his guides are still going strong!
Sally Erdle, Editor, Caribbean Compass

Don Street deserves his reputation as the "best God-damned rock pilot" in the Caribbean. If Don says there's a rock there—there is a rock there. (And he probably found it the hard way!)
**Captain Fatty Goodlander, Author: Chasing the Horizon
And other books about the Caribbean sea gypsy lifestyle.**

Books by Donald M. Street, Jr.

A Cruising Guide to the Lesser Antilles
A Yachting Guide to the Grenadines
The Ocean Sailing Yacht, Volume I
The Ocean Sailing Yacht, Volume II
Seawise

Street's Cruising Guides to the Eastern Caribbean:

Transatlantic Crossing Guide

Puerto Rico, Spanish, U.S. and
British Virgin Islands

Anguilla to Dominica
Including Anguilla, St. Martin, St. Barthélemy, Saba,
Sint Eustatius (Statia), St. Kitts, and Nevis,
Antigua, Barbuda, Montserrat, Redonda,
Guadeloupe, and Dominica

Martinique to Trinidad
Including Martinique, St. Lucia, St. Vincent, Barbadoes,
Northern Grenadines, Southern Grenadines, Grenada,
and Trinidad and Tobago

Venezuela
Including Isla Margarita and Adjacent Islands, Los Testigos,
La Blanquilla, La Tortuga, La Orchila, Los Roques, Las Aves,
Aruba, Bonaire, and Curaçao

Street's Cruising Guide to the Eastern Caribbean

Martinique to Trinidad

Donald M. Street Jr.

Sketch charts by Morgan B. MacDonald III
and Alan Wilkenson of Imray, Laurie, Norie & Wilson Ltd.

AN AUTHORS GUILD BACKINPRINT.COM EDITION

Martinique to Trinidad
*Including Martinique, St. Lucia, St. Vincent, Barbados, Northern Grenadines,
Southern Grenadines, Grenada, and Trinidad & Tobago*
All Rights Reserved © 1974, 2001 by Donald M. Street, Jr.

No part of this book may be reproduced or transmitted in any form
or by any means, graphic, electronic, or mechanical, including photocopying,
recording, taping, or by any information storage or retrieval system,
without the permission in writing from the publisher.

AN AUTHORS GUILD BACKINPRINT.COM EDITION
Published by iUniverse.com, Inc.

For information address:
iUniverse.com, Inc.
5220 S 16th, Ste. 200
Lincoln, NE 68512
www.iuniverse.com

Originally published by W.W. Norton & Company

ISBN: 0-595-17356-X

Printed in the United States of America

Dedication

The idea for this cruising guide was conceived in 1963, and it was only through the hard work, perseverance, courage, and self-sacrifice of my late wife, Marilyn, that the original book got off the ground.

Fortunately for myself and my daughter, Dory, I met Patricia Boucher, now my wife, on the beach in Tyrell Bay. She has presented me with three active sons yet has had time to help in business, sailing *Iolaire*, and exploring. Although she had hardly sailed before our marriage, she has taken to sailing like a duck to water. Her love of sailing was largely instrumental in my decision to keep *Iolaire* when I was thinking of selling her to reduce expenses.

It is only because of Trich's hard work keeping our various enterprises going in my absence that I have been able to keep the third love of my life, *Iolaire*.

Iolaire has been my mistress for thirty-three years; at age eighty-five, she is still the type of boat Michel Dufour would appreciate: She is "fast, beautiful, and responsive." She first arrived in the islands in 1947, remained for a few years, and cruised back to Europe in 1949, directly from Jamaica to England. In 1950, under the ownership of R.H. Somerset, she won her division's RORC Season's Points Championship at the age of forty-five, returned to the islands in 1951, cruised there during the winter of 1951-52, sailed in the Bermuda Race in 1952, then cruised back to Europe and the Mediterranean. In 1954, she returned to the islands, where I purchased her in 1957.

In 1975, we celebrated *Iolaire*'s seventieth birthday by cruising to Europe via Bermuda, New London, New York, Boston, Halifax, and then a fifteen-day passage to Ireland. We cruised on to Cowes, took part in the fiftieth anniversary of the first Fastnet Race, and then raced to La Rochelle, La Trinité, Benodet, and back to the Solent—four races, totaling 1,300 miles, in twenty-one days.

After Calais, we went up the Thames to St. Katherine's Dock in the Pool of London under Tower Bridge, then back down the Thames and up the Colne River in Essex, where we lay alongside the dock in Rowhedge, where *Iolaire* had been built seventy years earlier. Then we went to Plymouth, Glandore (Ireland), Madeira, the Canaries, and back across the Atlantic in eighteen-and-a-half days to Antigua.

We arrived in Antigua seven months and seven days after our departure, having sailed 13,000 miles and raced 1,300 miles—all without an engine—and having visited all the places people had said we would never get to except under power.

We decided that *Iolaire* should celebrate her eightieth birthday in 1985 by retiring from round-the-buoys racing. Her swan song in Antigua Week of 1985 was wonderful—third in the cruising division (seventeen boats), first in the boats twenty years old or older.

Then we took *Iolaire* on a 12,000-mile double-transatlantic jaunt. In seven months, we visited Bermuda, five of the Azores islands, Ireland, Vigo (Spain), the Salvage Islands and the Madeiran archipelago, five of the Canary Islands, and three of the Cape Verde Islands. Then we rolled on home in fourteen days and four hours from the Cape Verdes to Antigua—not a record but a good, fast passage for a heavy-displacement cruising boat.

We spent the winter of 1989-90 exploring Venezuela and crisscrossing the Caribbean, finalizing update information for all volumes of this guide. After that, we sailed from Antigua directly to the Azores, then on to Ireland, down to Vigo, the Canaries, and the Cape Verdes—visiting all the islands we had not visited before in order to eliminate all secondhand information from the *Transatlantic Crossing Guide*. Again we did 12,000 miles in twelve months, without the aid of an engine. We did the Cape Verdes-to-Antigua leg of the trip in fourteen days and twelve hours—with the spinnaker up the last five-and-a-half days. Not bad for an old girl of eighty-five!

In 1990, *Iolaire* came out of retirement to sail in the new Classic Regatta and won her division! She is not ready to race against her younger sisters, but she is still ready, willing, and able to take on the classic boats.

Iolaire has eleven transatlantic passages under her belt. I have sailed her at least 140,000 miles. Who knows how many miles she has sailed during her lifetime? There is little of the Caribbean that has not been furrowed by her hull—and as some of my good friends will point out, there are few rocks that have not been dented by her keel!

To my three loves—Marilyn, Trich, and *Iolaire*— I dedicate this book.

Contents: Martinique to Trinidad

	Dedication	*v*
	Contents of Other Volumes	*ix*
	Foreword	*xi*
	Publisher's Preface	*xviii*
	Preface	*xx*
	Acknowledgments	*xxiii*
	Charts	*xxvi*
	List of Charts and Sketch Charts	*xxix*
	Prologue	*xxxi*
1	*Sailing Directions*	*3*
2	*Martinique*	*19*
3	*St. Lucia*	*49*
4	*St. Vincent*	*66*
5	*Barbados*	*78*
6	*Northern Grenadines*	*87*
7	*Southern Grenadines*	*109*
8	*Grenada*	*140*
9	*Trinidad and Tobago*	*171*
	Bibliography	*193*
	Index	*195*

Contents of the Other Volumes in Street's Cruising Guide to the Eastern Caribbean

Transatlantic Crossing Guide

List of Sketch Charts
Publisher's Note
Preface
Foreword
Acknowledgments
Charts
1 The Eastern Caribbean—
  a General Description
2 Preparations
3 Charts
4 Getting There
5 Wind, Weather, and Tides
6 Sailing Directions
7 Entry and Communications

8 Provisions and Services
9 Chartering
10 Yacht Clubs and Racing
11 Boats of the Eastern Caribbean
12 Leaving
Appendices
  Principal Navigational Aids
  Principal Radio Aids
  Principal Commercial
    Radio Stations
  Principal Holidays
  Chart Number Conversion Table
Bibliography
Index

Puerto Rico, The Passage Islands, The U.S. and British Virgin Islands

List of Sketch Charts
Publisher's Note
Preface
Foreword
Acknowledgments
Charts
U.S. Chart Number Conversion Table

1 Sailing Directions
2 Puerto Rico
3 Passage Islands
4 U.S. Virgin Islands
5 British Virgin Islands
  Bibliography
  Index

Anguilla to Dominica

List of Sketch Charts
Publisher's Note
Preface
Foreword
Acknowledgments
Charts
U.S. Chart Number Conversion
  Table
1 Anguilla

2 St. Martin
3 St. Barthélemy
4 Saba, Sint Eustatius (Statia),
    St. Kitts, and Nevis
5 Antigua and Barbuda
6 Montserrat and Redonda
7 Guadeloupe
8 Dominica

Venezuela

Dedication
Publisher's Preface
Foreword
Acknowledgments
Charts
List of Sketch Charts
Introduction to Venezuela
1 Sailing Directions
2 The Golfo de Paria
3 North Side: The Peninsula
    de Paria to Ensa Esmeralda
4 Isla Margarita and Adjacent
    Islands
5 The Peninsula de Araya and
    the Golfo de Cariaco

6 Cumaná to El Morro
    de Barcelona
7 Carenero to Puerto Tucacas
8 Puerto Tucacas and Chichiriviche
    Westward
9 Eastern Offshore Islands:
    Los Testigos, La Blanquilla,
    La Tortuga, La Orchila
10 Western Offshore Islands: Los Roques,
    Las Aves
11 Aruba, Bonaire, Curaçao
    Bibliography
    Index

Foreword

The Lesser Antilles stretch southward from St. Thomas to Grenada in a great crescent 500 miles long, offering the yachtsman a cruising ground of unequaled variety. Some of the islands are flat, dry, and windswept, their shores girded by coral reefs and their land barely arable. Others are reefless, jagged peaks jutting abruptly up from the sea, where they block the ever-present trades and gather rain clouds the year round; water cascades in gullies down their sides, and their slopes are well cultivated. The character of their peoples likewise varies —from the charming and unspoiled but desperately poor Dominicans to the comparatively well-to-do and worldly wise Frenchmen of Martinique.

Unless you have a whole season at your disposal, it is foolhardy to attempt all the islands in a single cruise. Not only will you not make it, but you will fail to enjoy the slow, natural, and relaxed pace of life in these tropical islands. The first measure of a successful cruise is how soon your carefully worked out timetable gets thrown away.

Rule number 1 in the Antilles is: Don't make any plan more than a day in advance, since you will frequently—in fact constantly—alter your intentions to suit the pace and attractions of the locale.

Rule number 2: Each night before turning in, read the sailing directions covering your passage to the next area, and study the detailed description of your intended anchorage. In some cases, this will seriously affect the next day's plans—particularly the hour of departure. Remember, for instance, that when you are on the east coast of Martinique, Guadeloupe, Antigua, and Grenada, you must be in the anchorage by 1400 hours. Otherwise the sun is in the west, directly in your line of vision, making it impossible to see any reefs until it is too late.

Rule number 3: Do not enter a strange harbor at night if at all possible.

Rule number 4: No chart can be absolutely accurate. In the Caribbean, knowing how to read the water is as important as knowing how to read a chart. Eyeball navigation is the key to safe and satisfying sailing in the islands.

Whether or not Puerto Rico to the north or Trinidad and Tobago to the south should be considered part of the Lesser Antilles is a question for the gazetteers to squabble over. For the purposes of this guide, we welcome all three into the fellowship of proximity. (And, of course, the guide also covers Venezuela and the Atlantic islands.) Taken as such, the Antilles conveniently break up into a number of areas suitable for two- or three-week cruises. The starting and end points of a cruise will be governed by your own tastes and the availability of air transportation. The air services into San Juan and Trinidad are excellent, for example, but neither of these places is a particularly good spot to begin a cruise. San Juan is dead to leeward of the rest of the chain—and who wants to start out with a hard slog into the wind against a strong current? Trinidad is not much better, unless you are going to Venezuela.

To get to most of these places, you must often rely on secondary local airlines with shuttle services. These vary from being fairly good from San Juan to St. Thomas and Tortola and the Venezuelan airlines, to downright disastrous with LIAT. LIAT's aircraft, pilots, and maintenance personnel are first rate, but the office staff has elevated the art of losing baggage and double-booking reservations to an exact science. There are various jokes about what LIAT actually stands for—some people claim it is an abbreviation for "Leave Islands Any Time," while others insist that it means "Luggage In Another Terminal." Still, it's all part of the adventure of a Caribbean cruise.

Which starting point you choose will say something of your tastes in cruising. If you prefer gunkholing and short jaunts between many little islands only a few miles apart, if you like snorkeling and little in the way of civilization, then it's the Virgins or the Grenadines for you. But you'd best hurry down, because real-estate developers and other sailors are fast making this situation a thing of the past. Mustique, for one example, was until recently

Foreword

a private estate in the hands of the Hazel family. But it was sold to a developer, who has worked it over at a pretty fast rate. Well-to-do Europeans have bought land and built houses, creating many new jobs for local labor but depriving the yachtsman of a wonderful hideaway.

For those of you who want to give boat and crew a good tuning-up for offshore racing, set out from St. Thomas up through the Virgins, then work your way across Anegada Passage to St. Martin or Anguilla, and finish with a final leg up to Antigua. In doing so, you will gain a fair sampling of island diversity and of French, Dutch, and English colonial temperaments. The Anegada Passage is a nice, hard drive to windward, which should uncover any weak points in rig or crew.

Those interested exclusively in the pursuits of diving, treasure hunting, or snorkeling should steer for the low-lying islands of Anguilla, Barbuda, Anegada, Los Roques, and Las Aves. The reefs in these areas are vast and inexhaustible. Fortune hunters still flock to these islands, where innumerable off-lying wrecks date back hundreds of years, some presumably undiscovered. Consult the source books— but remember that these islands are low, flat, encircled by reefs, and hard to spot. The charts are based on surveys done mainly in the middle of the nineteenth century. Coral grows, and hurricanes have moved through the area a number of times; earthquakes have shaken the islands, and sand bars have moved. In short, you must be extremely careful. Do not let your boat become the next curiosity for inquisitive divers!

Saba and Statia (Sint Eustatius) are two attractive islands that are too seldom visited. Their anchorages are exceptionally bad, but when the conditions are right, they certainly are worth a go. Their close neighbors, St. Kitts and Nevis, are of historical interest, figuring as they do in the lives of Alexander Hamilton, Admirals Nelson and Rodney, and Generals Shirley and Frazer. St. Kitts is well worth a visit to see the beautiful restoration of the old fortress of Brimstone Hill. A number of the old plantation great houses have been restored and opened up as hotels and restaurants. Renting a car to tour St. Kitts is a good scheme.

If you like longer sails, the bright lights of civilization, and a variety of languages and customs, the middle islands—from Antigua to St. Lucia—should keep you happy. The French islands of Guadeloupe and Martinique afford the finest cuisine in the Antilles. The local merchants offer an excellent selection of cheeses and meats from Europe and the best wines available outside France. The tourist shops are a woman's delight, and the perfumes are at about half the price in the States. Up until a few years ago, bikinis were so inexpensive (two for $US5.00) that the women bought them by the dozen. Regrettably, those days are gone—probably forever. There is still a fabulous collection of bikinis in Martinique, but the prices have gone up so much in France that the savings for an American no longer are substantial. Rough rule of thumb: The smaller the bikini, the more expensive it is. The string has arrived: its size—minuscule; its price— astronomical. One solution frequently used by the always economical French women was to buy only half the string at half the price. Others felt that even that was too expensive and sailed *au naturel*—not really showing off, just economizing!

The universal pastime of watching members of the opposite sex is alive and well in Martinique, and the visiting seafarer soon gets into the spirit of things. This pastime can be enjoyed in many ways, but the two most popular methods are strolling around the streets of Fort de France and rowing around in Anse Mitan (which today is likely to have 40 or 50 boats in it) and pretending to admire the boats while admiring the crews. An added bonus here is that at Anse Mitan, going topless seems to be *de rigeur*.

The women in Fort de France may not be the prettiest in the Caribbean, but they are far and away the most stylish. And the men, sitting at sidewalk cafés sipping their coffee or *punch vieux*, cut figures worthy of the boulevardiers of Paris. Newcomers, however, should take note: The punch will make a strong man weak-kneed and the coffee tastes not unlike battery acid.

The French and their chicory-laced coffee have distressed visiting foreigners for a great many decades. A story is told of Count von Bismarck touring France after the Franco-Prussian War. At the close of a fine meal in a country inn, he called for the maître d'hôtel and offered to buy all his chicory at 10 percent over the market price; the maître d' agreed and sold him what he claimed was all he had. Again the count offered to buy any remaining chicory, this time at 50 percent over the market price; the maître d' managed to produce a second quantity of the plant. For a third time, the count offered to buy any that remained—at *double* the market price—and the maître d' surrendered an additional small amount, insisting that this was indeed all that remained. Satisfied at last, the count concluded, "Very well, now you may prepare me a cup of coffee!"

H.M.S. Diamond Rock, off the south coast of

Foreword

Martinique, is the basis for many stories in folklore, most of them inaccurate. The story of Diamond Rock (now called Rocher du Diamant) is contained in *Her Majesty's Sloop of War Diamond Rock,* by Stuart and Eggleston.

Dominica is for the adventurous. A ride into the mountains by Jeep and horseback will take you to the last settlement of the Carib peoples. Here the natives fashion the distinctive Carib canoes that are also seen in Guadeloupe, Martinique, and St. Lucia. With nothing but a flour sack for a sail and a paddle for a rudder, the islanders set out in these boats against the wind to fish in the open Atlantic. Not an easy way to earn a living.

St. Lucia provides some superb anchorages at Pigeon Island, Marigot, and Vieux Fort, and the truly unbelievable one beneath the Pitons at Soufrière. The volcano and sulfur baths are an impressive spectacle, and it is well worth the expense to explore the island by car or Jeep, an adventure vividly recounted by George Eggleston in *Orchids on the Calabash Tree.*

St. Vincent, at the northern end of the Grenadines, is a high, lush island richly and diversely cultivated. The island has an intriguing history, highlighted by the almost continual warfare among French, English, and Caribs that lasted from 1762 until 1796, when the Caribs were expelled to Central America.

Bequia is the home of fishermen and whalers, an island where any sailor can explore, relax, and "gam" for days on end. The harbor is beautiful and life is relaxed.

After cruising the entire Caribbean and getting to know all the islands intimately, many experienced yachtsmen declare Grenada to be "the loveliest of the islands." The highlands produce enough rain to allow the farmers to grow a large quantity of fresh fruit and vegetables, but the south coast is dry enough to allow the yachtsman to live and work on his boat. The island also has a dozen different harbors, providing 60 separate anchorages. Most of these harbors are only short, one- or two-hour sails from each other.

The town of St. Georges is picturesque; the main anchorage, in the lagoon, is only a short dinghy ride from supermarkets, cable and telephone offices, banks, and other services. The island has yacht yards and a yacht club, providing slipways, a good stock of marine supplies, and—most important—a large stock of friendly people. In short, after some years of a topsy-turvy political situation, the island should, in years to come, reassert itself as the capital of Eastern Caribbean yachting.

Barbados is relatively remote and seldom visited by yachts, except those that are coming downwind from Europe. If your plane stops there en route to another island, arrange for a layover of a day or two. It is undoubtedly the best-run island in the entire Caribbean and everything is clean and neat (by West Indian standards). The people are charming, speak with the most wonderful accent, and are solicitous and helpful to visitors. The old Careenage in Bridgetown should not be missed.

It is a shame that Tobago is seldom visited by yachtsmen. It is dead to windward of Trinidad, and from Grenada it is 90 miles hard on port tack. Even if you manage to lay the rhumb line from Grenada, it will be a long slog, hard on the wind. Current and sea will drive you off to the west. It is fairly inaccessible except from Barbados, from where it is an easy reach southwestward.

The American and British Virgin Islands have been described laboriously in the various tourist guides, but whatever the evaluation of shoreside life, a sailor can pass a very pleasant month cruising in this area.

The character of the various island peoples is apt to vary broadly within a very small area. Even among the former British islands, each has its own peculiar flavor, its own outlook and accent. (In fact, natives are known to complain that they can't understand the English spoken on neighboring islands.) For the most part, the people are quiet and law-abiding. Actually, the sort of racially inspired violence that periodically has troubled St. Croix and St. Thomas has been far less of a problem in the islands farther south.

As the years go by, the Eastern Caribbean becomes more crowded; hence, yachtsmen are beginning to head west to Venezuela. In the 1950s and 1960s, cruising in Venezuela was looked on as a hazardous pursuit—not because of unfriendliness to yachtsmen but rather because Fidel Castro was smuggling guerrillas ashore in small fishing boats. The Guardia Nacional and the Navy frequently were guilty of shooting first and asking questions later, with the result that a number of yachts were ventilated by Venezuelan government agencies. All that is now a thing of the past. Although you may have to fill out a lot of documents, everyone is extremely friendly, and, to the best of my knowledge, there have been no nasty incidents involving yachts in Venezuela for many years.

Venezuela is a land of contrasts. The coast, with its mountains that rise directly from the sea to 9,000 feet, in some parts is dry and desolate like a desert; other sections, like the eastern end of the Peninsula de Paria, are covered with dense jungle. The easternmost tip of the peninsula rises 5,000 feet, with vertical slopes spilling into the Caribbean on one side and into the Golfo de Paria on the other. From the Golfo de Paria, one can visit Angel Falls and the Orinoco Delta, take excursions into the jungle, and see unbelievable wildlife right from the boat. This area is the original primeval jungle, occasionally visited by powerboats but seldom by sailing yachts. The windswept offshore islands provide some of the finest fishing, snorkeling, and diving in the Eastern Caribbean. They have not been fished out and they are generally uninhabited.

The north coast of Venezuela, as one progresses westward, begins with heavy jungle that tapers out to brush and ends up finally in Laguna Grande del Obispo. In the Golfo de Cariaco, one finds a fantastic harbor—the scenery ashore is like a lunar landscape, and it looks as though it hasn't rained here in 20 years!

Continuing westward, the mountains of Venezuela are always close to the coastline and always barren. The cities are exploding rather than simply growing. Side by side are sophisticated new marinas and tiny fishing villages. Offshore are low, deserted reef and uninhabited islands. After Puerto Cabello, you can pretty much forget the rest of the Venezuelan coast.

Los Roques, a 355-square-mile cruising area off the north coast, is almost as large as the American and British Virgin Islands, and at least 50 percent of it is unsurveyed. Venezuelan yachtsmen and a few Americans (such as Gordon Stout) have crisscrossed this wonderful place and spent as long as a week cruising here. This area would be ideal for a bareboat organization, and perhaps one will expand into this area. It will be interesting to see what develops here in years to come.

Yachting has taken hold in Venezuela, and modern marinas now can be found at Caracas (five, in fact), Cumaná, Puerto La Cruz (three), Puerto Cabello, and in Morrocoy National Park. Furthermore, there are hauling facilities in all of these harbors. In addition, at Centro Marina de Oriente, in Puerto La Cruz, you will find a brand-new yacht yard, repair facility, and marina—specifically built to cater to the needs of cruising yachtsmen.

Because of the devaluation of the bolívar, most things in Venezuela are inexpensive. Hauling and repair costs, for example, are considerably less than in the Eastern Caribbean, so more and more yachtsmen now are sailing to Venezuela for repairs and refits. This is especially true in summer, when boats head there for refitting and at the same time escape

from the hurricane belt. Everyone remembers the devastation caused by Hurricane Hugo in 1989, and one way to avoid being "Hugoized" is to head for Venezuela. (See "Reflections on Hugo," below.)

Once you get away from the major population areas, you will seldom have more than one or two other yachts in your anchorage—and the only time you are likely to find many boats in the anchorages is on the weekends.

One cruising technique used by yachtsmen in Venezuela is to arrive at a marina on Friday night as the Venezuelans are all departing and berths become available. Stay for the weekend, enjoy sightseeing, etc., on Saturday, go out on the town Saturday night, sleep late Sunday morning, and depart Sunday afternoon prior to the arrival of the returning Venezuelan yachts.

Unfortunately, the great welcome that the Venezuelan private clubs used to give visiting yachtsmen has cooled. As more and more sailors go to Venezuela, the behavior of some has been such that the door has been slammed shut against the rest of us in most private Venezuelan clubs. If you know a Venezuelan yachtsman, write to him ahead of time and he probably can get the door opened specifically for you.

Close to Venezuela are the ABC islands of Aruba, Bonaire, and Curaçao. Low and wind swept, they vary from the quiet, simple, and slow-moving Bonaire to the hustling, bustling, and very cosmopolitan Curaçao.

Fighting your way eastward along the north coast of South America is rough—especially once you pass Cabo de la Vela. By the time you reach the Golfo de Maracaibo, you are dead exhausted and would love to stop. It used to be a matter of pushing on to reach Aruba, but a few years ago I discovered (via the Venezuelan Hydrographic Office) that there is a small naval base at Los Monjes with a passable anchorage between the islands. Here you can stop, rest for a day or so, and then fight your way to Aruba.

In years gone by, Aruba was basically a low, flat island covered with oil refineries, but now the refineries have been dismantled, tourism has taken hold, and the island is covered with hotels. A new marina in Oranjestad offers all the amenities a yachtsman could want.

Bonaire is low, flat, and sparsely populated. Its shores rise so steeply from the sea bottom that it is almost impossible to anchor in its lee. But the anchorage problem has been solved with a new marina. Adequate supplies—fresh, frozen, and canned —are available. The people are very friendly and

Foreword

Bonaire has some of the best diving in the world—with excellent support facilities right at hand.

If you want to connect up with the outside world from the ABC islands, go to Curaçao, which has excellent air communications and first-class hotels. Curaçao also has superb harbors and all kinds of supplies.

I hope that with the aid of these books, you will enjoy the Caribbean islands and the Venezuelan coast as much as I have for more than three decades. Anyone contemplating a cruise is well advised to read the supplementary chapters, found in *Street's Transatlantic Crossing Guide,* which contain the general information not contained in the individual volumes on the island groups. Preparations, Charts, Getting Communications, Provisions and Services, Chartering, and Yacht Clubs are all covered. The *Crossing Guide* is the essential companion to any of the guides you have on board and will provide much background information. Not only will it explain why perhaps your charter skipper looks tired (he probably spent the last two days fixing his generator under sail while he was deadheading to pick you up), but they will also offer a better idea of what you can expect upon arrival in the islands. A host of important tips and facts that are not included in the average tourist or charter-boat broker's brochure will, I trust, be found in this book. And, needless to say, if you are planning to bring your own boat to the islands, you should read the whole book carefully with pencil in hand to make notes on what is applicable.

One caution in particular: In May, June, and July, the Caribbean is usually 12 to 18 inches lower than it is in the winter. Thus, at the time of a low-water spring tide in those months, the water is a full three feet lower than it is at a high-water spring tide in the winter. Although the soundings on the Imray-Iolaire charts are based on the lowest-level datum, not all charts or local knowledge take the difference into account. If you have any doubt about your situation, take soundings before you venture into questionable waters.

Probably the most important chapter in this book is chapter 1—Sailing Directions—and you should read and study it. Consult it regularly before finalizing the day's plans. While the navigational features and anchorages of the individual islands are described in the chapter concerned with that island, the routes *between* the islands are detailed in chapter 1.

Remember: Always be alert and cautious. Almost every place in the Eastern Caribbean where a yacht can anchor has been described or at least mentioned in the Street guides, but not all are easy to enter. Many of these anchorages can be used only in good weather and perfect visibility. Besides, some boats are handier than others and some sailors are more skilled than others. Thus, you must evaluate each anchorage for yourself before entering. The time of day, the weather, your abilities, the weatherliness of your boat—all influence the final decision.

Some advice to readers who operate bareboat charter fleets: Study this book carefully, make your judgments, and mark on the charts in the book the anchorages you want your charterers to avoid.

Finally, before you sail anywhere in the Eastern Caribbean (and particularly if you are going during hurricane season), I advise you to read and take to heart the advice that appears below.

Reflections on Hugo

The Eastern Caribbean is basically overpopulated with boats. All of the hurricane holes are so overcrowded that all you need for disaster is one or two boats that are anchored improperly and start dragging. (Of course, I well remember being told in prep school that all general statements are suspect, and even the statement—"all general statements are suspect"—is suspect!) Undoubtedly, there are a few hurricane holes that are not overcrowded or that people do not know about. Witness Ensenada Honda Vieques off Puerto Rico. To the best of my knowledge, almost no boats went to Vieques in 1989 during Hurricane Hugo; like lemmings, they all poured into Ensenada Honda Culebra—whereas Ensenada Honda Vieques, which is a better hurricane hole, had relatively few boats tucked up into the mangroves.

Further, throughout the Caribbean, anywhere there are bareboat fleets, the hurricane season creates what the local yachtsmen refer to as "bareboat bombs"—so called because the bareboat operations do not have enough labor to put a crew on every boat to ride out the hurricane, tend lines, or shift anchors, and the vessels become potential lethal weapons! Few bareboats are equipped with more than two anchors, and those may be sufficient for a 30-to-40-knot blow, but nothing more. Once one of the "bareboat bombs" starts dragging down on you, you have a problem. You may be lucky, and he will just bounce off you and do no damage, but it could be a disastrous situation: The bareboat hooks your *xvi*   *Foreword*

anchor, pulls you loose, and you both end up on the beach, high and dry.

One of the tragedies of this sort of situation is that the bareboat companies are all insured. The underwriters pay off the damage done to bareboats, but all of the courts consider the hurricane as an "act of God." If you are insured and a "bareboat bomb" drags down on you and your boat is damaged or lost, it is not fine and dandy, but at least it is not a complete disaster, as your insurance company will cover your loss. If, however, you are NOT insured, your chances are minimal of finding an admiralty lawyer who will entertain a case against a boat dragging down on you in a hurricane. Even if you find one, you will need to put up $US5,000 or $6,000 before he will even consider taking the case. This is just another good reason why cruising yachts should be insured. Insurance is particularly essential for cruising yachtsmen who have retired and are living aboard, with everything wrapped up in their boat. (See *Street's Transatlantic Crossing Guide and Introduction to the Caribbean* for information on insurance.)

In light of the damage done by Hugo, what is the solution to the hurricane problem? Go to sea! This sounds very drastic—going to sea in the face of a hurricane—and it is if you do it at the last minute. But it is a viable option if you do it 48 to 72 hours before the expected arrival of the hurricane.

The situation with hurricanes has changed radically over the years. Until the early 1950s, the hurricane warning system in the Caribbean was very poor. Hurricanes originated out in the Atlantic, and unless they were spotted by a passing ship that sent in a report, the Eastern Caribbean did not realize a hurricane was en route until the barometers started falling. And then the barometers usually dropped so fast that the bottom fell out, and there was little time—perhaps 18 to 24 hours—to prepare. Seamen could only hunker down in the nearest hurricane hole, lash everything down, and hope for the best.

In the early 1950s, however, the old B-36s were converted to weather planes and became hurricane hunters. For more than a decade, they spotted most of the hurricanes, tracked them, and provided fairly good warnings. But they did not find them all. Once, when one popped up just east of St. Barthélemy, the St. Barts people called St. Thomas to tell them a hurricane was on the way. St. Thomas said they had received no warning, and how did St. Barts know it was a hurricane? St. Barts replied, "Because our radio tower is about to blow down," and then they went off the air. Recognizing the danger, St. Thomas went into action and the warnings went out. The St. Thomas charter fleet (which, luckily, was quite small in those days) tried to get out and head to Hurricane Hole in St. John—a dead beat to windward. A few of them made it, but most of them were blown back into the harbor in St. Thomas, where they rode out the hurricane.

Each year, the hurricane tracking system has improved, and now, with sophisticated satellites, it's well nigh perfect. Normally, there is plenty of warning; it is only the freak hurricane, such as Klaus in late 1984, that catches the islands unaware. Klaus popped up just south of Puerto Rico, went northeast, and was very late in the year. Klaus was one of only three hurricanes in 100 years that tracked northeast below 22°N! Today, there is at least a three- or four-day warning of an approaching hurricane. The US government publication *Tropical Cyclones of the North Atlantic Ocean* (US Department of Commerce—NOAA—1871 to 1980, with an update to 1990) shows the tracks of all the known hurricanes in the last 120 years. You'll notice that, with very few exceptions, hurricanes follow a definite and predictable pattern as they approach the islands of the Eastern Caribbean. Admittedly, once they reach Puerto Rico, Haiti, and the Dominican Republic, they can execute a 180-degree turn, or a 360-degree one, or a right angle, or anything in between. They are not predictable once they pass through the islands. Thus, many experienced seamen have concluded that if you have a decent boat of 40 feet or more, well equipped, with an engine so you can power, and if there are light airs in front of the hurricane, the thing to do is pull up the anchor and go to sea. (In any case, if you don't have a boat that can handle 40 knots of wind, you should not be out sailing.)

The boats in English Harbour, Antigua, survived Hugo with relatively little damage, but many seamen figure they were just lucky. If the hurricane had followed a route 30 or 40 miles farther north, English Harbour would have been a disaster area, because even though it is a beautifully sheltered harbor, there were plenty of untended, poorly moored boats that could have become absolute bombs and destroyed the other yachts.

Three days before Hugo passed south of Antigua, it was easily predictable that the hurricane would hit Guadeloupe or Antigua or pass close to the north of Antigua. Thus, any boat in Antigua could have hoisted anchor and headed due south 48 hours before the storm was supposed to hit. They could easily have been 300 miles to the south, down near Grenada, by the time the storm arrived in Antigua,

Foreword

xvii

and they would have experienced nothing more than 30 knots of wind.

Similarly, the United States and British Virgin Islands, Puerto Rico, and the Passage Islands had plenty of warning. It was obvious that the hurricane was going to pass south of or through the Virgins, and the boats could have hauled anchor and headed due north (or, possibly better, north east), thus being 300 miles from the brunt of the storm.

Having seen the havoc caused in harbors by "bareboat bombs" and other poorly moored boats dragging through the fleet, I think that if *Iolaire* and I are ever in the path of a hurricane, we will got to sea rather than look for a hurricane hole.

Another solution to the hurricane problem is to sail south to Grenada and spend the hurricane season doing your repairs and refitting there. Grenada has only been hit three times by hurricanes, and even though many of them have passed fairly close to the north, the hurricane holes in the south coast are so sheltered (until yachting increases even more and produces the same kind of crowded conditions that exist in the Virgin Islands) that you would be safe in any of the hurricane holes there. If it appears that a hurricane is going to pass too close to Grenada, you can always pick up anchor and head a hundred miles south to Trinidad, thus avoiding even the edges of the storm.

To be absolutely safe, of course, go to Venezuela, which is out of the hurricane area. Just north of Venezuela, a few lows have developed, blowing 40 to 50 knots, that later turned into hurricanes when they reached the Western Caribbean, but, to the best of my knowledge, Venezuela has never had a bad hurricane and has only suffered heavy rain and massive ground swells from storms passing through the region.

But what about boats stored ashore? Yacht yards that have onshore storage facilities in the Eastern Caribbean are doing very well. People are storing boats on shore for a number of reasons: to avoid having their boat stolen by someone who wants to make a quick drug run and then pull the plug; to al- low the bottom to dry out, thus minimising the chance of osmosis. Finally, some boats are stored ashore in the misconception that a boat is safer there in a hurricane. This is a very erroneous assumption. Admittedly, if a hurricane just brushes an island, relatively few boats are damaged ashore. If it comes close, there is considerable damage. But if the hurricane hits dead-on, the boats all topple like pins in a bowling alley—a few on a near miss and al- most all in a direct hit. The marinas on the east coast of Puerto Rico were pretty well cleaned out by Hugo, with the exception of Puerto del Rey which survived with an acceptably low level of damage.

As a result of Hugo, not only have boat owners who had their boats stored ashore suffered, but the underwriters have been taken to the cleaners. The only ones that came out on top were the boatyards doing the repairs (often the same yards that made money by storing the boats).

It has been recommended that underwriters should not cover boats stored ashore north of Grenada unless the mast is removed. Further, if the boat has a deep-keel, fin-and-separate-rudder configuration, you should dig two holes and chock up the boat a foot or two off the ground, with the rudder and the keel in the holes. Chocked up this way, with the rig out, the boat should survive the hurricane. I realise this is an expensive procedure, but it is a hell of a lot cheaper than rebuilding your boat.

See notes in Epilogue for updates to 2001.

Probably the most important chapter in this book is chapter 1—Sailing Directions—and you should read and study it carefully. Consult it regularly before finalising each day's plans. While the navigational features and anchorages of the individual islands are described in the chapter concerned with that island, the routes between the islands are detailed in chapter 1.

Remember: Always be alert and cautious. Almost every place in the Eastern Caribbean where a yacht can anchor has been described or at least mentioned in the Street guides, but not all are easy to enter.

Many of these anchorages can be used only in good weather and perfect visibility. Beside, some boats are handier than others and some sailors are more skilled than others. Thus, you must evaluate each anchorage for yourself before entering. the time of day, the weather, your abilities, the weatherliness of your boat—all influence the final decision.

Some advice to readers who operate bareboat charter fleets: Study this book carefully, make your judgements, and mark on the charts in the book the anchorages you want your charterers to avoid.

Publisher's Preface

Donald M. Street, Jr., a veteran Caribbean sailor, is also known as an author and the compiler of Imray-Iolaire charts of that area, and as a worldwide yacht insurance broker who places policies with Lloyd's of London.

Mr. Street also serves as a design consultant on new construction, most notably recently on *Lone Star*, a 54-foot wooden ketch built by Mashford Brothers of Plymouth, England. He also acts as design consultant on rerigging existing yachts and finding good cruising boats for people who want a proper yacht. His latest project is a sailing and seamanship video series with *Sailing Quarterly*.

Street is known mainly as a cruising skipper, but he has raced successfully on *Iolaire* and other boats. *Iolaire*, now 87, has retired from round-the-buoys racing, but her skipper has not. He still races in the various Caribbean regattas as an elder statesman—usually as "rock pilot." It is said he is excellent at this, as he has bounced off every rock in the Eastern Caribbean that is slightly less than *Iolaire*'s draft of seven feet six inches.

His contributions to sailing in the Eastern Caribbean consist of his five-volume cruising guide and the Imray-Iolaire charts. Fifty Imray-Iolaire charts have replaced roughly 200 French, US, British, Dutch, and a few Spanish charts and are all that are needed to cruise the Eastern Caribbean, the Atlantic Island Groups of Azores, Mederian Archepelego, Canaries, and Cape Verdes.

As an author, Street is prolific. His original *Cruising Guide to the Lesser Antilles* was published in 1966, *A Yachting Guide to the Grenadines* in 1970, and an updated and expanded *Cruising Guide to the Eastern Caribbean* in 1974, with continual expansions and updates since then. This has now become *Street's Cruising Guide to the Eastern Caribbean*, a five-volume work that covers a 1,000-mile-long arc of islands, plus the Venezuelan coast and the Atlantic islands. In 1985, Street and *Iolaire* made two transatlantic trips (their sixth & seventh and eighth & ninth respectively). These trips provided a wealth of information which was incorporated into his rewrite of *Street's Cruising Guide to the Eastern Caribbean Volume I*. This revision, called *Street's Transatlantic Crossing Guide to the Eastern Caribbean*, contains detailed information on islands and harbors in the Atlantic islands group plus general information on them and the Eastern Caribbean. It is the essential companion volume to any and all individual volumes covering the Eastern Caribbean. In 1989, *Iolaire* again did a double transatlantic crossing. As a result of this trip a supplement was issued to this book, removing almost all secondhand information. The *Venezuelan* guide was completely rewritten and updated in 1991. In early 1993 the newest version of *Anguilla to Dominica* should be available. In 1992 and 1993 *Iolaire* will be reexploring *Puerto Rico Passage and the Virgin Islands* to rewrite and update this section of the guide completely.

Street has also written *The Ocean Sailing Yacht, Volume I* (1973) and *Volume II* (1978). *Seawise*, a collection of articles, came out in 1976. He is also working on *Street on Storms*, as well as *Iolaire and I*, the story of *Iolaire* and Street's lifetime of adventures and misadventures in the yachting world.

Street writes regularly for *Sail, Cruising World, Sailing, WoodenBoat, Telltale Compass, Yachting, Yachting World*, and *Yachting Monthly*, as well as for publications in Sweden, Germany, Italy, Ireland, Australia, and New Zealand.

For more than 20 years, Street owned land and two houses in Grenada, but, unfortunately, the houses are no more. They were taken over by the People's Revolutionary Army (PRA) in May 1979 to be used as part of its military base. The houses did not survive the United States liberation in 1983, when helicopter gunships targeted both of them. He hopes someday to rebuild on the old site. During the winter, he crisscrosses the Caribbean.

Since Street's main occupation is yacht insurance, he and *Iolaire* appear at all the major gatherings of yachts in the Eastern Caribbean. In the fall, he is always at the St. Thomas and Tortola charter-boat shows. Then he proceeds eastward via St. Martin

Publisher's Preface

xix

and St. Barthélemy en route to the Nicholsons Agents Week. Spring finds him at the Rolex and BVI regattas, after which he heads to Antigua for the Classic Yacht Regatta and Antigua Week. Then it is south to lay up *Iolaire* beyond the hurricane belt. Formerly, *Iolaire* was laid up in Grenada, but her berth has been moved south and west to Centro Marina de Oriente in Puerto La Cruz, Venezuela. In July and August, Street is usually in Glandore, County Cork, Ireland, skippering the family's 55-year-old Dragon, *Gypsy*, or trimming her sheets for his sons.

To update Street's activities. In 1994/1995 *Iolaire* received a major rebuild at C.M.O.—Castro Marina de Oriente, Puerto la Cruz, Venezuela—where the work was done by Mick 'Shortfuse' Jarrold of *Lilymaid*. Mick sailed *Lilymaid* all the way from Madagascar to Venezuela to do the job. 'Shortfuse' is a superior shipwright who learned his trade through a seven year apprenticeship in Camper Nicholsons in the 1950's when Camper's was considered one of the top boat yards in the world. Mick did the rebuild in six months with the aid of Street, Street's long time mate Les Duncan, Street his son Richard and various other people drafted in at various times to help out.

Once the rebuild was finished, *Iolaire* took off to St. Thomas, then on to Antigua and the Classic Regatta. Subsequently *Iolaire* went on to Bermuda, the Azores, Ireland and England and celebrated her 90th birthday with her 12th transatlantic passage (Street's 10th), and by taking part in the 1995 Fastnet Race. Then down to the Mediterranean to the Cannes and Niourlargue regattas, and was laid up in Sardinia for the winter. In 1996 *Iolaire* headed north to England, Ireland and France taking part in eight classic regattas. She laid up in St. Katherine's Dock for the winter.

In 1997 she acted as mothership to the Street family's two Dragon's. *Fafner* recently restored and owned by Street's eldest son DIII, is a the 1936 Dragon that had won the original 1937 Dragon Gold Cup. Also the family has for many years owned the Dragon *Gypsy*, a 1937 Johannsen. Thus giving 210 years of wooden boats were hanging on the same mooring during the 1997 Dragon Gold Cup.

1998 saw *Iolaire* cruise up the Irish Sea to the Fife Regatta in Scotland, through the Caledonian Canal, across the North Sea to Norway. Through the "Scary" Skerries off the west coast of Sweden, down to Copenhagen and other Danish ports, through the Kiel canal and back to England, where she laid up in Lime House Basin.

In 1999 she cruised from Lime House Basin, across the North Sea, through the Kiel canal, up to the east coast of Sweden through the "Scary" Skerries on the east coast, back to Kiel and back to Lime House Basin for the winter.

In 2000 *Iolaire* again sailed to Scandinavia, this time to the Mariehamn, the home port of the Ericson grain ships—through the "Scary" Skerries of the Åland islands to Hanko. Then on to Estonia, Gulf of Rigo, Poland

As mentioned, Street is an insurance broker, and, in fact, it is his main source of income. He has pointed out that many boats have trouble obtaining insurance coverage while in the Caribbean (and especially in Venezuela), so if you are having such difficulties, contact the author—D. M. Street Jr., Rock Cottage, Old School Road, Glandore, County Cork, Ireland Fax: +353 28 33927
E-mail: streetiolaire@hotmail.com
Or: D. M. Street Jr., C/o David Payne, Besso Ltd., Minories House, 2-5 Minories, London EC3N 1BJ, England, Tel: 0207-204-1800, fax: 0207-204-1830.

(Gdynia) and on to Kiel, back through the Kiel canal across the North Sea and on to Lime House Basin, London. Street points out that sailing up and down the Thames and Elbe Rivers, with no engine puts the sport back into sailing and makes it a little exciting for the crew. *Iolaire* is now for sale and the reason Street gives is that he has owned her now for 43 years, with each year the mast gets taller, the anchor gets heavier and the winches get smaller.

She is for sale in *The Sale of The Millennium* as she is offered for sale under the terms and conditions that a boat has never been offered for sale before. 10% of the selling price will be held in escrow for twelve months. If the new owner finds any structural defects that a surveyor did not turn up, the structural defects will be repaired with the money held in escrow. Further, Street is so confident in the rig, that he has stated that if the rig goes overside in the first twenty four months of new ownership, he will pay the insurance deductible. People have spent fortunes pulling Edwardian wrecks (Avel, Marigold, Partridge etc.), off mud banks—spend fortunes completely rebuilding them to Edwardian elegance. The rebuild is such that little is left of the original hull. It has been pointed out that *Iolaire*—destinctive in that she has been in commission every year since she was built (World War II excepted)—could easily be converted back to her original rig, deck layout and below decks restored to Edwardian elegance for much less than restoring an Edwardian yacht from a mud bank!!!

Street still keeps up with affairs in the Caribbean correcting charts, and updates the guides, by sailing up and down the eastern Caribbean in *Li'l Iolaire*; his 28 foot, miniature Myth of Malham She is 26ft. on the water, 7ft. 6ins. abeam and draws 5ft. 6ins She was a sloop until January 2000, when she was converted to a yawl. From a distance she looks quite like big *Iolaire*, as they have the same wide separation from the leach of the main to the Mizzen, to the extent that when people ask what happened, Street replied, "Well we took *Iolaire* to Europe after the rebuild she was a little bit dirty so we put her in a gigantic washing machine, then put her in a drier and hit the wrong cycle button and she shrunk!"

In Europe when not sailing on *Iolaire*, Street spends his spare time in Ireland (if there is any) racing the family's 1937 Johannsen Dragon *Gypsy*.

Preface

When I first bought *Iolaire* in 1957, I found on board what was then the only straight cruising guide to the Lesser Antilles—a mimeographed publication produced by the Coast Guard Auxiliary and edited by a Lieutenant Commander Buzby. Carleton Mitchell's *Islands to Windward,* published in 1948, was generally regarded as a good cruising yarn rather than as a cruising guide, but it did have some basic cruising information in the back of the book. Unfortunately, by the time I started sailing outside the Virgin Islands in 1959, *Islands to Windward* was out of print. In 1960, *The Virgin Islands* by George Teeple Eggleston was published, the result of a one-month cruise aboard Eunice Boardman's 55-foot ketch *Renegade.*

In 1961, Percy Chubb III, after a cruise through the Lesser Antilles, produced the small, privately printed *Guide to the Windward and Leeward Islands of the Eastern Caribbean.* In 1964, Linton Rigg wrote *The Alluring Antilles,* a combination guide and cruising adventure of a half-year sail from Puerto Rico to Trinidad aboard the 45-foot ketch *Island Belle.*

These seemed to suffice for the small amount of Caribbean cruising done in those days, but starting in the early 1960s, the charter-boat business suddenly began to expand, and many new boats arrived. It was Frank Burke of Island Yachts who inspired my entry into cruising-guide writing. Figuring that too many of the charter parties were missing the best spots in the Virgins because their skippers had not been in the islands long enough to get to know them intimately, he asked me to write a cruising guide to the Virgin Islands. I did so, and he had it privately printed. I received the magnificent sum of $100—which was a veritable fortune for me in those days.

This small volume later formed the basis of the Virgin Islands section of my *Cruising Guide to the Lesser Antilles,* published in 1966, after I showed it to Phelps Platt of Dodd, Mead, who encouraged me to expand it to cover the whole island chain. This was followed two years later by Tom Kelly and Jack

van Ost's *Yachtsman's Guide to the Virgin Islands,* and then by Al Forbes's excellent *Cruising Guide to the Virgin Islands*—notable in that, unlike many guide authors, he had sailed the area for many years before he wrote his.

In 1970, following eight years of cruising the Grenadines, I produced *A Yachting Guide to the Grenadines,* after which, in 1973, came Julius M. Wilensky's *Yachtsman's Guide to the Windward Islands,* which covered largely the same territory as mine. Also in 1973, Gordon C. Ayer produced an interesting small guide covering an island group that had never been detailed before—namely, the Passage Islands.

During the late 1970s and early 1980s, numerous guides to the Eastern Caribbean appeared. They covered individual areas such as the Virgin Islands, the northern Windward Islands, Anguilla, St. Martin, St. Barthélemy, St. Kitts, Nevis, and the Leeward Islands. Others keep popping out of the woodwork like mushrooms out of an old log.

If, in all this, you find that one guide reads surprisingly like another, I ask only that you refer back to my original works to see who said what first. If nothing else, it's a matter of pride. It is very easy to write a guide to an area if someone else has previously done all the hard work—i.e., extensive exploring, producing charts, and bouncing off uncharted rocks. Most of the rival guides have been written with an eye on the bareboat-charter market, so they concentrate on the well-known, popular anchorages and skip a tremendous number of excellent anchorages that are a bit out of the way.

As each year goes by, and more and more yachts cruise the Caribbean, the bareboat-charter organizations are expanding exponentially. The area is now flooded with boats. But if you are willing to go off the beaten track, you can still have anchorages completely to yourself—or almost so.

My suggestion for finding this idyllic world of deserted (or almost-deserted) anchorages is to buy the rival guides. (I know—why am I promoting people who have benefited from my earlier guides? But heed my advice.) Then circle in red in my guide all of the harbors that are not listed in the other books. If you head for the anchorages circled in red, you will be able to avoid most of the other boats cruising the Eastern Caribbean.

To illustrate this, I would like to quote from a letter I received: "My thanks to you for your cruising guides. I have enjoyed my season down here in the Caribbean and the myriad of information in your books has really been a pleasant and informative education and made my cruise more safe, interesting, and fun. Just a brief example: I've begun to seek out the less crowded anchorages, and armed with your guides and eyeball navigation have visited Sandy Island, Grenada; Grand Bay, Carriacou (caught 10 lobsters there in 1 1/2 hours); Petit St. Vincent, north side (6 lobsters); Grand Bay, Canouan; World's End (some help from other sources). Always we were the only vessel anchored. Nifty—we loved it. Soon I'll be going around to Antigua with your guide in hand. Thank you for an excellent job. Great sailing and best wishes, Ray Bachtle, *Alchemist.*"

In *Street's Cruising Guide to the Eastern Caribbean,* I have tried to include all the information I have gleaned in some 35 years of cruising these islands. I have drawn not only from my own experiences, but, as you can see from the accompanying Acknowledgments, also from the experiences of old friends who are, in addition, good sailors. Thus, I feel I have described probably every cove in the Eastern Caribbean where one could possibly think of anchoring.

If you find one I may have missed, please let me know. I boldly asserted in my 1966 guide that the book would never become dated because rocks do not move. Little did I realize how eagerly island governments would actually start moving them, along with creating new islands, making islands into peninsulas, building low bridges, and so forth, as the development of the Eastern Caribbean boomed. Further, any guide is destined to go out of date simply because the idyllic, uninhabited spot of one year becomes a thriving hotel and cabaña settlement the next. Indeed, one of my readers once took me to task because he was using my original guide and expected to anchor off an island described therein as uninhabited. As he rounded between Pinese and Mopion, he was greeted by a brand-new hotel ablaze with celebration, and he counted no fewer than 45 boats moored in the lee of Petit St. Vincent! Please . . . don't blame me!

I have largely stayed away from recommending restaurants and bars in the Eastern Caribbean, because these establishments—especially their cooks and bartenders—do change. A superb restaurant or bar one week can become rotten the next when the cook or bartender decides to move on to another challenge.

It is impossible for anyone to say he knows the Eastern Caribbean perfectly; even after three decades, I was still discovering new little anchorages. But then the time came to look to new fields —namely, Venezuela.

At various times, Venezuelan yachtsmen extolled the virtues of Venezuela and the offshore islands. I originally went to Venezuela to give a slide lecture to a yacht club and take part in a race. I then took *Iolaire* to eastern Venezuela for six weeks and later visited western Venezuela on *Boomerang.* There followed a month's cruise in 1978 and a two-week cruise in 1979. In the early eighties, we seldom visited Venezuela, as it was the most expensive place in the Eastern Caribbean. In fact, Caracas was rated as the most expensive city in the world.

But then came the collapse of the oil market— and the devaluation of the Venezuelan bolívar—in the 1980s. Venezuela became the cheapest cruising area in the Eastern Caribbean. At first we were unable to take advantage of this, but since 1986, we have spent six to eight weeks (somctimes 10 weeks) each winter cruising there. The result is *Street's Cruising Guide to the Eastern Caribbean—Venezuela,* published in 1991 and covering the Venezuelan coast, its offshore islands, Aruba, Bonaire, and Curaçao.

With the aid of many veteran Venezuelan yachtsmen, plus yachtsmen from the Eastern Caribbean (see Acknowledgments)—and as a result of all my own cruises—I think the area is now superbly covered. I defy anyone to find a good, safe anchorage suitable for boats drawing seven feet that I have not mentioned in my Venezuelan guide. In fact, I will buy drinks for the evening for anyone who does.

During the summer of 1985, *Iolaire* visited and explored the Azores, the Madeiran Archipelago, the Canary Islands, and the Cape Verde Islands. The information gained—combined with the information already in the first volume of *Street's Cruising Guide to the Eastern Caribbean*—came out under a new title: *Street's Transatlantic Crossing Guide and Introduction to the Caribbean,* the essential companion to my guides to the Eastern Caribbean. Not only does it contain transatlantic crossing information—plus cruising information on Bermuda, the Azores, the Madeiran Archipelago, the Canaries, and the Cape Verdes—but it also has important information on the Eastern Caribbean: preparation; wind, weather, and tides; universal tide tables; sailing directions; communications; provisioning and services; chartering; yacht clubs and racing; and lists of navigational aids for the Eastern Caribbean and the Atlantic islands. *(Street's Transatlantic Crossing Guide and Introduction to the Caribbean* should be used in conjunction with the volume that covers the area where you are planning to cruise.)

In 1989, *Iolaire* again crossed the Atlantic and did a double-transatlantic—*Iolaire's* tenth and eleventh such trips, my eight and ninth. With the aid of my two sons Donald III and Richard, plus other friends we did extensive explorations of the Canaries and Cape Verdes. The information gleaned on that trip has been included in a supplement to *Street's Transatlantic Crossing guide and Introduction to the Caribbean.*

Now I am extending the bet I have offered for a number of years: If you can find any anchorage safe for a boat that draws seven feet in the Eastern Caribbean, the Atlantic Islands, or along the Venezuelan coast that I have not mentioned in my guides, I will happily pay for an evening's drinks in exchange for the information on that unmentioned harbor. Also, I greatly appreciate the assistance that yachtsmen have been so willing to provide, so

please send suggestions for corrections, additions or deletions to: D. M. Street Jr., Rock Cottage, Old School Road, Glandore, County Cork, Ireland Fax: +353 28 33927; E-mail: streetiolaire@hotmail.com or D. M. Street Jr., C/o David Payne, Besso Ltd., Minories House, 2-5 Minories, London EC3N 1BJ, England, Tel: 0207-204-1800, Fax: 0207-204-1830 (Needless to say, this is also valid for anyone requiring marine insurance.)

Many cruising friends who knew the Eastern Caribbean in the early days have headed west to Belize, the Bay Islands, the River Dulce. They have been urging me to base *Iolaire* in that area for a few years and then write a cruising guide. I refuse to do that, as I do not feel you can cruise an area for a total of six to 12 weeks and then write a guide to it.

Others are urging me to do a guide to Cuba. The island is so big—600 miles long—it would be impossible to do enough exploring to write a proper guide in my lifetime!!!

It takes years to explore a cruising area adequately, and exploring is a young man's game. Those days are over for me; the "Old Tiger" has retired. It is time for one of the "Young Tigers" (daughter Dory or one of her three brothers, Donald, Richard and Mark) to take over *Iolaire* or *Li'l Iolaire* and explore new territory.

— D.M.S.

Acknowledgments

Yachtsmen who cruise the Caribbean should be thankful to Phelps Platt of Dodd, Mead, who saw my original draft of what was then going to be a privately printed guide to the Virgin Islands and liked it enough to encourage me to write a complete guide to the other islands. Yachtsmen should also thank Bernard Goldhirsh, founder of *Sail* magazine, who published the 1974 updated and expanded cruising guide.

Thanks are now due to Eric Swenson of W. W. Norton and Company, who not only agreed to publish a completely updated guide but also agreed that it should be expanded to include Venezuela, its offlying islands, and Aruba, Bonaire, and Curaçao, plus tremendously enlarged sections on "Getting There" and "Leaving." The guide has become so comprehensive that we have produced it in five volumes.

Special thanks should go to Harvey Loomis—a good literary editor and an excellent sailor. Finally, I have an experienced editor who has cruised in the Caribbean and understands the problems of sailing —and racing—in the Caribbean. For eight years he labored hard as editor of these guides, and he was a tremendous help in rewriting the sailing and piloting directions to make them clear to the reader. Both I, the author, and you, the reader, owe Harvey a vote of thanks.

I must also thank the many yachtsmen who have helped me with valuable information. Augie Hollen of *Taurus* (the only person I know who cruises in a genuine Block Island Cowhorn), Carl Powell of *Terciel,* and Ross Norgrove, formerly of *White Squall II,* all deserve a special vote of thanks for helping me update the Virgin Islands section. Jon Repke of Power Productions—a refrigeration expert, electrician, mechanic, sailor, and pilot—solved many of the mysteries of St. Martin/St. Barthélemy/Anguilla by spending the better part of a day flying me through that area. Carl Kaushold supplied an excellent chart and information on the Salt River. Ray Smith of Grenada was most helpful in his suggestions on tides and weather patterns in the

Caribbean, and in compiling the list of radio stations and radio beacons. His brother, Ron, solved the mystery of the whereabouts of Tara Island, off the south coast of Grenada, which is marked improperly on the chart. Carl Amour of the Anchorage Hotel solved the great mystery of the rocks off Scotts Head, Dominica. Dr. Jack Sheppard of *Arieto,* the late Dick Doran of *Laughing Sally,* and Carlos Lavendero of several boats made possible the inclusion of the Puerto Rico and Passage Islands information. Gordon Stout of *Shango* and Peter Lee of *Virginia Reel* made possible the inclusion of Tobago. Jerry Bergoff of *Solar Barque* and Sylver Brin of St. Barthélemy were most helpful in clearing up some of the mysteries of the eastern end of St. Barts.

Pieter van Storn, formerly of Island Waterworld, and Malcolm Maidwell and Peter Spronk, both of Caribbean Catamaran Centre, were most helpful in the Sint Maarten area. Hans Hoff, from the 90-foot ketch *Fandango,* is one of the few people who has won a bet from me on anchorages. The standing bet is that I will buy a drink for anyone who can find a good, safe anchorage with six feet of water in it that has not been mentioned in this cruising-guide series. I expect to be nabbed once in a while by a small boat, but not by the skipper of a 90-foot ketch! Hans found an anchorage inside the reef on the north coast of Anguilla. Where the chart showed nothing but solid reef, Hans managed to find himself inside the reef with 40 feet of water!

John Clegg, formerly of *Flica II,* Dave Price, formerly of *Lincoln,* and Gordon Stout have popped up continually with wonderful odd bits of information that they have gleaned on their cruises from one end of the Lesser Antilles to the other.

Numerous other skippers have, over the years, given me a tremendous amount of help. They include, in the Antigua area, Desmond Nicholson, of V.E.B. Nicholson and Sons, English Harbour, and Joel Byerley, skipper of *Morning Tide* (and former charter skipper on *Ron of Argyll, Mirage, Etoile de Mer,* and *Lord Jim),* to name but two. For finer

xxiii

xxiv   *Acknowledgments*

points on the exploration of the east coast of Antigua, I am deeply indebted to David Simmons of the little cruising/racing sloop *Bacco*. David is also head of Antigua Slipways and the senior marine surveyor in the Eastern Caribbean. Thanks should also go to Simon Cooper and David Corrigan, both of whom unfortunately have left the islands; Morris Nicholson of *Eleuthera*; Simon Bridger of *Circe* and other boats; Peter Haycraft and George Foster, harbor pilots and yachtsmen based in Tortola; Martin Mathias of the sportfisherman *Bihari*; Bert Kilbride, diver extraordinary of Saba Rock, Virgin Islands; and the Trinidadians Doug and the late Hugh ("Daddy") Myer of *Rosemary V* and *Huey II*. I want also to thank Arthur Spence of *Dwyka*, Marcy Crowe of *Xantippe*, Andy Copeland of various boats, Mike Smith of *Phryna*, Ken McKenzie of *Ti*, Dave Ferneding of *Whisper*, Chris Bowman of *Water Pearl of Bequia*, and others whose names I may have forgotten to include.

The Venezuela section of the guide has been made possible with the help of a tremendous number of Venezuelan friends and yachtsmen—most particularly Dr. Daniel Camejo of *Caribaña*, Rolly Edmonds, Otto Castillo (port captain of Sinclair Oil), Humberto Contazano, Daniel Shaw, Peter York, Pedro Gluecksman of *Bayola*, and especially Peter Bottome, who at various times loaned us aircraft so we could fly over the areas we describe in the guide. Sailing is a wonderful way to explore, but a plane allows vast areas to be covered in a matter of hours. This was particularly true for the Los Roques area, a huge archipelago that is mostly listed as UNSURVEYED. Trying to explore it in a yacht would be almost impossible, but from the air we were able to obtain a very clear view of the layout of the unsurveyed area.

Jim Young of Dive Tobago provided reams of information on Buccoo Reef at the southwest corner of Tobago, on Tyrrel's Bay at the northeast corner, and on many coves in between. The Tobago charts in this book could not have been done without his help. Molly Watson, her son Eddie, and all the members of the Trinidad Yachting Association have done a great deal to help get out the word on Trinidad. Curaçao yachtsman Dick Nebbling was most helpful with the Netherlands Antilles section.

Other yachtsmen in the Eastern Caribbean who helped with Venezuela information were Hank Strauss of *Doki*, Richard and Barbara Weinman of *Narania*, and Mike Jarrold of *Lily Maid*.

It is only with the help of experienced yachtsmen such as these that a book of this type can be written.

A special vote of thanks must go to my nephew Morgan B. MacDonald III, who labored hard for three months in Grenada putting together the sketch charts contained in two of the volumes in this series. Thanks to the staff of Imray, Laurie, Norie & Wilson, especially the late Tom Wilson, who decided to produce the Imray-Iolaire charts; his son, Willy Wilson, who is carrying on his father's efforts; and Alan Wilkinson, their cartographer, who has labored long and hard to draw the charts for all five volumes of the Street guides and who also draws all of the Imray-Iolaire charts of the Eastern Caribbean. Thanks to Jim Mitchell, who has done a superb job of drawing the local watercraft and preparing topographical views.

Admiral Sir David Haslam, retired head of the British Hydrographic Office, and his successor, Rear Admiral R. O. Morris, have been most helpful in supplying information and giving permission for material from the British Admiralty charts to be incorporated in this book. These appropriations have been made with the approval of the controller of Her Majesty's Stationery Office and the Hydrographer of the Navy.

I want to thank Patricia Street, my sister Elizabeth Vanderbilt, her husband Peter, and their son Jay, for their help in rechecking many facts.

Finally, a special round of thanks:

Maria McCarthy of Union Hall, County Cork, Ireland, labored long and hard during the summer of 1978 typing up corrections and inserts on a previous edition of this volume. Audrey Semple spent the winter of 1978-79 doing a magnificent job of cutting, gluing, correcting, typing, and fitting it all back together again. Geraldine Hickey, my secretary during the winter of 1979-80, did similar work under times of trying circumstance.

Aileen Calnan of Glandore, County Cork, not only worked with me in Ireland but also came on board *Iolaire* in the winter of 1983 as typist, secretary, crew, sometime babysitter, and sometime cook. She stayed through the summer of 1988, then went on to bigger and better things, working in a bank in New York. Her replacement came on board, started learning the ropes, and was beginning to do a very good job when she fell in love with our Venezuelan interpreter/expediter and departed in January 1989 with 24 hours' notice. Needless to say, we were up a creek without a paddle, but we were saved by Nick Pearson, an ex-British Army telegrapher who was wandering through the Caribbean on boats. He became our "hairy-legged" secretary and labored hard through the winter of 1989. Not only did he bang away on the typewriter, but he also was our number-one man for jumping overside in shoal

Acknowledgements

water, grabbing the anchor, carrying it onto the beach, and burying it.

In January 1990, Cheryl Tennant came on board, worked extremely hard as secretary and also helping train Venezuelan crew, but, unfortunately for the skipper, she fell in love with a crew member and got married. Now they are expecting an offspring!

Aileen Calnan returned in the summer of 1991 to help me put together the complete rewrite of this guide.

The help of all these devoted friends of the Street family and of *Iolaire* has been invaluable to the production of this book.

Thanks should also go to Diane O'Connor, production editor at Norton who has fought all the guides through the editors, copy editors, and printers. Finally, when she could no longer stand my bad typing and manuscripts glued together with last minute additions, she recruited Kathleen Brandes to do a combination job, copy editing and putting all the guides on computer discs. Kathleen has done a wonderful job as not only has she put the books on computer discs, but she has also copy edited them at the same time, and unlike other copy editors I have suffered through and fought with Kathleen is a sailor, knows and understands the pro- ject and problems and thus does a combination job of editing and copy editing at the same time. Modernity has finally arrived to Street's guides.

In the winter and spring of 1992, Nancy White made possible the rewrite of the *Anguilla-to-Dominica* volume. Sophie Munroe worked hard as secretary during the winter and spring of 1993 to help me put together the *Puerto Rico, Passage Islands, and Virgin Islands* volume.

I am also grateful for the help of Dale Mitchell, who sailed as mate on *Iolaire* from December 1991 through June 1993, helping us explore all sorts of places *Iolaire* had never before visited. In April 1993, when I was ashore in St. Martin, Dale and Sophie and Caroline Schmidt did a magnificent job of sailing

Iolaire out of Marigot Harbor when an unexpected northwest squall blew in and swung her stern toward the breakwater. Dale hoisted the main, Sophie dropped one anchor line and cut the other, and Caroline backed the mizzen. *Iolaire* fell off and gathered way when the stern was only 10 feet from the breakwater. They managed to save her from massive damage. The squall was so sudden that three boats with engines, anchored near us, ended up on the breakwater!

For the latest update of the guide thanks must go to Hal Roth fellow yachting author, and sailor who convinced me to join the Author's Guild about twenty years ago. through the Author's Guild and the wonderful help of Julie Kaufmann out of date books published by Author's Guild members are being electronically published by iUniverse.com. Lori Brown of iUniverse.com has been extremely helpful in putting together this guide and by bending the rules a little bit.

Thanks must also go to my secretary Frances MacMahon who with the aid of her computer has transcribed my taperecordings, with the updates, and with the aid of my son Richard who edited them into shape so they would fit the space available.

Thanks must also go to my son Richard for correcting, updating and altering the various charts in the various guides.

Also thanks to my daughter Dory Street-Vogel who, living in Genoa, Nevada with access to phone, fax and email, was able to organise communications with W.W. Norton, Author's Guild and Laurie Brown of the iUniverse.com and was very helpful in organising and helping redesign the covers for the guides.

Last and not least I really want to thank my long suffering wife Trish who has sailed with me this past 33 years, largely raising our family of four children on the boat or holding the fort down in Glandore and raising the children while I have been out sailing and exploring on *Iolaire* and *Li'l Iolaire*.

All the Imray-Iolaire Harbour Charts are to WGS 84. However,
Many of the other harbour charts are not to WGS 84.
Therefore, do not use GPS for final approach, use visual
navigation. ie. Bearings, soundings by lead line, fathometer,
or colour of the water.

Charts

REMEMBER: DO NOT ENTER STRANGE HARBORS AT NIGHT!

I used to carry on board *Iolaire* about 200 United States, British, French, Dutch, and a few Spanish charts—all of which were out of date; that is, even though they were new charts, the various government offices had not accurately corrected and updated them. The British Admiralty will correct charts of a foreign area only if the government concerned officially notifies the BA. Much worse, US charts are corrected *only* when a whole plate is corrected; if you buy a new chart of Puerto Rico and it is a 12-year-old edition, no corrections will have been made on that chart since the date of the edition 12 years earlier!

Furthermore, BA and US charts often are on the wrong scale for inshore navigation by a yacht. The charts covering Grenada, the Grenadines, and St. Vincent are 1:72,000, while the famous old Virgin Islands chart is 1:100,000, which is even worse. You need a magnifying glass to find small anchorages and coves. In addition, it cuts Virgin Gorda in half. Several of the US and British charts break up the St. Vincent and Grenadines area in odd splits not conducive to use by the average yachtsman. The US chart of the Grenadines has an excellent enlarged inset for the Tobago Cays, but it does not have tidal reference points. The British chart does have this valuable information. Furthermore, the US and BA charts are based on surveys made in the 1890s. The latest NOAA and Admiralty charts have new deep-water information but retain the old inshore errors.

As a result of all these difficulties, I signed a contract with Imray, Laurie, Norie & Wilson (usually known simply as Imray)—which traces its ancestry back to 1670—to do updated and accurate charts specifically tailored to the needs of the yachtsman. Our information has been gathered from US National Ocean Survey (NOS) and Defense Mapping Agency (DMA) charts, British Admiralty charts, French and Dutch charts, plus unpublished US and British Admiralty surveys, topographical maps, and aerial photography, backed up by the information I

have gathered in more than 30 years of exploring the Eastern Caribbean. Information also has been supplied to me by other experienced yachtsmen. Although it may be true that I know the Eastern Caribbean as a whole better than any other yachtsman, there are people who know individual islands and areas much better than I do. These yachtsmen have been tremendously helpful in sharing their knowledge.

Our charts come in one standard size, 25 inches by 35 1/2 inches, and three colors. Blue denotes deep water; white denotes water five fathoms or less; yellow indicates one fathom or less. Detailed harbor charts are inserted in the margins of the general charts. Useful ranges (transits) are shown to guide the mariner clear of dangers. Various overlapping coverages and often contradictory information found in the various French, US, Dutch, and British Admiralty charts have been eliminated.

Imray-Iolaire charts are kept up to date through careful attention to the British Notices to Mariners, my own observations, and comments sent by users of these charts and readers of these cruising guides. Important corrections are inserted by hand at Imray prior to shipment; all corrections are logged in on the master sheet so that even minor corrections are included in new editions. Seldom do we go more than six months between printings of a chart. (The most popular Imray-Iolaire charts—those of the US and British Virgin Islands, and Anguilla, St. Barthélemy, St. Martin, and Antigua—are available on waterproof paper.)

As of this writing, forty-nine Imray-Iolaire charts now cover the entire Eastern Caribbean, replacing the 200 plus government charts (which had numerous inaccuracies) I formerly carried on Iolaire. Further, we have expanded the charts to cover the Atlantic Island groups: Azores, Mederian Archipelago, Canaries, and Cape Verdes. Each group is covered by a single chart with the detailed plans of the major harbors shown on the chart as insets.

xxvi

The Imray-Iolaire charts have become the accepted standard; the US Coast Guard, as well as the St. Vincent and Grenada Coast Guards, use Imray-Iolaire charts rather than government charts. Very few chart agents in the Eastern Caribbean continue to stock the government charts.

In short, I strongly recommend that yachtsmen use the Imray-Iolaire charts instead of British Admiralty or US government charts.

Most of the harbor charts in this volume have been taken from the relevant Imray-Iolaire charts. The few sketch charts included here are just that—sketches. They are as accurate as I can make them, but they are *not* official publications, so they should be used only in conjunction with *reliable* navigational charts, common sense, and eyeball observations.

NOTE: Keep in mind that the sea level in the Eastern Caribbean is roughly 12 to 18 inches lower in May, June, and July than it is the rest of the year. Imray-Iolaire chart soundings are based on this low, low datum. Other charts may not be.

No chart can be absolutely accurate, but I feel that the Imray-Iolaire charts are the most accurate ones available. They can be kept that way only if experienced yachtsmen continue to fee information and corrections to us to correct the small errors that may still exist or to update charts where the topography has been changed by hurricanes, earthquakes, or dredging.

Please send information regarding chart corrections to me:

By Post: Rock Cottage, Old School Road, Glandore, Co. Cork, Ireland.

Or, By E-mail: streetiolaire@hotmail.com

Since the above was written much has happened. In 1994 Imray turned over to me the job of trying to get all the Imray Iolaire Charts to the single WGS84 datum. I succeeded in doing this over the next eight months. People ask me am I trained cartographer and I reply "No". Then they ask how could I get all the Imray Iolaire Charts to WGS84.

I point out to people that I Majored in History (to the English, I read History) at Gothic University, Washington DC., and with the library at Congress in the city, as a student you were forced out of the Catholic University Library down to the Library at Congress. The University Library did not have enough information. Hence I learned how to do research. I learned that if you don't know the answer to something, research hard enough and you will find out who does have the answer.

The aeroplanes obviously know where their runways are, so I bought an aircraft chart. No good. the scale was so poor that a pencil line was 600 yards wide. I then contacted NOAA's aeronautic division and discovered that they had a book which gave the centre line of every runway in the entire Caribbean and South America. By locating the centreline of a runway we could then move the whole island. Also I discovered that NOAA had redone the Puerto Rican charts to WGS84, the DMA had redone the Venezuelan charts to WGS84 and the British had done some of the islands of the Eastern Caribbean to WGS84, but not all and had some off sets of some of the others. I also discovered that the French had re-established Martinique and Guadeloupe to WGS84.

So with the aid of all these charts and all this information out living room floor for the summer of 1994 became a gigantic jigsaw puzzle. But by the end of the year all the information was collated, cross checked. Alan Wilkinson of Imray then began the process of putting all Imray-Iolaire Charts to WGS84 or noting on the charts an off set originally express- ed to bring your GPS position to it's correct place on the chart.

Originally this off set was expressed in degrees and minutes and tenths of minutes, and in latitude and longitude. This is difficult to plot when doing a series of positions. In 1998 I finally recalculated all the off sets (with the aid of my sons, Richard and Mark, cross checking all my calculations). The offsets are now all expressed in not only latitude and longitude, but also in bearing and distance. This makes it much easier to plot.

It should be noted that in 2000 the military has cut down the built in error in GPS. Some of the very fancy units will not only say how many satellites are being tracked, but also state the degree of accuracy. This will of course vary as to the lay out of the satellite. There are some where it is recorded on conventional GPS where the difference is down to ten or twelve feet.

All the charts from Grenada to U.S. & B.V.I. have on the back, sailing and piloting directions pulled from Street's Guides. A chart and a guide in one. By the time you read this the Puerto Rican charts will probably be the same. Not only that but the Puerto Rican charts will have the sailing and piloting directions in both English and Spanish.

Hopefully by the end of 2001 the Venezuelan coast, the close off shore islands and the Aves islands will have sailing and piloting instructions on the back of the charts and also be in Spanish and English.

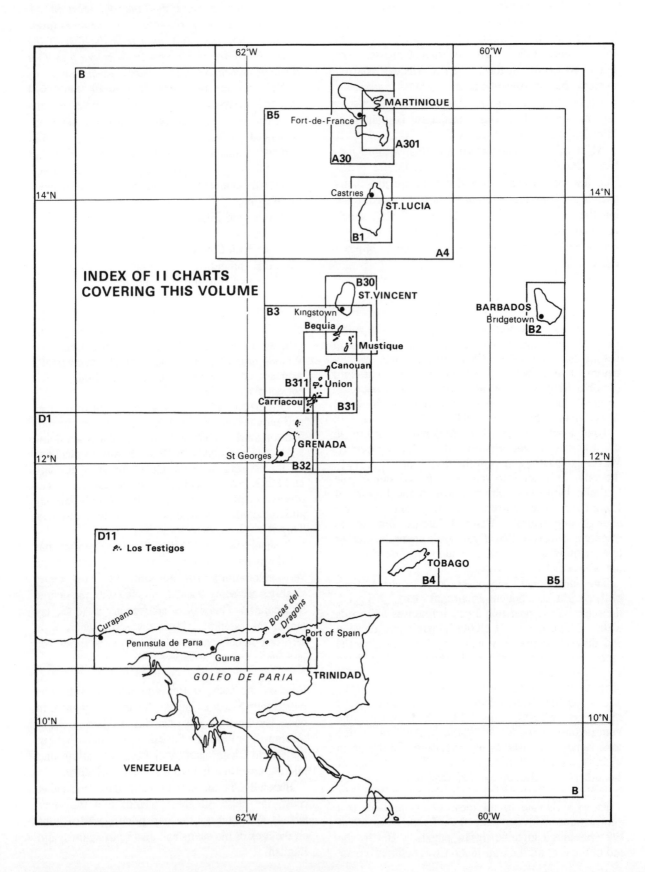

List of Charts and Sketch Charts

SAILING DIRECTIONS
Sketch Chart A

MARTINIQUE
1. Rade de Fort de France
2. Pointe du Bout
3. Martinique—South Coast
4. Cul-de-Sac Marin
5. Martinique—East Coast, Southern Part
6. Martinique—East Coast, Northern Part
7. Cul-de-Sac Tartane/Baie du Trésor (sketch)
8. Havre de la Trinité
9. Rade de St. Pierre

ST. LUCIA
10. Port Castries
11. Rodney Bay and Yacht Harbour
12. Grand Cul de Sac Bay
13. Marigot Harbour
14. Soufrière Bay and the Pitons
15. Laborie Bay
16. Vieux Fort Bay and Point Sable Bay

ST. VINCENT
17. Kingstown Bay
18. Calliaqua Bay and Blue Lagoon
19. Cumberland and Wallilabou Bays (sketch)
20. Chateaubelair Bay

BARBADOS
21. Bridgetown Harbour (Carlisle Bay)

NORTHERN GRENADINES
22. Bequia—Admiralty Bay
23. Bequia—Friendship Bay
24. Mustique—West Coast
25. Baliceaux and Battowia
26. Canouan—South End
27. Canouan—North End (sketch)

SOUTHERN GRENADINES
28. The Grenadines
29. Tobago Cays
30. Tobago Cays (sketch—proposed ranges)
31. Mayreau Island
32. Union Island—Clifton Harbour
33. Union Island—Chatham Bay (sketch)
34. Petit St. Vincent
35. Carriacou—Tyrell Bay
36. Carriacou—Hillsborough Bay
37. Carriacou—Northeast Coast (sketch)
38. Carriacou—Southeast Coast (sketch)
39. Carriacou—Southwest Point (sketch)
40. Ile de Ronde

GRENADA
41. St. Georges Harbour
42. Morne Rouge Bay and Long Point (sketch)
43. Grenada—Southwest Coast (A)
44. Grenada—Southwest Coast (B)
45. Grenada—Southeast Coast
46. Great Bacolet Harbor (sketch)
47. Marquis Island (sketch)
48. Grenville Harbour
49. Grenada—Northeast Coast
50. Halifax Harbor (sketch)
51. Dragon Bay (sketch)

TRINIDAD AND TOBAGO
52. Bocas del Dragon
53. Port of Spain
54. Trinidad—North Coast
55. Tobago—Scarborough
56. Kings Bay
57. Tyrrel's Bay
58. Buccoo Reef
59. Plymouth
60. Man of War Bay

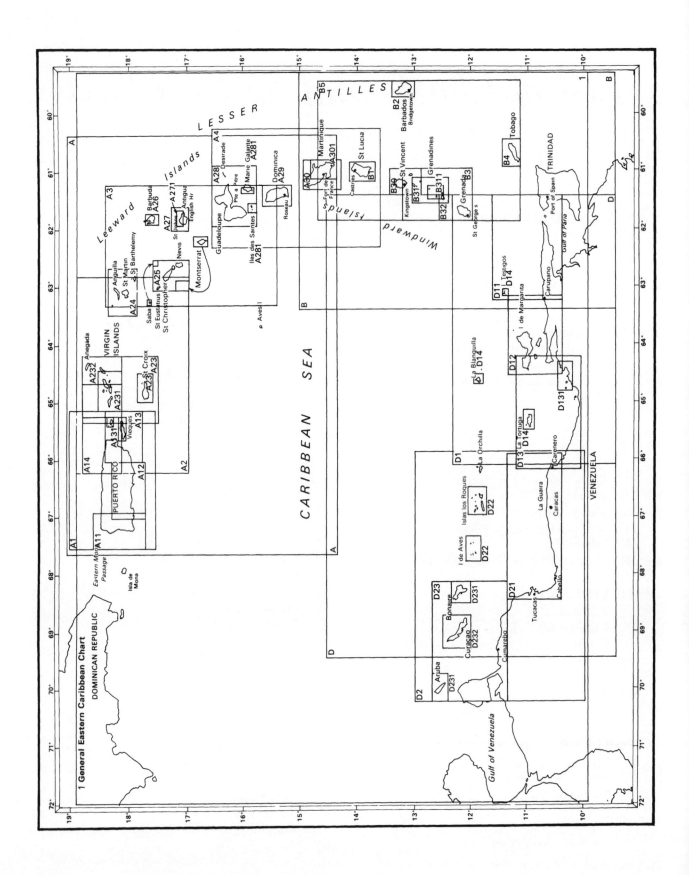

Prologue

If this guide does not read smoothly at all times please remember it was written many years ago, but luckily rocks don't move—unless a new harbour is created or breakwater built. Electronic printing has made it possible to re-publish these guides but the amount of new material that could be included is strictly limited.

For navigational dangers and sailing directions these guides are completely up to date to year 2001. As to the marine oriented infrastructure, no guide can be completely up to date. However, all the islands that have a real marine industry put out each year a free marine guide. Immediately upon clearing customs and immigration pick up the marine guide and you will be all set. On islands that do not produce a marine guide I refer the reader to an Old Timer in the business that will know the answers to the questions you ask as to where things can be bought or repaired.

For bars, restaurants and hotels pick up the free yearly printed tourist guide. It is impossible for a marine guide to cover the marine scene and also the bars, restaurants and hotels. The author would have to eat three meals a day each one at a different restaurant 365 days of the year to cover the restaurants. To cover the bars, to do a decent job, the author would certainly either become an alcoholic or die of cirrhosis of the liver.

Immediately upon arriving at any island pick up the FREE Marine Trade Guide locally produced every year. Also there is a FREE tourist guide— These will be much more up to date than any cruising guide can possibly be.

Every two years a supplement will be available through Imray with whom I published the Imray Iolaire charts. Cost of the update will vary as to the size of the update and the amount of work I have to do to gather the information.

These guides should be used in conjuction with the latest Imray-Iolaire charts. Free updates of the Imray-Iolaire charts are issued every six months and are available from Imray Chart Agents or direct from Imray (Imray, Laurie, Norie & Wilson Ltd., Wych House, The Broadway, St. Ives, Cambridgeshire PE17 5BT, England.
Tel: +44 (0)1480 462114; *Fax* +44 (0)1480 496109.

People always ask when did I get to the Caribbean and how did I end up in the writing business. The short and brief of it is After spending some time in Uncle Sam's navy in a submarine, during the Korean war, I finished Catholic University DC in 1954 where I majored in American History. I landed a job as paid hand on Huey Long's Ondine A beautiful 53 foot Aberking and Rasmussen Yawl. I was hired as paid hand and a month later they fired the skipper. I ended up as skipper, with no increase in wages! An interesting couple of years followed includ- ing racing in Europe

Our parting of the ways came just before the Fastnet Race when I made a Pier Head jump onto Lloyds' Yacht Club boat *Lutine, a 57 foot* . J Laurent Giles designed yawl built by Camper Nicholson in 1953 I sailed the rest of the season on her, bounced around Europe for about nine months, and sailed back across the Atlantic on Arabella, a 46 foot yawl, as cook and apprentice navigator.

The summer of 1956 I spent sailing delivering boats, helping friends out in boat yards doing odds and ends. Everyone was after me to take a real "job" I asked "Why?" I had money in the bank, did not owe anything on my car, I was making more than I was spending. But, the pressures mounted and I ended up in the job market. I landed a job, at Frank B. Hall & Partners, big ship Marine Insurance brokers on John's Street —in the canyons of New York.

One of the conditions on taking the job was that I had to shave—the weekend before I was to start, I shaved off my beard. We were racing frostbite dinghies in Larchmount and Dick Ronan said, "my God, Don you are the only person in New York who has chap stick on your entire face." I thought about it, and decided I didn't like cold weather.

At the age of 55, after three cases of ulcers and two minor heart attacks, fighting the canyons of New York and commuting my father had to retire— living in that atmosphere my mother had two cases of ulcers—At the age of 70 I haven't had an ulcer or a heart attack, I give them!!

You can't change the weather, but you can fly to where the weather is good. Also a friend had just come

xxxii   *Prologue*

back from the Virgin Islands and told of the wonderful climate, the good sailing and an evolving economy

So, for $45.00 I bought myself a ticket on the "Vomit Comet" a Pan-American DC6—so called because in those days the propeller planes couldn't fly over the storms they flew through them! They didn't really take off from Idlewild (now Kennedy) they just flew down the runway, the runway ended, they pulled up the wheels and staggered off across Jamaica Bay. The rate of climb predicated by how fast the fuel was used up When they hit an air pocket the plane would drop around 500 feet, the "barf" bags would come out, and the Puerto Ricans would have their rosary beads going round like a bicycle chain.

I landed in San Juan in the wee hours of the morning—and picked up for $10, the Carib Air flight to St Croix.   A few days later I ended up in St. Thomas, and landed a job as a land surveyor.

People ask how did I do that, having graduated with a History Major On Friday I borrowed a book on basic surveying. Monday and Tuesday were bank holidays. By Wednesday morning I convinced them I was a surveyor—in the land of the blind the one eyed are king.

Not too long after I arrived in St. Thomas I met the late Captain Bob Crytzer who owned three boats. *Little Electra*, a sister ship to the 44 foot academy yawls, big *Electra* a 56-foot Camper Nicholson ketch (Owen Aischer's original *Yeoman*) and *Iolaire*, 45foot engineless cutter—owned for many years by Bobby Sommerset. *Iolaire* had been across the Atlantic five times and was presently engineless (that is a story you can read in *Caribbean Capers*) Glenda Crytzer was trying to convince her husband that he really didn't need three boats Bob took a liking to me, one thing led to another and I purchased Iolaire for $3,000 down, $1,000 a year for four years, with no interest and no repossession clause!

I slowly drifted into the charter business. Then the exploratory business and then the writing business and all of that is described in great detail in *Iolaire and I.*

Those who like my writing can thank John Steinbeck, John Fernly and Burt Cheveleaux

My first charter after rebuilding *Iolaire* when she had been wrecked in Lindberg Bay was John Fernly (He had been casting director for Rogers & Hammerstein for many years) and his good friend Burt Cheveleaux who had just written *Something Funny happened on the Way to the Forum* (one of the most amusing characters I have ever met in my life). We stopped at Caneel Bay to have cocktails, then dinner with John Steinbeck—very good friends of John Fernly.

A week or so later on the charter we came back and had another evening with cocktails and dinner. The subject came up on writing and talent. It was kicked around for quite a long time, until finally Steinbeck said, "Hell forget all the B.S on talent, becoming a good writer depends on your ability to put your ass on a hard wooden chair and look at the G.D. typewriter for six hours a day, seven days a week and pound something out. Eventually an editor will accept your work "

Later that evening he turned to me and said, "Kid you tell a good story. Why don't you try writing?" To which I replied, "But Mr Steinbeck," "Never mind Mr Steinbeck, call me John," "John, I can't spell." To which Mr. Steinbeck replied, "What the hell do you think secretaries and editors are for? Try writing. Go get me a drink." I went to the bar to get Steinbeck a drink and had to report the bar was closed   Steinbeck said, "My God, this is a great place for newly weds and nearly deads. I don't know what you characters are doing, but I'm going back to my room to wrap myself around my bottle of scotch. Good night " That started my writing career.

Carlton Mitchell had done a cruise through the islands on "Carib" in the late 1940's and written a book *Islands to Windward*. It was the story of his cruise, not really a cruising guide and long since out of print when I arrived on the island Eggleston wrote a book in 1960 of the Virgin Islands as the result of a one month cruise Also Linton Rigg was writing a book *The Alluring Antilles*—a cruise through the islands, and not a cruising guide.

I have always had an exploratory instinct and began to think about writing a guide I had started on the Virgin Islands about the time Frank Burke of Island Yachts, (also known as "Frank Lurk the friendly Chinaman" count your fingers after you have shaken hands with him), approached me complaining that the new charter skippers didn't know the islands well enough and were missing a lot of the good spots—would I write a guide for them.

I said I would sell him the Virgin Island section of my proposed guide but no copyright. He mimeographed it off and sold it, (note mimeograph this was the days before the photocopying). Frank paid me the magnificent sum of $100.00 (remember this was in the days of 25¢ beer), for the manuscript. Subsequently after printing a couple of hundred I discovered he was selling them at $10.00 a piece.   He made a fair piece of change on it.

A couple of years after I wrote the V.I. section of the guide and was working on completing the guide, I met Carlton Mitchell who was in the Eastern Caribbean with *Finisterre*—his little 39-foot centreboarder with which he won three Bermuda races. He was doing a cruise through the islands to write a series of articles for National Geog- raphic. At this point Carlton Mitchell was probably yachting most famous writer and certainly the most highly paid yachting author in the world.

He looked me up in Grenada to pick my brains. We had a pleasant evening and I told him about my Virgin

Prologue

xxxiii

Island guide. About two years later I ran into Mitch and he told me a most amusing story.

He arrived in the Virgin Islands and went in to see Frank Burke at Island Yachts. He said he had heard there was a young guy named Street who had written a Virgin Island guide. Frank said "yes he certainly has" and handed him a small mimeographed guide with the price on it of $10.oo. Mitch. looked at the $10 oo price tag and said, "Gee this is expensive." To which Burke replied, "Look that is really good solid information. This Street has written a guide that is a hell of a lot better than anything Carlton Mitchell has written in *Islands to Windward* or in Eggleston's *Virgin Island guide*, and it is worth the $10.oo Mitch thumbed his way through and decided he liked it. It was worth the $10.oo. He handed over the money and as Frank took it he looked up and said, "By the way, I'm Frank Burke." To which Mitch. replied, "I'm Carlton Mitchell." Burke didn't blink an eye, just said, "I still say the information is better than *Islands to Windward* or Eggleston's book." Mitch walked out the door and related the story to me much later. Luckily Mitch has a good sense of humour.

I took the bare bones of the book with me to New York on a delivery. I visited eight or ten publishers, and got thrown out on my ear by all of them. I am a persistent soul and I started going back again. Phelp Platt of Dodd Mead, just to get rid of me, said he'd publish the book.

It is worth noting that as long ago as my first cruising guide (1966), I pointed out that the best sailing of the year occurs in May, June and July—when the wind blows at a steady 12 to 15knots day after day, and no fronts come blasting on through.

June and July are the beginning of hurricane season so you must be wary. After mid-July I would not think of cruising in the Caribbean, north of Martinique I say this because if a hurricane is approaching and you are in Antigua and decide to head south, unless you have a very large boat and can turn on the engines and head south at 8- or 9-knots you have a long way—300 miles from Antigua to Grenada—to go to get out of the hurricane belt. If you are in the area of Martinique or south, and a hurricane approaches you only have 150 miles to get all the way down to the south coast of Grenada and the various anchorages completely sheltered other than when a hurricane runs right over the top of Grenada—a very unlikely occurrence in the light of past history.

WHEN TO COME AND WEATHER

The weather patterns in the Caribbean—and especially the northern end of the Caribbean—have changed drastically in the last three or four decades

When I first came here some 40 years ago, the fronts coming out of the Bahamas would stall in Hispaniola We heard about them, but they didn't affect our weather. Come the 1960s, they pushed on through the western end of Puerto Rico, and the main effect in the Virgins was that the trades would die out once in a while and come in very light from the northwest In recent years, fronts have pushed farther and farther east—through Puerto Rico and down to the Passage Islands in 1993, when we were anchored at Buck Island in St Croix, the wind was blowing 15 knots from the west!

From November to July, winds will be 15 to 20 knots from the east. These are referred to as the northeast trades, but that is a misnomer. In early winter, they are generally east to east-northeast, sometimes crawling around to northeast or north-northeast. Traditionally, the weather report reads, "East-northeast to east-southeast, 10 to 15 knots, higher in gusts." Some of us feel that this is a recording put on in early November and played until April. Then it is replaced by a recording that reads, "East to southeast, 10 to 15 knots, higher in gusts." When fronts come through, it will blow 20 to 25 knots, sometimes for a week or more.

The above is that all charter brokers and dreamers speak of as the Eastern Caribbean weather. However, at various times it can pipe way up to where it will be blowing for days on end 20-25 knots with stronger gusts. Those gusts, i.e. small squalls easily go up to 30 to 35 knots. These periods of heavy weather normally last 2/3 days but can last for weeks, as they have done a couple of times. In the extreme weather of 1998, when for almost all of January and the first week of February in the Antigua area it was exceptional when the wind dropped BELOW 25 knots.

A further example of the changing climate is in 1957, sailing from St. Thomas to Caneel Bay, inside the Caribbean you occasionally ran into patches of Sargasso Weed, the size of a football field. In 1958 they were down to the size of tennis courts. In 1959, only small patches of Sargasso weed could be seen, then it completely disappeared from the Eastern Caribbean until 1989 when small patches of the weed reappeared. Not only that but the Caribbean was warmer than usual. People regularly quoted water temperatures as high as 81° and occasionally 82° instead of the normal 77°

Needless to say, everyone was very worried that hurricanes might be generated. yet only one hurricane came into the Caribbean that year—Hugo. Hugo the single hurricane did a huge amount of damage. See Reflections of Hugo.

In 2000 we have again seen small patches of Sargasso weed within the Caribbean, what does that mean???

UTC	LOCAL	STATION & REPORT DESCRIPTION	FREQ	MODE	
0930	0530	NMN Offshore Forecast	A	Voice	USB
1000	0600	WAH VI Radio Repeat NMN Offshore Forecast	4357	Voice	USB
1035	0685	Antillies Emergency & Weather Ham Net(Eric)	3815	Voice	LSB
1100	0700	Caribbean Maritime Mobile Ham Net	7241	Voice	LSB
1100	0700	Albatross Weather Report (Alex)	4054	Voice	USB
1115	0715	Caribbean Maritime Mobile Ham Net(George)	7241	Voice	LSB
1130	0730	Caribbean Maritime Mobile Ham Net(George)	7086	Wefax	LSB
1145	0745	Albatross Weather Report(Alex)	8155	Voice	USB
1200	0800	Trop Pred Ctr 0600 Tropical Surface Analysis	C	Wefax	USB(Note 1)
1205	0805	ZBVI Morning Marine Report Mon-Fri (David)	0780	Voice	AM(Note 2)
1230	0830	Caribbean Weather Net David)	8104	VoicE	USB(Note 3)
1230	0830	Trop Pred Ctr 24/36hr Winds/Seas Forecast	C	Wefax	USB(Note 1)
1250	0850	Trop Pred Ctr 1200 High Seas Forecast	C	Wefax	USB(Note 1)
1350	0950	Trop Pred Ctr 1145 Goes-8 Trop Sat Image	C	Wefax	USB(Note 1)
1600	1200	NMN Offshore Forecast	B	Voice	USB
1915	1515	Trop Pred Ctr 00 12hr Winds/Seas Forecast	C	Wefax	USB(Note 1)
1950	1550	Trop Pred Ctr 1745 Goes-8 Trop Sat Image	C	Wefax	USB(Note 1)
2000	1600	Southbound II (Herb)	12359	Voice	USB
2030	1630	Cocktail & Weather Net	7086	Voice	LSB
2045	1645	Cocktail & Weather Net (George)	7086	Wefax	LSB
2200	1800	NMN Offshore Forecast	B	Voice	USB
2235	1885	Antillies Emergency Weather Net*	3815	Voice	LSB
0028	2028	V.O.A. Windwards/Leewards Forecast	9945	Voice	AM
0330	2330	NMN Offshore Forecast	A	Voice	USB

WWV has World Marine Storm Wannings (Voice) at 8 min., and Solar Flux (Sunspot) number
at 18 minutes after each hour on:
2.500, 5.000, 10.000 15.000, 20.000 MHz (USB).

Frequencies:

A.	4426 6501 8764
B.	6501 8764 13089
C.	4316.0 8502.0 12788
	4817.9 8503.9 12789.9

Notes: (Note 1) Tropical Prediction Center via US Coast Guard, New Orleans Louisiana
USB. Tune 1.9 kHz below listed frequency. 120 LPM. 576 IOC,
(Note 2) ZBVI Morning Marine Report with David Jones, Mon-Fri 8:05am. Sat 7:45am, Sun 9:45am
Hourly weather forecasts every hour on the 1/2 hour. 7·30am - 9:30pm.
(Note 3) Annual subscription. required for custom forecast,
* temporarily off the air

As well as 4357. WAH also does a simultaneous broadcast on VHF 85. in range. Also included besides the NMN repeat is a weather summary, the east Puerto Rico and Virgin Islands local forecast, the Tropical Weather Outlook, and hurricane co-ordinates as appropriate. Updated broadcasts are also at 1400 and 2200 AST. A continuous broadcast can be heard on VHF WX 3 in range. The Antilles Emergency and Ham Weather Net does the same at 0645 AST on 7163 LSB

In St Vincent, there is a local forecast on VHF 06 at 0900.
The Safety and Security Net now begins at 0815 AST on SSB 8104.

Thanks to William Mills of Toucan I and John and Melodye Pompa of Second Millennium & Compass Publications *for radio information.*
Note: NMN = US. Coast Guard Station, Chesapeake, Virginia.

WEATHER REPORTS - ISLAND BY ISLAND

South bound to Herb	12359Khz.	16.30
Amateur Weather	3815Khz.	06.30 + 18.30
Amateur Marine Mobile Net	7230Khz.	07.00

Contact Dave at Z.B.V.I., Roadtown, Tortola, B.V.I.
Caribbean weather Centre Ltd.,:
www.caribwx.com;   e-mail: weather@caribwx.com
Tel: 284 494 7559;   Fax: 284 494 5358

British Virgin Islands.

Because of the volcano eruption on Monserrat Radio Antilles is no more. However, there is a new weather report from Tortola done by a private weather forecaster by the name of David Jones Z.B.V.I. at 0805 Monday to Friday, 0745 on Saturday and on Sunday at 0945. Then there is a forecast every hour on the half hour—0730 to 2130. Further you can receive a customer weather forecast payable by the month.

Martinique to Trinidad

Martinique

In Martinique you should check with the Harbor Masters Office and the Port Captains office as they post a very good weather report every 24 hours. Complete with weather maps.

St. Lucia

In St. Lucia at Rodney Bay Marina they usually post a weather report and weather map

St. Vincent

In St. Vincent to Grenada you should listen to the radio weather reports. See the complete table of weather reports below.

Trinidad

In Trinidad after the evening news on TV6 at 1900 Eric Mackey comes on—usually between 1930 and 1955—and gives a weather report which covers not only the lower end of the Eastern Caribbean but more important it covers Trinidad. This weather report is excellent as Eric is a Trinidad yachtsman who interprets the weather for Trinidad backed up with his own local knowledge. His average on accuracy is very high.

RAIN

The rainy season is the same as the hurricane season —roughly July to October (although hurricanes have occurred in June and November). Even then, it very seldom rains day after day but rather a maximum of three hours a day. The rest of the day is sunny. However, at times the rainy and dry seasons reverse themselves, confusing everyone. In 1993, for example, during the "dry season", our longest stretch without rain was only 36 hours. So be sure to have on hand a raincoat or a foul weather jacket. Trousers and boots are not really necessary, as the air is warm enough, but you will get tired of having a wet tail, so if you have a full-length raincoat with a hood, you won't be sorry.

Amazingly, however, the best months for sailing the Eastern Caribbean are May, June, and July—the weather patterns tend to be more stable.

SUN

Despite the fact that you might have spent time in Florida or the Bahamas and not suffered from sunburn, that does not mean that you will be safe when you get to Puerto Rico and the Virgins. Remember that Florida is 26°N; the Virgin Islands are 18°30'. You will get a tan in the Virgins even if you keep all your clothes on. Be sure you have a broad-brimmed hat, at least one long-sleeved white shirt, long cotton trousers, and plenty of sunblock. And use it all! If you have a tiller-steered boat, be especially careful to put sunblock on the tops of your hands and the tops of your feet. Men's cotton pyjamas or doctors' scrub suits make good cover-ups to keep you from getting too much sun.

If you intend to spend a large portion of your life sailing in the tropics, it is essential that you cover up and use the strongest sun block you can find on your hands and face. I have done that most of my life. Although I am known as "Squeaky" I could be known as "Swiss Cheese" due to all the holes made in me by doctors removing skin cancer. At times I' come out of the skin specialists feeling like a blown out Genoa rather than a sailor. Cover up and use the sun block

WHAT TO WEAR

Travel light. If you can't fit everything into the standard duffel (generally measuring 26 inches long by 12 inches in diameter), you have too much gear Dress in most places is casual. In town, women should wear a skirt and blouse or long shorts and a blouse, bare midriffs and bikinis are not acceptable. For a fancy night out, women may want a long dress and men may want a jacket and tie. Plus, if you go to any of the mountain top restaurants in Puerto Rico, St. Thomas, or Tortola, be sure to take along a jacket or light sweater; you lose a degree of temperature for every 150 feet of altitude. The temperature can easily be in the upper 60s (and feel quite chilly) at one of these areas. On the south coast of Puerto Rico, where the cold air comes down off the mountains at night, the temperature drops quickly to the 60s. On any of the really high islands like Guadeloupe or Dominica the cold air comes down off the mountains at night and the temperature drops quickly to the upper 60s.

On the trip down, carry some clothing in your hand luggage—a bathing suit, a hat, and a change of clothes— incase your baggage doesn't arrive at the same time you do. There is nothing worse than walking around San Juan or St. Thomas or Tortola wearing your winter duds.

To beat the heat in the airports most of which are not air-conditioned, my technique is to change out of my winter duds and into my tropical clothes before the plane lands. Then when standing in the Immigration & Customs line you don't die of the heat and perspiration. Similarly when flying out of the islands, I go through the airport and on board the aircraft wearing tropical attire carrying my winter duds in my bag. Once in the aircraft I change and all is well. I haven't climbed on the aeroplane in a pool of sweat

DINGHIES

In the eastern Caribbean one finds all sizes of Dinghies and tenders. Varying from small dinghies like our six foot clinker pram that we use on Li'l Iolaire through to nice rowing dinghies like those we carry on Iolaire, or inflatables, very small soft bottom ones, which are willing, eager and desirous of running out from under you when you step into them and dumping you in the drink. I have fallen out of a dinghy twice in my life both times were from one of those soft bottomed tiny inflatables. Then there are those big RIB's thirty feet long, and valued at $40,000 and RIB's of all sizes in-between

Losing dinghies or the larger boats, called launches, is endemic in the Caribbean. However, it is not all down to the locals One third of the ships boats that are lost are just not tied up properly. For that reason on Iolaire or Li'l Iolaire, when ever we are anchored in a harbour that is open to the west, I insist that the dinghy be tied on with two <u>separate</u> lines, going on the supposition that a person may miss tie one line, but is unlikely to miss tie two lines. Another third of dinghies are stolen by the locals. Another third stolen by a "fellow" yachtsman. More than once a culprit has been caught stealing a dinghy and when his boat is visited by the police they have found five or six deflated dinghies inside the boat.

The normal safety precaution is to shackle a wire onto the dinghy, and padlock the dinghy to the dock or the boat with the other end of the wire. However, quarter inch 1/19 is not good enough. The thieves come around with wire cutters and slip right through ¼ inch. If you have a valuable ships tender/launch my advice is to use a piece of $5/16^{ths}$ of 1/19 as cutting through that requires more effort and a bigger cutter than the average thief is likely to have. However, the only way you can be absolutely sure of not losing your dinghy at night is to have it sling rigged attached to your halyard and haul it clear of the water. That is the only reliable way. In some areas, there is little or no dinghy stealing, and in other areas it is rife. Thus the prudent mariner asks among his fellow yachtsmen, especially from the bareboat managers, about the dingy stealing situation locally.

SECURITY

If you are flying down and chartering a boat with a skipper and crew they will know what the security situation is and keep you advised so you can sit back and relax. If you are bareboat chartering, check with the bareboat managers and they will advise you of any security problems. Generally there are very few security problems from Guadaloupe north. From Guadaloupe south, i.e. Dominica south, St. Lucia, St. Vincent, the Grenadines, the security problems do arise.

Again if you are cruising through the islands in your own boat, check with the bareboat managers and skippers. They are very friendly and they will keep you advised as to security problems.

People who cruise through on boats ask about guns— forget about them, leave them ashore. They are more hassle than they are worth. The thing to remember is that in my entire yachting life, I have never ever heard of a boat being robbed that has had a barking dog on board A small barking dog is enough to keep the thieves away. There is no need for a great big huge guard dog

FISH POISONING

Fish poisoning is a major problem in Anguilla, St. Martins, St. Barts area Occasionally fish poisoning has been reported to Antigua Barbuda area, but I have never heard of an authentic case of fish poisoning from Guadeloupe south.

I have no idea how to avoid the fish poisoning known as ciguatera, although it's easy to find people who will give you advice on the matter. I have never heard reports of anyone dying of ciguatera, but people have said that it makes you feel so terrible you wish you were dead!

One of the problems is determining what fish are likely to be poisonous. What's poisonous in one area is not necessarily so in another area. In St. Croix, barracuda is consumed by the ton. In the northern Virgins, on the other hand, no one eats barracuda because it is alleged to be poisonous if found on the northern side of the islands and non-poisonous if found on the southern side of the islands. How do you tell whether you have caught a travelling barracuda?

One recommendation is to cook fish with a silver spoon; if the spoon stays shiny, the fish is fine. Well, we tried that once on *Iolaire*. Four of us ate the fish, with mixed results. Our West Indian cook ate a lot and was very sick; two American friends, Marv and Carol Bernning, ate a moderate amount and were moderately sick; I at a little and did not get sick. On another occasion, when we were given a fish, part of the crew went to a friend's house and cooked half of the fish. Some of them were fine, some slightly sick, some violently ill Aboard *Iolaire*, where five of us ate the other half, we were all fine. Who can figure it out?

In St. Barts, the advice is to cut out the fish's liver and put it down for the ants; if the ants eat the liver the fish is fine. If they don't eat it, you shouldn't either. some suggest offering some of the fish to a cat and waiting 24 hours. If the cat is fine, go ahead and eat the fish; if the cat gets sick, throw out the rest of the fish.

The best advice is to check with the locals. In general, if they would be willing to eat it, you should be too

COMMUNICATIONS

Communications are expanding so rapidly that whatever I write to day would be out of date by the time it is printed. In the big fancy yachts they can pick up a phone and call anywhere in the world and in the medium sized yachts there is the SSB. With this you can get patched through to a shore side station to enable you to make phone calls. Ashore on all the islands, with the aid of a credit card, you can call anywhere in the world

On the French islands it is sometimes difficult to get an English speaking operator to explain what you should do. On St. Martins I think I can say, without fear of contradiction, that the Dutch side of St. Martins historically has had the worst and most expensive phone system in the world The U S A. direct phones seem to work pretty well, but for calling anywhere else, my advice is that if you are in Phillisburg, go to Dockside and use their phones and pay them. If in Simpsons Bay or Simpson Lagoon go to Mailbox and avail of their services. Both organisations also have photocopying, fax, secretarial services—the works.

On Anguilla, Antigua and Dominica with the aid of a credit card you can more or less call anywhere in the world. The only problem is that Cable & Wireless change their procedures and they don't change the new directions in the phone booths.

Mobile phones are coming in on the islands. At the time of writing each island has their own mobile phone system so when travelling from island to island, your mobile phone is useless. However, I am told by 2001 and certainly by 2002 you will be able to have a chip put into your mobile phone, that will enable you to use your mobile phone up and down the eastern Caribbean.

Mail and general delivery is not too hot an idea on most of the islands. It is better to look at the guide, check with the marina or yacht yard. Write to them and make arrangements with them to hold your mail when you arrive.

RENTAL CARS

Rental cars are available everywhere in the eastern Caribbean. You should shop around as the rates vary widely. Also you should drive very defensively as the accident rate on many of the islands is right out the window.

TIDES

You can try to predict the tides on the islands if you refer to Street's Transatlantic Crossing Guide and the information shown on the back of Imray Iolaire charts. It should be noted at the spring and autumn equinox the tide will be extremely high, as much as two feet, sometimes as much as two and half feet in areas that normally have no more that eighteen inches rise and fall of tide. Also a most important thing, for deep draft vessels, or even moderately drafted vessel, THE CARIBBEAN IS EIGHTEEN INCHES TO TWO FEET LOWER IN MAY, JUNE, JULY AND EARLY AUGUST than it is the rest of the year. Thus the channels that you can go up and down all winter long with no trouble, often with 6 inches of clearance, may have you wedged like a cork in a bottle in these months,

at spring tides and may have to wait 6 hours to float off For this reason for the past thirty years I have been urging installation on of tidal gauges in channels where depth is a problem. As each year goes by the yachts bet bigger and bigger, and it becomes more and more essential to have tidal gauges installed They should be installed Nanny and Wickhams Cay, Tortola, Simson Bay entrance to Simson Lagoon, St. Martins, Jolly Harbour, Antigua. Rodney Bay, St. Lucia, Blue Lagoon, St. Vincent, the Lagoon St. Georges and Secret Harbour Grenada. With a proper tidal gauge installed, one can tell at a glance exactly what the controlling depth is in the channel at any moment

GROUND SWELLS

Ground swells are produced by storms in the North Atlantic and have absolutely nothing to do with local weather They used to arrive completely unannounced, but now the weather reports from Puerto Rico usually predict them Each year, ground swells put at least one boat up on the beach. Anytime you see an especially beautiful sandy beach, you know the ground swells have done their bit to create it. When in any volume mention is made of an anchorage subject to ground swells be sure to use a Bahamian moor (see *Street's Transatlantic Crossing Guide and Introduction to the Caribbean),* or your boat may be the one up on the beach.

BUOYAGE

The French islands buoyage system is excellent as they have always had a buoy tender based in Guadeloupe. When a French buoy comes adrift it is replaced almost immediately. On the other islands if a buoy comes adrift it may be years before it is replace.

In the ex-British islands, they are often not buoys but booby traps that catch the unwary yachtsman. Throughout the islands the privately maintained buoys frequently go adrift and are frequently altered. The privately maintained buoys are not marked on the charts, because they are too subject to change. Basically, anywhere there is likely to be a buoy, you should be able to use eyeball navigation. Judge depths by the colour of the water: Brown is reef, white is shoal water, light green usually is deep enough to sail in, and blue is deep water. A good test of your skill is to try to guess the depth of the water and then turn on the fathometer to check.

Don't sail at night; enter all harbours when the sun is still fairly high. When heading eastward, you can enter as late as 1700, because the sun is behind you, but if heading westward, you should be in harbour by 1600 at the very latest. Similarly, before leaving a harbour in the morning, take a good look around. Check the access to the channel and the bearing to the sun. In the morning, the sun may be right in your eyes, making it hard to see anything, so you may have to delay your departure until 1000 or 1100

LIGHTS

Despite what other guides say, the lights in the Caribbean are NOT all reliable. In the French islands, the lights are excellent and reliable; in the American islands, they are good and fairly reliable, but not absolutely, in the British (and ex-British) islands, it looks as though the lighting and buoyage system was established to keep harbour pilots, ship wreckers and salvagers from starving to death. DO NOT RELY ON THESE LIGHTS

DIVING

Throughout the islands there are diving organisations. If you wish to do any diving it is best to make contact with the diving organisations as they know the area, the best diving sites, have the equipment and they take all the hassle out of diving. There are a few exceptions.

Many charter skippers do not conduct diving tours as the local divers know the areas so much better than they do and are so much better equipped with suitable boats. Diving from a charter boat, except for those specifically built to cater for it, is pretty much a no no. Further, immediately on checking in with Customs & Immigration you should check what the local regulations are regarding diving, fishing and anchoring as in many of the islands, as of 2001, diving from your boat is NOT LEGAL. It is also very very important that as soon as you have checked in with Customs & Immigration you check what the local regulations are regarding anchoring, fishing with hand lines off the end of a boat and rod and reel fishing. The regulations are regularly being changed and I cannot summarise it here.

In many areas spear fishing is prohibited. In other areas even trolling from a boat is prohibited.

CUSTOMS AND IMMIGRATION

The situation is on arrival on most of the islands, Customs and Immigration is fairly lenient. When you arrive you should hoist the Q Flag and the skipper should go ashore to clear customs and immigration. However, in most islands if you arrive outside office hours, no one will object to the crew going ashore for drinks and dinner with the skipper clearing the next morning.

The trouble comes when you are flying in to join a boat, sailing off the island and flying back from another island, or joining the boat and not flying out. Immigration at the airport will immediately insist on seeing you flight ticket to get out of the island. If you don't have a ticket out all sorts of problems ensue. The way around this is to have a letter from the owner or captain of the boat, addressed to the immigration officer, stating that you are joining the boat and leaving the island on board the yacht. If worse comes to worst, and you have not received a letter sit down and write a letter to yourself Forge the skipper's signature—it works everytime.

The exact location of the Customs & Immigration on each island is noted on the Imray Iolaire charts.

HURRICANES

See *Reflections on Hugo* in the Forward Page *xv*

The entire Caribbean is hurricane territory, and hurricanes are more frequent than most people realise. The Virgin Islands, for example, have been hit or sideswiped by 32 hurricanes since 1871. In 1916 alone, there were three hurricanes. In 1889, 1891 and 1979 there were two hurricanes in the same year.

Puerto Rico has been hit by 34 hurricanes, of which three were in 1916 and two were in 1891, 1898, 1899, 1901 and 1979. The Antigua/Guadeloupe area has had 32 hurricanes (three in 1933), plus the area has been sideswiped by 10 or 12 tropical depressions. The Martinique/St. Lucia area has had 44 hurricanes, plus about a dozen tropical depressions

The frequency of hurricanes in St. Vincent and the Grenadines is much lower than farther north, BUT there are really no hurricane holes in the area The first hurricane hole south of St. Lucia is all the way down on the south coast of Grenada—an area that has had only about five hurricanes in its history.

Amazingly, Isla Margarita in Venezuela has been hit by two hurricanes in the last 120 years, even though no hurricanes have struck the Venezuelan mainland.

You can find the tracks of all the known hurricanes in the U.S. government publication *Tropical Cyclones of the North Atlantic Ocean* (national Climatic Data and Information Center, Ashvill, North Carolina 28801, U S.A.—NOAA—1871-TI 1980, with an update to 1993).

In light of the above, one must figure on a major hurricane every four to five years, no matter where you are in the Caribbean. For the best odds, head for Grenada, Trinidad, or mainland Venezuela—and I urge that underwriters offer discounts to boats that arrange to be in those areas between July and November

Bill Skokl, of the 42-foot double-topsail, gaff rigged schooner *Media*, took off southward, singlehanded, from Isleta Marina in Fajardo, on the east coast of Puerto Rico, 48 hours before Hugo hit. He experienced no more than 30- to 40-knot gusts of wind, huge but long swells, and no damage whatsoever to his boat. When he returned to isleta Marina, he found nothing but utter destruction. Go to sea; don't try to ride out a hurricane in an over crowded harbour.

Prologue

Remember: Always be alert and cautious. Almost every place in the Eastern Caribbean where a yacht can anchor has been described or at least mentioned in the Street guides, but not all are easy to enter. Many of these anchorages can be used only in good weather and perfect visibility. Beside, some boats are handier than others and some sailors are more skilled than others.

Thus, you must evaluate each anchorage for yourself before entering. the time of day, the weather, your abilities, the weatherliness of your boat—all influence the final decision.

Some advice to readers who operate bareboat charter fleets. Study this book carefully, make your judgements, and mark on the charts in the book the anchorages you want your charterers to avoid

OVERALL VIEW

For an overall view of the entire Caribbean you should carefully read a copy of Street's Transatlantic Guide, study it's sections of Transatlantic Crossings and "getting there" from the States, leaving—the States, Europe and Panama, supplies, communications, touchdowns, wind weather and tides This really is an essential companion to the other guides.

To find more about the islands and also some good advice, very carefully read the Foreword, Acknowledgements and the section on Charts

Finally, before you sail anywhere in the Eastern Caribbean (and particularly if you are going during hurricane season), I advise you to take to heart the advice that appeared above.

Street's Cruising Guide to the Eastern Caribbean, Volume III— Martinique to Trinidad

[The Islands] are accessible in every part, and covered with a vast variety of lofty trees, which, it appears to me, never lose their foliage, as we found them fair and verdant as in May in Spain. Some were covered with blossoms, some with fruit, and others in different stages, according to their nature. The nightingale and a thousand other sorts of birds were singing in the month of November wherever I went. There are palm-trees in these countries, of six or eight sorts, which are surprising to see, on account of their diversity from ours, but indeed, this is the case with respect to the other trees, as well as the fruits and weeds. Beautiful forests of pines are likewise found, and fields of vast extent. Here is also honey, and fruits of a thousand sorts, and bird of every variety. The lands contain mines of metals, and inhabitants without number. . . . [Their] harbors are of such excellence, that their description would not gain belief, and the like may be said of the abundance of large and fine rivers, the most of which abound in gold.

> —Christopher Columbus, on his return
> to Spain from the Caribbean, 1494

1

Sailing Directions

Introduction

In the Eastern Caribbean during the winter months, the wind will vary from east-southeast to east-northeast, occasionally going all the way around to north. The current sets generally west at a knot or more. Thus the greatest problem encountered by the yachtsman new to the area is that of allowing his boat to sag below the rhumb-line course. At the end of the day, he suddenly realizes that the anchorage is well to windward—a hard slog against wind and tide. My advice to avoid this situation is to keep a hand-bearing compass handy and take continual bearings; if you can't see the island ahead, take stern bearings.

This problem is complicated in the Grenadines by variable currents that can at times veer strongly to windward. Since the currents will almost always be on the beam, they will rapidly push you off course if you sail strictly by the compass. Hence the reason for ranges; stay on them and you will stay out of trouble.

It is also important to read the sailing and pilot directions for the area concerned the night before, in order to plan the next day's run, and to calculate your departure in time to guarantee arrival at the next anchorage while the sun is still high.

Regarding tides, read *Street's Transatlantic Crossing Guide and Introduction to the Caribbean,* chapter 6. This is most important, as correct analysis of the tides will drastically affect your times of departure.

Proceeding South

MARTINIQUE TO ST. LUCIA

From the east coast of Martinique, you can pass to windward or leeward of St. Lucia, an easy reach either way. From Fort de France on the west coast, it is still not too rough a sail to Castries. Do not be discouraged if, when you clear Cap Salomon, you are almost hard on the wind. Usually the wind hooks around the southern end of the islands, coming in south of east, backing to the east as you sail offshore and to the northeast as you approach Castries. Thus, as you leave Martinique, especially in the region of Pointe du Diamant, do not fight your way up onto the rhumb-line course; frequently there is a tide-against-the-wind situation that can make it very rough. Better to ease sheets and alter course to south or even slightly west of south until you are clear of Rocher du Diamant. Then start to work your way up to the rhumb line, but don't work too hard to lay a course to Castries Harbor. As you approach St. Lucia, the wind tends to back and lift you; if you are below the rhumb line, you'll be able to work your way back up to it. Being hard on the wind the last six or eight miles is not all that bad, since you're under the lee of St. Lucia and in calm water.

ST. LUCIA TO ST. VINCENT

In proceeding south to St. Vincent, remember that there is usually wind on the lee side of St. Lucia from 1000 until about 1700, but it is likely to be calm the rest of the time. And it is a long sail down to Kingstown, the entry port of St. Vincent, or to Bequia. Thus, plan your departure to make sure you are clear of the Pitons by 1700 or you're likely to have to spend the night under the Pitons—a scenic but not swift trip.

Most yachtsmen sail from the Pitons to the west coast of St. Vincent on course 205° magnetic, which normally gives a very easy reach. However, they usually run out of wind in the lee of St. Vincent, and then from the southwest corner of St. Vincent have either a hard slog against the wind and current up into Kingstown Harbor or a fairly close fetch across to Bequia and then a beat up into Admiralty Bay.

I prefer passing to windward of St. Vincent, setting a course from the Pitons of 190° magnetic with adjustments for leeway and current. In most conditions it is an easy reach; at worst, a close fetch. Sail down the windward coast of St. Vincent on an easy reach, enjoying the beautiful scenery. If it really pipes up, stay well offshore, as a heavy Atlantic swell will crest in 18 feet and break in 12. When you get to the southeast corner of St. Vincent, run dead downwind and anchor in Kingstown Harbor. Or, usually better, broad-reach across Bequia Channel and enter at Bequia, an easier process than entering at Kingstown.

ST. VINCENT TO PETIT ST. VINCENT

Departing St. Vincent from Kingstown Harbor, Young Island anchorage, or the lagoon presents no difficulties. It is almost always a reach to Admiralty Bay. On the other hand, if you want to go to windward and east of Bequia—"over the top," as the locals say—you must hold high in the event of a lee-going ebb tide. Once around, you can stand southeast to Baliceaux or south to Mustique. The only danger here is Montezuma Shoal.

Leaving Admiralty Bay under sail is a good test of seamanship, since you will be running dead before the wind. Once past West Cay, stand south, leaving Canouan to either side. Windward of Canouan, beware of the reefs that extend well offshore. These carry seven-tenths of a mile windward of Friendship

CHART A

Range 1.   Peak of Petit Martinique bearing 162°–342° magnetic leads between Pinese and Mopion.

Range 2.   N sides of Baradal and Petit Bateau in line with S side of flat land on Mayreau, 100°–280° magnetic, leads through boat pass.

Range 3.   Glossy Hill, Canouan Island, in line with E tip of Mayreau 037°–217° magnetic passes Grand de Coi to the E.

Range 4.   Catholic Island between Red Island and Union Island, 022°–202° magnetic, leads W of Grand de Coi and also into entrance Windward Side, Carriacou.

Range 5.   Petit Tobago one finger open from Fota 012°–192° magnetic leads between Palm Island and to W of reef at N end of Saline Bay, Mayreau. If more than half a finger's width of Petit St. Vincent shows to E of Palm Island, bear off, or you will fail to clear the dangers at N end of Saline Bay.

Range 6.   Taffia Hill in line with Channel Rocks, 036°–216° magnetic, leads E of Break Rock.

Range 7.   NW side of Channel Rocks open slightly from the summit of Friendship Hill, Canouan Island, 059°–239° magnetic, leads W of Break Rock.

Range 8.   Petit Tabac in line with Jamesby, 127°–307° magnetic, leads into Worlds End Reef anchorage.

Range 9.   Middle hill on Palm Island under High North, Carriacou, 043°–223° magnetic, leads through S entrance to Tobago Cays.

Range 10.   SE point of Petit Rameau in line with NW point of Petit Bateau, 071°–251° magnetic, leads through S entrance to Tobago Cays.

Range 11.   Speak of Mayreau bearing 126°–306° magnetic clears Worlds End Reef to the S.

Range 12.   Peak of Petit Martinique bearing 047°–227° magnetic clears Worlds End Reef to the E.

Range 13.   Cliff on NW end of Saline Bay, Mayreau, in line with midpoint of dock. To locate wreck of *Paruna*, proceed along this range until intersection with Range 14.

Range 14.   Peak on Petit Martinique between easternmost two hills of Palm Island, 004°–184° magnetic, leads over wreck.

Range 15.   Sail Rock three fingers open from NW corner of Petit St. Vincent 070°–250° magnetic. To enter Windward Side, Carriacou, follow down this range until intersection with Range 16.

Range 16.   Fota closing with SW corner of Petit Martinique 123°–303° magnetic. From where this range meets Range 15, the channel through the reef may be eyeballed.

Range 17.   Westernmost hill on Mayreau over western low land of Palm Island clears the 1.2–fathom spot off Petit Tobago to the W, 018°–198° magnetic.

Range 18.   Hill on Frigate in line with 290–foot hill and radio mast on Union Island. The hill between the Pinnacle (741 feet) and Mount Taboi (999 feet) leads clear inside shoal spot (4 feet) inside Jack a Dan, 026°–206° magnetic, to Hillsborough, Carriacou.

Sailing Directions

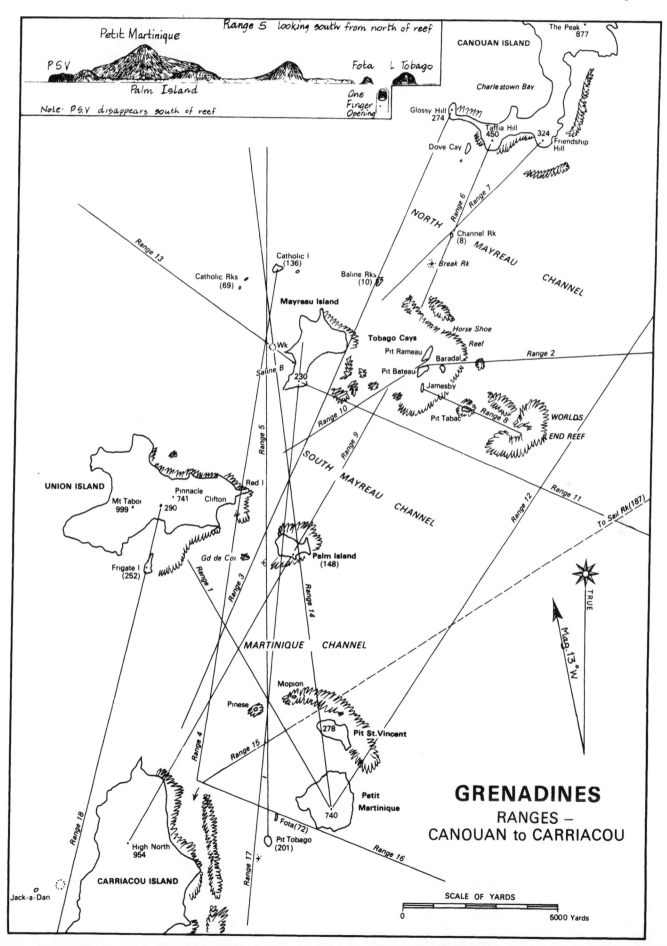

Hill. There is one danger to look out for between the southeast corner of the reefs off Canouan and Baline Rocks. The course leads directly across the breaking rock southwest of Channel Rocks. The best route is to pass Channel Rocks close aboard to the southeast and run to the west until Channel Rocks opens slightly from Friendship Hill, Canouan (Chart A, Range 7). Turn to the southwest and maintain this range, 239° magnetic, until close by Baline Rocks.

Passing to leeward of Canouan, there are no dangers between it and the Tobago Cays. Steer course 204° magnetic, making allowance for the current and passing between Baline Rocks and the reef northwest of the Tobago Cays. The sailing directions within the Tobago Cays are included in chapter 7, so I will not repeat them here. Basically, eyeball navigation will be required to get you clear of the inner reef; then sail southeastward until the middle hill of Palm Island (formerly Prune Island) lines up with High North, Carriacou (Chart A, Range 9). This range will guide you south between the windward and leeward reefs of the Tobago Cays. If your plan is to pass to windward of Palm Island, go east until the peak of Petit Martinique bears 190° magnetic. Sail that course until south of Palm Island, then sail southwest magnetic until you reach Range 1, with the peak of Petit Martinique bearing 162° magnetic. If you maintain this range, you will come right between the two sand islands off Petit St. Vincent. But remember to follow the range rather than the compass course, since the currents will be tending to throw you off one way or the other.

If you are proceeding from the southern entrance to the Tobago Cays to the west of Palm Island, a course of 239° magnetic—and an allowance for current—will take you between the reefs of Union and Palm islands. There are no reliable ranges, and a good deal of precautionary eyeballing will be necessary. Also, keep a sharp lookout for Grand de Coi, which must be avoided. There is a new post with a light on it mounted in 12 feet of water on the western side of Grand de Coi. (For a short history of classic groundings here, see chapter 7.) It can be passed to the westward by staying west until Catholic Island aligns itself between Union and Red islands (Chart A, Range 4) and following this range on southward. To pass eastward of Grand de Coi: Once the reefs of Palm Island are cleared to port, head up until Glossy (Glass) Hill joins the eastern end of Mayreau Island (Chart A, Range 3). This range should be maintained, keeping clear of the shoal at the southeast corner of Palm. And if your

destination is Petit St. Vincent, hold this range until the peak of Petit Martinique bears 162° magnetic. Follow 162° midway between Pinese and Mopion. Once you have passed beyond the reefs, you may alter course to Petit St. Vincent.

SOUTH AND WEST FROM PETIT ST. VINCENT

From Petit St. Vincent to Windward Side, Carriacou, head west until Sail Rock is three fingers off the northern end of Petit St. Vincent. Continue heading 250° magnetic (Chart A, Range 15) until Fota is overlapped by the southwestern corner of Petit Martinique (Chart A, Range 16). At this point you will be inside the reef. From here on southward along the coast, use eyeball navigation. A skillful reef pilot in a boat drawing no more than seven feet with a crew member aloft could continue south all the way through Watering Bay into Grand Bay.

A less taxing course from Petit St. Vincent is to sail southwest until the westernmost hill on Mayreau lines up with the western low land of Palm Island (Chart A, Range 17). Turn south along this range, which will carry you safely to the west of the 1.2-fathom spot southwest of Petit Tobago. Once past this danger point, alter course to clear the reef off the eastern point of Carriacou, after which you can steer a course approximately southwest, passing to either side of Ile de Ronde and Grenada.

The west coast of Carriacou is far less formidable. From Petit St. Vincent to Rapid Point is a straight-line course with no hazards. Around Rapid Point it is an easy reach down the coast of Carriacou with no dangers until Jack a Dan, at which time you should hook up with the next range (Chart A, Range 18), defined by the peak on Frigate Island placed under the first peak west of the easternmost peak of Union Island. This will carry you clear inside the shoal spot between Jack a Dan and the mainland of Carriacou.

CARRIACOU TO GRENADA

From Hermitage Point at the southwest corner of Tyrell Bay to Diamond Island (Kick 'em Jenny) and David Point, Grenada, it is 228° magnetic without taking account of current. This is normally a very broad reach or a dead run. If the wind is in the north, it may be a good idea before you leave the lee of Carriacou to rig your main boom foreguy to starboard and set your jib on the pole to windward. This will save you a lot of rolling and slatting on the way down.

Once round David Point, the wind tends to hook around the island, often putting you dead before the wind most of the way to Black Bay, Grenada, where it will tend to come more abeam. If your destination is St. Georges, the course from Molinière Point is 178° magnetic, hugging the shore. If you are bypassing St. Georges and heading directly to the south coast of Grenada, a course of 214° magnetic from Molinière Point will clear Long Point Shoal.

Work your way up the south coast of Grenada, continually tacking inshore to stay out of the westward-flowing current and the sea. Consult the chart, use watchful eyeball navigation, and carefully read the sailing directions given under "St. Georges to Carriacou via the South and East Coasts of Grenada."

If you sail down the lee side of Grenada and continue around Point Salines and eastward to Prickly Bay (Anse aux Epines), it means that at the end of your trip you'll have a good, hard slog to windward. For this reason, many people heading for the south coast would rather pass to windward of Grenada; then you have a glorious beam reach along the weather side of the island; you can ease sheets around the southeast corner and run dead downwind for half an hour, then jibe over and reach into Prickly Bay. Once again, keep a careful eye on the depth of the water if the sea is running high. Breaking crests can demolish a boat in short order. This happened to Mike Forshaw's *Tawana*, which took a breaking crest on board and sank almost instantly. Luckily, the dinghy had been tied on the cabintop with rotten old line, and the dinghy popped to the surface minutes after the boat sank. The crew righted the dinghy, bailed it out, and drifted ashore in it.

When running along the south coast of Grenada downwind, you should be careful about the reefs spreading south from Hog Island and Mount Hartman Bay. A good plan is to clear the south end of Calivigny Point by a half mile or more and continue on a course of west 270° magnetic until Prickly Point bears 300°. Then you have to sail inside The Porpoises, which are exposed rocks southwest of Prickly Point with deep water all around—*except* for a rock with only six feet over it, 40 yards north of The Porpoises.

GRENADA TO TRINIDAD

The sail from Grenada to Trinidad usually is an easy beam reach. The only difficulty is an occasionally strong current, along with some tide rips that will set up between the two islands. The normal procedure for most yachts making the passage is to leave Grenada at about 1800, steer 170° magnetic (or 165° if your boat makes a lot of leeway) until you spot the Chacachacare light, and alter your course accordingly. This is a very powerful light, which can be seen as far as 25 miles away on a clear night. Do not head right for it, as it marks the westernmost *boca* (mouth) of the Bocas del Dragon, and the current will be pulling you in that direction anyway. Most boats favor entering the Golfo de Paria through the easternmost *boca* in order to save a lot of windward effort. This should put you in Port of Spain early in the morning.

ALTERNATE ROUTES

Although the distance from St. Thomas to, say, Antigua is only about 200 miles, the course is practically dead against the wind all the way. There are plenty of islands in between that afford the opportunity to lay over, rest, and sightsee, but the windward legs still will be pure hell. In a small boat of 30 or 35 feet, your progress against heavy trades may be reduced to nothing.

Bear in mind that there are other ways to reach the middle or southern islands. Depending on the time at your disposal, you can sail from the Virgins directly to Grenada, St. Lucia, or Martinique, and from any one of these islands you can work your way north in easy stages off the wind to Antigua. The strategy is to define the southern extent of your cruise and to proceed north from there. If you are chartering a bareboat and are willing to pay the deadhead fee (for someone to deliver it), you should consider picking up the boat on one of these southern islands. Otherwise, sail the passage yourself. With a break in the weather, you can lay a straight course from St. Thomas Harbor to Martinique (143° magnetic), making it in two and a half or three days. This is not a great deal of time to give up if you are planning a cruise of two or three weeks. The disadvantages are that you will be close-hauled the entire way, and if you have just arrived by air from the United States, setting out on a long sail from St. Thomas allows no time for the crew to get its sea legs or to build up a tan against the sun. Therefore, a preferable course is to work your way eastward from St. Thomas through the U.S. and British Virgins for a few days. This gives you the time to shake down the crew, pick up some precious easting and a tan in sheltered waters, and then to take off through Necker Island Passage for

Grenada. The course is 170° magnetic; the distance—420 miles—an easy reach. Even if the wind veers to east-southeast, you will still be under slightly eased sheets and going like mad. If it is east to east-northeast, as is usual, you can make the trip in three days. Let me repeat that if you have the time to invest in this passage, I can recommend no better way of positioning yourself for a cruise of the southern islands. You will have reached the southernmost of the Antilles without having strained to windward and with no serious windward work before you.

The course from St. Thomas Harbor to Grenada direct is 163° magnetic, 423 miles. You will have to hold one point high on the course for the first 50 miles in order to clear the eastern end of St. Croix, but once clear, you can ease the sheets for a nice, comfortable reach to Grenada. The chances are relatively slim that the wind will swing so far south as to put you hard on the wind. If the wind should really pipe up, its direction will back and give you a real sleighride. A heavy blow won't faze a small boat, as it will be aft of abeam. For the remainder of the passage, there are two things to watch out for:

First, don't run up on Aves Island, which will be right on your track. Aves Island is low and hard to find; it is a nesting area for turtles and the site of enough disasters and near-disasters to fill a book. It has also been mischarted by almost everyone. According to the most recent British Admiralty information, it is located at 15°42'10" N. latitude and 63°37' W. longitude. This may or may not be where it is on your chart, because it has moved three or possibly four times during my three decades in the Caribbean!

Now the Venezuelan government (which, amazingly, owns Aves Island) has established a well-lighted military base on the island. No navigation lights have been set up yet, but if you are in the area and see something that looks like a cruise ship hove-to, it's probably Aves Island. Give it a wide berth.

Second, take sights frequently to ensure that you are not falling off to leeward. It would be an awful waste of time to have to beat the last 50 miles or so to Grenada. The current runs to the west through here as fast as three knots. Against a three-knot current in the same direction as the wind, you would need to make six knots through the water to hold your own tacking in 120°.

Proceeding North

TRINIDAD TO GRENADA

It is best to depart Trinidad in time to arrive at Point Salines, Grenada, by dawn. More than one boat has grounded on Long Point Shoal tacking up from Point Salines to St. Georges. Most yachts can hold a course of 015° from the easternmost *boca* to Grenada. Soon after you pick up the lights on the hills of Grenada, airport lights will appear. If entering at Prickly Bay (Anse aux Epines), keep these high lights on the starboard bow but don't approach the coast till dawn, or you may come to a sudden stop on The Porpoises. A better course is to head for Point Salines and round close aboard. Hug the coast and short-tack up the beach, passing close to Quarantine Point (the local name for Long Point). This way, you will avoid Long Point Shoal, which is most difficult to spot at night. There is no difficulty entering St. Georges Harbour at night: Anchor in the northeast corner and proceed at dawn to clear.

SOUTH COAST OF GRENADA TO ST. GEORGES HARBOUR

Do not leave harbors like Bacaye or Calivigny until the sun is high, because in the early morning the path of the sunlight is directly in line with the exit course. Once clear of the harbors on the south coast of Grenada, it is best to head directly for Glover Island, keeping an eye open for The Porpoises (Grampuses); pass close south of The Porpoises and then head for Point Salines. As I mentioned earlier, reefs do extend well offshore between Calivigny Island and Prickly Point. Check bearings and ranges carefully, as described above.

If you head directly for Point Salines, you will discover that the wind shifts to the south at Hardy Bay and you will end up dead downwind, whereas if you stay offshore, as the wind shifts you may head southwest for Point Salines and still be on a reach. Once you have rounded Point Salines, favor the shore. Stay close in to avoid the sea and to take advantage of better wind shifts than you could find offshore. When approaching Long Point, be sure to favor the Morne Rouge beach area, and stay inshore to avoid Long Point Shoal. If under power, motor directly from Point Salines to Long Point, leaving Long Point 100 yards off the starboard side, and proceed directly to St. Georges Harbour or Grand Anse Bay, clear of all dangers.

Sailing Directions

GRENADA TO CARRIACOU

When proceeding north from St. Georges, you must make plans to arrive at Carriacou early in the day and in no event later than 1700. This necessitates a very early departure from St. Georges. Many boats motorsail all the way up the coast to David Point and then set sail for Carriacou. If you choose to sail the coast, it is best to do it close inshore. Every time you get a mile offshore on starboard tack, you should tack back in.

There is little or no wind on the lee coast of Grenada until after 0800, and it dies drastically after 1700. Grenada's highest point is almost 2,800 feet, and the main line of mountains is approximately 2,000 feet. Do not make the mistake of standing offshore to find more wind. Nine times out of ten, you won't find any. *Stay in close.*

When you reach David Point (Tanga Luanga, locally known as Tangle Angle because of the way the current sweeps around it and causes tide rips), it is again important to tack to the eastward. In fact, you should tack to the east as far as Sauteurs and frequently to Levera Island before setting out for Carriacou. The current runs as much as two and a half knots (normally it is one to one and a half knots) to the west through this passage. (Remember that many boats make as much as 15° leeway when on the wind.)

Occasionally, with the wind in the southeast, it is possible to lay the course from David Point to Carriacou, but this is very much the exception. Most Grenada—Carriacou races have proved that it is worth tacking to Sauteurs, even with a windward-going tide. In any event, be careful of the shoal spots between Levera Island and the town of Levera, as they can break in heavy weather. Proceed east until you can lay Ile de Ronde, and then set out. Pass between The Sisters and Ile de Ronde and stand north on starboard tack until you reach smooth water in the lee of Carriacou.

The best time to arrive at David Point is when the tides have just begun to run to windward. This will give you four hours of either slack water or weather-going tide, enough to reach Tyrell Bay before the tide changes.

As you approach Carriacou's southwest point, you should note the tide. If you wish to go to Saline Island or One Tree Rock on the south coast of Carriacou, do so only if the tide is running to windward; otherwise it is almost impossible to get up to Saline Island unless you have a very powerful engine. It should also be noted that it is best not to tack east after Diamond Island (Kick 'em Jenny), as

this will put you into the worst of the current. Instead, stand north into the lee of Carriacou; you can then make good progress on port tack in smooth water.

ST. GEORGES TO CARRIACOU VIA THE SOUTH AND EAST COASTS OF GRENADA

When proceeding from St. Georges to the south coast of Grenada, be careful of the shoals extending from the Islander Hotel over to the Silver Sands Hotel (Chart 41, Range C).

Long Point Shoal off Long Point (locally referred to as Quarantine Point) is most dangerous. The northeast corner of the dock transit shed in line with Government House will clear Long Point Shoal to the northwest (Sketch Chart 42, Range B). Government House is easy to identify, as it is situated on the ridge northeast of town and is a large, dark-colored building with large verandas on both first and second stories. It is the only house on the ridge with two flagpoles—one east and one west of the house.

The other route commonly used by yachts is to head from St. Georges Harbour to Long Point, leaving Long Point to port 100 yards off. When Long Point Shoal comes abeam, head for Point Salines, which course will clear Long Point Shoal to the southeast; or use Range A on Sketch Chart 42, course 062°–242° magnetic. There is deep water along this entire shore, and you may sail 200 yards off with no danger and in smooth water. If it is blowing more than 10 knots, tie in a reef before rounding Point Salines.

When rounding Point Salines, give it a 200-yard berth, because when they built the airport, they blew up and carted off the hill; most of it was used for fill for the airport, but much fell into the sea. No survey has been done of the area since the hill was removed.

Upon rounding, unless you draw more than 10 feet, the best procedure is to stay close inshore. This will keep you out of the swell and current. Each time you make a long tack offshore, the current and sea will set you to leeward.

Between Point Salines and Prickly Point, there are few difficulties as long as a lookout is kept during starboard tacks inshore. If beating to windward under sail, short-tack along the shore as close as possible, as it will keep you out of the swell and the foul current, and usually will give you port-tack lifts; watch for shoals on starboard tack. From Prickly Point eastward, this coast has numerous reefs and sandbanks. All are clearly visible as long as the sun is fairly high.

For a long time, it was generally thought that there was a good two fathoms of water everywhere between Glover Island and the mainland. Deep-draft boats have sailed happily between the two without a thought. However, there is at least one seven-foot spot. We discovered it in *Iolaire* while racing along the south coast. We were on a direct line between The Porpoises and Point Salines, absolutely upright doing about eight knots and with the point that forms the west side of Hardy Bay bearing about northwest. We felt a tremendous crash as we bounced off the top of a rock. Subsequently, I have gone back and looked for the rock but have been unable to find it. It must be just a small pinnacle rising up from the bottom.

When proceeding eastward along the south coast of Grenada under power, stay close to shore and keep an eye out for the various shoals. Remember, of course, that you should subtract at least three feet from any depths quoted on the charts, and frequently as much as a fathom. Eastward beyond Fort Jeudy Point, there are a number of shoal spots well offshore: off Westerhall Point, Menere Point, and Marquis Point.

During the winter, if the wind is out of the east or northeast, it is unwise to beat up the east coast of Grenada. It can get very rough, with seas breaking fairly far offshore. On the southeast coast, there is also roughly a one- to two-knot current dead on the nose.

Now that The Moorings has a base in Secret Harbour (Mount Hartman Bay), on the south coast of Grenada, sailing up the east coast of Grenada becomes a very viable method of reaching Carriacou. This route is most feasible if you have chartered one of the good boats that sail well to windward and if it is not blowing hard out of the northeast. You can spend a couple of days exploring the south coast of Grenada (which some of us feel has among the best anchorages in the Eastern Caribbean), then work your way eastward from Secret Harbour for the first and possibly second days of your cruise, shaking down both your crew and your boat. Then take off from Egmont/Calivigny Harbour, or possibly La Sagesse.

If you elect to proceed up the east coast, be sure to note how far offshore the shoals extend off Great Bacolet Point. Bear in mind that the current will be setting you onshore. Once you reach Telescope Point, set a course for Black Rock (Anthony Rock), which will take you clear of the shoals. The current between Telescope Point and Green Island sets very strongly to the south—so strongly that the old sailing directions warn vessels about passing and getting south of the entrance of Grenville. The old square-riggers were not too good to windward. Thus, if by mistake they sailed past Grenville, they were advised to continue south, around Point Salines, up the west coast of Grenada, and try again. It seems a long distance to go a few miles, but in years gone by, the sailors had plenty of patience, especially in adverse conditions.

Be very careful not to get involved with the three-fathom spot between Black Rock and Sandy Island, as the ground swell breaks continually on this spot in heavy weather. If you keep the eastern side of Sandy Island directly in line with the western peak of Ile de Caille (Chart 49, Range E), you will pass clear to windward of this breaking shoal spot.

There is deep water between Sandy Island and Green Island, between Green Island and Levera Island, and between Levera Island and Bedford Point, but favor the Levera Island side of the channel for deepest water. From the northeast corner of Grenada, it usually is an easy sail to Carriacou.

CARRIACOU NORTHWARD

The usual course is to pass along the west side of Carriacou, stopping at Tyrell Bay. When leaving this harbor, pass north of the middle ground, hug the coast, and make allowance for the rocks, which extend about 200 yards offshore from Lookout Point (the point south of Cistern Point). Under power or sail, the best course from Cistern Point to Hillsborough Bay is between Mabouya Island and Sandy Island, being careful to avoid the reef on the southwestern tip of Sandy Island. Other than that, there are no dangers in this area unless you have a vessel drawing 12 feet. Beating to windward through this gap is good fun, as there is no sea and usually plenty of wind.

Between Cistern Point and Hillsborough, deep-draft boats can easily run aground. The old schooner range is still a safe one. Put Cistern under the stern and the hospital building at the top of the mountain on the bow and proceed straight to the anchorage. Once past Sandy Island, you can shift course slightly toward the Hillsborough jetty. North of Hillsborough there is one danger, between Jack a Dan and the mainland. This is a 3/4-fathom spot with quite a few dents in it. You can pass it inside by placing the hill on Frigate Island directly in line with the 290-foot hill on Union Island, which is the hill just west of the highest and easternmost range

Sailing Directions 11

on Union (Chart A, Range 18, course 026° magnetic). Be sure to stay on this range, as this shoal is particularly hard to spot.

Under power, you can steer direct from Rapid Point to the dock of Petit St. Vincent and clear all dangers. Under sail, it will be a dead beat to windward. On port tack, beware of the shoal off Little Carenage Bay and the shoal on the north end of Watering Bay. On starboard tack, watch out for Pinese and Mopion, the two sand islands northwest of Petit St. Vincent. (Pinese may not be visible; it has been reported as under water.) There is ample water between these two islands, but eyeballing is called for, as they both are continually growing and shifting.

Grand de Coi is now marked by a buoy west of the reef. For discussions on the buoy and its problems, see chapter 7.

To head north from Petit St. Vincent, pass midway between the two cays and continue on course until Fota and the east side of Petit Tobago are one finger open (Chart A, Range 5, course 012° magnetic). This will take you east of Grand de Coi and east of the detached reef off Palm Island. Care must be exerted here, as the current will be at a right angle to your course and will tend to sweep you leeward. Thus, you need to check continuously that you are still on range. If you do not keep a good lookout, you may come to a sudden stop before you realize you are too close.

An alternate route clear of Grand de Coi is provided by Range 3 on Chart A, course 037° magnetic. This is Glossy Hill (Glass Hill), on the western point of Canouan, in line with the eastern end of Mayreau Island. Glossy Hill will appear as a detached island west of Taffia Hill, as it is

CHART A

Range 1.   Peak of Petit Martinique bearing 162°-342° magnetic leads between Pinese and Mopion.

Range 2.   N sides of Baradal and Petit Bateau in line with S side of flat land on Mayreau, 100°-280° magnetic, leads through boat pass.

Range 3.   Glossy Hill, Canouan Island, in line with E tip of Mayreau 037°-217° magnetic passes Grand de Coi to the E.

Range 4.   Catholic Island between Red Island and Union Island, 022°-202° magnetic, leads W of Grand de Coi and also into entrance Windward Side, Carriacou.

Range 5.   Petit Tobago one finger open from Fota 012°-192° magnetic leads between Palm Island and to W of reef at N end of Saline Bay, Mayreau. If more than half a finger's width of Petit St. Vincent shows to E of Palm Island, bear off, or you will fail to clear the dangers at N end of Saline Bay.

Range 6.   Taffia Hill in line with Channel Rocks, 036°-216° magnetic, leads E of Break Rock.

Range 7.   NW side of Channel Rocks open slightly from the summit of Friendship Hill, Canouan Island, 059°-239° magnetic, leads W of Break Rock.

Range 8.   Petit Tabac in line with Jamesby, 127°-307° magnetic, leads into Worlds End Reef anchorage.

Range 9.   Middle hill on Palm Island under High North, Carriacou, 043°-223° magnetic, leads through S entrance to Tobago Cays.

Range 10.   SE point of Petit Rameau in line with NW point of Petit Bateau, 071°-251° magnetic, leads through S entrance to Tobago Cays.

Range 11.   S peak of Mayreau bearing 126°-306° magnetic clears Worlds End Reef to the S.

Range 12.   Peak of Petit Martinique bearing 047°-227° magnetic clears Worlds End Reef to the E.

Range 13.   Cliff on NW end of Saline Bay, Mayreau, in line with midpoint of dock. To locate wreck of *Paruna*, proceed along this range until intersection with Range 14.

Range 14.   Peak on Petit Martinique between easternmost two hills of Palm Island, 004°-184° magnetic, leads over wreck.

Range 15.   Sail Rock three fingers open from NW corner of Petit St. Vincent 070°-250° magnetic. To enter Windward Side, Carriacou, follow down this range until intersection with Range 16.

Range 16.   Fota closing with SW corner of Petit Martinique 123°-303° magnetic. From where this range meets Range 15, the channel through the reef may be eyeballed.

Range 17.   Westernmost hill on Mayreau over western low land of Palm Island clears the 1.2-fathom spot off Petit Tobago to the W, 018°-198° magnetic.

Range 18.   Hill on Frigate in line with 290-foot hill and radio mast on Union Island. The hill between the Pinnacle (741 feet) and Mount Taboi (999 feet) leads clear inside shoal spot (4 feet) inside Jack a Dan, 026°-206° magnetic, to Hillsborough, Carriacou.

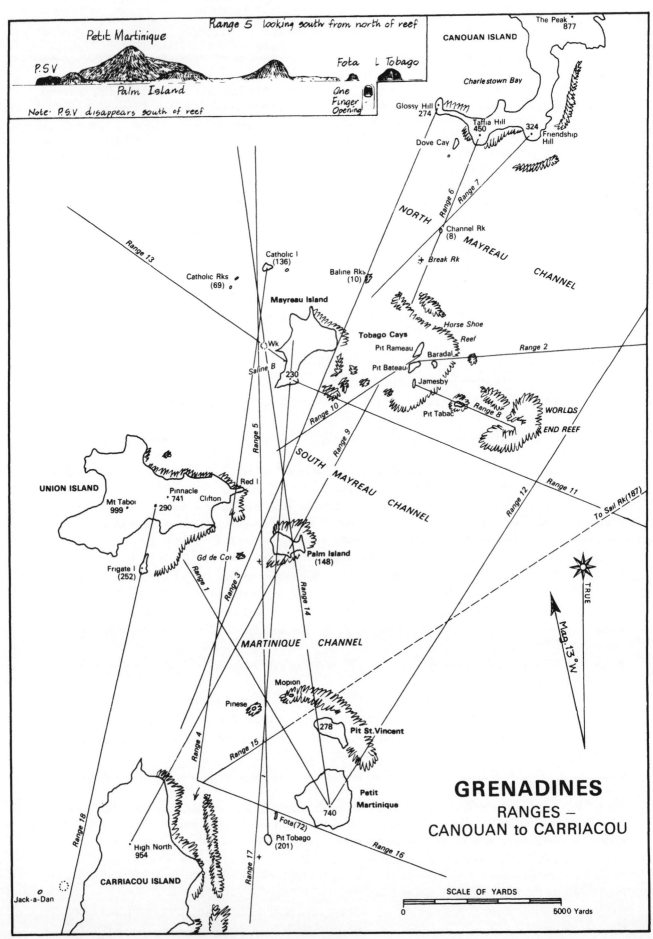

Sailing Directions 13

connected to Canouan only by a low sandspit.

Beating to windward from Rapid Point to the region of Union Island, you will want to avoid Grand de Coi. Catholic Island placed between Union Island and Red Island passes clear to the west of Grand de Coi (Chart A, Range 4, course 022°–202° magnetic). North of Grand de Coi, you will have to tack to the east to clear the reefs to windward of Union Island.

North beyond Palm and Union islands is about the most dangerous area of the Grenadines. A reef at the north end of Saline Bay has damaged many yachts proceeding north along the lee coast of Mayreau. To clear the end of this reef, put Fota one finger open from the east side of Little Tobago (Chart A, Range 5, course 012°–192°). As you approach Grand Col Point at the north end of Saline Bay, Mayreau, check to see if any of Petit St. Vincent is showing east of Palm. If Petit St. Vincent is at all visible, bear off to the west or you will come to a sudden stop on the reef off Grand Col Point. With this reef behind you, there are no other dangers standing north from Mayreau to Canouan.

APPROACHES TO THE TOBAGO CAYS

When approaching the Tobago Cays from the west, if you are coming in under power, no problem—just head for the buoy northwest of Baline Rocks and pick up the newly installed range. (The range is 139° magnetic.) This leads directly to the anchorage in the slot. If, however, you are beating to windward under sail and cannot lay the range, be careful of the nine-foot spot approximately 800 yards southwest of Baline Rocks—really a case of eyeball navigation.

If you are coming from Petit St. Vincent, sail west until the peak of Petit Martinique bears 162° magnetic over the stern, come to course 342° magnetic, eyeball your way between Pinese and Mopion, and, once clear of these two islands, come hard on the wind until the eastern peak of Petit St. Vincent bears 192° magnetic. Stay east of this line of bearing until Union Island Airport bears due west magnetic. Then bear off until the middle hill on Palm Island lines up with High North on Carriacou (Chart A, Range 9, course 043° magnetic). Stay hard on this range until you have passed between the eastern and western reefs. The western one may be spotted by a small sand island. However, remember that these sand islands are prone to disappear at irregular intervals.

If you are coming from between Palm and Union islands and heading for the southern entrance to the Tobago Cays, you must fight your way up to windward until, again, the middle hill on Palm Island lines up with High North on Carriacou (Chart A, Range 9). Follow this bearing into the cays.

Or if the range to the south is obscured, a second range on the northwest corner of Petit Bateau just touching the southeast corner of Petit Rameau 070°–250° also leads into the southern entrance of the Tobago Cays.

TOBAGO CAYS TO CANOUAN

From the northern end of the Tobago Cays to the western end of Canouan, there are no dangers. Glossy Hill is easily laid from Baline Rocks. If you are bound for the windward side of Canouan and are tacking below Channel Rocks, I urge that you set out in slack water or a fair tide. Great care must be taken to avoid the submerged rock one-half mile southwest of Channel Rocks. This rock is covered and breaks in a swell. Friendship Hill touching the northwest side of Channel Rocks passes clear to the west of the breaking rock (Chart A, Range 7, course 059° magnetic). Channel Rocks in line with Taffia Hill passes the breaking rock clear to windward (Chart A, Range 6, course 036°).

CANOUAN TO BEQUIA

This trip should be made at slack water or when the tide is running to windward. The distance is 15 miles, and should the tide be running its full limit of two knots to the west, a vessel making five knots through the water would have to steer 045° magnetic, as opposed to the 028° rhumb line. Unless the wind were southeast, this would put you very close on the wind. During the winter, with the wind toward the north and a leeward-running tide, you stand very little chance of laying West Cay, leaving you a tough beat into Admiralty Bay. Against a foul tide, be sure to hold high on the course, passing close aboard to leeward of Pigeon Island. There are no dangers on the course to Bequia. If you depart during a weather tide, the only difficulty will be a strong tide rip off the northern end of Canouan. Once you reach Pigeon Island, Isle Quatre and Petit Nevis serve to break the swell, giving a glorious sail the rest of the way in with plenty of wind and smooth water.

Once you have rounded West Cay, you may turn

on the iron genoa and head for the anchorage at Port Elizabeth with no dangers in the way, or you can put the sport back into sailing and beat up into the harbor, but be very careful of the shoals on its south side.

BEQUIA TO ST. VINCENT

Bequia Channel has the well-deserved reputation of being exceedingly rough at times. This brief eight-mile passage has done in any number of small boats and dinghies over the years. The water is smoothest during a leeward tide. A windward tide will offset your leeway, but it will also manage to churn up a nasty, steep sea. I have seen the waves making up into almost boxlike shapes—six feet high and six feet between each crest—a great place to lose a dinghy under tow.

From Admiralty Bay, round up close aboard Point Peter (Fort Point), watching out for Wash Rocks 100 yards off Devil's Table. Play the wind shifts close to the Bequia shore and keep inshore until you feel you can comfortably lay Young Island. If this does not seem logical, let me note that the 45-foot gaff-rigged schooner *Stella Maris* twice beat *Iolaire*—a 45-foot marconi-rigged yawl—between Bequia and Young Island in just this way, tacking northeast along the Bequia shore before setting out.

Young Island is easily identified by a high peak just south of it on Duvernette Island, which looks like a vertical loaf of French bread. Kingstown will also be readily visible to leeward.

ST. VINCENT TO ST. LUCIA

There are two routes to St. Lucia from the south coast of St. Vincent. The more usual is to proceed up the west coast in easy stages, stopping off at Wallilabou Bay. The lee of St. Vincent is frequently becalmed, so you may be forced to stoke up the engine. Hold high the course across St. Vincent Passage, as the current sets strongly northwest; at the southwestern corner of St. Lucia, it becomes even more severe. If you fall four or five miles offshore when Beaumont Point comes abeam, you are going to have a rough beat inshore.

It is extremely important that you stay east of the rhumb line between the lee side of St. Vincent and Beaumont Point (the rhumb-line course is 015° magnetic). To be certain you are staying to windward of this course and not sliding off to leeward, take back bearings continually. Frequently

St. Lucia will not be visible from St. Vincent, thus the necessity of stern bearings. This is when a good hand-bearing compass is worth its weight in gold.

When you get discouraged about the sea conditions, remember that Vieux Fort, out to windward, tends to break the sea. Once you are halfway across, the seas should ease up. The last quarter of the trip will be in comparatively smooth water, with the seas hooking around the south coast of St. Lucia and coming much more on the beam. Similarly, the wind frequently hooks around the southern end of St. Lucia, lifting you to windward and enabling you to ease sheets as you approach the coast of St. Lucia. This effect is generally only felt to windward of the rhumb line. To leeward of the rhumb line, you will not be getting the lift and will have to fight your way up to the Pitons against wind and current.

The sail from St. Vincent to St. Lucia used to be a very long one, because you had to go all the way to Castries to clear. It was illegal to stop anywhere in St. Lucia along the way. Finally, in 1985, the St. Lucia government did something I had been urging in print for 15 years: They made Soufrière a preclearance station. This shortens the run by 12 miles. You still cannot stop first in the Pitons, though—preclear in Soufrière and then backtrack to the Pitons.

The other way to St. Lucia is to head southeastward from Young Island or Blue Lagoon until you are off soundings. When the swell eases up, tack and head directly for Vieux Fort, a distance of about 45 miles. This is a course for boats that are able to windward and should be undertaken when the tide is running eastward. This is an excellent sail when the wind is in the east or south of east, and less than excellent if it veers northeast.

ST. LUCIA TO MARTINIQUE

Castries to Fort de France is one of the finest sails in the Caribbean. The first five miles are sheltered by Pigeon Island on the northeast corner of St. Lucia—smooth water and plenty of wind. On leaving Castries, it is best to come hard on the wind till north of Pigeon Island, and then to bear off direct for Rocher du Diamant (Diamond Rock). The course is 005° magnetic, usually a splendid close reach across 18 miles of open water. The wind swings farther aft under the southeast corner of Martinique. Quite likely you will become becalmed briefly under Cap Salomon, but a good breeze resumes once you enter the bay of Fort de France.

If you are making this trip at night, watch out for the unlighted Fond Blanc red pillar buoy on the northeast corner of Banc du Gros Ilet; it is dead on a line between Cap Salomon and Fort de France. In years gone by it was unlighted and nailed more than a few boats.

MARTINIQUE TO DOMINICA OR GUADELOUPE

I prefer to head south, gunkholing around Martinique's east coast, before taking off from Cul-de-Sac Tartane, clearing Presqu'île de la Caravelle, and laying a course for Scotts Head, Dominica, 45 miles away on a broad reach. If you wish to bypass Dominica, steer 010° magnetic for the light on Iles de la Petite Terre southeast of Guadeloupe, a magnificent reach all the way.

If you decide to sail up the west coast of Martinique, don't set out before 1000, as there is no wind before this time. With any luck, you will pick up a light breeze along the coast before clearing the lee of the island and setting out for Scotts Head.

NOTES

NOTES

2

Martinique

(Imray-Iolaire Charts 1, A, B, A-30, A-301)

Martinique is one of the largest and most populous islands in the Eastern Caribbean, with 425 square miles and 340,000 people. The spoken languages are two strains of French—one fairly pure and the other an indecipherable patois. The natives, who in fact are French citizens, regard themselves as French rather than West Indians, and this is reflected everywhere. Fort de France is a sort of Paris of the New World. Its women are beautiful and well dressed, and the sidewalk cafés are always filled with an assortment of types sipping their *punch vieux* and admiring the passing scenery. The restaurants are of a very high quality, and the local boutiques offer many of the latest fashions.

Martinique is high and lush. Mountains tower over vast fields of cane and banana. Country roads vary from beautiful four-lane highways to grotesque contours of rubble and mud. The good beaches are on the east coast for the most part, and difficult to reach except by boat.

In the last 20 years or so, tourism has arrived in wholesale fashion. As recently as 1965, it was considered noteworthy to see 10 yachts moored off the Savane. In December 1973, I counted 86; in February 1985, there were almost 100 boats anchored off the Savane and another 100 in Anse Mitan, and all 120 berths in the Marina du Pointe du Bout were filled. Monsieur Le Breton, former head of Customs and Immigration for yachts, reported that during January and February of 1985, 50 to 60 boats cleared every day. It's a far cry from the days when there were so few yachts and things were so informal that the recommended method of entering a yacht in Martinique was to write out your crew list and hand it to the first gendarme you saw, who probably would lose it.

The Customs and Immigration office is open seven days a week, from 0800 to 1200 and from 1500 to 1700. Take your ship's papers and passports to the office at the head of the water and fuel dock at the western end of the anchorage. In the past, you were greeted there by Monsieur Le Breton—affectionately known to his yachting friends as 007—who handled the entrance and clearance with tremendous enthusiasm, cheerfulness, and no charge. Now that he has retired, his replacements are just as cheerful and efficient but nowhere near as picturesque. Other islands should take note of the swift, efficient, and free customs and immigration service provided in Martinique—no wonder the yachtsmen flock there to spend their money.

The amount of paperwork the French require is substantial, but they do supply pens, paper, carbon paper, and a running commentary about why the French islands are far superior to the former British colonies.

You may enter at St. Pierre, Fort de France, Cul-de-Sac Marin on the south coast, or La Trinité on the north coast (if you can find the Customs officer), but you can only clear out of Fort de France. However, your boat does not actually have to be in Fort de France; if you are on the east coast, you can grab a bus, taxi, or car from the boat to town, fill out the papers at Customs and Immigration, and return to the boat. Similarly, when entering, it is perfectly acceptable to anchor in Anse Mitan, hop on the ferry, go over to Fort de France to enter, and then return to the boat via ferry. At least that was allowed as recently as July 1991.

Flight service in and out of Martinique is excellent, with direct flights from Paris and the

United States, plus interisland service to the rest of the Eastern Caribbean.

Cruise ships ply in and out all winter long. I have seen as many as three enter Fort de France on a single day. Hotels and guest houses are found throughout the island. Most of the new ones are expensive, geared to the needs and lifestyles of the modern tourist. Some of the old-fashioned ones not only are less expensive but also are much more fun and have better food. There are many fine small restaurants on the island that are not listed in the travel brochures. On a French island, you never need to worry about the outside appearance of a restaurant. Simply arrive around 1230 and observe the clientele. If it is predominantly French-speaking Martinicans (or Martiniquais), sit down and enjoy a meal. Like the French, the Martinicans demand good food and value for money spent.

A stop at the tourist office is well worthwhile, as there you can pick up a brochure covering the vast majority of hotels and restaurants in Martinique. Cross-check with the locals, who will be able to recommend which ones are best at the moment.

Out in the countryside, there are a number of restored estates that serve as restaurants, guest houses, and hotels. It is a long ride from town, but Plantation Leyritz on the northeast side of the island, in the foothills of Mont Pelée, has an extremely good reputation. Several others are also worth visiting.

The yachtsman who doesn't want to travel for dinner or sightseeing should remember that the restaurant on top of the yacht club has received excellent reviews—and it's only a dinghy ride away.

Martinique is a prime spot for stocking up on foods of all kinds. The various self-styled "supermarkets" carry an excellent selection of imported meats, cheeses, and poultry. *A word of caution, however, about French poultry:* It is frequently sold plucked and frozen but not cleaned. Be sure to gut it as soon as it thaws. (Buying chicken in Martinique is something of a risk anyway. The last time we purchased chicken in Martinique, my excellent mate and cook Alston Blackett prepared it in his normal superb fashion. After dinner, we decided that Alston had made a large error: After cooking the chicken, he should have thrown it overboard and served us the roasting pan, which would have been easier to chew than the chicken. We concluded it had flown under its own steam all the way from France.)

The yachting industry has grown so much in recent years that some of the stores offer free delivery to the yacht landing. For further information about this, check with Yacht Services Martinique (YSM), the small office at the head of the dock. (YSM also stocks the Street guides and, I hope, Imray-Iolaire charts.) Also at the dock, you can purchase diesel, gasoline, outboard oil, and water. Just a short walk to the west beyond the Customs and Immigration trailer is the ice plant, where you can buy chip or block ice.

For years, Philippe Vatier has supplied yachts with wine, champagne, and liquor. His inventory of wines is superb, varying from cheap to the finest of the fine. We have always ordered from the bottom (cheap) end of his list and have never had a bad bottle. He is located underneath the Ship Shop marine hardware store. Place your order when you arrive and they will arrange delivery just before you leave; you must present your clearance papers before they will hand over the order.

When it comes to stocking the boat with food, there is an enormous selection from which to choose. But I can recommend the second street in from the waterfront, Rue Ernest Déprog, where among other stores you'll find a greengrocer and some wholesale food shops that sell sacks of onions, potatoes, and so on.

The most picturesque market in all of the Eastern Caribbean was the old covered market in Fort de France. It was a wonderful 1890 shed, supported by ornate cast-iron pillars. Unfortunately, when engineers surveyed it in the mid-1980s, they decided it was verging on collapse, so it was torn down. The original plans were to rebuild in the same style, but in the end it was rebuilt in a modern style—nowhere near as beautiful, but probably more efficient. It's well worth visiting the market for all your fresh produce. Even though the produce costs about the same as what you'll see in the supermarket, it is much fresher and the selection is infinitely greater. The one problem is that you arrive at the market with a few icebags, fill them with fresh fruit and vegetables, and then have to lug them back to the dinghy landing. In years gone by, there were porters available who would happily carry 150-pound loads on their heads, but like many other picturesque aspects of the Caribbean, they are no more. Take along your icebags and a couple of strong crew members.

There is another small produce market—and also a fish market, an ice house, and some new supermarkets—on the east bank of the River Madame, 300 yards upriver from the mouth.

The easiest way to get to and from the market is via dinghy. Land at the small fueling station and tie your dinghy alongside the dock, using a couple of

Martinique

fenders. The secondary market up the River Madame has a larger and more convenient dinghy landing, where you can load everything directly into the dinghy. There are now numerous small and medium-size supermarkets within a short walking distance of the dinghy landing in River Madame, so you can visit the produce market, dump the fruits and vegetables in the dinghy, buy fish and ice, and then get most of the remaining food you'll need from the supermarkets. All this is much easier than shopping in the center of town.

A word of warning: The River Madame is also the local sewer. Don't fall in. I don't know which would be worse—drowning in the river or being rescued from it. If you have a leaky dinghy, be sure you are wearing seaboots, or your toenails will dissolve in the bilgewater.

Don't arrive at the market too early—the French don't really get going until about 0830.

I cannot think of a better way to wind up a morning of shopping than to sit down at the open-air bar at the Impératrice or on the balcony of the Gallia, order a cold beer, and watch the splendid scenery. One can debate as to whether or not the women of Martinique are the most beautiful in the Eastern Caribbean, but they certainly are the best dressed and have the most fantastic carriage. The local boutiques offer the latest fashions, but at a price that is so high I think the extremely chic women of Martinique must make their own clothes.

For marine supplies, visit the Ship Shop on Rue Joseph Compère; around the corner, on Rue François, you will find SCIM, which has some marine supplies and plenty of fishing gear. Unfortunately, if you want marine paint, you may have to hop in your dinghy and go all the way around to the eastern side of the Baie du Carénage, where you'll also find the Ship Shop's 50-ton Travelift. They run a good operation that is building up an excellent reputation (although I would be very leery of hoisting a heavy boat on that Travelift), and when the franc is soft on the dollar, the Ship Shop's hauling facility offers excellent value. It has the advantage of being right on the edge of the main dry dock. Thus, all the shops that service the dry dock can also service a yacht in the Ship Shop facility.

You are allowed to do your own work there or hire outside labor; men are available to do excellent repairs on fiberglass, and there are facilities for spray painting, sandblasting, marine painting, engine repair, welding, electrical repair, inflatable repair, and life-raft servicing. Practically anything you want done can be done in Martinique if you track down the right person.

On the way to the Ship Shop on Rue Ernest Déprog, you will find Sea Services, which has a good supply of marine hardware as well as (wonder of wonders) one of the few swaging machines in the Eastern Caribbean. It is a small machine that I refer to as a Tinkertoy, as the swage must be fed through the dies a number of times. Most riggers feel that the only way to fit swages is to use the huge rotary machines, but even swaging done on the big machines does not last long in the tropics. The ones made by the Tinkertoy have an even shorter life, but if you must have swage fittings because of the way your rig is set up or because of your lifeline stanchions, then visit Sea Services. They'll come to your rescue in any number of languages. (By the way, for wire-end fittings, I personally recommend Sta-Lok or Norseman for 5/16 and larger wire, and Nicro-Press for smaller sizes.)

If there is anything you cannot find at Sea Services or the Ship Shop, visit the Captain's Shop over at Anse Mitan, on the road between Anse Mitan and Marina du Pointe du Bout. They have an amazing collection of marine supplies, one of the best in the Eastern Caribbean, and they are very good at ordering parts and having them shipped in rapidly.

Both the Ship Shop and the Captain's Shop stock the Street guides and the Imray-Iolaire charts.

Since I obviously cannot list all the facilities available in Martinique, the best thing to do is find someone who knows the island well and also speaks French and English; hire him as an interpreter and set out to solve your problems. Miguel at Yacht Services Martinique is excellent, and yachtsman Hank Strauss highly recommends Fok Chak Lindsay, who usually can be found around the Ship Shop hauling facility.

Large yachts, of course, can haul in the big main dry dock, but that is practical only for vessels of more than 90 to 100 feet. One word of caution regarding the main dry dock: Hauling there during hurricane season is tricky, for if a hurricane comes anywhere near the area, the gate on the dry dock is removed and the dock is flooded. If you happen to have a few planks out, or some plates off the bottom of a steel boat, that's tough; you are sunk in the dry dock. This has happened more than once in years gone by. Bob Elliot, owner of the brig *Unicorn* of Vigie Cove, St. Lucia, reports that the dry dock has now become quite efficient. The last time he hauled *Unicorn*, he pulled a number of fastenings, removed the propeller and shaft, replaced some bearings in the stern tube, and had the propeller rebuilt—and everything was done quickly and efficiently. Although the work was not inexpensive, he reported that it was very reasonable considering the amount of work that was done.

Martinique now boasts five sailmakers. Fidol has been holding fort for well over 20 years at Pont de Redoute, voie no. 2. Helenon is at 34 Boulevard Allegre, the road on the east side of the River Madame. At Anse Mitan, sailmakers can be found at the Bakoua Marina; they do quick repairs right there, and they make sails and do major repairs at their main loft on the east side of the road between the Hôtel Bakoua and Anse Mitan. West Indies Sail (Quai West PB 704) is found on the west side of the main dry dock.

The newest sailmaker is upstairs in Hangar Number One in the main docking area. It's a little hard to find, as you cannot walk from Quai West through the dry-dock area to the hangar. Rather, you must go outside and around all the buildings. The best solution is to take the dinghy into the inner basin by the cruise-ship dock, climb up the wall, and look for Hangar Number One. They are North agents, and their biggest advantage over the other sailmakers is that they have a huge loft floor—about 60 by 90 feet.

Underneath the sailmaker is Multicap Caribes, which is building catamarans with WEST System epoxy and also is repairing chopped-mat fiberglass catamarans.

For paint, Camic is the main supplier. They have a small intown office at Immeuble Somarec, Pointe Simon, Fort de France 97026, a five-minute walk from the dinghy landing. Their main office is on the west side of the main dry dock. They stock paint and fiberglass and also sell, repair, service, and certify life rafts and rubber dinghies.

Freshwater showers have always been hard to find in Martinique. Showers are available at Club de Voile on Pointe Simon (introduce yourself to the manager as a member of another club and you should get guest privileges) and also at the restaurant on the fueling pier. None of these showers are all that clean, however. If you don't mind a public shower, try the open-air arrangements free to all at the eastern end of the Savane beach. (Actually, showers in Martinique are usually a blast of water from a pipe, since all the shower heads seem to have disappeared.)

At Anse Mitan, there are open-air showers by the pool at the Hôtel Méridien. At the small marina under the Hôtel Bakoua, people sometimes hold the hose over their heads and have a clean, airy, but rather public wash.

The French take a two-hour lunch, so the shopping hours are slightly different from those on the English-speaking islands: 0800 to noon and 1430 to 1730, with a large number of small shops also opening at 1600 and closing at 1800.

Overseas telephone calls are difficult. Using the phones in the main post office is a slow, costly, and frustrating experience. Pay phones ("taxe phones") are excellent in that you can call anywhere in the world once you ascertain the code. First, though, you have to find a phone that works, then have handy a stack of five-franc coins. Finally, you have to find the right code. So the best phoning deal we found was at the Hôtel Méridien in Anse Mitan, where the operators are fast, efficient, extremely friendly, and speak English. Telexes can be sent from the Ship Shop, from the main post office, and by anyone you find who has a telex and who is in a friendly mood. Although some firms still use telex, most nowadays rely on faxes for communications. You'll need to inquire about access to a fax machine.

Public transport around Martinique is excellent. Some routes are covered by buses, others by public taxi—*taxi pays* or *taxi collective*. Just go to the taxi parking area by the fueling pier, look for a *taxi collective* with the destination you want painted on its side, and hop in; the ride is fast and cheap. When taking a *taxi collective* to a distant part of the island, though, be sure to note when the last one returns in the evening; if you miss it, you could face a very expensive regular taxi ride.

Depending on the dollar-franc exchange, you may find renting a car in Martinique to be relatively inexpensive. You can spend a few interesting days exploring the island this way. A word of warning, however, if you decide to go swimming in any of the rivers: Flash floods sometimes rush down the river gorges, sweeping everything before them; woe betide anyone in the water at the time. Friends of ours who are good swimmers very nearly lost their lives in one of these floods.

Among the unique sights in Martinique are the *gommier* races. The Carib canoes are about 30 feet long and carry a massive cat-ketch rig. Spritsails are set loose-footed on both masts, with the main overlapping the mizzen like a genoa jib. A crew of five men hang over the weather side on hiking poles (the sliding seat and the trapeze are nothing new to the West Indies).

According to experts, there are three types of boat referred to generically as *gommiers*. The original canoes were carved out of single logs; nowadays the bottom is a single log, with frames and planks added to provide the necessary freeboard.

Basically there is no keel, but they have a long ram bow. Apparently the original cat rig had one small sail forward—the long ram bow acted like a centerboard to keep the bow from blowing off to leeward.

A later version, called a *yole*, looks similar but is built up with a proper keel, frames, and planks. The newest addition to the fleet is the *petit yole* class, started in 1984. These are approximately 18 feet long (instead of 25 to 30 feet), carry the same rig, and are sailed in the same way—but by kids, usually the Sons of the men racing the big boats. The hope is to get the kids hooked on the sport early so they will keep it going in the future. (I am told there are also rowing races in *gommiers*.)

All these canoes are commercially sponsored and are raced with tremendous enthusiasm and skill. They provide a real spectacle—as long as you can figure out the racing schedule. It seems to be a military secret, but basically there are about 20 races a year, of which 12 occur in July, August, and early September. I have been told that if you check with the Office du Tourisme, B.P. 520, Fort de France, you might be able to get a copy of the schedule.

I have never seen a *gommier* race in Martinique, although I have spent the better part of 30 years chasing them; fate was always against me. Finally, however, I did see them—on Irish television, of all things. I happened to be in the Marine Hotel in Glandore, County Cork, having a pint of Guinness, and what should come on the "telly" but an excellent 15-minute color film featuring the *gommier* races in Martinique. The races are extremely exciting and closely fought, and the winners receive cash prizes. Masses of people follow from the shore and on the water—definitely worth watching one way or another.

Small-boat sailing in general is popular in the Baie de Fort de France—an ideal location, as it is large enough to give plenty of room for exploring; the land to the east breaks any sea but is low enough so it does not block the wind. Boardsailing is extremely popular, and there are at least two schools where beginners can learn—one at the Hotel Méridien and another on the open beach at Anse Mitan.

Martinique is one of the best-charted islands in the Caribbean. The US National Ocean Survey publishes three charts of Martinique and the British Admiralty has two. The French, on the other hand, publish six, all of which not only are up-to-date but also are the most modern charts in the entire Lesser Antilles. This resulted from the fact that during World War II, the French Antilles sided with Vichy France, and an aircraft carrier, numerous destroyers, and a cruiser loaded with all the gold from the Bank of France took refuge in Fort de France Harbor. The US Navy blockaded these ships from the time of the fall of France in 1940 until the Free French took over in mid-1944. The officers of the blockaded fleet had nothing to do, so they set to work recharting the islands of Martinique and Guadeloupe, and they did a superb job.

From all these charts—French, British, and American—and from my own observations, I have developed two Imray-Iolaire charts, A-30 and A-301, which cover Martinique at a scale useful for yachtsmen. These two charts are all you will need for normal cruising on the south and east coasts of Martinique, but if you really want to poke in and out of the reefs, I advise you to buy the *Cruising Guide to Martinique*, by Philippe Lachesnez-Heude and Jérôme Nouel. Philippe is a Bekee, a descendant of the first settlers of 1640, and a yachtsman who has spent his life sailing the coasts of Martinique. Jérôme is a French yachtsman who has spent more than 10 years exploring the island.

Incidentally, make sure you have on board the latest versions of the Imray-Iolaire charts, because the French are continually adding new buoys, lights, and ranges. **They have now switched from the European buoyage system of green/right/returning to the North American system of red/right/returning.**

Baie de Fort de France
FORT DE FRANCE HARBOR
(Chart 1; II A-30, A-301)

On approach the red buoy is now lit so it is not a problem. However, approaching the Savan anchorage at night it is difficult to find space. The fueling pier is gone, block ice seems to be unobtainable. In Fort de France cube ice is obtainable from the gas station across the river Madame.

Baie de Fort de France is commodious, containing many anchorages and coves that will provide shelter in all weathers. If one of these becomes rough under certain conditions, you only have to move a short distance to a more favorable spot.

When entering the harbor at night, the course from Cap Salomon to the anchorage at the Savane leads almost directly across the position of a large, unlighted, red pillar buoy (number 1) in the middle of the harbor. Keep a good lookout for it, because it is big enough to do substantial damage to your boat.

The principal yacht anchorage is off the town at the Mouillage des Flamands. Anchor southeast of the covered pier, due west of the north end of Fort St. Louis (formerly Fort Royal). Feel your way in with the leadline and anchor at a convenient depth.

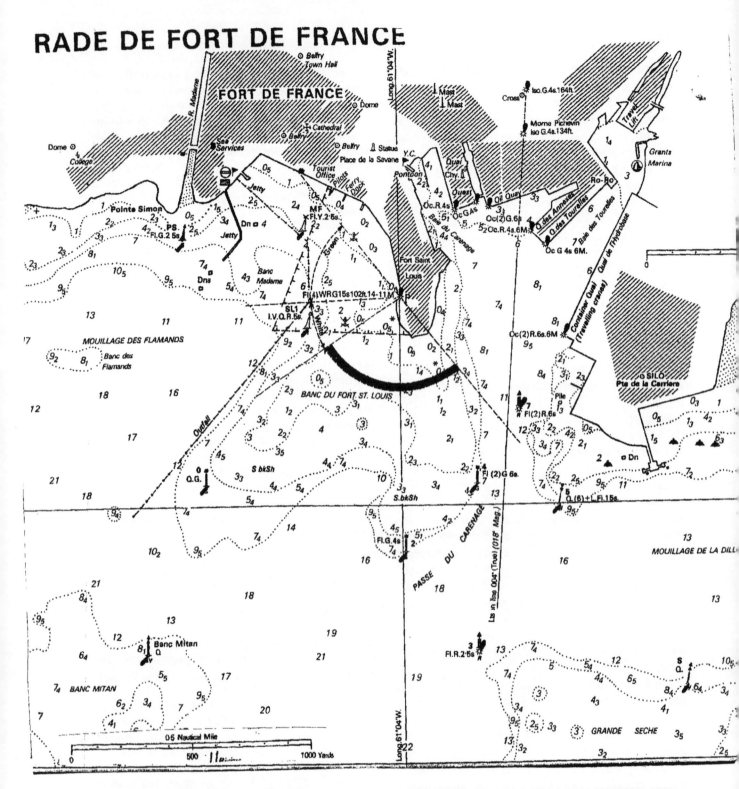

RADE DE FORT DE FRANCE

The bottom shoals very gradually. If you are spending the night, keep an eye on your outboard. Some islanders find them exceedingly adaptable to their fishing canoes. The anchorage is satisfactory in normal weather; when the wind swings around to the south or southwest, it is time to move along. If this happens, I would advise crossing the harbor to Anse Mitan.

The advantage of anchoring off the Savane is that it is only a short dinghy ride ashore. You can tie up to the fueling pier, where fresh water and ice are also available. Or you can take the dinghy up the River Madame to the market for fresh fruit and vegetables; the ice house is alongside the fish market and some small to medium-size supermarkets are nearby. Everything is in one place. This way, you can load the dinghy and avoid the traffic jams at the other supermarkets.

The holding in the Savane anchorage is not particularly good. The inner part of the anchorage has good holding but is too crowded for visiting yachts to find space. The eastern part of the anchorage must be kept open for the launches that go back and forth to Anse Mitan and Marina du

Martinique 25

Pointe du Bout. Anchoring is forbidden east of the ferry piers (see Chart 1). The outer and western part of the anchorage has very poor holding, so make sure your anchor is well dug in. I remember once arriving back at the fuel dock after a rain squall to discover no *Iolaire*. Then I spotted her sailing up from the west. A squall had blown through, the anchor had come loose, and by the time my mate Leslie, my wife Trich, and my secretary Aileen had retrieved the anchor, taken the awning down, and gotten squared away, they were about two miles to the west! They had to set sail and sail back in.

BAIE DU CARENAGE
(Chart 1; II A-30)
East of Fort St. Louis, this is the home of a yacht club—a good shelter if you are willing to put up with heat, dirt, odor, and noise. The yacht club has a well-stocked bar, shower rooms, and fresh water. Boats drawing 6 ½ feet can moor stern-to for short periods. The smell is so atrocious, however, that I can't imagine anyone staying more than an hour or so. On the east side of the bay are the steamer docks and the main dry dock. Baie du Carenage now has a pontoon for visiting yachts.

BAIE DES TOURELLES
(Chart 1; II A-30)
East of the steamer dock, Baie des Tourelles has a first-rate yacht yard that was run for many years by a gentleman named Jean Grant. Some charts of this area do not show that deep water now carries all the way up the mouth of the river just east of the yard. Favor the eastern shore.

Unfortunately, Monsieur Grant, a wonderful person whose yard had much to do with keeping *Iolaire* going in my early years of owning her, is no longer with us. Gabriel, a fellow who worked with him for 55 years (yes, he started working at the age of 10), has now retired but still lives at the yard.

Draft at the yard is limited to six feet, but at full high-water springs, they were able to get *Iolaire's* seven feet six inches on the cradle. If you own a wooden boat, be aware that many of the old shipwrights who worked on *Iolaire* more than two decades ago are still there today.

There is a vast supermarket at Monoprix, within walking distance of Grants; thus, you can take your dinghy to Grants, walk to the supermarket, do your shopping, get a taxi ride back, load stores into the dinghy, and he off. Alternatively, take *taxi collective* Famentir from town, do your shopping, and take the taxi back to the dinghy landing.

The Baie north east corner of des Tourelles has now been dredged out 9 feet pretty much everywhere. Ship Shop has a hauling facility in the north east corner. Grants Marina has been expanded but it is completely overcrowded and there is no space for a visiting yacht.

ANSE MITAN
(Chart 2; II A-30)
This is an indisputably fine anchorage that is understandably popular with the French. It has one of the few decent beaches in the area within easy access to the town—a three-mile reach coming and going.

A word of warning to those sailing from the anchorage off the Savane: Do not head directly for Anse Mitan or else you will come to a resounding halt against Bane du Fort St. Louis, which extends southwest from Fort St. Louis. Instead, keep west of the line bearing 210° magnetic from the Savane pier. When green pillar buoy number 0 approaches the port beam, head for the Hôtel Bakoua at the northern end of the anse.

Another hazard to be reckoned with on the way to Anse Mitan is a shoal with coral heads about 500 yards due west of the hill on the north end of the beach where the Hôtel Bakoua is located. You can avoid it by laying a course from the shoal off Fort St. Louis direct to Pointe du Bout and thereafter hugging the shore south to the Anse Mitan anchorage.

So many boats have hit this reef, which lies right on the line from the Anse Mitan anchorage to that at Fort de France off the Savane, that the locals call it Caye des Couillons, or Idiots' Reef. The reef is marked by a spar buoy—or at least it should be, but don't count on it.

On weekends, Anse Mitan is inundated by the French from Fort de France. They love to tear around the bay at full throttle in their little hot-rod outboards. Swimmers take heed: If you want to get ashore safely from your boat, row.

Anse Mitan remains a good refuge from the crowded, dirty anchorage of the Savane, with excellent ferry service both to the dock at Anse Mitan and to the Marina du Pointe du Bout, from which it is only a short walk through the hotel to the anchorage on the beach.

Excellent meals are available at Anse Mitan. The Méridien and the Bakoua are first-class international hotels, sometimes featuring lavish entertainment. Elsewhere on the beach are too many restaurants to be listed here. If you are staying at Anse Mitan for a week or so, a great occupation is to have lunch at a different restaurant each day and dinner at a different restaurant each evening; all are good—some are just better than others.

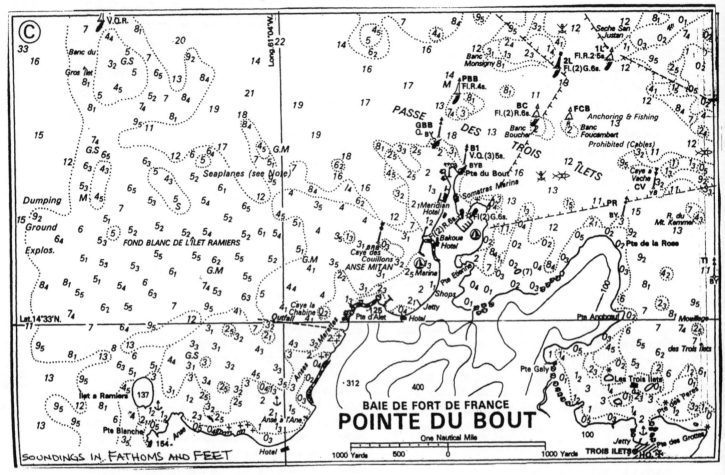

CHART 2   Pointe du Bout

Happily, we discovered several years ago that all supplies are available in the Anse Mitan area. Among the facilities are a supermarket in Marina du Pointe du Bout, a bank (closed on Mondays but open on Saturday mornings), restaurants, a small marine store on the road that leads to the Hôtel Méridien, and a newsagent. Down in the middle of Anse Mitan, near the sailboard Pedalo establishment, an excellent *pâtisserie* sells fresh bread, sticky buns, and croissants at 0700. Up the small road next to the pâtisserie, on the left-hand side, is an excellent greengrocer; farther up you'll find a superb butcher and a nice little supermarket. One thing not available at Anse Mitan is block ice, but cube ice can be bought from the hotels or from the marina at the Bakoua. Here you can find water, fuel, bread, pastries, and books (including the Street guides and Imray-Iolaire charts).

You can get back and forth between Anse Mitan and Fort de France via two ferries: the Méridien—Bakoua ferry, which is a big, fast catamaran that leaves town on the half hour and leaves Marina du Pointe du Bout on the hour; and the smaller and more erratic Anse Mitan—Anse à l'Ane ferry. This ferry leaves Anse Mitan sometime between a quarter and half past the hour, goes to Anse à l'Ane and then back to Fort de France, whence it leaves on the hour.

About the only thing that seems to be lacking in Anse Mitan is a post office; the nearest one is at Trois Ilets. A bus goes from Anse Mitan to Trois Ilets on the half hour and returns on the hour.

Leaving Anse Mitan for Fort de France, hug the shore until past the Bakoua, and then head for the buoy marking the shoal off Fort St. Louis. If you are bound for Pointe des Nègres, again stay inshore until the Bakoua is abeam, as otherwise you may clip the three-foot spot that lies on the line between Anse Mitan and Pointe des Nègres.

MARINA DU POINTE DU BOUT

(Chart 2; II A-30)

East of Pointe du Bout is a marina, perfectly sheltered, with 10 feet and possibly a little more water inside. It is entered from the north through a buoyed channel that, while narrow, is wide enough to accommodate the big, high-powered catamaran that serves as the ferry from the Savane to Marina du Pointe du Bout.

The marina provides a place to lie alongside, with showers, water, and electricity for the yachtsman who wishes to spend some time in Martinique. However, the place is absolutely jam-packed, and I doubt if you will find space. The boats are literally shoe-horned in there, and you may have to move two or three boats to extract yourself when you are ready to leave. It is an absolute disaster waiting to happen. Despite its being completely sheltered from the sea, I am sure that if a hurricane were to pass overhead, the damage inside Marina du Pointe du Bout would be incalculable.

Do not try to enter the marina without first anchoring at Anse Mitan or in the lee of Pointe du Bout and walking over to see if there are mooring slips available (there's no room to turn around); every time I have seen the marina, it has been crammed, and people tell me there is a waiting list to obtain docking space.

I don't know anyone who has explored the eastern side of the Baie de Fort de France in a yacht, but if I were to do it, I would certainly have on hand the detailed French Harbor Chart 6892.

In general, remember that the Baie de Fort de France can be a veritable death trap if a hurricane passes over the island, or even if one passes north of it. This would build up a large westerly swell, which makes all normal anchorages completely untenable. Some boats may try to hide in Cohe du Lamentin (see below), but since it is a commercial anchorage, it is likely to be loaded with freighters. If the marina is not filled, smaller boats can get up the creek to that haven, as described below. Trois Ilets (see below) is well sheltered but has poor holding. The carenage east of Fort St. Louis would he disastrous, as a strong surge pours back and forth through there, making it impossible to anchor or get secure to the dock.

If a hurricane threatens, do not go to Cul-de-Sac Marin, as it is so loaded with "bareboat bombs" that your chances of survival would be minimal. With the massive expansion of the bareboat fleets in Martinique, all of the harbors on the island's east coast will be so overcrowded that they would not be safe during a hurricane. Therefore, I suggest that you plot the expected hurricane track, and, 48 hours before the storm is to hit the Eastern Caribbean islands, pick up your anchor, go to sea, and head north or south—depending on the track.

TROIS ILETS
(Chart 2; II A-30)
In the southwest corner of Baie de Fort de France, Trois Ilets is an out-of-the-way spot, difficult to reach

by car and seldom visited by yachts. The anchorage (due north of town) is mud bottom, and it frequently is used as a hurricane hole. The holding is not too good, but if you drag, you'll only end up on soft bottom.

When sailing to Trois Ilets from Fort de France, be careful of the numerous shoals that litter the eastern side of the bay. They are all buoyed, however, and there is plenty of water between them.

A better idea is to anchor at Anse Mitan and take the bus to Trois Ilets. It's worth an afternoon visit anyway. La Pagerie, the museum of Josephine Bonaparte, is there, as well as a botanical garden. It's a nice, old-fashioned Martiniquais town with tiled roofs, and it boasts a number of small restaurants and a post office.

This is one area where all charts were wrong. The French charts done in World War II were extremely accurate. However, the boys were definitely drinking too many petit Punch when they did the chart of this area. Following the Imray-Iolaire chart which was drawn from the French chart, was most embarrassing, *Li'l Iolaire* ran hard aground. We re-explored the area and completely redid the chart. Now the Imray-Iolaire chart and the chart in this guide are correct. The other charts, unless they have been corrected from the Imray-Iolaire chart are still wrong!!

COHE DU LAMENTIN
(II A-30; French 6892)
In the northeastern most corner of Fort de France Harbor, this area offers the Port Cohe Marina, an excellent hurricane shelter. Draft in the channel is limited to six feet, though, and once there, you are in the middle of nowhere, as the airport is two kilometers away on a rough road.

I have never been there, so I will rely on the directions supplied by Philippe Lachesnez-Heude and Jérôme Nouel: "Steer 100 degrees from the red buoy marked CAR situated in the middle of Cohe du Lamentin, proceed toward the entrance of the small channel, which is hard to see from a distance but identifiable once you draw near a grounded barge, which must be left to port." In theory, at least, the rest of the channel is marked by gas lights. The marina is 400 yards inside the entrance.

ANSE A L'ANE
(Chart 2; II A-301)
As you leave Anse Mitan and head for Cap Salomon and the mouth of Baie de Fort de France, you come to Anse a l'Ane. It is a real sleeper—one of the more attractive anchorages in the area—and until recently was seldom used by yachtsmen.

It is quieter, with nowhere near as many people as Anse Mitan. Yet it has an attractive hotel at its western end and a number of restaurants along the beach. The easternmost one is a drinking man's delight: a classic *petit punch* for four francs; three dollars' worth would send almost anyone down in flames.

Another attraction of Anse à l'Ane is a hand-powered, carved wooden carousel equipped with an amazing set of bearings: One shove spins it three full revolutions. Think how fast it could get going at fiesta time with a bunch of well-lubricated celebrants spinning it around!

Ashore at Anse à l'Ane it is only a short walk to a small grocery store and an interesting shell museum. The ferry dock is a good place to tie up the dinghy, but be sure to use the southwest side, since the ferry comes along its northeast face.

When sailing from Anse Mitan to Anse à l'Ane, pass outside the shoal due west of Pointe d'Alet. Then watch out for the four-foot spot out from the center of Anse à l'Ane beach. Both of these hazards had marks on them in 1985; don't count on their still being there. Incidentally, the reefs west of Pointe d'Alet provide excellent snorkeling.

A somewhat erratic ferry connects Anse à l'Ane with Anse Mitan, as described above; you can also make the trip by a perfectly pleasant dinghy ride in sheltered water.

In normal trade-wind weather, Anse à l'Ane is a well-protected anchorage. If the wind backs to the north, or a ground swell starts coming in from the northwest, it will definitely become uncomfortable (as will Anse Mitan)—but probably not dangerous, since the beach is flat. (Remember that you can tell when a beach is dangerous in northwest ground-swell conditions: It is always very steep-to, with soft sand.)

The rule of thumb for comparing the Savane anchorage with those of Anse Mitan and Anse à l'Ane is the same as that for comparison between Basseterre, St. Kitts, and Charlestown, Nevis. If the anchorage is calm in the Savane, it is likely to be choppy on the other side of the harbor; similarly, if the wind goes into the southeast, when Anse Mitan and Anse à l'Ane are sheltered, the Savane will be rough.

If you have an exploratory urge, you can have a lot of fun with a dinghy or outboard in the various rivers and canals that radiate from the harbor of Fort de France. Many of them extend quite far inland to towns east of the harbor.

ILET A RAMIERS
(Chart 2; II A-30)

This is the little island at the southwest corner of Fort de France Harbor. The preferred anchorage is in the channel between the island and the mainland. Anchor in 10 feet of water over a white-sand bottom. Drop the hook when the dock on the island bears due north. This channel shoals to six feet east of Ramiers. Here, too, the swimming is excellent.

Unfortunately, you are no longer allowed ashore here, and the wonderful old fort that we used to explore in years gone by is now forbidden to visitors. When it was first closed, we decided that at least it must be a secret missile site. It turns out that all the secrecy is merely to conceal a private club for the French military!

ANSE NOIRE AND ANSE DU FOUR
(II A-30)

These two small coves, which I have only looked at, are notable for the fact that although they are side by side, one has a white-sand beach, the other a black-sand beach.

In the winter, the ground swell would make them uncomfortable or even untenable. In periods when there isn't a ground swell, or in the summer, either of these bays could make a quiet, secluded anchorage.

At Anse du Four, you'll find a white-sand cove, a fishing village, a small shop, a restaurant, and an excuse for a road leading up the valley. If you anchor too close inshore, the fishermen may ask you to move so that they can shoot their nets.

At Anse Noire, you will find, in addition to the black beach, the Coconut Grove, a thatch-roofed restaurant with its own lobster tank. Apparently it's a nice little place to visit.

For a chart of these two coves and more specific directions, consult the Lachesnez-Heude/Nouel *Cruising Guide to Martinique.*

Southwest Coast

GRANDE ANSE D'ARLET
(II A-30)

This is the first cove south of Cap Salomon and one of two good anchorages on the southwest coast. The bottom is white sand and good holding, with two

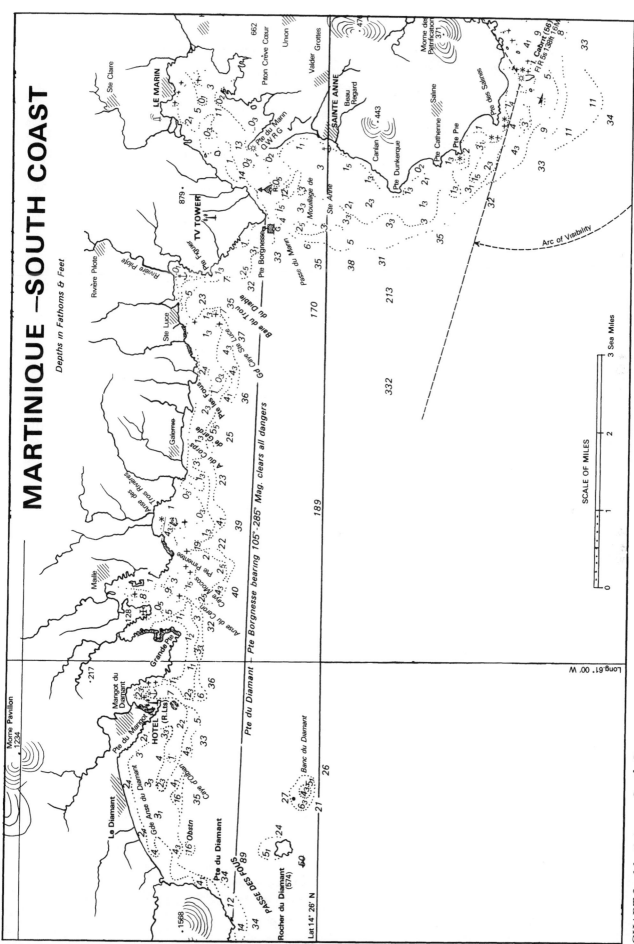

CHART 3   Martinique—South Coast

fathoms in the southeast corner of the harbor. A slight roll is not too bothersome. The swimming is excellent.

What you want to do, ideally, is feel your way in to the extreme southeast corner and anchor in two fathoms, being sure to get your hook onto the edge of the shelf, since the bottom drops off steeply. But the fisherman shoot their nets here, as in Anse du Four, and there has been friction between them and yachtsmen in the past. So it's wise not to get too close inshore. Stay about 200 yards off and you should be okay.

There is no real town at Grande Anse d'Arlet, only a fishing village with a variety of çanoes, nets stretched out to dry, dogs, cats, goats, roosters, and bare-bottomed urchins running to and fro. As is usual in any small French village, there is a restaurant and bar.

At the north and south ends of the beach are some beautiful small cottages owned by wealthy citizens of Martinique, who come here in the summer to beat the heat of Fort de France. The cove is likely to be crowded with local yachtsmen on Saturdays and Sundays.

PETITE ANSE D'ARLET

(II A-30)

This is the next cove south of Grande Anse and not as sheltered, but it has the advantage of a good restaurant and ferry communication to Fort de France. Anchor off the town, but be careful of the coral bank at the northern end of the harbor; here, too, the bottom drops off steeply. The anchorage in the northeast corner usually avoids the swell. If you want to get away from town, a little cove to the south, Anse Chaudière, provides privacy, good snorkeling, and, in settled weather, a good anchorage in two fathoms. It's within dinghy distance of town. Avoid the sunken wreck south of the town dock.

The well-to-do citizens who come here from Fort de France used to travel by boat to avoid the kidney-busting roads. Now the roads are so improved that they commute by car. Still, the town has apparently kept its quaint character. Philippe Lachesnez-Heude calls this one of the best preserved of the old Martinique towns.

PETITE ANSE DU DIAMANT

(II A-30)

A small white-sand beach but not very good anchorage. I do not advise stopping here.

The most spectacular sight on the south coast of Martinique is the Rocher du Diamant, or, as the British prefer, HMS Diamond Rock—so called because in 1781 Admiral Hood somehow managed to establish a gun battery at the top of the mountain. The guns swept the channel between Diamond Rock and the mainland, closing it to all coastal traffic. Against the best efforts of the French, the British succeeded in holding out for some 18 months. When they finally surrendered, the French arranged for their immediate exchange as prisoners, as it was felt that men so brave and resourceful should not be left to rot away in prison. How wars have changed!

How the French have changed! They have lost their sense of humor. Some years ago, their navy was sending a squadron to Martinique to celebrate a national holiday. Two young Englishmen decided to have some fun. The night before the squadron's arrival, they scaled the cliffs of Diamond Rock and hung a huge white ensign, the symbol of the British Navy. In the morning, as the French sailed past HMS Diamond Rock, the white ensign was clearly visible on the south face. The French admiral was apoplectic; he ordered a helicopter to lower a man onto the rock to destroy the flag. The French complained through diplomatic channels, and before the dust settled, it had become something of an international incident.

For those who are interested in the history of the rock and its British occupation, the fighting, and the French recapture, there are two fine books: *Her Majesty's Sloop of War Diamond Rock,* by Stuart and Eggleston, is an extremely readable account of the affair. Dudley Pope turned the historical event into an excellent novel in *Ramage's Diamond.*

South Coast

This coast offers few really good anchorages until you get to its eastern end, and with the excellent harbor of Sainte Anne beckoning from there, it would be my inclination to skip right on by the rest. Nevertheless, there are a number of small stopping places (which I haven't been in), and if you are a good reef pilot, have a small boat, and are into gunkholing, then these out-of-the-way spots might be a lot of fun.

A general warning, though: The water along this south coast is not as clear as it usually is elsewhere in the Caribbean. Furthermore, the shoal water extends as much as a mile offshore in some places. (Cave Sainte-Luce, for instance, which breaks only in heavy weather, is a full half-mile offshore.) To complicate matters, a strong westerly current works along the coast.

So even though getting inshore on the shelf will get you out of the current, the water will be choppier as the swell comes up on the shelf, and will also be much harder to read. Basically, a safe policy is to tack offshore as soon as you see bottom. And keep a lookout in the bow and a chart on deck at all times.

Back bearings on the southwest tip of Martinique are a useful guide. If your bearing on Pointe du Diamant is 285° or more, you should be in deep water. If the bearing gets less than 285°, watch out for shoal water. A good hand-bearing compass is a big help here.

The distance from Petite Anse d'Arlet on the southwest coast to Sainte Anne is only 13 miles, but it is best to allow the better part of the sailing day for the trip because of head winds and the strong westerly set. As you get closer inshore, the wind will become variable; play the lifts and the headers for all they are worth and you'll save some time. Do not try to push on beyond Sainte Anne after 1100, because you will be unable to reach the east-coast harbors before the light fails.

MARIGOT DU DIAMANT
(Chart 3; II A-30, A-301)

This is a proper little harbor, location of the Diamond Rock Hotel. Be careful of the reefs that extend out from Pointe do Marigot. A small dock under the hotel in the southwest corner offers fuel and water alongside. Do not go north of the buoys in the center of the harbor, since it shoals rapidly here. This is a good anchorage, in clear water, and sheltered in all winds except those from the south.

To the east of Marigot du Diamant, anchorages of sorts can be found at Anse du Ceron (two little coves for the brave and careful), at Anse des Trois Rivières, at Sainte-Luce, and at Rivière Pilote. All are shown on Imray-Iolaire Chart A-301, and also on Chart 3, but for these nooks and crannies, I highly recommend that you carry the *Cruising Guide to Martinique* by Lachesnez-Heude/Nouel; it has greater detail and a better scale. The newest edition of their guide has color aerial photographs of the harbors taken from a point vertically above each harbor. For navigational purposes, they are the finest aerial photographs I have seen in any guide.

In settled conditions, when the wind is not in the south, all these villages offer moderately good anchorages. If you like to explore, anchor off Rivière Pilote, as you can take your dinghy all the way up the river to within a couple of hundred yards of the little village of Rivière Pilote. Needless to say, since large areas of this river are uninhabited, I am quite sure that if you drift or row down the river from Rivière Pilote, there will be excellent bird-watching.

CUL-DE-SAC MARIN
(Chart 4; II A-30, A-301)

This has now become a huge yachting center - see Notes at the end of the chapter.

Cul-de-Sac Marin is a large harbor with numerous coves. When approaching the harbor, check the chart and the buoys red/right/returning (i.e., green buoys on the port hand, red buoys on starboard). Leave the buoy off Pointe Borgnesse to port, steer a course of approximately 088° magnetic, which would lead you to starboard of the next buoy, the four-foot spot of Bane des Trois Cayes. Leave the next buoy to port, as that marks the shoal Bane du Singe. Head on in to Pointe do Mann, then come to port. Stay in the deep water, following the markers inside the harbor.

There are too many anchorages within the harbor to describe all of them; just look at the chart and take your choice. However, when heading to the inner harbor, leave the day marker on Banc Major to port, then take a short dogleg due north until you pass the day markers on Bane do Milieu. Once clear of that marker, swing to the northeast and head for the inner harbor.

Monsieur Bruno Mabille de Poncheville points out that when boats leave the ATM Marina, and also the town, all too frequently they head directly for the beacon on Bane du Milieu, turn too soon, and run right up on the bank. That beacon should be given a good berth; pass well northwest of it until the beacon bears south, then take your dogleg south to clear Bane Major.

Club Med has an establishment on Pointe du Marin. Visitors are not welcome ashore unless they are members of the club—an attitude that will be made clear to you in no uncertain terms.

West of Club Med is not a good anchorage because the bottom drops off steeply down to 60 feet, but you can find an anchorage near a white-sand beach on the shelf north of Pointe du Marin. Here you'll not only be sheltered from winds in all directions, but also have excellent scenery ashore: The northern Club Med beach seems to be the one preferred by those who like to swim and sunbathe *au naturel.*

As you go on into the harbor, be careful. Most but not all of the shoals are marked by beacons, some lighted. Eyeball navigation is the rule. There are too many coves to enumerate here. My advice is to anchor right inside the harbor off Club Med, get in your dinghy, spend an hour or so exploring Cul-de-Sac Marin, then pick an anchorage that suits your taste. Some of the offlying cays have good anchorages, and there will be good snorkeling around the edges of the reefs. Other anchorages are tucked up inside mangrove groves and provide excellent fishing and bird-watching (of the feathered variety). The land east of Cul-de-Sac Marin is low, so the trades are unobstructed, making the area cool and relatively bug-free.

Things have changed here over the years. In 1985, when we were in Cul-de-Sac Marin, there were no more than 20 boats anchored in the harbor, and another 15 at the yacht club on the northeast corner. At that time, I described this as a good, safe anchorage and an excellent hurricane hole, plus a good place to practice small-boat sailing and sailboarding. The last two points are still true, but a hurricane hole IT'S DEFINITELY NOT. If a hurricane came over the area—as Hugo did over Culebra and the east coast of Puerto Rico in 1989— it would be an absolute disaster. As I urged earlier in this chapter, stay away from Cul-de-Sac Marin if a hurricane approaches. (See "Reflections on Hugo" in the Foreword to this volume.)

The reason for this warning is the huge number of boats now using the harbor. The French have a complicated tax dodge whereby if you buy a boat and put it in the charter business in the French islands, you receive something like a 200 percent write-off over a five-year period—plus other advantages. The result of this is that the French boatbuilding industry is turning out boats like Detroit did with cars in the early 1980s, and they can sell them as fast as they produce them. The Caribbean is flooded with bareboats—to the extent that when I visited ATM recently, I discovered that in Cul-de-Sac Marin alone they have 107 bareboats! When you add in the various other companies, there are close to 200 bareboats in the harbor, plus probably another 50 or 60 private boats.

However, every cloud has a silver lining. . . . There is now a Customs and Immigration facility at the main dock by the new pier, right on the beach. Officially, the agent is there six days a week from 0800 to noon. (What does he do in the afternoon? Have a really big French lunch and then go to sleep? What a life!) Also, even though there are supposed to be office hours on Sunday, I have heard various reports of yachts that have tried to clear on Sunday but had to wait until Monday.

Fuel and water can be picked up at Club Nautique, and cube ice can be bought many places, but I am told that no block ice is available.

Along the shore behind the customs office, you will see a sign for outboard repairs, and above that a sail-repair shop. For hull repairs, it's a case of heading out of town to the large Annette supermarket, about a mile west on the Fort de France road, where you will find a German who builds wood-and-epoxy boats. He probably could be talked into repairing a wood or fiberglass boat that has had a hole knocked in it.

In the northwestern cove where the chart shows CHYS (an old sugar factory), a yacht yard is under construction. They hope to be operational by late 1992 or early 1993.

In the summer of 1991, construction was well underway on a large new marina, including a 60-ton Travelift. However, I have had so many conflicting reports about its facilities and completion dates that I advise you to go in person and check it out.

The shopping is fair in town, with a number of small supermarkets—including two Annette supermarkets through which you can contact the main store on the outskirts. They will either send a car for you or you can hop in a taxi. Some people insist you can walk from town, but that's only for those who really enjoy walking—and on the return trip, you'll be laden with packages.

Needless to say, as in any town in Martinique, there are restaurants. Just ask around and look for the one with the most Martinicans—the locals always know the best restaurants.

The town of Marin is not one of my favorites, as I almost died of thirst before I could find a bar. But it does have four banks—whereas the neighboring town of Sainte Anne has none.

MOUILLAGE DE SAINTE ANNE
(Chart 4; II A-30, A-301)

This is one of the most attractive anchorages in the whole area and an excellent shelter in normal trade-wind weather. The entrance is simple and straightforward.

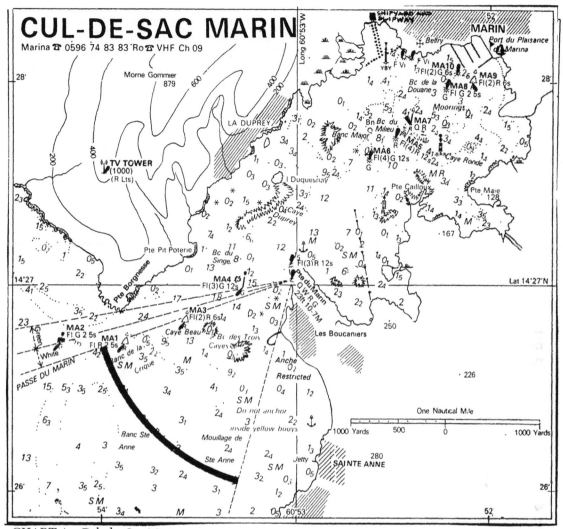

CHART 4 Cul–de–Sac Marin

The anchorage off Sainte Anne and northward is littered with yellow buoys. Supposedly you are not allowed to anchor inside these buoys, but I saw many boats in there. Off the town, there are more yellow buoys, but south of town, off the Hôtel Caritan (see below), there are none. It probably is best to anchor off the Caritan, but anchor at the northern end of the beach, as the water is shoal at the southern end.

This is basically a resort town, so the stores tend to be open seven days a week until late in the evening. A fish market, a small vegetable market, two or three unsuper supermarkets, a source of block ice, and a post office supply all the basic necessities—everything except a bank, which you'll find in Cul-de-Sac Marin.

On the beach is the Filet Bleu, with a glass dance floor. Underneath the floor are the lobsters you can have for lunch or dinner. Also along the beach are various typically French seaside snack shops.

In town, the Hôtel Dunette has a pleasant bar and restaurant overlooking the harbor. A short walk south takes you to the restaurant Au Mahogany, which has been serving delicious meals to locals and visitors for a couple of decades.

In the next bay south is the Hôtel Caritan, mentioned above. It is a most hospitable place with boutique, restaurant, swimming pool, nightly music, and a helpful and efficient telephone operator. There is an attractive small beach south of the hotel.

The anchorage in Mouillage de Sainte Anne extends over a mile and a half of very pleasant territory and is never too crowded with yachts.

East Coast

This coastline is thoroughly charted by Imray-Iolaire Charts A-30 and A-301. The east coast should be explored only by an experienced yachtsman sailing a good, weatherly boat, a cruising guide in one hand, the appropriate Imray-Iolaire or French chart spread before him, and a crew member on the pulpit—or, better, in the spreaders. It offers wonderful cruising in an area where you are not likely to encounter many yachts. It may be rough or windy at times, but there are any number of harbors and coves that are completely sheltered and as calm as a millpond. At Le François, Le Robert, and La Trinité, food and supplies are available. Lobster is plentiful and inexpensive. *Sudon*, the Caribbean cherrystone clam, can be found in the shoal-water areas.

In planning a trip up the east coast, bear in mind that this is a lee shore with a strong current setting on it. Until you go through Passe du Vauclin, there will be no protection from offlying reefs. Once you get behind the reefs, however, they will dampen the swell to give you a great sail. But you must stay on your toes as you thread through the reefs; afterward, it will not seem as bad as you anticipated.

On the subject of tides and currents on the east coast, I quote from the Lachesnez-Heude/Nouel *Cruising Guide to Martinique:* "The current seems, based on personal observation, to run roughly parallel to the coast and most often to bear northward to the north of Cap Ferré, and to the southwest south of this cape. Except in the vicinity of large points of land, the current is less than one knot. Near areas such as Pointe des Salines, Cap Ferré, and Presqu'île de la Caravelle, it can attain two knots or even more in combination with tidal currents [especially at springs—D.M.S.]."

CAUTION: Deep inside bays, the tidal range can, under unusual circumstances, attain as much as one meter (three feet).

When rounding the southeasternmost point of Martinique, off Ilet Cabrit, one can frequently experience a strong westerly current. As explained above, once around the corner, the current sets north-and-south up the east coast of the island. Thus, when standing northward on starboard tack, stay well offshore, as there will be a weather-bow current setting you toward shore.

Imray-Iolaire Chart A-301 has all the information you need for normal cruising on this coast. Once again, though, if you are in a shoal-draft boat and have the time to explore every nook and cranny of the coast, I advise you to have the Lachesnez-Heude/Nouel cruising guide aboard. It is based on the authors' own experience and is not plagiarized from other guides.

I first cruised this coast in *Iolaire* in 1964, and I believe she was one of the very first nonlocal yachts

to do so. One other foreigner I know to have cruised here in the early days is John Guthrie, who visited Cul-de-Sac des Anglais several times in his engineless Brixham trawler, *Pas de Loup.* But how he beat to windward out of that place in a Brixham trawler is beyond me. To tack one of those boats, you put the helm down, lash it, throw off the jib and jib-topsail sheets, leave the staysail sheeted, and go below and grab a cup of coffee. When you get back on deck, the staysail is aback, she has started to fall off on the other tack, and you are in time to unlash the helm and sheet in your headsails!

The French have always been very conscientious about establishing good buoyage systems, and Martinique's east coast is no exception. In fact, it is being expanded and improved so often that even the French charts are often out of date. The Imray-Iolaire charts are hand-corrected to conform to the latest Notices to Mariners, but they, too, sometimes cannot stay *au courant* with the latest changes, so be on your guard.

This coast makes a wonderful cruising ground, but it should be approached only in good light. Many leading lights guide local fishermen as they return home at night through the reefs, but no yachtsman should try it after dark on his own.

Furthermore, I strongly advise against running dead downwind through any passes to get behind the reef. It's better to approach from north or south and find a range that gets you through a pass on a reach.

If you are coming in from the north, pass to weather of Presqu'île de la Caravelle. Once Pointe Caracoli is abeam, bear off for Ilet de Ramville, or jibe around and head into Cul-de-Sac Tartane. The former course will put you to leeward of Loup Bordelais, the unbuoyed, northernmost shoal of the offlying reefs. If you are heading south, just stay in blue water and you'll be all set.

In approaching from the south, stay well offshore in deep water until you pick up the buoys at the southern end of Passe Sud du Vauclin; then ease sheets and run up behind the reef. In heavy weather, don't even think about trying any of the passes through the reef between Vauclin and the pass east of Cul-de-Sac Frégate. It would be like running a New Jersey inlet in foul weather. On the other hand, once you do get behind the reef at Vauclin, you'll find comfortable sailing.

If you are coming from St. Lucia to explore the east coast, stop at Sainte Anne, check in, spend the night, and go around the next day. It is virtually impossible to get from St. Lucia to Passe Sud du Vauclin by 1200 on the same day, and if you get there any later than that, you will be running dead downwind into harbors with the sun in your eyes—a guaranteed way to get yourself into serious trouble.

When you leave Sainte Anne for the east coast, you have to get around the corner. In the winter months when it's blowing hard, this can be a problem. In these conditions, beating around Ilet Cabrit (the southeasternmost part of Martinique) is to be avoided at all costs—the Atlantic swell shortens as it comes in on the island, humps up, and becomes horrendous.

Instead, stand south on a close reach after passing Pointe Dunkerque until you are in good deep water, then come on the wind and sail southeast. Tack north when you think you can clear Cap Ferré by a good bit (Cap Ferré looks like an island from the distance). Do not allow yourself to fall down on the coast, as the sea becomes so steep and confused that tacking is difficult. Remember, too, that even after you pass Cap Ferré, the coast (and particularly its reefs) tends northeast for another three miles. It should be noted that the current at Cap Ferré turns south. If this is backed up by the tide, it can reach two knots, so allow for considerable leeway when beating up this coast around Cap Ferré. Once north of Cap Ferré, the current should be under your stern and life will be much easier.

Once around the corner off Grande Anse Macabou, you can ease sheets and head for Passe du Vauclin, which is well marked. Leave the red lighted buoy to starboard and stand north inside the reef. Put a crew member in the bow or on the spreaders to help you avoid the various unbuoyed shoals north of the pass.

When it's blowing hard, I recommend that you go right to Cul-de-Sac Frégate and avoid all the harbors south of that—Vauclin, Anse du Sans Souci, Cul-de-Sac Grenade, etc. They are for gunkholing in calm weather.

General warning: When sailing on the east coast of Martinique, you must remember that almost all the entrance channels lead due west. Entrance should therefore be made before 1400; otherwise, the sun will be in your eyes and eyeball navigation will be impossible. Similarly, when leaving harbors and heading due east, it is extremely difficult to see the reefs before 1100, as the sun will be in the east and in your eyes.

When sailing from Sainte Anne around to the east coast, it is very important that you make an early morning start, as it is 20 miles from Sainte Anne to Cul-de-Sac Frégate, with a hard beat around the southeast corner of Martinique, then it is a full 12 miles to the first possible anchorage northward—Cul-de-Sac Ferré.

You should also remember that in periods of heavy weather, there is nothing between you and Africa, and the sea will hump up and break in three or four fathoms of water. Thus, when sailing up Martinique's east coast and using the Imray-Iolaire charts, be sure to avoid all the areas of white, because in these areas you may not run aground, but you can get into trouble by running into breaking seas that will demolish a boat in very short order.

CUL-DE-SAC DES ANGLAIS
(Chart 5; II A-30, A-301)

Note: Chart 5 is more up-to-date than Imray-Iolaire Chart A-301, but the best chart to use is Chart 15 in the Lachesnez-Heude/Nouel *Cruising Guide to Martinique*. Remember, however, that all soundings in the French guide are in meters.

Tackling the entrance to Cul-de-Sac des Anglais in bad weather is, once again, like running a dangerous New Jersey inlet. Furthermore, there's not much room to round up once you are inside. But in favorable conditions, the entrance is straightforward and the rewards are generous. This is an excellent anchorage, with lots of possibilities for exploration.

Enter from the southeast on a course roughly northwest. Watch out for the rocks on the port side as you come in and round up under Ilet Hardy. Proceed as far north toward shoal water as your draft will permit, then anchor.

It is possible to take seven feet up into Cul-de-Sac des Anglais. Its inner harbor is nothing more than soft mud with mangroves around the sides—good fishing, I suspect, and excellent bird-watching; peace and quiet in the mangroves and an enclosed anchorage. The *Cruising Guide to Martinique* has detailed directions for doing this.

The dinghy can be taken northeast to Ilet Lézards, a mile away across reef-sheltered water and white-sand bottom. This area would be superb for boardsailing, as the wind sweeps unobstructed across the reef, while the reef breaks the swell completely.

A distinctive feature of this area is the fishermen who work from long, narrow bamboo rafts that they pole along just as if they were punting on the Thames. They sit on chairs secured to the raft; from 300 or 400 yards, though, you can't see the raft, which is almost flush with the water. So all you see

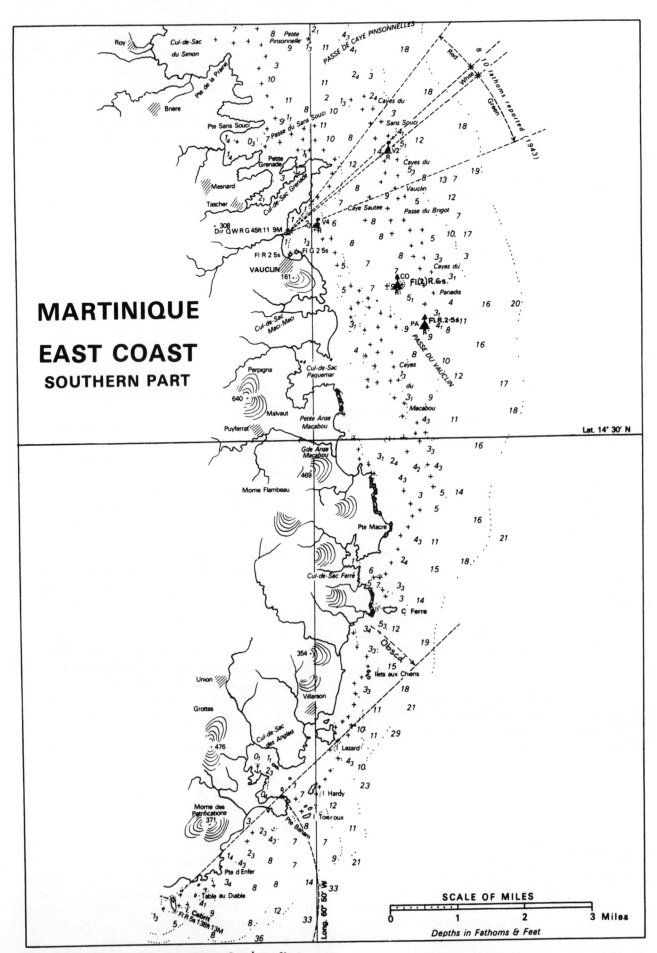

CHART 5   Martinique—East Coast, Southern Part

are men sitting on chairs in the middle of the sea. It's very startling.

The French chart shows an entrance between Pointe Baham and Ilet Toisroux. I am told that there definitely is no passage between these two islands. If you are coming up from the south and trying to sight Cul-de-Sac des Anglais, look for the black cliffs on Toisroux.

CUL-DE-SAC FERRE; CUL-DE-SAC PAQUEMAR; CUL-DE-SAC MACI-MACI

(Chart 5; II A-30, A-301)

These are all summertime anchorages for shoal-draft boats. Consult the *Cruising Guide to Martinique* for details.

VAUCLIN

(Chart 5; II A-30, A-301)

This is the first town of any size that you will encounter going up the east coast. It is easily spotted from seaward by its church, which has a green roof. The chart shows a white, green, and red sector light that provides a night-time range through the channel between Cayes du Sans Souci and Cayes du Vauclin. This is strictly for small-boat fishermen returning home or for someone who really knows the area. It should not be attempted by yachtsmen under any circumstances. Among other things, if you were running downwind with a big swell, steering control would be minimal.

The basin behind two breakwaters at the southern end of Baie du Vauclin is strictly a small-boat refuge with five feet of water at its outer edge and three feet in the main part.

The bay itself is wide and shoal and provides an anchorage of sorts, but there's no real shelter when the trades are up because the reef is so far to the east that there's room for a sizable chop to build up. There seems to be an anchorage due east of town behind the unnamed islet south of Baril de Boeuf. On the beach south of town is a sailboarding school and a campsite; thus, as you sail up the coast, you will see sailboarders flitting across the flats south of town—a great place to do this, as there's white-sand bottom only three feet down.

CUL-DE-SAC GRENADE

(Chart 5; II A-30, A-301; French 384, 385)

Cul-de-Sac Grenade is not very well spoken of by the French, but I found it a delightful spot, a perfect anchorage, and a wonderful place to try out the sailing dinghy or explore with an outboard. In fact, with a dinghy one can stay inside the inner reefs and visit almost all of the remaining east coast of Martinique, all the way to Le Robert, 10 miles to the north.

Spotting the break in the reef that leads to Cul-de-Sac Grenade is none too easy unless you have someone high up in the rigging. (In fact, put a crew member in the rigging when cruising *anywhere* on the east coast of Martinique.) In the spring of 1973, a Morgan 41 missed the channel entrance, hit a coral head, and sank. The outer part of the channel is deep, with seas breaking on the reefs on both sides, giving a definite line of demarcation. Once you spot the break, the course is about southwest by south.

In 1963, I found the channel to have a depth of nine feet, sounding with a leadline. In the late 1970s, a Gallant 53 drawing seven feet nine inches got in and weathered a hurricane. However, I've heard that the channel has shoaled up in recent years, so I advise sending in a dinghy to sound the channel before you enter. Remember that if there is a swell running into the channel, the safe depth will be reduced to six or possibly only five feet.

Once you do get in, the place is indeed a perfect hurricane hole. Put anchors to the west, tie your stern to trees, and sit it out safe and sound.

As you pass between Petite Grenade and Pointe du Vauclin, you will notice a low spit of land to port; round up behind the spit of land and anchor. It is a beautiful cove with 20 feet of water right up to shore; you can put out a stern anchor and run your bow line to a tree. There is a beautiful white-sand beach on the point, but it turns out to be a great disillusionment—there are only six inches of beautiful white sand over soft, gooey, black mud.

At the head of the cul-de-sac is a small fishing village where you probably could find a taxi or a bus for a ride to Vauclin.

Baie des Mulets, northwest of Petite Grenade, is a good deserted anchorage. Although there are few soundings shown on the chart, I found fairly regular depths of eight feet through most of the bay, gradually shoaling as we approached the inner edge of the reef. I had no difficulty finding a break in the reef for the dinghy, allowing me to enter Passe du Sans Souci.

PASSE DU SANS SOUCI
(Chart 5; II A-30, A-301)

This is another good anchorage with plenty of water and no town or village of any sort. Anchor near the mouth of the pass, as the land is low and swampy at the head of the bay, where it's likely to be hot, airless, and bug infested.

GRANDE PASSE DU SIMON
(Chart 5; II A-30, A-301)

This passage is fairly open to the east. It is littered with reefs that are so steep you could round up under just about any one of them and drop your anchor right on it. If no contact with shore were desired, you could comfortably spend the night with the likelihood of a pleasant cool breeze.

On the south side of Grande Passe du Simon is Pointe Cerisier, with a reef and shoal water extending quite far to seaward. You can work your way into an anchorage behind this curving reef.

There are several tight little anchorages behind bits of reef at the west end of Cul-de-Sac du Simon.

CUL-DE-SAC FREGATE
(Chart 6; II A-30, A-301)

Easy to spot and easy to enter. On the north side of the entrance is Ilet Thiery, a good landmark. On the island's northeast point is a large white house encircled by a big veranda. Also on the east side of Ilet Thiery is a black cliff with a large cave at the water's edge. When entering, sail between the two easily spotted reefs, which are always breaking. But before you ease sheets, make absolutely sure of your bearings: You should be looking down between Ilet Anonyme (Ilet Aubert) and Ilet Long at a bearing of 260° magnetic. If, coming north, you bear off too soon, you can get tangled up with the 10-foot spot that always breaks in heavy weather. (Some of the gray hears in my beard were caused by doing just this, many years ago, with the late Sam Lane on board. Fortunately, he was an excellent sailor and good helmsman, and he realized our error and suddenly headed up and tacked without asking for orders.)

Favor the reefs on the north side of the channel; they are more steep-to and more clearly defined than the reefs on the south side. Once you have definitely established your position, run on in and anchor in the lee of one of the many islands.

We found the anchorage off the house of M. Hayot the best. Run along the north shore of Ilet Long past the small cove with the fishing boats, give the point to the west of the cove a berth of 100 yards, jibe over, then harden sheets and round up in the next cove. There is a white house with a small marine railway to the east of it. There's plenty of water close to shore, so run in until the eastern point of the cove lines up with the western point of Ilet Thiery. This anchorage is perfect no matter what direction the wind blows, and the holding is good. If you would like to be nearer diving water, you can move to the lee of Ilet Thiery, but be careful of the detached coral heads.

Although the chart shows coral heads and no soundings, a draft of five feet may be taken between the western end of Ilet Anonyme (Ilet Aubert) and the mainland. Go slow, keep your leadline going, and try to make some sense out of the private stakes placed by the locals to mark the shoals. Pass close to the western shore of the island, holding a course of west-northwest; you should spot two stakes that mark the channel. However, be careful and don't rely too much on local marks. There is also a dinghy pass around the western end of Ilet Long into Grande Passe du Simon.

LE FRANÇOIS
(Chart 6; II A-30, A-301)

This is one of Martinique's typical middle-size French towns where full-scale tourism has not yet arrived. It is especially attractive for the sailor, as there is a drainage canal that leads right to the edge of town, where you can tie up the dinghy among the French fishing boats. Here there is an active fish and vegetable market early in the morning. After making your purchases, walk to town, where you will find various markets that are more than adequate, and an excellent bakery. Buy your supplies, and if they are too heavy, grab a taxi at the main square. Halfway down to the dinghy landing on the north side of the street is a cold storage warehouse where block ice is available. Also here, of course, are a post office, a pay telephone booth, and various small bars and restaurants.

This whole area around the towns of Le François and Le Robert is especially interesting, as many people live on the various islands and in little mainland coves not connected to the main roads. As a result, there is a continual flow of canoes to and fro, some rowing, some sailing, and some motoring, almost completely hidden by their great bow waves.

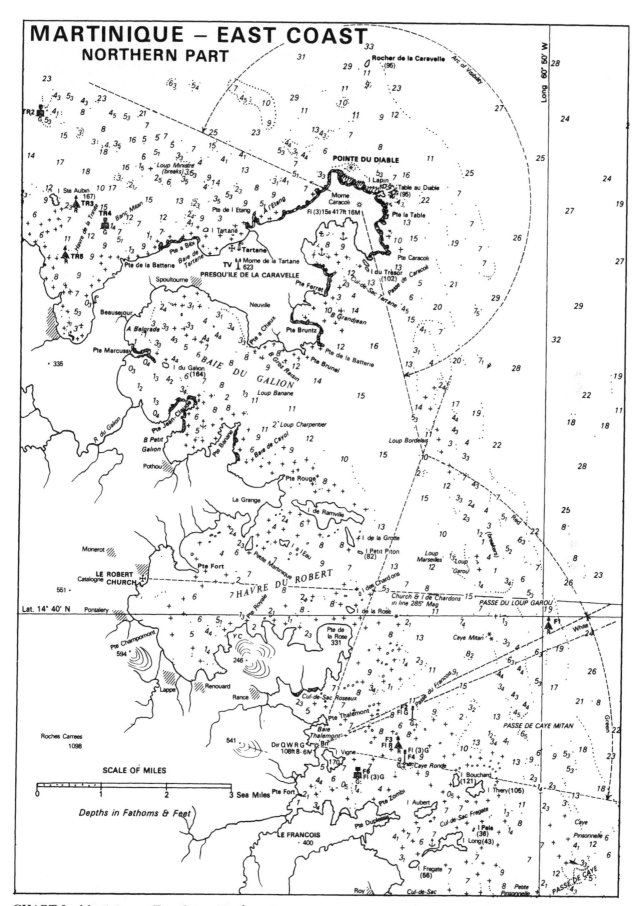

CHART 6 Martinique—East Coast, Northern Part

MOUILLAGE DU FRANÇOIS
(Chart 6; II A-30, A-301)

You can enter this excellent anchorage by either Passe du François or the channel between Ilets Thiery and Bouchard and the reefs to the northwest. If you use this southern entrance, be careful of the seven-foot spot north-northeast of Ilet Thiery. (A bearing aligning the eastern end of Thiery with the eastern end of Ilet Long extends right over this shoal.)

The northern pass leads between Petite Caye, which always breaks, and Caye Brigantine, and is now marked by two buoys. A line between buoys F2 and F3 bears 033° as you enter, but the centerline of the channel is more or less north-south, so it's a reach either way. Even if the wind is around in the north as you leave, you can stand well to the eastern side of the channel and then easily lay out the course on starboard tack. When entering, you can be sure you're on the right line if you keep the buoy on Caye Ronde (F4) between the other two.

I strongly advise against entering Le François by the eastern passage, Passe de Caye Mitan; it's dead downwind and unmarked.

Once inside the harbor, keep your eyes peeled for the various shoal spots. There are three coves on the south side of Mouillage du François. The first two west of Pointe Zombi have picturesque fishing villages on their shores. However, I would not advise spending the night, as I think they would tend to be hot, airless, and full of bugs. A better anchorage is in the third cove, where there is a yacht club with showers, a restaurant-bar, fuel, water, and what-have-you. Dockage is available or you can anchor out. On Sundays, French people from all over the east coast of Martinique come here for an all-out three-hour banquet. The fact that there are few foreigners means that it must be very good indeed.

From here you can visit Le François by taxi or by outboard; if you go by outboard, take it easy—you may churn up mud at various points in the canal. And don't capsize: as I mentioned earlier, I don't know whether it would be worse to drown in a Martinique canal or to be rescued from one! The canal is hard to spot, but if you continue southwestward alongshore from the yacht club, you will have no trouble picking it up.

Behind Ilet Vigne is an excellent anchorage with deep water right up to the shore. Swing around the southern end of the island, sail north, and round up when the slot between the two hills faces east. You will have absolutely calm water, yet the wind will sweep across the hills, guaranteeing a cool and bug-free anchorage. Do not be put off by the muddy water southwest of Ilet Vigne—it is only a tidal eddy that stirs up the mud. Behind the island, the water is clear and clean.

Swimmers can then take the dinghy, visit the outer reef anchorages, and have a fine time snorkeling and spearfishing, although the latter will probably be unprofitable, as the area is pretty well fished out. With the aid of the sketch chart in the *Cruising Guide to Martinique*, a boat drawing five feet or less can explore probably a dozen anchorages in Mouillage du François.

CUL-DE-SAC ROSEAUX
(Chart 6; II A-30, A-301)

This is just north of Le François. I have not visited it, but I did climb to the top of Pointe de la Rose and enjoyed a commanding view of the entire area. The main harbor of Cul-de-Sac Roseaux is easy to enter, but of course the shoal water must be navigated by eyeball. On the north side of the harbor, along the south shore of Pointe de la Rose, are two coves. The easternmost of these, Anse Coco, has deep water right up to the shore, not too much vegetation to gather mosquitoes, and a narrow entrance through the reef. Even the entrance channel is sheltered by offshore reefs. In short, this is a good hurricane hole or, in fact, a good stop at any time. Check the chart carefully and enter only with good light and a person on the bow or in the rigging. The western cove, Anse des Roseaux, is even more sheltered, as it has high hills on three sides and a good hurricane hole, but otherwise it is likely to be hot, airless, and bug-infested.

A path leads from a small dock up the hill to the road; the climb is well worth it—follow the road westward and you will come to the ruins of an old sugar mill from which you can survey the entire area.

There is another cove to the west of Pointe de la Rose that has plenty of water. It makes a good hurricane hole and is a nice spot to visit by dinghy. Don't spend the night, however. The hills rise vertically on three sides, and no air reaches the cove. Looking down on it from the hill above the fishing village, I could not see a single ripple in the water, even though the trades were blowing so hard at the time that they almost knocked me off the ridge. The western part of Cul-de-Sac Roseaux is shoal at its head, and you would have to anchor

Martinique 41

quite far offshore. There is little or nothing to attract one ashore.

This area is described in excellent detail and covered by good sketch charts in the *Cruising Guide to Martinique*. If the *Guide*'s sketch charts should ever disagree with Imray-Iolaire Chart A-301, proceed with extreme caution, but rely more on the *Guide*. Lachesnez-Heude and Nouel have done inshore work on places along this coast that I on *Iolaire*, with a draft of seven feet six inches and no engine, could not do justice to.

HAVRE DU ROBERT

(Chart 6; II A-30, A-301; French 7088)

The largest harbor on the east coast and a sister town to La Trinité, Havre du Robert is beautifully shown on the French Chart 7088. This harbor is wide and easy to enter, with innumerable coves on both sides. There is an anchorage at its head near the town of Le Robert. The town itself is perched on the edge of a hill. Right next to the dinghy dock is a delightful open-air restaurant. The one difficulty with the restaurant is that they have no menu and no one on the staff speaks a word of English; I can vouch for the *sudon* and the *langouste*, however. As is typical of French towns, there is plenty of bread, cheese, wine, fresh fruits and vegetables, and seafood.

The east coast of Martinique is so featureless that strangers may not know exactly where they are. Some of the towns are not even visible from the sea. Let me list the key Le Robert landmarks to watch for: Vauclin—church with a restored roof; Ilet Thiery—large house on the northeastern end with a veranda all around, and the black cliff with caves on its eastern shore; Caye Pinsonnelle—the reef always breaks and the wreck of a sunken steamer is visible at the southern end; Loup Garou—a small, bleach-white sand island off the entrance of Le Robert.

When standing north toward the entrance to Le Robert, remember that the shoal water east of Pointe de la Rose extends well east of the point. Even after you have passed this shoal, don't bear off until you are north of Ilet des Chardons. Then run down into the harbor, which has so many anchorages that you'll have to choose by throwing a dart at the chart.

The charts give ranges for entering Le Robert, but these ranges are for large vessels standing in from seaward and not for inside the harbor itself.

When running into the harbor, I would not pass much west of Petite Martinique, as the anchorage off the town tends to be choppy; the water is not clear and is not well marked. Just west of Pointe Fort is a new fish farm, and the locals do not appreciate having yachts anchor in that area.

The south side of the inner harbor is shoal and muddy. Stay out near the entrance and visit the town by dinghy. The bottom off the town is soft mud, with plenty of grass—all right for an old-fashioned fisherman anchor, but not good for a plow or a Danforth.

Behind Ilet à l'Eau, or northwest of it in the basin, an excellent anchorage is sheltered from the sea but has plenty of wind. I would imagine the snorkeling is good here, since it has crystal-clear water.

Another excellent anchorage on the north side of Havre du Robert is behind Petite Martinique. Deep water runs right up to the shore, and you can literally run aground and jump off the bow of the boat onto shore. Be careful, though, as the wind curves over the top of the hill and comes back from the west—even though it may be blowing thirty knots from the east on the southern tip of the island. We discovered this to our chagrin while exploring here in April 1985; we ended up aground on a steep-to shore and had an interesting time getting off.

Another anchorage is west of the bluffs. An even better one can be had just west of the buildings on the northern end of Ilet de la Grotte; deep water goes right up to the shore, with sand bottom, good holding, and no swell; it's breezy and bugless as well. There is a dinghy passage between Ilet de Ramville and Ilet de la Grotte. There is good snorkeling, and the area is a good place to teach children to swim—great sand flats with only a foot of warm water over them between the two islands. If you wish to visit Rocher de la Grotte, it is best to leave the dinghy at Ilet de la Grotte and wade across from the island.

The cove of Ilet de la Grotte on the south side of Ilet de Ramville is shoal- and reef-encumbered. I would not advise entering it in anything but a dinghy.

The first anchorage on the south side of the harbor is to the west of, and in the lee of, Ilet des Chardons. There is deep water right up to the reefs on both sides, and there are dinghy passages among the reefs, excellent diving, and lobsters galore. Very close to this anchorage is another in the lee of Ilet de la Rose. Deep water carries close to shore on the western side; a long arm of the reef extending out to the north and a solid reef across to Pointe de la

Rose give complete protection. Both these anchorages are good, and there should be plenty of wind to keep you cool and bug-free.

To the west of Pointe de La Rose is Baie de Saintpée; be careful of Banc de la Rose when entering. The best anchorage is under the lee of the reef with the northern end of Pointe de ha Rose bearing east. There is plenty of water all the way to the head of the bay, but the head is all mud flat and mangroves. Take a dinghy, tie it to the mangroves, and walk up the hill to the old sugar mill: a wonderful view, a cool breeze, soft grass, and a big, spreading shade tree.

The next cove, unnamed, between Pointe du Sable Blanc and Pointe Hyacinthe, is completely sheltered and deep. Watch out for Banc Guillotine when you enter; four feet could easily bring you to grief. The pond at the head of the bay is full of mosquitoes; I would advise mooring near the mouth of the cove, where there is a breeze.

East of Pointe Royale is the last noteworthy cove on the south side of the harbor. It is easily spotted: an old sugar mill with a modern house next to it, a number of old cannons pointing seaward, and three or four boats moored in the cove. There is never a problem with bugs and always a breeze in this perfect shelter. The house is used mainly as a summer residence.

(A word is in order about the holiday habits of the Martinicans: Like the French, they take their vacations in late July and August, desert the city, and go to the beach. At that time of the year, the west coast of Martinique is hot, muggy, and wet, while the east coast not only is cool and dry but also has the sand beaches. Hence in the summer you will find the east coast heavily populated, but in the winter the various summer residences will be empty. The locals will tell you that it is winter and cold, even though the temperature is in the low eighties all day.)

BAIE DU GALION
(Chart 6; II A-30, A-301)

A large, open bay with several anchorages but not much to warrant more than a lunch stop. A reef runs south from the mainland east of Pointe Brunel, giving good shelter from the sea. Moor close to the reef at its northern end, as close to shore as you dare. This puts the boat out of the swell, but there is still plenty of wind sweeping across the reef. Another good anchorage is north of Pointe Brunel, off an old farm that is still in operation. There are numerous reefs in the bay and the water is none too

clear, so be careful. I circled Ilet de Galion in the dinghy and found nothing of interest except to a mountaineer eager to practice belaying. I did not visit the village of Galion, but I did find an old jetty near the cane cutters cottages on the western shore of Baie du Galion. The cottages are below the old sugar plantation. A landing can be made at the jetty; a short walk up the hill brings you to the main road, where there is frequent bus service to La Trinité. A taxi may be hired for the ride back; the driver will take you down the hill to your dinghy. If you speak French, it might be possible to get a tour of the sugar estate.

There are other small coves in this bay to be visited; again, consult the *Cruising Guide to Martinique.*

CUL-DE-SAC TARTANE
(Chart 6, Sketch Chart 7; II A-30, A-301)

Now a national park. See update notes on page 47.

Also referred to as Baie du Trésor, reputedly because this was a pirate hideout in days of yore, this is one of the most beautifully sheltered harbors I have ever seen. This is now a nature reserve. No spear fishing, fishing or gathering of shells is permitted. Check locally for the latest regulations regarding anchoring. We were there in September 1964 when a hurricane up north was kicking up a ground swell more than six feet high along the east coast of Martinique—large enough for the seas to crest in 15 feet of water lying in the northeast corner of Cul-de-Sac Tartane, we felt not the slightest motion: It was as smooth as a millpond, with a pleasant breeze hooking around Pointe Caracoli, and no bugs. The water is either shoal or very deep and everywhere steep-to. I was able to lay *Iolaire* parallel to the shore so close that we could step from the port side of the boat into one foot of water. We put a tackle on the main halyard and heaved her down far enough to paint the waterline. Even so, there was water enough to dive between the sandbank and the boat's bottom and to come up on the other side.

When entering the harbor, it is easy to see the reefs on both sides, as they always break; once in the pass, head for the lighthouse on the hill, skirting the western edge of the reef that will be in your path and rounding up north of the reef. Shoot across on the back side of the reef, drop your hook off the stern, snub up, and drop a bow anchor once you have actually reached the reef. Be sure to lay your anchor on the reef, or on the beach. They are both a near-vertical drop into 50 feet of water. Make sure that your stern anchor is well set; when the wind

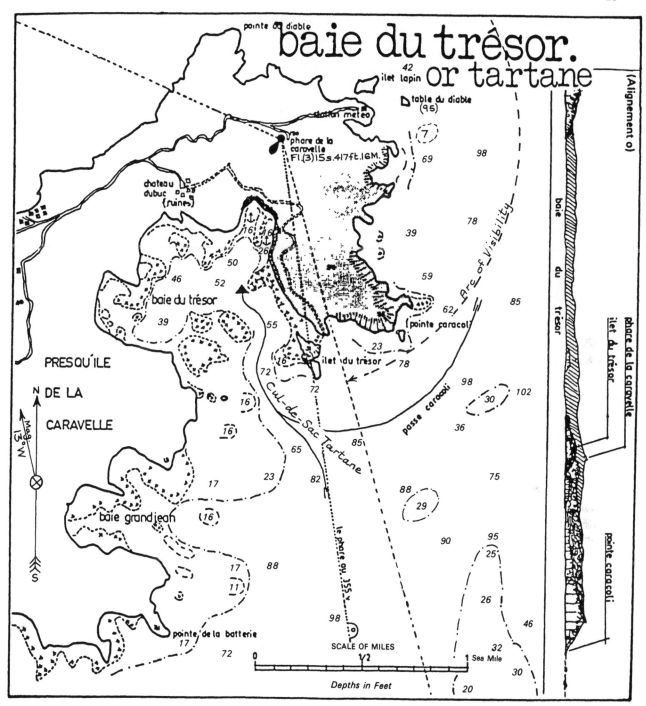

SKETCH CHART 7 Cul–de–Sac Tartane/Baie du Trésor
REPRODUCED FROM GUIDE TO MARTINIQUE TROIS RIVIERES. REPRODUCED WITH PERMISSION. AREA NOW A NATIONAL PARK. CHECK LOCALLY FOR LATEST REGULATIONS.

drops at night, the current running out over the top of the reef will tend to shove you into shoal water.

In April 1985, when we revisited this anchorage, we sailed on in and literally ran the bow up on the beach, jumped ashore with an anchor, dug a hole and buried it, and ran a stern anchor out. Although it was blowing 20 knots outside, we had an absolutely calm anchorage with a nice breeze across the boat.

The whole area is a wildlife preserve that offers the bird-watcher a field day: great herons, blue herons, turnstones, plovers, and yellow-legged sandpipers are just some of the birds that are here.

There are numerous small fishing boats, all

chasing squid, and I can vouch for the lobsters in the area—I caught one while checking the anchor. In the western side of the bay, behind the main reef, are still more anchorages. Although the northwestern corner of the bay is encumbered with reefs, it does provide some perfect hurricane moorings. The water is deep between the reefs; it is possible to place the anchors on top of the reefs and run stern lines to trees ashore. With hills on three sides and overlapping reefs at the entrance to the harbor, it would be hard to find a more ideal spot.

For those who like to explore, there are the ruins of an old estate, the Château Dubuc, which is also reputed to have been a pirates' or smugglers' hideout. It is high on a ridge but so overgrown that it is impossible to spot from seaward. In its day, this must have been quite a place: It included a reservoir (now a mudhole) and a dam some 30 feet high that must have held a good-size pond two centuries ago. Old bits and pieces of iron abound, some huge molasses pots known as people pots (what they cooked missionaries in), sugar-cane machinery, an old powder magazine—you could easily spend a whole morning rummaging about this place. To find the old castle, land the dinghy in the cove to the west of the middle point projecting out into the bay where a group of fishermen are always making fish pots or working on their canoes. From there, a path leads up the hill to the ruins.

It's easy to see why this might have been a bad guys' paradise in the old days: A lookout posted at the top would have been able to see all the way south to Cap Ferré, and northwest to the northern parts of Martinique. Anyone coming to interfere with smugglers or pirates would have had to arrive by ship, since there was no overland route in those days, and any ship would have been spotted almost a full day's sail away (remember that square-riggers were not very good to windward). If the lawmen came from the north, the bad guys could scoot south; if the danger came from the south, it was only a short beat out of the harbor, around the corner, and off to the north. A perfect setup.

Above the ruins you will find a road eastward to the Caravelle lighthouse, where the keepers are most happy to give you a tour. There is also a road west to the towns of Tartane and La Trinité.

North Coast

(Chart 6; II A-30, A-301)

Along the northern coast of Presqu'île de la Caravelle are a small cove east of Pointe de l'Etang and the fishing village of Tartane. Both are strictly summertime stops for small boats, and they are well covered in the *Cruising Guide to Martinique.*

Otherwise, La Trinité is the only port worth mentioning on Martinique's north coast. It is an excellent harbor when the trades are south of east; in winter, though, the swell from the north makes the anchorage pretty rolly. Witness the beautiful white-sand beaches on the south and east sides of the harbor, proof of a good surge.

When sailing from Cul-de-Sac Tartane to La Trinité, stand southeast on the port tack, then tack back to the north and pass between Pointe Caracoli and the five-fathom spot southeast of the point—it can break in heavy weather. Head northeast, ease sheets, and pass outside Table au Diable. Continue north in the deep water, staying out beyond the 10-fathom shelf, as the Atlantic swell coming into shoal water can really hump up. Once you turn west, there are two choices:

1. Sail west until Ilet Tartane bears 230° magnetic, then run in on this line of bearing until the southern end of Ilet St. Aubin bears 285° or you can line up the buoy on Banc Mitan on a bearing of 278°. Run west along either of these lines of bearing (don't sail *over* Banc Mitan!) and then pick up the entrance buoys to La Trinité.

2. Alternatively, pass north of all the shoals, staying in deep water until the center of the beach at the head of La Trinité Harbor bears approximately 195°; jibe over and run south on this line of bearing, which will put Loup Ministre on your starboard hand. When you get into the harbor, anchor on the eastern side, off the beaches.

As for going the other way—from La Trinité to Cul-de-Sac Tartane—if it's blowing hard, I wouldn't. If you must, stand well north from La Trinité and do your windward work in deep water. The winter trades roil the sea over the shoals, making it very hairy to tack safely through them. In spring and summer, though, when the wind is south of east, you can easily short-tack up the beach and stay out of the current.

LA TRINITE

(Chart 8; II A-30, A-301)

The town of La Trinité is much the same as the other towns on the east coast of Martinique, except that it is larger, with good road communication to Fort de France. La Trinité is a port of entry for Martinique, but only for Customs. (You'll have to clear out of Fort de France.) It is best to take a taxi

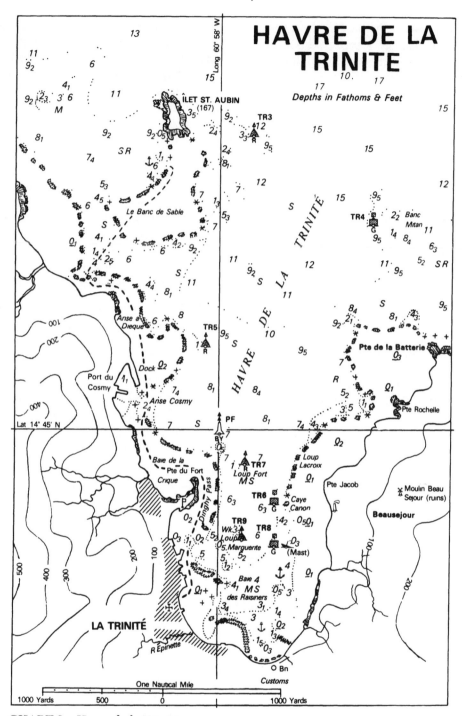

CHART 8   Havre de la Trinité

collective into Fort de France to clear, a one-hour ride that costs about US$3.00.

The harbor would certainly be more convenient if the dinghy landing facilities were better. There are two small docks. One is by the fish market, and is also near a vegetable market, a supermarket, an ice storage plant with block ice, a couple of small, friendly bar/restaurants, a phone booth, and a nice waterside park. Be sure, though, to throw out a stern anchor to keep the dinghy from beating against the pier. The other dock is 200 yards south; here there is a beach, and if your dinghy is light enough, you can slide it up on the beach above the high-water mark.

While at La Trinité, it is worth visiting the Hôtel St. Aubin, a wonderful old turn-of-the-century

French Victorian hostelry that I admired from afar. I am sure it would provide a perfect setting for a delicious three-hour French lunch. Call the hotel and arrange for a taxi.

ILET ST. AUBIN
(Chart 8; II A-30, A-301)

I visited this place for the first time in 1985, and I feel we discovered an anchorage that was not included in any previous guides. That this was a good anchorage was news even to Philippe Lachesnez-Heude, who has spent his lifetime cruising Martinique's waters.

Approach it from the east as you would La Trinité, swing around the north end of St. Aubin, jibe around the island, head south, eyeball your way right up behind the reef, and anchor in 50 to 60 feet of water, depending on how close to the reef you want to get. If you anchor really close to the reef, I strongly advise anchoring bow and stern, as I am sure that during the night, when the wind dies down, a change in tide would swing you against the reef.

The swell hooks around Ilet St. Aubin in a great circle and catches the western corner of the reef, so it's best to anchor about a third of the way down the reef (where the anchor is shown on the latest Imray-Iolaire charts). You will be guaranteed privacy and a calm, bug-free anchorage with a huge area to snorkel and dive. The number of fish-pot markers on the edge of the reef suggests that there must be a fair amount of fish around.

One of the great advantages of this anchorage is that you are only 1½ miles by dinghy from La Trinité; almost the entire trip can be made behind the reef, sheltered by the outer reef. (The dinghy pass is shown on Imray-Iolaire Chart A-30 and Chart 8, the plan of Havre de la Trinité.)

It is possible to sail south from Ilet St. Aubin through the pass between the end of the St. Aubin reef and the reef on the mainland; there is ample water and even room for *Iolaire* to tack in the passage.

West Coast

ST. PIERRE
(Chart 9; II A-30)

The town here was totally destroyed by the eruption of Mont Pelée in the early twentieth century. It appears that the best anchorage is south of the town where the chart notes "old Battery". Every time I pass St. Pierre this is where the yachts have been anchored. A

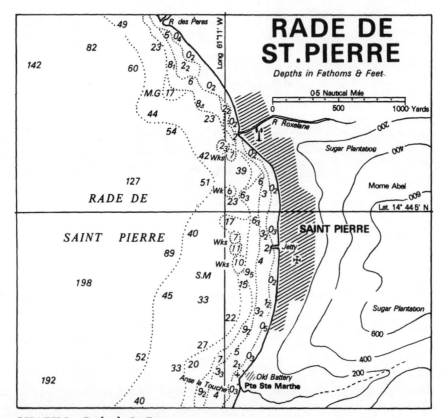

CHART 9   Rade de St. Pierre

museum commemorating the catastrophe is a spectacular tourist attraction. The anchorage is not good, however. For the most part, it is an open roadstead; the swell usually runs in and the bottom drops off very steeply. Make sure that you are on the shelf before you let go the hook. Many a boat has almost lost its anchor when its depth gauge registered bottom—on the second time around the dial.

The best anchorage is off Pointe Ste. Marthe, where there is a restaurant right at the water's edge and a group of *gommiers* are pulled up on the beach.

There is good diving on the wrecks of the ships sunk when the volcano blew in 1902—only one ship out of about 13 or 14 escaped destruction. The wrecks are plotted in the *Cruising Guide to Martinique*. The guide recommends that you contact the Carib Scuba Club at the Hôtel Latitude Carbet; they run regular diving tours to the area, know the wrecks, and are fully equipped to take you diving.

St. Pierre is a good place to stop if you have had a rough trip from Dominica and arrived late in the day and want to rest before heading south to Fort de France. Conversely, if you have left Fort de France at midday or later, then St. Pierre is a good place to stop for the night prior to an early morning departure for Dominica.

The weather conditions in Rade de St. Pierre are variable—sometimes flat calm, sometimes blowing like mad, and other times with hard gusts suddenly dropping down off the mountains. Take care.

CASE PILOTE
(II A-30)
Case Pilote is a small town with a breakwater about halfway between St. Pierre and Pointe des Négres. This little habor is well described in Chris Doyle's guide, but after having inspected the little village and the harbor formed by the breakwater, I cannot imagine why any yacht would ever want to visit here. The dock does not offer much protection, and available space seems to be taken up with broken-down yachts that don't appear ever to move.

WARNING—fish farming has arrived in Martinique.
½ mile south west of Cove Pilot approximate position 14 37.9°N 61 08.5°W marked at night by lights flashing every 3 seconds.

In years to come this business may expand so be careful - and check for the biannual up dates of this guide

POINTE DES NEGRES
(II A-30)
This is an excellent shelter in normal weather. The only difficulties are posed by deep water and the lack of swinging room. In the past, arrangements could be made to moor bow-and-stern to the dock, but I have been informed that this is now a private club for the French military and is closed to visitors.

In conclusion, I would say that Martinique probably is the most underrated island in the Caribbean for the average yachtsman. After having spent three years in the mid-1980s reexploring the Caribbean from Mona Island to Trinidad and Tobago, and having hit every island in between, my wife and I have come to the conclusion that Martinique is our favorite. Do not judge the island by the anchorage at Fort de France off the Savane, or the pleasant but crowded Anse Mitan. Go explore the other harbors, especially those on the east coast.

The only problem we have found with the east coast is drinking water. After leaving the Fort de France area, the only place with even a possibility of getting water alongside is Club Nautique in Cul-de-Sac Marin—and even that is iffy. So take a minimum of eight five-gallon collapsible water jugs and be prepared to carry your water out in the dinghy.

Otherwise, the east coast is a cruiser's delight. Don't miss it.

CUL-DE-SAC MARIN
(Chart 4; II A-30. A-301)
This has now become a huge yachting centre. There is now something like twelve bareboat organisations. Customs & Immigration is available at the marina and the hours now seem to be 08.00 to 16.00. No one seems to be particularly worried about coming in after 16.00 and not clearing before the next day.

The shipyard is now upgraded with a 60 ton travelift. There is also a floating dry dock which is very popular amongst the multi-hull fraternity.

Pick up the Martinique Marine Guide and you will discover that practically anything you need done to a yacht can be done. If you have difficulty in finding people to repair equipment the best thing is to introduce yourself to one of the bareboat managers and ask his advice. Both the Moorings and SunSail are maintaining large fleets of boats and know just about all there is to know about the facilities on the island of Martinique

NOTES

3

St. Lucia

(Imray-Iolaire Charts 1, B, B-1)

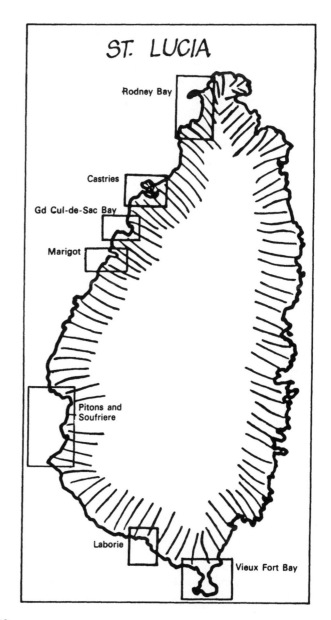

St. Lucia, an independent member of the British Commonwealth, lies between Martinique to the north and St. Vincent to the south, and on most days it is visible from both of these islands. There are two good harbors and sundry anchorages on its western side. The harbors were the cause of violent clashes between colonial powers in the eighteenth and early nineteenth centuries. Castries, the capital of St. Lucia, was important to the British as a fleet harbor in the eighteenth century and as a coaling station in the nineteenth. It was continually built up and fortified until the early years of the twentieth century. During the 1920s, its importance declined with the passing of coal-burning ships, and the island fell into economic depression. The activities of World War II and the establishment of a large American airbase at Vieux Fort revived the economy for a brief period, but soon after the war, the base was closed and the island returned to Third World oblivion. In the very earliest colonial days, the island had grown rich from its sugar; now a second economy based on sugar, bananas, and tourism has been established, and St. Lucia is stirring again.

Because of its many hills and mountains, St. Lucia is one of the wetter islands of the Eastern Caribbean. During the wet season, it seems to rain almost continually, tapering off in the dry season to a couple of short squalls per day. Although the island is high, it is not a solid block like Dominica but rather more like a series of ventilated hills. Thus, there usually is a breeze close inshore along the western coast.

The tides are so minimal that they are not listed in the tide tables. I found an old British chart that listed the HWF&C (high water full and change: the average interval between the transit—upper or lower—of the full or new moon and the next high water) as "2h 30m." The current north and south of the island sets into the Caribbean at a knot or more.

Because of inaccuracies in both the British and the American charts, I recommend using Imray-Iolaire Chart B-1 exclusively.

St. Lucia has a number of good hotels and restaurants, although the island's restaurants open and close with great frequency. It is best to ask the various marina operators which restaurants are currently recommended.

Air communication into St. Lucia is excellent in that it is served by Island Air, LIAT, and Air Martinique, all of which "island hop" to St. Lucia through Vigie Airport, which is right next door to the harbor of Castries. The old American airbase near Vieux Fort is now Hewannora International Airport, where the runways have been extended to accept even the biggest jumbo jets, so there are direct flights here from many parts of the world.

There is only one fly in the ointment. When it was decided that the old airbase would become St. Lucia's major airport, the British government financed a beautiful highway from Vieux Fort to Castries to reduce the driving time from three hours on a treacherous road to one hour on an excellent road. As part of the deal, a bus service was to have been installed from the airport direct to Castries, Vigie Airport, and the hotels just north of the town at Rodney Bay. However, this has never come to pass. Thus St. Lucia is a very poor transfer point, as one flies in from Europe and then gets stung for an EC$50 taxi ride to Castries, to the hotels, or to Vigie Airport for transportation to other islands in the Eastern Caribbean.

There is a good open-air market in the town of Castries, and there are three or four stores where frozen foods, canned goods, and so forth, are available. The yachtsman will have no problem securing all the normal food supplies.

A visit to Bagshaws, two miles or so out of town, is a must. Here you will find dresses, skirts, and decorative yet practical household items made of silk-screened cotton, silk, and linen. There are also lengths of material to be made up by the nimble-fingered, and the visitors are welcomed to the studio to see how it's done. Go by taxi and ask the driver to wait.

A very worthwhile excursion when visiting St. Lucia is a trip on Bob Elliot's *Unicorn,* a brig fully rigged to the royals—she looks like something out of the last century. Needless to say, she has a diesel engine, but given favorable wind conditions, Bob and his excellent crew really sail the boat. Even the most experienced ocean racer will get a thrill out of this and be extremely interested in the sailhandling of the handsome square-rigger.

When approaching St. Lucia from the north, there are no dangers lying off the coast. Castries is easily identified during the day by the forts on Vigie Point, and at night by the lights on either side of the harbor entrance. Do not stop at Pigeon Island before entering Castries; wine smuggling is a great occupation here, and the authorities take a dim view of yachts that stop before clearing at Castries. (Alternatively, you can clear at Rodney Bay in the lagoon—depth eight feet. Alert Customs and Immigration by calling on VHF channel 16.) When coming from the south, unless you are heading for Vieux Fort (a port of entry), head directly for the Pitons, which are very easy to spot from a great distance, appearing like two loaves of French bread standing on end on the southwest corner of the island. There is only one hazard. On the lee side of St. Lucia, off Grande Caille Point north of the Pitons, the rocks extend 200 to 250 yards offshore. They have only a few feet of water and a tide rip over them most of the time. Give them a wide berth.

Castries is the main port of entry to St. Lucia, but there are also Customs offices on the west coast in Rodney Bay Marina and Marigot Bay (Hurricane Harbour Hotel), as well as at Vieux Fort, on the extreme southern tip. Contact them via VHF channel 16 to give advance warning before you enter.

The good news is that you can now also get preclearance at Soufrière. Anchor bow-on to the beach and clear with the local police sergeant. His clearance will cover you until you get to an official port of entry. This welcome development is a vast improvement over the old days when there was no entry point south of Marigot Bay on the west coast. It meant that anyone coming to St. Lucia from the south who succumbed to the temptation to anchor at the Pitons or Soufrière along the way was illegal and in danger of incurring fines or even jail. (I'd like to think that my sounding off about this situation in earlier guides had something to do with the change.)

Beware, though. I hear through the grapevine that Customs *still* takes a dim view of yachts anchoring at the Pitons before clearing. Now, however, Soufrière is just a stone's throw away from there.

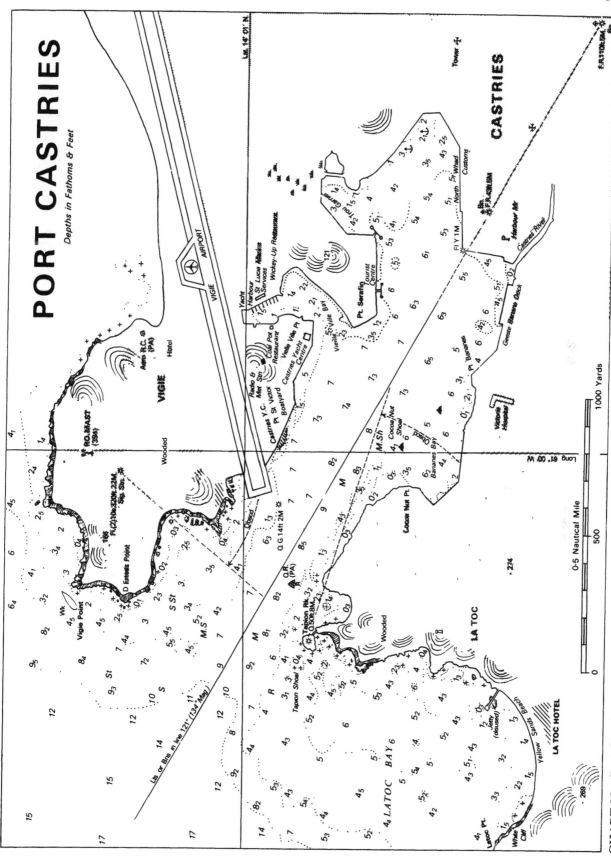

CHART 10 Port Castries

CASTRIES

(Chart 10; II B-1)

The harbor is deep, well sheltered, and easy to enter. So easy is the entrance, in fact, that during World War II a German submarine entered after dark, sank a freighter along the dock, and departed, allegedly leaving an unexploded torpedo embedded in the soft mud under the town.

If you must enter at night (I advise against it), follow the range—two fixed red lights—right into the harbor. The range may seem to put you very close to the south shore of the harbor, but this is correct and there is nothing to worry about except that the dredging companies are notoriously lax about lighting their equipment. In a contest of yacht against dredge, the dredge will win. Keep an eye out.

To clear customs, anchor off the north side of the east-west wall of the steamer dock. You may tie up alongside the dock, but this is not advisable, as Castries has long had a reputation for having the most unfriendly, and foulest-mouthed, longshoremen in the Lesser Antilles. Their language will blister the paint right off your boat. Better to anchor off the dock and row ashore in the dinghy to Customs and Immigration, which is right on the dock.

When anchoring here, stay clear of the turning basin; be sure you are positioned east of the white, unlighted quarantine buoy. If you are anchored in the turning basin, the pilot launch will tell you in no uncertain terms to move.

Under no circumstances should you anchor at Vigie Cove and proceed to town to clear. This will cause much (and sometimes expensive) trouble. Either go alongside the dock or anchor in the northeast corner clear of the turning basin and go to Customs and Immigration by dinghy.

After clearing at Castries, if you're not ready to move on to Rodney Bay, Marigot Bay, or other more scenic spots, it's best to go back to Vigie Cove on the north side of Castries Harbor.

The harbor improvements have created problems in Vigie Cove. The main harbor has been dredged right to the mouth of the cove, and the east and northeast sides of the cove have been covered with riprap. Now the cove, which used to be a semi-hurricane shelter, has become untenable whenever the northwest ground swell comes in. The swell ricochets off the stone riprap and finds its way into the innermost reaches of the cove.

Furthermore, when you anchor in the mouth of the cove, you find an almost vertical slope, as the bottom drops off suddenly from 10 to 35 feet. If you let out enough scope, your swinging circle (the wind frequently dies during the night and comes in light from the west) is just too large. Either use a Bahamian moor or anchor bow-and-stern.

Be aware that the *Unicorn*, Bob Elliot's brig replica, lies in Vigie Cove and makes daily trips down to Soufrière. Leave him room to maneuver when he is entering and leaving the cove.

If you have time, a trip on the *Unicorn* is well worth the investment, as it is unlike most of the replica pirate-ship cruises that chug along under power with guests drinking rum punch—to the point where by the end of the trip the only sober thing on board is the engine. Although the *Unicorn* cruise does provide drinks, food, and a band, it also provides (weather permitting) a memorable sail down the coast. Bob is an enthusiastic sailor who singlehanded his own boat across the Atlantic in the 1950s (before the days of reliable self-steering gear) and still enjoys sailing. He has well-trained crew members who set all sails in a minimum amount of time, and, given a beam or broad reach, he does not spare the horses. Where else except St. Lucia would you have a chance to jump on a square-rigger that really sails? Admittedly, if the wind is around to the north when you are returning from Soufrière, you will be reduced to a chug-chug: Going to windward is definitely not a square-rigger's best point of sailing.

At Vigie Cove you'll find St. Lucia Marine Services, formerly known as Ganter's, where for 20 years Gracie Ganter took care of itinerant yachtsmen and charter skippers, acting as fairy godmother to us all. Now Gracie is back in England and various people have taken over the operation, but no one seems to have established a first-rate marina. Still, St. Lucia Marine Services is useful for taking on fuel, water, and a fair selection of food supplies from their commissary. They also have showers. Eight feet can be squeezed into the docks.

More yacht facilities are available now at the Castries Yacht Centre, newly established on the north side of the harbor, just east of the airport runway. They have a 30-ton Travelift and provide hauling and long-term storage facilities (Box 120, Castries, St. Lucia; telephone: 809-452-6234 or 5348). Also, adjacent to the yard is Derek Morton, a qualified English mechanic who is a diesel specialist (telephone: 809-452-1317; fax: 809-452-5313).

To get bottled gas in Castries, take your bottles to the Texaco depot in town; it's a bit hard to find, as it is in a lumber warehouse about two blocks south of the western end of the commercial docks. Leave the bottles and they will be filled by the following day.

(You can also get bottled gas in Rodney Bay, at Sun Sail Stevens (formerly Stevens Yachts), where Ian Cowan, with his usual efficiency, can fill your bottles while you wait; if a bottle is half full, he'll charge you only for what he puts into it.)

Ice on St. Lucia used to be cheap in 200-pound blocks; now it's available at the cold-storage plant only in small 10-pound blocks, or at St. Lucia Marine Services by the bag in cubes.

Laundry services are extremely expensive, and the commercial laundry in town is a dead loss. It is best to find a local laundress—but check the price first. (Or, again, wait until you get to Rodney Bay, where Sun Sail Stevens has laundry machines.)

Near St. Lucia Marine Services is a small restaurant formerly known as the Wickey-Up. Originally Gracie Ganter's private apartment, then converted to a restaurant, it has gone through many hands. Happily, all of the owners of this restaurant have kept it simple, informal, and reasonably priced. It is now called Jimmy's, and the place has built up an enviable reputation as an excellent seafood restaurant.

If you're interested in diving, Bob Elliot can put you in touch with his brother-in-law, Mr. O. Alcée, whose Dive St. Lucia operation is on Vieille Ville Point (Box 412, Castries).

PIGEON ISLAND AND RODNEY BAY
(Chart 11; II B-1)

This is an excellent anchorage for yachts. However, it is illegal to put in to Pigeon Island if you are coming from Martinique. You must enter through Castries, Rodney Bay, or Marigot Bay beforehand. Pigeon is an island in name only, as it is connected to the mainland by a causeway. This gives full shelter from the sea hooking around the northern corner of the island, and the causeway is low enough that it doesn't block the wind, allowing for a cool and bug-free anchorage in 12 feet of water. The causeway has created a wonderful harbor, although it has spoiled the seclusion of Pigeon Island, which once was a bird sanctuary. I suspect the influx of cars and day-trippers has driven the birds away.

If you are approaching Pigeon Island from Castries, hug the coast. There are no hazards and you should be able to make it in one tack. Head for the thatched huts on the southern side of the island, round up behind the causeway, and anchor about 200 feet offshore. But stay south of the dock on Pigeon Island, since the water shoals to three or four feet directly off the dock. Do not anchor too close to the

east coast of Pigeon Island, as this can be a lee shore. The causeway and the island of St. Lucia to windward will break any sea, although you may experience a small chop.

If you want a calmer anchorage, work your way up to the northeast of St. Croix Roads. (The US chart is wrong here—use Chart 11 in this book.) In December 1978, we found an excellent anchorage in 10 feet of water with the fort on an eastern peak of Pigeon Island bearing 315°, a distinctive cliff north of the causeway bearing 035°, and the breakwaters forming the entrance to Rodney Bay bearing 155° magnetic. Feel your way in with the fathometer and/or leadline.

Pigeon Island was formerly owned by Mrs. Josette Leigh, better known in yachting circles as Madame Snowball. Her thatch-roofed cottage hotel on the beach vied with Mary Pomeroy's Beachlands on Nevis as the most famous and hospitable hotel in the Lesser Antilles. Mrs. Leigh sold out some years ago, however, and the hotel is no more, although the thatched cottages still stand. Visitors are welcome to tramp about or explore the old ruins. A climb to the top of the watchtower at Fort Rodney is well worthwhile.

These waters may be the only place in the world where fish are still caught with rocks. Two or three mornings a week, about 25 dugout canoes assemble off the beach. Nets are strung out at right angles to the shore and canoes are laden gunwale-deep with rocks gathered from shore. The canoes arrange themselves in a line a few hundred yards off, where the fishermen wait for a school of fish to come along. When the fish are sighted, the natives throw the rocks to drive the fish into the nets, which are then looped together and dragged ashore. This is a wonderful opportunity to get some good photographs, as well as to obtain fresh fish at reasonable prices. The fishermen are friendly and enjoy having strangers help them haul the nets.

South of the village of Gros Islet is the dredged channel to the lagoon of Rodney' Bay Harbor, originally' referred to as "Rotten Bay" by the charter skippers of the Stevens fleet who arrived in the early stages of the development when nothing much was there. The channel to Rodney Bay has been dredged to 12 feet in November/December 1999. the dredging is presently (April2000) going on inside the harbor. In general the depths of the harbor are approximately as per Chart 11. But there are various humps that have been missed by the dredging. Proceed slowly and you will not get into trouble as it is soft mud. Admittedly, prior to the dredging a couple of the Swan 65 skippers who knew and understood the

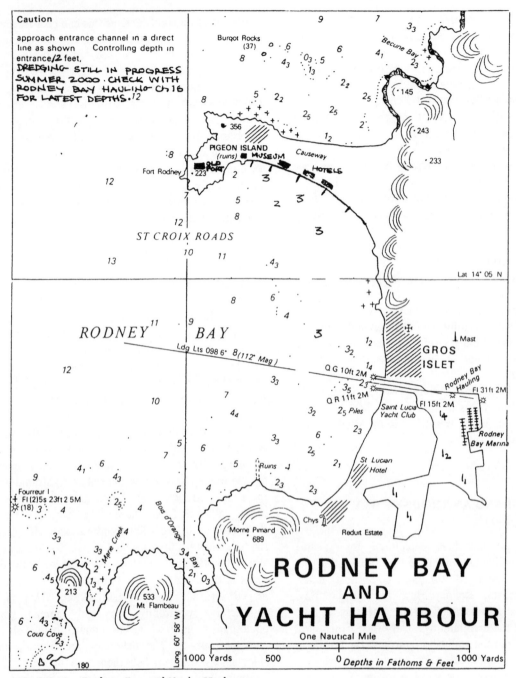

CHART 11 Rodney Bay and Yacht Harbour
SOUNDINGS IN FATHOMS AND FEET

tides can coax a Swan 65 into Rodney Bay Harbor on high-water springs, but that only gives them six days a month when they can get in and out. A day late in leaving can mean a 10-day delay.

In 1979, dredging was proposed again, and the talk was still going on in 1991. Rodney Bay will never be fully developed until the channel and the basin in the yacht harbor are dredged to 12 feet.

The harbor does finally have a full-service marina, though. It has good docks, water, electricity, marine supplies, a restaurant, and a specialty grocery store with goodies from Martinique.

In order to accommodate the flood of boats that arrive from across the Atlantic with the ARC (Atlantic Rally for Cruisers), dockage was greatly expanded at Rodney Bay Marina before the 1991 race. For a week or 10 days after the regatta, the marina was full, but once the ARC fleet departed, half of the docks were empty. This means that you can be assured of finding dock space here throughout the rest of the year. It also means that if you are looking for a sheltered marina to lay up your boat during hurricane season, Rodney Bay fills the bill.

There are many shops in Rodney Bay Marina, but none have the basic everyday items that yachtsmen need and want. Thus, if you want to do any stocking up, you have to get a bus to town or to the supermarket near Vigie Airport, collect what you need, and take an expensive taxi back to the boat.

When you visit the showers at the marina, I recommend you arrive with a wrench and pliers, as the faucet handles are likely to be missing. As with other such facilities in the Eastern Caribbean, the shower situation at Rodney Bay Marina is rather ridiculous. They probably spend as much money paying someone to collect for the showers as they take in; plus, of course, there is the difficulty of accounting for it all—i.e., how much the employee takes in from yachtsmen versus how much the employee passes on to the employer! Like dinghy landing fees, shower fees are a dead loss. The only place in the Eastern Caribbean where this problem has been solved is at Village Cay Marina in Tortola, British Virgins. They installed a meter on the shower, so you go to the desk, buy a token, insert the token in the slot, and you get a specific number of gallons of water. The token-operated shower (which is specially made and therefore rather expensive) paid for itself rapidly. It changed the Village Cay shower situation from being a disaster and a money loser to an operation that made so much profit they could pay someone to clean it out seven times a day and still laugh all the way to the bank. (The shower units are available from Dick Morris at R.E.M.S. Co., Ltd., Box 208, Hassia Estate, Roadtown, Tortola. BVI; telephone: 809-494-2694.)

Finally, based on my own experience, DO NOT change francs to EC currency at the Rodney Bay Marina. In January 1990, we dropped off a load of books in Martinique and were paid in French francs, which I figured would be easily convertible to US or EC currency. When we arrived at Rodney Bay, a staff member at the marina office cheerfully said they could handle the currency exchange, so I sent my son up to change about US$600 worth of francs into EC currency. That evening, when I counted up and did some quick figuring, I realized that the francs had been discounted roughly 20 percent. Assuming there was some sort of error, I went back the next morning to the marina office, where they assured me I had received the correct rate. So I decided, fine, if that's the rate, I'll buy francs with my EC money and at least won't take too much of a beating. But the response was, "We don't sell francs, we only buy them." With the discount I was given, any profit I made on my books

in Martinique ended up in the pockets of the Rodney Bay Marina! Be forewarned. If you have French francs in St. Lucia and you are heading south, find a yachtsman going the other way and strike a deal.

Telephone service from Rodney Bay Marina is via phone cards. Of course the only trouble there is that sometimes the cards are not available anywhere at the marina. If you have an emergency and need to make a phone call, the office staff is not likely to help you out and let you use their phones—from my experience, they are less than cooperative. You have to use the outside phones and that's it. No emergency will allow you to use the office ones. In a *real* emergency, contact Ian Cowan at Sun Sail Stevens. Although they DO NOT like anyone to make outside calls, at least it can be done in an emergency (for a fee).

There are a number of other charter companies besides Sun Sail Stevens operating out of Rodney Bay Marina, but the charter business is in such a state of flux at this point—with companies coming and going at a great rate—that anything I report here probably will be out of date by the time you read this book. Thus, for more information on charter companies operating out of St. Lucia. consult the latest issues of the yachting magazines.

Stevens Yachts (now Sun Sail Stevens) has rented space in the marina for many years, and, thankfully Ian Cowan is still in charge. Besides its charter business, Stevens also has a very good sail loft run by a fellow named Inse, who has been repairing sails and rigging boats for Stevens for the last 20 years. Needless to say, he is good.

NOTE: Sun Sail Stevens is not more - January 2000. But Ian Cowan is still in Rodney Bay running Rodney Bay Shipyard. His shipyard can organise just about anything you may want to have done on a yacht. He has been in the Caribbean running bareboats for 30 years and has been in St. Lucia for 20.

Ian also runs a marine chandlery, and what he doesn't have, he will order from the United States or the United Kingdom and get it shipped out very rapidly, duty-free. Plus, since he is not tying up money in inventory, his markup is considerably less than that of other marine suppliers. So it's very worthwhile to order equipment through him. As noted above, he also fills propane bottles, sells BLOCK ice and runs one of the best laundry services in the Caribbean. His assistant, Ince, does awning and sail repairs, and also makes excellent dodgers. When in St. Lucia contact Ian or his wife Rosemary—as what they can't do they can arrange, and in an emergency will help out with an engine repair. This man of many talents has also helped me compile information for the Imray-Iolaire charts, which he stocks in the chandlery along with Street guides.

56 Street's Cruising Guide to the Eastern Caribbean—Martinique to Trinidad

There is also a duty-free marine hardware store in Rodney Bay Marina. It should be a bargain, but because of the markup needed to cover money tied lip in inventory (which sometimes is on the shelves for many months), plus high rental fees, the supposed bargain is not always such a good deal. Check prices carefully.

Sails can also be repaired at Top Sail. Call them at 809-452-7773 and they will pick up and deliver. They also do fiberglass repairs on dinghies, and other small tasks.

The marina on the north side of the Rodney Bay yacht harbor operates a fueling pier, hauling facilities with a 50-ton Travelift, and repair facilities that handle woodworking, fiberglass repairs, painting, machine tooling, and engine and electrical repairs. There is also ample space for dry-storing boats. This operation is rapidly building up an excellent reputation as a good place to haul, store, and paint a boat.

St. Lucia is on the southern end of the hurricane track, so chances of getting a hurricane here are far less than in the northern islands, but hurricanes still do come through. Thus, boat storage is still a big concern As has been mentioned elsewhere in the Street Giudes, one wonders about the advisability of storing yachts with their rigs in, perched up high with little ballast in the keel. Chocked this way, they are prime candidates for blowing out of the cradles as happened in Antigua, St. Thomas, and Puerto Rico during Hurricane Hugo in 1989. (See "Reflections On Hugo" in the Foreword to this volume. Also *Street's Transatlantic Cruising Guide and Introduction to the Caribbean* has an extensive discussion of the dangers of hurricanes.)

If you have problems in St. Lucia. a good person to contact for help is Chris Kessel (telephone: 809-452-4499: fax: 809-452-3544), who has lived here for more *THAN* 20 years. He is a surveyor accepted by most insurance companies, does light machining himself, and can organize practically anything on the island. When you meet Chris, do not be fooled by his youth. He is young, but he started young—working for Bob Elliot of the brig *Unicorn* at the age of 14. While still in his teens, he was sailing as mate on *Unicorn,* and in his early twenties he was doing an excellent job of skippering the vessel. He still skippers her whenever Bob is in a jam and cannot make a trip or has to leave the island for business trips.

You must be very careful when entering this harbor: Various storms have dislodged rocks from the breakwaters. If you are off to one side of the channel, you are sure to hit solid rock. Stay absolutely in the center of the channel.

From the gate of the marina there is excellent, cheap bus service to town. Before you get in, though, make sure it is a bus: The buses and taxis look the same, but the bus fare to town is EC$1.00 and the taxi fare is EC$14 per person. Be careful!

Within Rodney Bay Harbor are numerous restaurants that jut out over the water; an evening's pub crawl can be done by climbing in your dinghy and visiting the various establishments. Since there seems to be considerable turnover, you'd better get up-to-date local information about what's open and what's reliable.

On the south side of the entrance to the lagoon is the St. Lucia Yacht Club—typical of the West Indian yacht club in that although its sign reads "Members Only," that also means "and visiting yachtsmen." So don't be put off. The club is active on weekends only, but an afternoon with the local yachtsmen is time well spent.

Over Whit Weekend (\Vhitsunday is a movable liturgical feast), the St Lucia Yacht Club hosts a three day version of the fun and games of Antigua Week's Lay Day festivities. It is also coupled with the WIYA match-racing championships. Member clubs send teams, and Sun Sail Stevens and the Moorings provide the boats for a Congressional cup-type match-racing series.

In October, the club runs the Interline series, similar to the Interline series held in Tortola. Sailing enthusiasts from international airlines fly down to spend a week racing and partying. It's absolutely wonderful if you work for an airline and have free transportation. Plus needless to say, it generates tremendous publicity for the charter organizations involved in the series.

Beware, another guide of this area praises the Saturday night jump-up in Gros Islet, which can be a lot of fun, but the major problem is that you may get mugged on your way back to the marina, so make sure you return in a large group capable of defending yourselves. The drug situation in the area seems to be getting out of hand; some yachtsmen report that the drug pushers are likely to approach you before the dock boys who are supposed to handle your lines.

GRAND CUL DE SAC BAY

(Chart 12; II B-1)
Two miles south of Castries, this bay is not too attractive. It has become a deepwater oil port,

St. Lucia

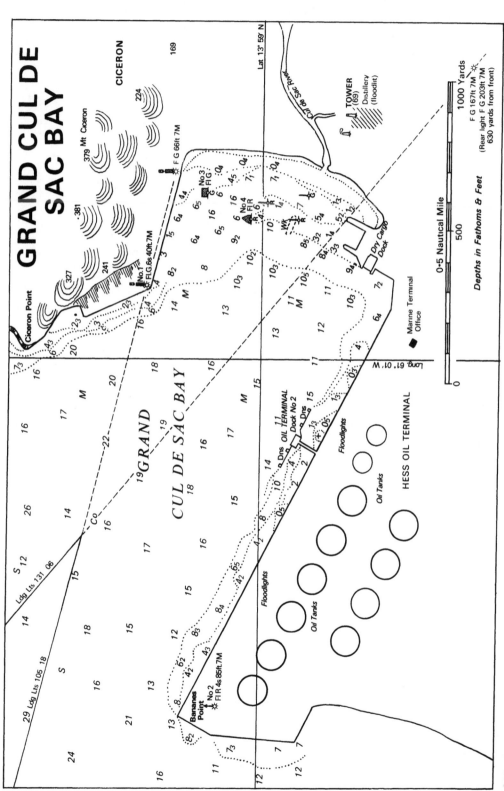

CHART 12   Grand Cul de Sac Bay

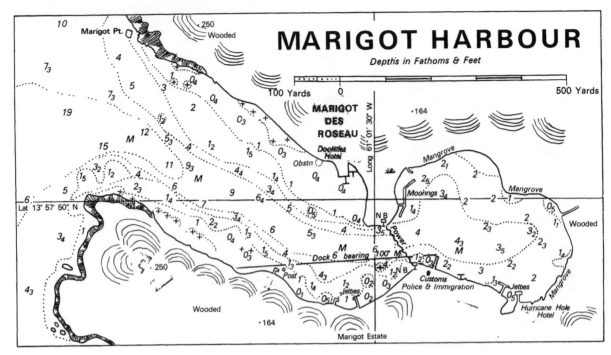

CHART 13   Marigot Harbour

where large tankers—300,000 to 400,000, possibly 500,000, tonners—come to offload their oil into storage tanks, which then are transferred to small tankers, mere 100 tonners. Obviously not a yachting anchorage.

MARIGOT HARBOUR
(Chart 13; II B-1)

Four miles south of Castries, this is a narrow, deep harbor. In years gone by, before the construction of the hotel and guest houses, yachts usually sailed right by Marigot without taking notice. Now it has become a popular anchorage. You will notice small cottages along the water's edge on the north side of the harbor, and a lot of new houses on the steep hillside forming the south side. Entering is easy: Favor the south side of the outer harbor; shoal water extends 200 yards west by north from the southern tip of the palm-covered spit on the north side of the entrance. Shoal water can easily be spotted in this outer section of the harbor.

When entering the inner harbor, stay north of the line of bearing of 090° on the end of the Customs jetty on the south side of the harbor or you may come to a grinding halt (as *Iolaire* once did) on a rock with six feet of water over it a hundred yards west of the Customs dock. Otherwise, tacking through the narrow neck to the inner harbor is no problem because there is deep water close to shore. In fact, it is perfectly possible to lay a large vessel alongside the end of the palm-covered spit on the north shore and tie up to the trees in plenty of water. If you do this, set an anchor out to the southeast to hold her off. The one disadvantage of palm-tree anchorages, however, is mosquitoes. For this reason, I prefer the middle of the inner basin off the new hotel and dock.

On the south side of the harbor at the ferry landing is Customs and Immigration, ably run by Scotty, who—like Monsieur le Breton who used to run Customs and Immigration in Fort de France, Martinique—is a friend of yachtsmen. Scotty is cooperative, humorous, and helpful.

Marigot Harbour is sheltered in all weathers, even in a hurricane. For many years it has been considered an excellent hurricane hole, but this is no longer true, as the Moorings operation (the Tortola-based bareboat-charter service) now has about 70 yachts based in Marigot. Add to that the 20 or so visiting yachts, plus the number of yachts that will come pouring into the harbor as a hurricane approaches, and you have another situation like what occurred in Culebra during Hurricane Hugo in 1989—a time bomb ready to explode. Even if you are properly moored during a hurricane in Marigot Harbour, you are very likely to be demolished by a bareboat "bomb"—a maritime hazard described under "Reflections on Hugo," in the Foreword to this volume, and in *Street's Transatlantic Crossing Guide and Introduction to the Caribbean.*

Fuel and water are available in Marigot Harbour, but they are very expensive. If heading north, try to get to Martinique to fill up; if heading south, load up in St. Vincent.

The Moorings has repair facilities, but the spare-parts operation is duty-free ONLY for their own repairs. They are legally prohibited from selling spare parts to visiting yachtsmen, so don't bother asking. They also have sail-repair and laundry facilities. The Moorings has taken over Doolittle's Hotel cottages, plus the sandspit on the north side of the harbor. The hotel is still called Doolittle's—named after the Rex Harrison movie *Dr. Doolittle,* which was filmed here. It has excellent meals at a reasonable price and also a beach bar, where you can swim between drinks. The only problem is that it has the hungriest no-see-ums I have ever encountered. After more than 30 years in the Caribbean, I am pretty impervious to these creatures, but Doolittle's takes the cake.

The south side of Marigot Harbour has been developed as the Moorings base (VHF channel 85). The Moorings should receive a real pat on the back for this. For a change, a firm has come to the Caribbean and developed an area sensibly. Instead of bringing in a foreign architect (I often say an architectural degree is merely a license to charge a lot of money for a bad design), they have built their buildings in traditional West Indian style, with a huge porch around the structure on all sides—the most attractive and practical type of architecture for this region. When a porch encircles a building and a slow-speed overhead fan is installed in a room, air-conditioning is not necessary. It has been said that in most areas of the Caribbean air-conditioning is merely an excuse for damned poor architecture.

The Moorings facility includes a supermarket, water (expensive), diesel, ice, and sail repair, but no marine hardware.

Doolittle's has a small launch that shuttles back and forth to the landing stage on the other side of the harbor—the signal for the ferry is three blasts on a car horn. If you are anchored in between and want to go ashore, the launch will oblige. An underwater power cable crosses the bay, running southeastward from the tip of the sandspit, and this is marked with warning signs at either end. Do not anchor on top of it.

While anchored in Marigot Bay, read *Ramage and the Freebooters* by Dudley Pope (in the United States it's called *The Triton Brig);* part of this novel is set in Marigot Bay.

MARIGOT HARBOUR TO GRANDE CAILLE POINT
(II B-1)

There are a number of anchorages along this stretch that could be used as daytime stops for a swim: Anse la Raye, off the village of that name, and Anse Cochon, which has always looked attractive when we have sailed by. In May 1991. while flying northward on LIAT, I was able to examine the cove from the air. The first cove south of the village of Anse la Raye, it has a beach with a stream running onto it, plus palm trees on the beach—it looks absolutely perfect. I have no idea what the bug situation would be at night. Obviously, when the wind dies down in the evening, you would waltz around on your anchor and thus should be anchored either bow-and-stern or, as I prefer, with a proper Bahamian moor. (See *Street's Transatlantic Crossing Guide and Introduction to the Caribbean* for details on both methods of anchoring.)

Day-trippers might come in here for a few hours, but certainly in the evening you would have the entire anchorage to yourself. There's no road, not even a track, to this beach. Where else in the Caribbean can you find a sand beach, palm trees, a stream, and no other people?

South of Anse Cochon is Anse des Canaries—here you do find a beach backed by a small village. Whether or not you would want to spend the night here is questionable, as yachtsmen and St. Lucia fishermen have not always had the best of relationships.

Anse Cochon and Anse des Canaries area has developed so much in recent years that they have placed mooring in both harbors, some are day time only, some can be used overnight, exactly what the regulations will be regarding anchoring or picking up moorings I have no crystal ball. Check for mooring and anchoring regulations when checking into St. Lucian waters. The area is referred to as CMMA—Canaries Marine Management Area.

ANSE CHASTANET
(Chart 14; II B-1)

Those who like to dive should check out the Anse Chastanet Hotel, as there is an excellent diving operation run by Nick Troobiscoff. Moor bow-and-stern, go ashore, and find out the details. You can have an excellent dinner at the hotel or arrange with Nick to go diving. Be forewarned, though, that the whole area is a national park, so do not anchor on the easily damaged coral. The ground swell can build up either on a Bahamian moor or bow-and-stern anchorage, but for reasons I don't understand, I have been informed that they do not appreciate your running a line ashore. Use your own anchors.

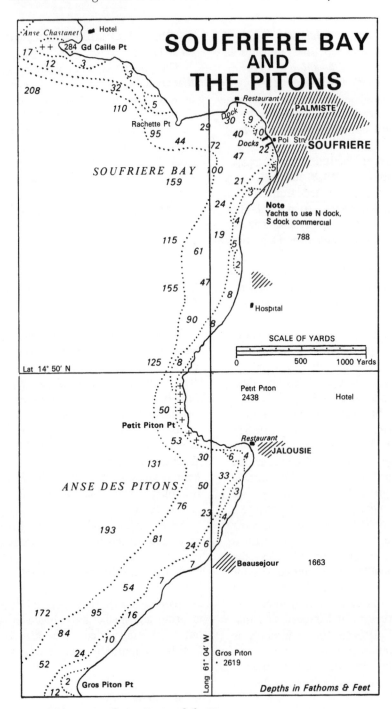

CHART 14   Soufrière Bay and the Pitons

SOUFRIERE
(Chart 14; II B-1)
South of Rachette Point north of Petit Piton, Soufrière is the second largest town on St. Lucia, and, although it is not a port of entry, you can get preclearance here, as mentioned above.

A marine park has been established covering most of the Soufriere area. Kai Wulf is responsible for the area who have a recognized association. All the boat boys who are members of the association carry identification badges. I strongly advise not dealing with anyone other than the boys in the association.

Mooring buoys have been established in Soufriere Bay and Anse des Pitons. Basically no anchoring is allowed in either area other than bow on to the beach at the Hummingbird, or bow on to the beach a Jalousie. Check for the latest regulations when entering St. Lucia waters.

Anchoring off the town of Soufrière is virtually impossible, as the bottom drops off almost vertically. There are now two docks (will they survive the ground swell generated by the latest hurricanes?): the southern dock is the commercial dock, the northern one is for yachts. I have been told by several yachtsmen, however, that the yacht dock is useless, as the surge makes it impossible to lie alongside. Apparently the only way you can lie to

lookout to starboard. Once the reef is abeam to starboard, head northeast toward the church, round up, and anchor wherever it is convenient. The harbor has about nine feet of water.

Mike Smith of *Phryna* has warned that you should keep an eye on the rain clouds before entering Laborie. In heavy rainfall, the stream that empties into the harbor spews out so much mud that it is impossible to find one's way in or out. Thus it might be wise to avoid this anchorage during the summer rainy season, or in periods of southeast winds. Phil and Joan Cardon of the Whitby 42-foot ketch *Glissade* report that they have made three visits to Laborie, enjoyed all the visits, found the people extremely friendly, and saw no other yachts. They pointed out, though, that a misprint in my 1974 guide resulted in a wrong range for this entrance. They favor the bearing, mentioned above, of 016° magnetic on the western end of town, which will keep you close to the eastern edge of the reef. (It's always better in a channel to touch on the windward rather than the leeward reef.) If you'd rather be dead center in the channel, though, you might prefer a bearing of 020° to 025° magnetic.

VIEUX FORT BAY
(Chart 16; II B-1)

On the southern end of St. Lucia, this is a large banana-loading port as well as a port of entry. Well to the east on the way north, it is difficult to lay from St. Vincent and is seldom visited by yachts. However, if you are disposed to visit Laborie and the Pitons without going to Castries first, you might do well to clear through Vieux Fort. In normal trade-wind weather, this is a good anchorage. Use the area southeast of the large pier. (North of the pier is a prohibited anchorage.) When coming from the south, approach with Cross Hill (the hill north of Battery Point) in line with Morne Belle Vue, one mile northeast, bearing 045° magnetic until the pier bears 073° magnetic. (Be aware, however, that reclamation work was in progress at the head of Anse Rafale in 1990.) Go to the head of the harbor and anchor. Hoist your "Q" flag, go ashore, and find the Customs office at the head of the new steamer dock. Since the harbor is being developed, exactly what the situation will be when you arrive is problematical.

There is not too much else ashore at Vieux Fort, but there is excellent reef diving and lobstering thereabouts. If you are the lazy sort, it's cheaper to buy lobsters here than elsewhere in the Eastern Caribbean.

The Vieux Fort area has a number of restaurants, including Cloud Nine, which dates back to World War II. Sometimes it's open, sometimes not—you need to get to Vieux Fort and inquire. Kimatri is high on the bill and overlooks the anchorage—a great spot for a sunset drink. Isla Pirata is west of the anchorage in an area where there is a lot of surf. I definitely would not advise visiting Isla Pirata with your dinghy; it's hard enough trying to get in through the surf, but getting out after a good dinner (including drinks, wine, and brandy) is a guaranteed recipe for disaster. Tie up your dinghy in town and take a taxi to the restaurant.

One advantage of anchoring southeast of the main steamer dock is that it is out of the swell and only 500 yards across the spit of land to Point Sable Bay. I am told that the beach of Sable Bay is a full mile long, has pure white sand, and is completely deserted—an ideal walk for those enamored of beaches.

Anchorage in Vieux Fort Bay is on the eastern side of the harbor. Either north of Noir Point or south of it in Anse Benson. Anchoring is not permitted anywhere else in the harbor. To visit town take the dinghy over to the new fishing harbor, check locally as to whether you are permitted to tie your dinghy up within the fishing harbor as in some places people have discovered to their chagrin that dinghies were not welcome by fishermen—as in the new fishing harbor in the south east corner of des Hayes. There are various well recommended restaurants ashore. Take a look around, find one that is populated by the locals.

POINT SABLE BAY
(Chart 16; II B-1)

I have seen Point Sable Bay from the sea and from the air, and it intrigues me as an anchorage—but I haven't tried it yet, nor have I talked to anyone who has. It looks as though a good anchorage would be in the lee of Maria Island, with its northern hill bearing about southeast, tucked in behind the reef. Pure speculation on my part—but it looks like a good spot to get away from it all. Exploration of this anchorage should be done only by experienced sailors under *ideal* conditions.

The eastern shore of St. Lucia has some small coves that are used by the locals for launching canoes, but there is nothing that can be really called a harbor. I know of no yacht that has visited this area.

A fishing harbor—depth unkown—has been built at Dennery and is possibly worth investigating in a shoal draft boat in summer when it is not blowing hard.

One last word of warning: *Under no circumstances should you swim, wash, or even paddle in St. Lucia's streams.* There is a parasite in the water that can enter the bloodstream through the skin and cause all kinds of trouble. The resulting debilitating disease is called schistosomiasis or bilharzia. (This same parasite plagues the upper reaches of the Nile in the vicinity of the Aswan High Dam.)

Gros Piton for US$5 or 10. If the weather has been dry, it will be about a two-and-a-half-hour scramble. The route swings around to the south of Gros Piton at roughly 600 feet and climbs the west ridge from there. At the top you will find yourself in the thick of a mahogany forest. Climb a tree and take a gander. The view will prove well worth the struggle.

George McLellan, who has also made this trip, recommends contacting Tonka Prosten in Soufrière; ask for him at the Texaco service station in the middle of town. He can rustle up a taxi driver who will take you to the closest approach to Gros Piton, about a mile outside Soufrière; he knows the way up quite well. McLellan advises setting out around 0700 so you can get back down to town or the harbor by noon or so, before it gets too hot.

The hike to Petit Piton is another worthwhile struggle. Again, you will need a guide. The route goes up the col from the anchorage toward Soufrière to about 800 feet, then down again to about 200 feet before winding its way up the northwest ridge. For the most part, the trip is a pretty standard scramble through thorn scrub, with the exception of a 30-foot patch of rock, where some knowledge of basic climbing techniques may be required. The top of the piton is open and breezy. If you clamber down about 150 feet and climb a tree, you can get a good shot of your boat anchored at Jalousie. Allow about six hours for the entire trip up and back. Be damned sure to take along some liquid refreshment.

LABORIE
(Chart 15; II B-1)

Laborie, on the chart but seldom visited, is a most intriguing anchorage. This harbor should be entered only under ideal conditions, with the sun high. The person who made the Admiralty chart appears never to have seen the harbor. The reef on the eastern side of the entrance to Laborie Harbor is not as indicated on that chart; it extends at least 150 yards westward from the eastern point.

To enter, bring the houses on the western side of town to bear about 016° magnetic and keep a good

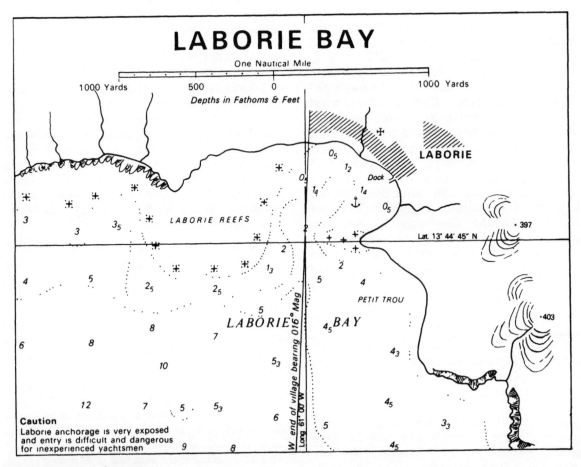

CHART 15   Laborie Bay

lookout to starboard. Once the reef is abeam to starboard, head northeast toward the church, round up, and anchor wherever it is convenient. The harbor has about nine feet of water.

Mike Smith of *Phryna* has warned that you should keep an eye on the rain clouds before entering Laborie. In heavy rainfall, the stream that empties into the harbor spews out so much mud that it is impossible to find one's way in or out. Thus it might be wise to avoid this anchorage during the summer rainy season, or in periods of southeast winds. Phil and Joan Cardon of the Whitby 42-foot ketch *Glissade* report that they have made three visits to Laborie, enjoyed all the visits, found the people extremely friendly, and saw no other yachts. They pointed out, though, that a misprint in my 1974 guide resulted in a wrong range for this entrance. They favor the bearing, mentioned above, of 016° magnetic on the western end of town, which will keep you close to the eastern edge of the reef. (It's always better in a channel to touch on the windward rather than the leeward reef.) If you'd rather be dead center in the channel, though, you might prefer a bearing of 020° to 025° magnetic.

VIEUX FORT BAY
(Chart 16; II B-1)

On the southern end of St. Lucia, this is a large banana-loading port as well as a port of entry. Well to the east on the way north, it is difficult to lay from St. Vincent and is seldom visited by yachts. However, if you are disposed to visit Laborie and the Pitons without going to Castries first, you might do well to clear through Vieux Fort. In normal trade-wind weather, this is a good anchorage. Use the area southeast of the large pier. (North of the pier is a prohibited anchorage.) When coming from the south, approach with Cross Hill (the hill north of Battery Point) in line with Morne Belle Vue, one mile northeast, bearing 045° magnetic until the pier bears 073° magnetic. (Be aware, however, that reclamation work was in progress at the head of Anse Rafale in 1990.) Go to the head of the harbor and anchor. Hoist your "Q" flag, go ashore, and find the Customs office at the head of the new steamer dock. Since the harbor is being developed, exactly what the situation will be when you arrive is problematical.

There is not too much else ashore at Vieux Fort, but there is excellent reef diving and lobstering thereabouts. If you are the lazy sort, it's cheaper to buy lobsters here than elsewhere in the Eastern Caribbean.

The Vieux Fort area has a number of restaurants, including Cloud Nine, which dates back to World War II. Sometimes it's open, sometimes not—you need to get to Vieux Fort and inquire. Kimatri is high on the hill and overlooks the anchorage—a great spot for a sunset drink. Isla Pirata is west of the anchorage in an area where there is a lot of surf. I definitely would not advise visiting Isla Pirata with your dinghy; it's hard enough trying to get in through the surf, but getting out after a good dinner (including drinks, wine, and brandy) is a guaranteed recipe for disaster. Tie up your dinghy in town and take a taxi to the restaurant.

One advantage of anchoring southeast of the main steamer dock is that it is out of the swell and only 500 yards across the spit of land to Point Sable Bay. I am told that the beach of Sable Bay is a full mile long, has pure white sand, and is completely deserted—an ideal walk for those enamored of beaches.

POINT SABLE BAY
(Chart 16; II B-1)

I have seen Point Sable Bay from the sea and from the air, and it intrigues me as an anchorage—but I haven't tried it yet, nor have I talked to anyone who has. It looks as though a good anchorage would be in the lee of Maria Island, with its northern hill bearing about southeast, tucked in behind the reef. Pure speculation on my part—but it looks like a good spot to get away from it all. Exploration of this anchorage should be done only by experienced sailors under *ideal* conditions.

The eastern shore of St. Lucia has some small coves that are used by the locals for launching canoes, but there is nothing that can be really called a harbor. I know of no yacht that has visited this area.

One last word of warning: *Under no circumstances should you swim, wash, or even paddle in St. Lucia's streams.* There is a parasite in the water that can enter the bloodstream through the skin and cause all kinds of trouble. The resulting debilitating disease is called schistosomiasis or bilharzia. (This same parasite plagues the upper reaches of the Nile in the vicinity of the Aswan High Dam.)

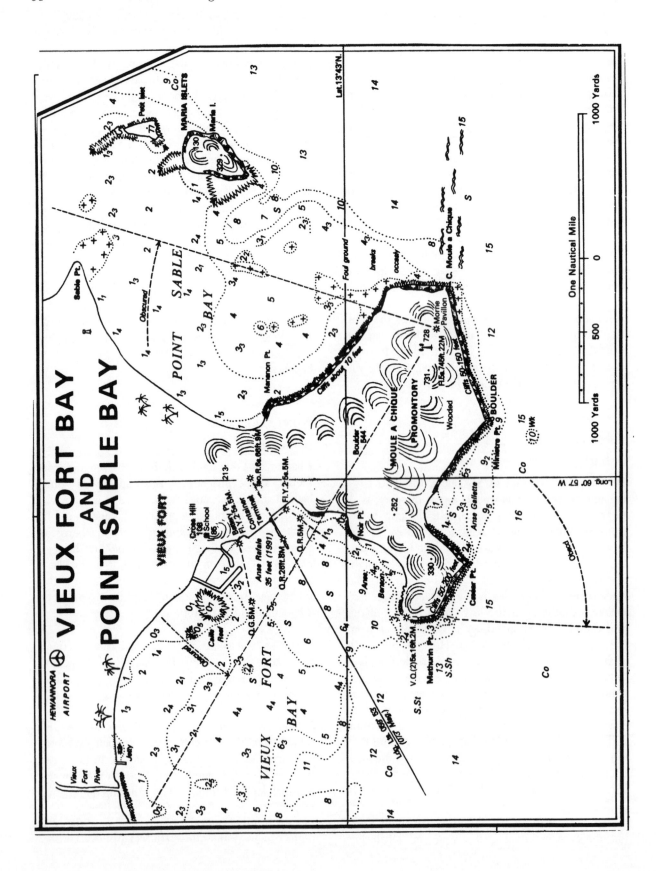

NOTES

4

St. Vincent

(Imray-Iolaire Charts 1, B, B-3, B-30)

IMPORTANT NOTE: As this book was being finalized, we discovered that the St. Vincent government was in the process of completely redoing the buoyage system in St. Vincent and the Grenadines. They are replacing missing buoys, and in many cases installing steel piles to mark reefs previously marked by buoys placed so far away from the danger that the mariner often became confused and hit the reef he was trying to avoid. The chartlets in this book have been corrected, but your charts may not have been; in case of discrepancy, rely on the book, not the charts.

I stand by my oft-repeated statement: Do not rely on buoys or lights in Eastern Caribbean waters in the ex-British islands, as they are set up so pilots, ship wreckers, and salvage operators would not starve to death.

St. Vincent is somewhat smaller than St. Lucia, its neighbor to the north. It is a lush, wet island with peaks rising to well over 3,000 feet. Sections of it have been cultivated lavishly, the crops laid in neat green tiers reminiscent of the English countryside. From the sea, Kingstown presents a pleasing aspect, nestled in a hollow with mountains rising around.

The island was discovered by Columbus on his third voyage to the New World. Like Dominica, it had been populated by Carib Indians who resisted every attempt to colonize the island. Only when the Caribs became embroiled in their own civil war were the Europeans able to establish a presence on the island. In 1675, a slave ship bound from Africa went down off St. Vincent. Many of the slaves swam ashore and settled, producing through intermarriage the black Carib of today.

The story of St. Vincent is one of continuous

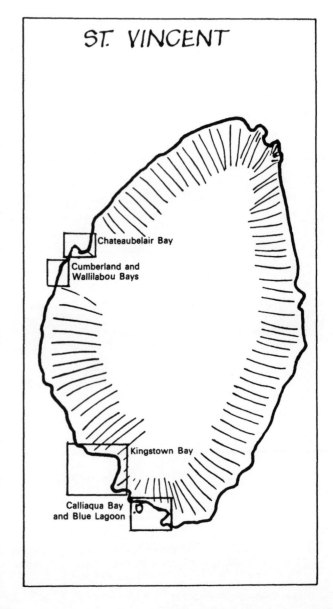

warfare. The Caribs entrenched themselves at the northern end of the island while the British settled and fortified the southern communities of Kingstown and Calliaqua. The Caribs were supported against the British by the French, who imported other Caribs as mercenaries from neighboring islands, primarily St. Lucia. These hired Caribs always landed on the northeast and northwest corners of the island, regrouped, and proceeded south overland against the British. It is for this reason that many of the old fortifications on St. Vincent—such as those on Duvernette Island, Dorsetshire Hill, Richmond Peak, and Sion Hill, as well as the earliest ruins at Fort Charlotte—all have their cannons aimed inland.

When the Caribs finally were conquered, about 5,000 of them were placed on the island of Battowia and later shipped to British Honduras (present-day Belize). How they managed to cram that many people onto an island the size of Battowia is very difficult to imagine, and I suspect the loss of life was heavy.

There are a number of good hotels on St. Vincent. The best thing to do is to pick up a local tourist guide that lists all the hotels. They are varied, and you are sure to find accommodations to suit your taste and budget.

The shopping situation, from the yachtsman's standpoint, has been improving gradually over recent years, and there are now four supermarkets of varying quality in the Kingstown area. The open-air market is excellent and operates every day from 0800; if you want to get the best selection, arrive early. Ice is available at the ice cream factory. Fuel is obtainable by appointment with the Shell agent at Hazel's store, and you can make arrangements for it to be delivered at the steamer dock.

The dock clearly was not designed with yachts in mind. It is a miserable place to lie, especially when the ground swell is running. Unfortunately, however, this is the only spot in Kingstown Harbor where fresh water can be obtained.

There is deep water all along the jetty. The best place to anchor at Kingstown, a port of entry, is around the northeast corner. Get your bow close to shore, drop anchor, and ease your stern into the dock right next to the steps where the small bumboats offload.

During Hurricane Klaus, in November 1984, a small freighter sank in the northeast corner of the harbor; it was in deep water and wouldn't have caused a problem except that its mast was sticking up to within seven feet of the surface. As of January 1991, the obstruction was still there. The mast may

have been cut off by the time you read this, but don't count on it. Once you have cleared, I advise moving out of Kingstown to another anchorage as soon as possible.

I suggest you *not* spend the night in Kingstown—and so does no less a personage than the Honorable James ("Son") Mitchell, prime minister of St. Vincent. He has told me that any yachtsman is crazy who does anything in Kingstown but clear and leave. The problem is that dinghy and outboard pilferage is rife, and the authorities so far haven't been able to do much about it.

One large yacht was the victim of a particularly galling theft. Its St. Vincentian crew had a girl friend ashore, and he asked permission to take the dinghy and leave it tied up overnight to the St. Vincent Coast Guard vessel *Captain George McIntosh*. The yacht's skipper figured that would be safe, so he gave permission. Next day the dinghy arrived back, but the outboard was gone. The deck watch on the *McIntosh* (which keeps a 24-hour watch) gave the usual West Indian reply: "Me no know," and a shrug of the shoulders.

If you are coming from the north, I hardly think it worthwhile to clear through Kingstown at all. From Johnson Point it is a hard beat to the jetty in the northeast corner of the bay. Much time is lost in maneuvering safely to the jetty, and thence through Customs. Once cleared, you are required to leave, and from the jetty it is two and a half miles against wind and current to the nearest amenable anchorage, at Young Island.

The better way by far is to take a beam reach from Johnson Point to Bequia and then a short sheltered beat up to Admiralty Bay (Bequia). This is a fine (if crowded) anchorage where you may clear at your leisure and spend the night. If you then wish to visit St. Vincent, you can sail directly to the anchorage at Young Island or Blue Lagoon, thereby postponing indefinitely the suspect pleasures of the Kingstown jetty.

If, after all of the above, you still decide to clear at Kingstown, call the lighthouse at Kingstown Harbor on VHF channel 16 and ask that a message be relayed to Customs and Immigration so they will expect you. The procedure then is to go alongside the landing stage at the northeast corner of the main ship jetty, not the small easternmost jetty used by the local schooners. There is usually a surge, so make sure you have plenty of fenders and strong springlines. Customs is right there on the dock, and they usually will summon the Immigration officer by telephone. Otherwise, walk south along the front street; Immigration is located on the ground floor of the police department. The Immigration officials nearly always insist on boarding the boat, even if you are anchored, and they come aboard with boots that usually have gravel lodged in the soles—not too good for paintwork and teak decks.

One charter skipper had a solution to this problem—he anchored out and dumped a couple of buckets of water into his dinghy before rowing ashore. When the Immigration people complained, he apologized, saying he had a leaky dinghy. By the time the officials came aboard, however, their shoes were somewhat cleaner and a bit squishy and therefore less damaging to his paint and varnish. The next time the boat came in and he arrived with his "leaky" dinghy to clear, the officials, remembering their previous experience, cleared the boat without going on board.

Back in the early 1970s, St. Vincent levied a tax on all charter boats entering her waters. The tax itself was not too high, but the precedent it set was scary. Since all the islands are independent or semi-independent, a charter yacht visiting all of the Lesser Antilles during a six-week cruise would have to shell out taxes to 13 different governments. This, of course, would have to be passed on to the charterer, thereby increasing the cost of chartering.

Then, in January 1979, the St. Vincent government began to charge private yachtsmen huge fees. In order to make sure these were collected, Chateaubelair and Canouan were made Customs clearance stations, and the St. Vincent government bought a number of police launches. Predictably (since the life expectancy of a police launch in the Eastern Caribbean seems to be three years), the Customs stations in Chateaubelair and Canouan were closed three years later.

Over the winter of 1984-85, I had to stop off in the Grenadines to check on a few things for an earlier revision of *Street's Cruising Guide*, a....! it cost me more than EC$99 to spend 48 hours in St. Vincent waters!

Now I'm glad to report that things have changed. James ("Son") Mitchell, who was elected prime minister by a landslide in 1984, has done much to make St. Vincent's waters more hospitable to yachtsmen. Fees for charter boats have been much reduced; there is no fee for visiting yachts; the head of Immigration has been replaced; and there is a much more realistic attitude toward yachts. Also, a Customs and Immigration station has been established at Wallilabou Bay, which means that you can avoid the hassles of clearing out when heading north and entering when heading south.

St. Vincent is not without its oddities, although my favorite traffic sign was taken down some time ago. This sign said, "Windward traffic, keep right. Leeward traffic, keep left."

The Catholic and Anglican churches in Kingstown are across the street from each other. The Anglican establishment is so "high church" it is hard to tell which church you have wandered into; if you hear what sounds like a good old-fashioned Catholic mass, you're undoubtedly in the Anglican church.

Tourism is making its mark on the island. Hotels, restaurants, shopping centers, and cruise ships have arrived in the customary profusion. The expansion, however, has been hampered by the lack of a good airport. For years it was assumed that it was impossible to build an airstrip on St. Vincent, until a young Grenadian engineer designed and executed a small one for DC-3s. To get around the space shortage, he built the strip on an incline. The planes landed uphill and took off downhill, with gravity doing the extra work in both cases. Flying out in one of those old DC-3s fully loaded was the experience of a lifetime, and if it was blowing really hard in the wrong direction, you just didn't take off—and that could even mean two or three days. Sometimes the stewardess would take the passengers from the last four rows and cram them up against the door of the cockpit so that, with the weight in the plane forward, the pilot could get the tail off a little faster. It worked fine in the islands, but I wonder how an FAA inspector would have reacted to the procedure.

With LIAT Avro airplanes, there is no problem landing or taking off; it is more a question of when LIAT is motivated to dispatch a flight to St. Vincent. The St. Vincent government has extended the runway; night landings are made regularly; and LIAT's schedule has been rearranged so that you no longer are stranded in Barbados trying to get to St. Vincent—unless they have fouled up your reservations, which they do with alarming frequency.

It is interesting to note that Ron Smith, the young Grenadian who designed the airport in 1960, was the head engineer for Grenada's new international airport.

A taxi ride around St. Vincent is definitely worthwhile. You can rent a car, but it's better to take a taxi, for then you'll get an explanation of the agriculture, culture, cuisine, etc., of the island. Check with the hotels for the name of a reliable and interesting driver.

The botanical garden in Kingstown is a must for those interested in flora, as it is by far the best botanical garden in the Eastern Caribbean.

St. Vincent

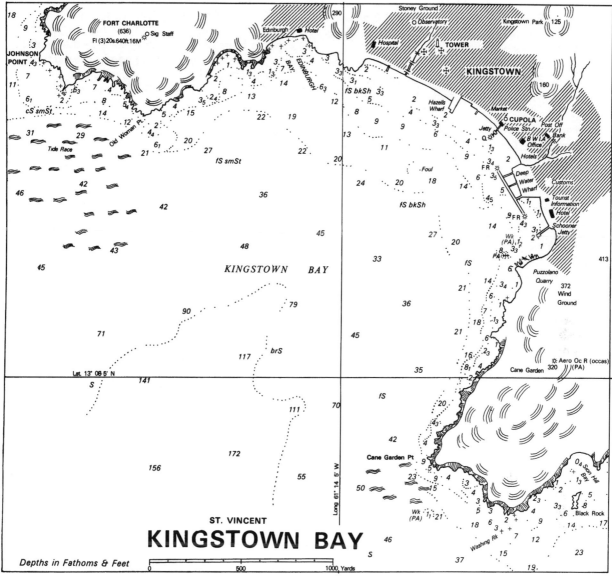

CHART 17   Kingstown Bay

KINGSTOWN BAY

(Chart 17; II B-30)

If possible, avoid Kingstown Bay, for the reasons already discussed above. If you decide you must anchor here, do so in the northeast corner of the harbor, as that is the only place you will find water shoal enough to anchor. Beware of the previously mentioned wreck. The wind will box the compass, so set a Bahamian moor, or moor bow-and-stern.

Shopping in St. Vincent in years gone by was a complete disaster. I often wondered what people ate, as the selection of food here in comparison to Grenada was incredibly poor. It is still not too good, but the situation has improved, as there are two supermarkets in town—Shop & Save and Graves—plus two supermarkets out at the airport. Needless to say, with an island as wet and tropical as St. Vincent, the open-air market at the western end of town is excellent. I strongly advise you to buy all your fresh produce at the market, then hit the other shops.

Unfortunately, only cube ice is available from the ice cream factory. Water may be obtained (with difficulty) at the main steamer dock. Because of the surge, drop a bow anchor, swing the stern in, run a line ashore, connect up every possible hose, and pray that you can find an adapter to reduce the diameter of the main hose to a suitable diameter to fill your tank.

Fuel can also be obtained, but only by the tanker-truck load, so this is suitable only for large yachts.

For marine supplies, contact St. Vincent Sails and Service which, by the time you read this, should be located opposite the ferry dock. If you can't find something there, ask Paddy Punnett—he is a yachtsman himself and probably will point you in the right direction. I say this because in the West Indies (and other island locales) you sometimes find what you want in the least logical place. For example, in Martinique for years you had to buy yeast for breadmaking at a bicycle-repair shop. Who would ever have figured that out? In Los Cristianos in the Canary Islands, I discovered block ice underneath the post office— something I think few others had found. Why should there be a deep-freeze room underneath the post office? As I said, on islands, the most illogical things happen.

There is shopping ashore in Kingstown along Bay Street, but it is no great shakes. However, if you are stuck in St. Vincent taking on fuel or water or clearing through Immigration. some members of the crew may find it interesting to wander around town.

There are so many ferries going back and forth to Bequia that there is absolutely no room to anchor a yacht in the north east corner of Kingston Harbor. Basically yachts just stay out of Kingston Harbor.

YOUNG ISLAND
(Chart 18; II B-30)

For many years, this has been the most popular anchorage in St. Vincent, but you need to exercise great care in anchoring here. It is frequently crowded, and when the tide starts running to windward, the boats have a tendency to roam about a little erratically. Many a bow pulpit has been bent out of shape at the change of tide. I strongly recommend a Bahamian moor.

We used to anchor with great success off the northeastern tip of Young Island, on a Bahamian

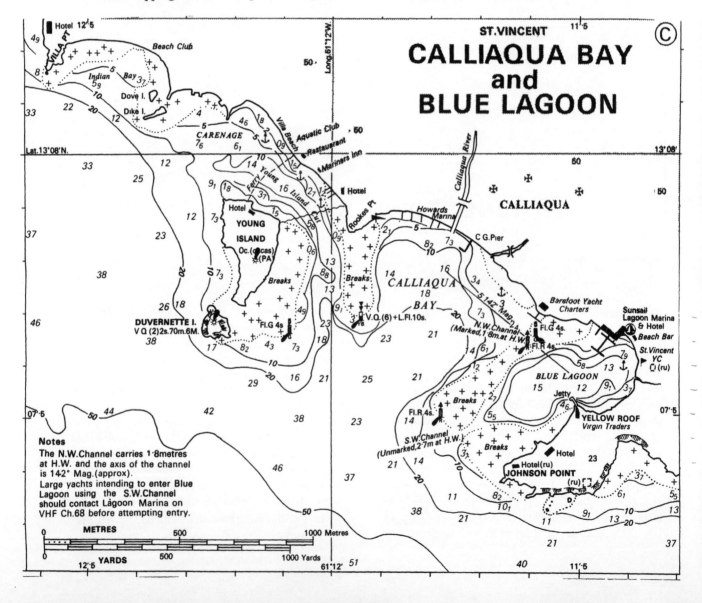

moor in 10 feet of water immediately behind the submerged power cable. But when we sailed in there in 1985, we found 65 to 70 feet of water over our old spot. It turns out that the ground swell that came in as a result of Hurricane Klaus in November 1984 completely changed the underwater topography of the area. We then spent three days dragging from one end of the anchorage to the other. The locals told us that the only decent anchorage now is in the northwestern corner of the Young Island anchorage, off the sand beach west of the Aquatic Club—if you can find room. But moorings have now been established at the Young Island stop, which greatly relieves the dragging-anchor problem. Exactly who owns which mooring, or what the charges are, I have not been able to ascertain. Thus, my advice is to tie up to one of the empty moorings, row ashore to any of the establishments, and inquire whose mooring you are on and how much it costs. No matter what the charge, if you are only going to be there for a couple of days, it will be well worth it. When I think of the number of times I have dragged up and down the Young Island anchorage in the past, I will never complain about paying a fee when I pick up a mooring there.

On top of Duvernette Island are four 24-pound guns and two eight-inch mortars—at least that's what I have been told they are. I saw them probably 30 years ago. We climbed to the top of Duvernette and almost killed ourselves in the process, as all the steps were crumbling. Now I have been told that the steps have been restored and are in good shape, but the climb is still not for anyone with a weak heart or acrophobia. The view is spectacular and the siting of the guns is rather interesting. They are not facing out to sea but rather in over Calliaqua Bay and the town behind. Duvernette was not established to keep naval forces from attacking Kingstown—rather, it was set up by the British to stop the French and Caribs from attacking from the land side.

Once you do finally get anchored in the Young Island slot, as it is called, there are various facilities. If your anchors are well set and you can swing your stern in, you can take on water from the Aquatic Club, now run by Stilly Frazer, who also operates a nightly disco in a soundproof building; supposedly the noise does not disturb the neighbors.

Then comes a French restaurant, run by Simon Despointes; he has a lobster pound, so you can point to the lobster you want for dinner. Next is what I am told is a good and efficient laundry service, after which you'll find Mariners Water Sports, Mariners Windsurfing School, and Mariners Inn, a small hotel with bar, restaurant, and public showers.

Dive St. Vincent, run by Bill Trewes, an Australian, has established a string of dive shops throughout St. Vincent and the Grenadines. In addition to the Young Island operation, he has stations at Wallilabou Bay, Mayreau, and Bequia. He is fully trained, certified by PADI-NAUI, and learned his diving techniques on the reefs off Australia and in Papua New Guinea. If you make arrangements with him, you will be able to dive throughout the Grenadine chain.

Mariners Water Sports runs a sailboat for charter and offers diving trips, diving equipment, water skiing, and so on. They also have a boutique and a mail drop, sell Imray-Iolaire charts and Street guides, and stand by on VHF channel 16. With difficulty, they can arrange to fill your water tanks and to have laundry done. This new organization, which has high hopes for success, is run by MacGregor Brisbane and Eric and Susan Holbrick, Box 639, St. Vincent.

Young Island Hotel is extremely attractive; a stroll through the buildings and gardens is well worthwhile. Check out the bar's excellent punches; there is entertainment some evenings, and dinner is reported to be very good but expensive.

CALLIAQUA BAY
(Chart 18; II B-30)

An open, turbulent, and generally unattractive anchorage, unless you want to stop for a short while, row ashore, and watch the fishing boats being hauled up on the beach in the afternoon. These are interesting native boats, although not as well finished or maintained as the boats of Bequia.

In Callliaqua, you will also find Buhler's Fibreglass, a boatbuilding operation that turns out multihulls by the foam-sandwich method. Apparently they are doing an excellent job, and orders are coming in from all corners of the world. It is a heartening example of someone bringing something to the islands that not only is providing employment but also is manufacturing a product that is competitive on the world market. There are also always a couple of schooners in the process of construction onshore, and you'll have a good chance to see how these local boats are built. De Frietas hauling facility is no more. Now one finds in Calliaqua Howards Marine, Phone: 784 457 4328; Fax: 784 457 4266. They have a railway and haul boats up to 60-feet, they are catamaran specialists and also have a marine supply store attached to the operation.

Calliaqua is also the home of the St. Vincent Coastguard whose ability to be helpful is rather minimal as boats that have run aground trying to enter the southwest entrance of Blue Lagoon have not been aided by the Coastguard which has stood by and left the salvage operation to the bareboat organisations based in Blue Lagoon.

A passable anchorage can be found in the north east corner of Calliaqua. Run plenty of anchore rode as you are anchoring on the back side of a sudden drop off.

BLUE LAGOON
(Chart 18; II B-30)

There are two entrances to Blue Lagoon. The one used most frequently is the northwest entrance, which is strictly limited in draft. Basically, it is a six-foot channel (despite what other guides may say to the contrary), although greater draft may be squeezed through the channel at the right state of the tides, particularly in winter when the Caribbean is higher than in summer. (Similarly, at low-water springs, in late April, May, and June, you can touch with only five feet!) It would certainly be a boon to all yachtsmen if the St. Vincent government would set up a tidal gauge at each end of the channel so that with binoculars one could read the controlling depth at various stages of the tide.

The other entrance, in the southwestern corner of the lagoon, used to be marked with a stake; now it is completely unmarked. The sea has changed the channel slightly so that it is now rather a dogleg, and the controlling depth in this channel has shoaled to around nine feet. Approach this entrance from the southwest with a lookout in the rigging and you will spot the channel. Access to the channel is about 067° magnetic. Run in on this course with good way on and sail between the breakers. As the reef to the northwest comes abeam, alter course to starboard, eyeballing it for the deepest waters. In periods of heavy weather, the swell breaks completely across this entrance, making entering somewhat like running a New Jersey inlet: only for the brave and the skilled.

Over the years numerous boats have gone aground using this south west channel—sometimes guided by a local who claims to be a Pilot but is not!!!

If in the least doubt of your ability to negotiate the southwest channel call the bareboat organisations on CH16 and they will happily send out a pilot free of charge.

They feel it is much easier to pilot a boat in than pull a boat off the reef that has gone aground!!

The old CSY marina has been taken over by a combination of Tortola Marine Management and a new company of the combined SunSail, Stardust and Sun Yachts fleets.

It is reported—July 2000—that they have established a 50 boat marina in Blue Lagoon—how I can't figure out—whether space will be available for visiting yachts is porblematical.

The harbor is crowded and whether or not there is space inside for anchoring or coming up bow on the beach is problematical. Check with one of the above organisations via the VHF and find out if there is room available.

St. Vincent is not over endowed with facilities for yachts. Also the situation changes so rapidly it is impossible to keep up to date in a guide. The best thing to do is to introduce yourself to the managers of one of the organisations and ask guidance from him.

Blue Lagoon is now not only the home of not only Tortola Marine Management, Barefoot Yachts and also Sun Yachts.

West Coast

CUMBERLAND BAY
(Sketch Chart 19; II B-30)

One of the few anchorages on the west coast of St. Vincent, this spot used to be popular with boats bound from St. Vincent to St. Lucia. From Young Island to Castries, at the northern end of St. Lucia, it is an 80-mile sail, which is longer than most charter parties care to make. Hence, Cumberland became the natural spot for an overnight layover. The bottom here drops off abruptly from the shore, so the best method is to ease in slowly, checking for bottom. As soon as you see it, drop a stern anchor and continue on ahead toward shore. Then you can either row the bow anchor into the shoal water or nudge your bow against the shoal, drop from there, and haul back on your stern line. Make sure your bow anchor is well set, or tied to a palm tree, or you may find yourself drifting out to sea during the night. If you are entering the bay from the south, give the southwesternmost point a wide berth. There is a rock with six feet of water over it. A number of yachts have cut too close and have left behind large portions of their keels to commemorate the oversight.

Also see *Notes* for updates on this area on page 77.

Cumberland Bay has had a terrible reputation for years because of the rowdy and belligerent attitude

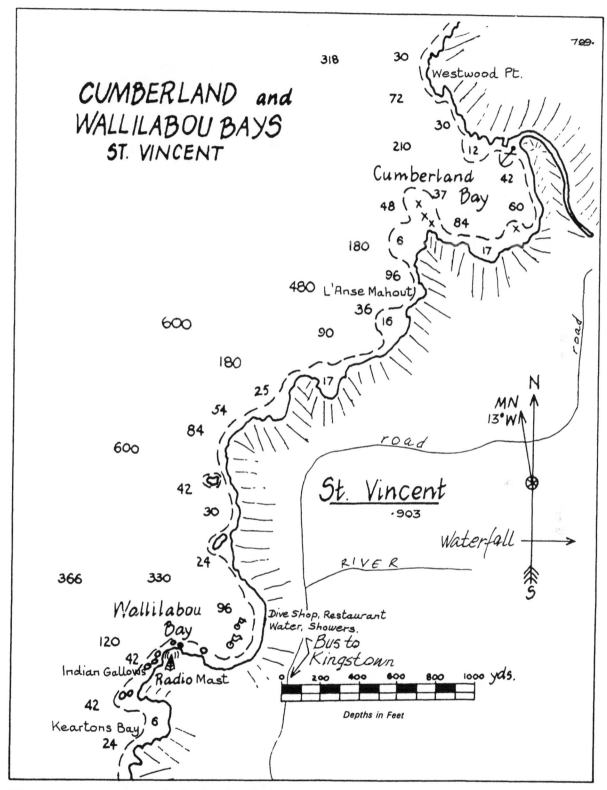

SKETCH CHART 19   Cumberland and Wallilabou Bays

of the boat boys on the beach and, tragically, because of the murder of Carl Schuster aboard his yacht there in 1976. Times change, though, and now it has been reported to me that the behavior of the local inhabitants has improved so much that the bay is an acceptable anchorage again.

Another improvement is the establishment of the Stevens Bar, a disco and restaurant run by Elford Stevens (an ex-policeman who served in both Antigua and St. Vincent) and his wife. They serve meals at a reasonable price, and if you make arrangements beforehand, you can order island specialties. Like many new operations, the restaurant has received mixed reviews. Be sure to call early to check the menu and the prices. (Check whether the prices are quoted in US or EC currency, as this will avoid embarrassment later.)

Mr. Stevens has also built a beach bar staffed with a couple of tough bartenders who are under orders to see that the boat boys behave themselves. When coming in to anchor at Cumberland Bay, my advice is to call the Stevens Bar on channel 16 to ascertain the situation and to request the name of a reliable boat boy who can take a line and keep an eye on your dinghy. (Inquire what the fee would be.)

I also urge you to secure your dinghy and your outboard well with wire and locks—or take them aboard at night—as dinghies and outboards still tend to "go adrift" at Cumberland Bay.

WALLILABOU BAY
(Sketch Chart 19; II B-30)

Because of the local problems in Cumberland Bay, nearby Wallilabou Bay became the preferred anchorage in the area. The radio tower is incorrectly listed on the British and American charts but placed correctly on Imray-Iolaire Chart B-30. (As is evident on Sketch Chart 19, it is on the hill forming the southern corner of Wallilabou Bay.)

About 30 years ago, the Stevensons (mistakenly referred to as the Livingstones in a previous edition of this guide) built a craft shop where they produced batik-printed goods. The shop, on the water's edge, offered the batik at what was described as the best buy in the Caribbean. However, after 25 years of dealing with the St. Vincent government and fighting with the local boat boys, the Stevensons finally gave up and sold the business to their niece Jan and her husband, Steve Tattersall (no relation to the well-known doctor from Tortola). They were young and full of drive and enthusiasm, but it still was an uphill battle against the St. Vincent fishermen and the boat boys. Finally they too gave up. The place has now been taken over by Randolph Russell, a St. Vincentian who has opened a bar and restaurant. Also here is John Monaghan, an ex-British policeman who runs a dive shop associated with Bill Trewes of Dive St.

Vincent. Monaghan (surely his predecessors came from Ireland!) is an excellent diver, and, being an ex-cop, he has been able to bring some order among the boat boys at Wallilabou Bay.

Randolph Russell's bar and restaurant offers trash pickup, free showers, and fresh water (make sure you have a long hose) at a price much cheaper than in St. Lucia.

Moorings are being installed here so that you can pick one up and run a bow or stern line ashore. Do not tie directly to a mooring, however, as you are anchoring on a vertical slope. No matter how heavy the mooring, if the surge comes in, it will quickly pick up the mooring and deposit it in very deep water, requiring Monaghan and his divers to do a lot of extra work retrieving the thing.

Exactly what the anchoring situation will be when you read this is difficult to predict, so my advice is to contact Russell's bar/restaurant or Monaghan's dive shop on channel 16 and find out the current routine for anchoring.

One of the nicest things about this anchorage is the beautiful small waterfall that's about a 15-minute uphill walk along the river road. Go about four in the afternoon; it will be a bit hot and tiresome, but then you can dive into the pool under the waterfall, take a shower, wash your hair and clothes, and no one will complain about how much water you're using. By the time you're through, it's cool enough so that even after the walk downhill, you're still feeling refreshed.

Another attraction here is the freshwater crayfish sold by the boat boys; it beats saltwater shrimp seventeen ways to Sunday. The boys will ask astronomical prices, but they are negotiable; check around to find out the going rate. And since the boys sell the crayfish by the dozen and not by weight, check their size—which ranges from tiny to very big—before settling on a price. The boys spear the creatures at night, so put in your order in the evening for the next morning. Since speared crayfish don't last as long as netted ones, you should eat them quickly.

CHATEAUBELAIR
(Chart 20; II B-30)

This is the northernmost town on the island of St. Vincent. Here again—although the charts do not show it properly—the bottom drops off very abruptly to 30 or 40 fathoms within a hundred yards of shore. The only way to anchor is with one anchor ashore and a second one to seaward. The best anchorage is on the small shoal north of the Fitzhughes estate, as marked on the NOAA and Imray-Iolaire charts. This is good only in calm weather when the swell is down, but it's the best spot from which to set forth to explore the northern end of St. Vincent.

My good friend George Freeman, who is no longer with us, told me once that you can sail between Chateaubelair Island and the mainland; he did it a number of times in his *Rosemary V*, drawing six and a half feet.

There are the ruins of an old estate at the village of Wallibou, north of Chateaubelair. This is reputed to be one of the most primitive areas of the Lesser Antilles, by romantic accounts not unlike regions of darkest Africa.

In years gone by, as has been described in previous editions of this guide, one of the most interesting excursions on St. Vincent was to climb to the rim of Soufrière volcano, look down onto Crater Lake, and on a clear day look south along the whole length of the Grenadines. It was a stiff uphill walk, not a mountain climb, but it was essential to take a water bottle and wear heavy shoes and foulweather gear in case it rained. Sometimes it was a great trip; other times, a complete waste: You would arrive at the rim of the crater, the clouds would roll in, and you would see nothing but a good Maine pea-soup fog. The supposedly dormant volcano started sputtering off and on in 1973, an island appeared in Crater Lake, and then it all quieted down until it went off again with a bang in the spring of 1979, covering the island with ash and largely destroying the rich agricultural land along the east coast.

The 1902 explosion of Mont Pelée, on Martinique, is the one that always had captured people's imaginations, since some 30,000 people died, but in 1979, when Soufrière on St. Vincent blew up, 2,000 were killed—no minuscule number. Amazingly, small pieces of flying rocks killed some people all the way down in Kingstown. People in Kingstown heard the explosion and rushed outside to see what had happened; many were then struck down by the debris from the eruption.

You used to be able to get up to the rim of the volcano from the west coast by taking a dinghy up to the village of Morne Ronde, hiring a guide, and climbing. Alternatively, you were able to assault the peak from the east by taking a cab to Orange Hill and following a fairly well-defined trail. I don't know if this is still possible, however, and have not been able to find anyone who does.

There are undoubtedly other anchorages on the west coast of St. Vincent that have not been

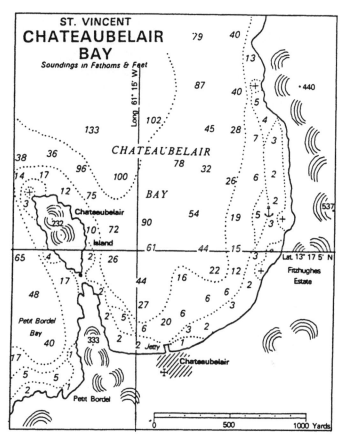

CHART 20   Chateaubelair Bay

mentioned in this chapter, as I have done little exploring in this area. There is no wind along the lee of St. Vincent from 1600 or 1700 straight through to noon the next day, and even then it is a sometime thing. However, if you have the inclination to explore, here are some anchorages that might prove attractive, working from south to north: the first cove north of Johnson Point (unnamed); then Questelles Bay; Anse Cayenne; the northeast corner of Buccament Bay; Layou Bay; Anse Bonaventure; and, in summer when there's no ground swell, Petit Bordel, just south of Chateaubelair Island.

Via the grapevine I hear that a small resort is being developed at Byahaut, between Anse Cayenne and Buccament Bay. I have not visited the place, and seeing is believing: What appears to be a development one year may be nothing but empty shacks the next. Thus, when you arrive in St. Vincent, check what the situation is. It certainly is off the beaten track, and there is no road connection to the outside world, so it should be different and worth investigating.

A final place of interest to yachtsmen in St. Vincent is the waterfall at Grand Baleine Bay at the northern end of the island. The falls are quite spectacular and make for a good day trip from Chateaubelair. You can go the six miles from Chateaubelair to Grand Baleine either by dinghy or under sail. If you sail, you must leave crew on the boat to stand off under shortened sail while the rest visit the falls. There is no hope of anchoring at Grand Baleine, as the cliffs are vertical to a great depth.

In a way, this is typical of the problems faced by the yachtsman in St. Vincent. There is much to be seen ashore, but there's a definite shortage of dependable anchorages from which to set out.

NOTES

WEST COAST OF ST. VINCENT

This area has over the years had a very varied reputation as to boat boys and being hassled by them. Exactly what the situation will be when you visit the West Coast of St. Vincent I don't know. However, if you are coming from the south in Admiralty Bay check with the local yachtsmen and charter skippers. If coming from the north in St. Lucia check with the bareboat managers and find out what the situation is. My personal experience on *Iolaire* and *Li'l Iolaire* on the West Coast of St. Vincent has been shall I say, less than happy.

OTTLEY HALL MARINA

(Chart B-30 Kingston Bay insert—north west corner.)

Ottley Hall shipyard and marina was built in the middle 1990s and seems to be a case of a lot of money being spent to build a big repair facility in the wrong place. Despite the tremendous amount of money poured into the operation it has never really got off the ground. In its short life it has been through various legal hassles and a couple of either bankruptcies or near bankruptcies. The facilities are superb. There is a large travelift, a syncro lift with side tracking that could haul even the largest mega yachts, a dry dock, covered sheds—the works. However, it appears to have been built at a spot where two strong tides meet and periodically a big surge builds up inside the harbor making it impossible to haul the boats. Or, in some cases, even to get ashore. I would not advise stopping at Ottley Hall until one has first visited it by car and ascertained what the present day situation is.

5

Barbados

(Imray-Iolaire Charts 1, B, B-2)

Barbados lies 80 miles due east of St. Vincent. It is a hard windward slog to reach it, and very few of the boats that cruise the Lesser Antilles ever try to go there. As good as *Iolaire* is to windward, I've found that nothing goes into the wind quite as well as a LIAT plane, and to my mind this is the best way to get to Barbados. In most cases, the yachts you will see in Barbados have arrived there from Europe.

Too bad that Barbados is so far to windward (and has so poor an anchorage once you get there), because it is a very attractive island. Despite its being one of the most heavily populated areas in the

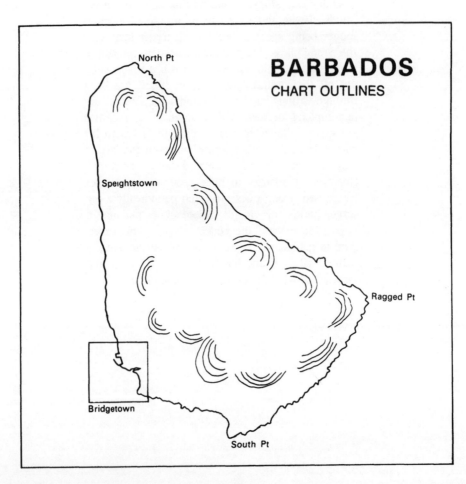

Barbados

world, with 1,400 people per square mile, it is neat, clean, and orderly. Certainly it is the best run of the Lesser Antilles. The people, who are polite, friendly, and helpful, speak in the soft, musical tones of the Bajan accent and regard themselves as Englishmen rather than West Indians. For centuries Barbados has been referred to as "Little England," and justly so. The beautifully tended landscape little suggests a tropical island. There are neatly clipped lawns, a racing turf, a cricket field, and a proper little bandstand. The police are impeccably dressed, and the harbor police in their straw hats and white sweaters look like something out of another era. The spoken language is English; there is no patois or corruption with a foreign language. In short, the island shows clear signs of being the only one in the entire West Indies that has remained under a single flag.

The northeast trades have been the lifeblood of Barbados, making travel from England a simple matter. By the same token, the trades were its protection from rival colonial powers to the west. In those days of wooden ships and iron men, the windward ability of a warship was roughly that of a bathtub toy. It was impossible for the French to keep a fleet assembled through a long beat out to Barbados. They tried once or twice, became hopelessly scattered, and had to give up.

Despite the generally low aspect of Barbados, its highest peak, Mount Misery, is 1,069 feet, and this is altitude enough to produce clouds that often serve as a landmark well before the island itself comes into view. Barbados is well lighted and well charted; making a landfall at night presents no real difficulties. All corners of the island are marked with lights visible at great distances. While there are no offlying hazards, bear in mind that there are a number of reefs along the coasts of the island, so do not hug the shore too closely. On the southeastern coast especially, the reefs extend offshore one and a half miles in places, and the current sets onshore. The current can mount to two knots at times, so, again, do not approach too closely. There are a number of small-boat passages through this reef, but a good deal of local knowledge is required.

Barbados was for years the traditional landfall for yachts crossing the Atlantic. In the winters of 1978–79 and 1979–80, it was estimated that roughly 300 yachts cleared through Barbados during the periods of December through early March. However, for various reasons, that huge influx of yachts has dried up almost completely.

In years gone by, when a yacht rounded Needham Point, lighthouse keepers spotted the running lights and reported to the harbor police, who came out immediately and were waiting when the anchor went down. The harbor police, picturesquely dressed in the costumes of sailors of Nelson's day, were efficient and cheerful; the yacht was cleared instantly and the crew was free to go ashore within an hour after dropping anchor.

Then the Deep-Water Harbour was created, and the harbor police were pretty much disbanded. Skippers who went to the Deep-Water Harbour were usually chased out and had to anchor off and then go around trying to enter at the various government offices, which were often less than interested in taking care of yachtsmen. I have heard tales of people spending *three days* in Barbados trying to enter.

In addition, the government began slapping all sorts of clearance fees on yachts, to the point that if you cleared at the wrong time of day or on the wrong day (i.e., Sunday), you could get stuck with approximately US$100 in customs, immigration, and landing fees. This was bad enough, but rumors through the yachting grapevine made it sound worse, jacking up the cost to US$300 (it probably was EC$300—a little more than US$100), so that by the winter of 1985, yachts were avoiding Barbados like the plague.

Furthermore, Antigua was temporarily well lighted and Guadeloupe had built an excellent marina, so yachts were heading for those two islands rather than for Barbados. The drop-off of yacht entries was so dramatic that the government decided to try to entice transatlantic cruising yachts by reducing the fees drastically. If you entered between 0600 and 2200 any day, the fee was reasonable.

In addition, the Knowles brothers established a dock, restaurant, bar, and laundry service and acted as expediters and advisers to visiting yachtsmen.

Then, in 1986 Jimmy Cornell instituted the Atlantic Rally for Cruisers (ARC), which brought almost 300 boats into Barbados during a 10-day or two-week period. This flooded the island and strained the facilities, but the government of Barbados, the chamber of commerce, the yacht clubs, and the tourism office all pulled together and did an amazingly good job of handling the situation. However, there were some difficulties that could not be surmounted. Barbados had no marina whatsoever, and the yachts that had crossed the Atlantic had to berth at Deep-Water Harbour or the Careenage; many ended up lying offshore rocking and rolling their guts out. The ARC finished in Barbados in 1986, 1987, 1988, and 1989; everyone

80 *Street's Cruising Guide to the Eastern Caribbean—Martinique to Trinidad*

worked hard to accommodate the yachtsmen, but their best was not good enough for Jimmy Cornell. He moved the finish of the race to St. Lucia, because Archie Mariez of Rodney Bay Marina promised to expand the marina berths to accommodate the transatlantic yachts. Thus, Barbados lost the ARC and St. Lucia acquired a tremendous number of new yacht slips—which are only filled for about three weeks of the year.

There is continual talk of building marinas in Barbados, but God knows whether one will ever come to fruition. Seeing will be believing. Some yachts coming across the Atlantic still make their landfall in Barbados. Those that do, usually stay there over Christmas, as they are guaranteed some good parties and some good racing. For example, Mount Gay, the popular Bajan rum company, sponsors a regatta over Christmas.

If you arrive outside of clearing times, drop anchor in Carlisle Bay, hoist your "Q" flag, and go to bed. Then, first thing in the morning, call the harbor authority on channel 12 and request permission to proceed to Deep-Water Harbour for clearance. If you do not have a radiotelephone, get a neighboring yacht to call for you.

Once you have cleared, move back and anchor in a convenient spot in Carlisle Bay.

From the Antilles, Barbados is best approached from a point north or south of the island, depending on the season. In the spring and summer, when the wind is in the southeast, the best place from which to start is the southern end of Grenada. Put to sea on starboard tack and check your progress by RDF (Barbados Radio at Black Point: 705 MHz; Grantley Adams Airport Beacon: 345 kHz) or celestial sights. The current runs to the northwest, so watch that it doesn't set you north of the island. Barbados is low-lying, and it is possible to miss it. Native schooner captains have a way of returning to their homeports in the islands with the explanation that "Barbados done sunk. We was where she is, but she ain't dere no more."

In the winter months, with the wind in the northeast, it is best to set out from Martinique or St. Lucia. Here is the method used by the schooners from St. Lucia: Stand north from Castries until the light of Ilet Cabrit—the southeastern corner of Martinique—is abeam. Go about on port tack and stay as close to the wind as you can; if you don't see Barbados in 24 hours, turn around and try again. Those are not the most explicit sailing directions in the world, but they seem to work one way or another.

When approaching Barbados from the east, stay well offshore when rounding the southeastern point. Many boats have come to grief here, as the highest land (the first seen) is on the northeastern corner of the island, the current sets onshore, and the reefs extend two miles offshore in some places. So be careful.

BRIDGETOWN HARBOUR (CARLISLE BAY)
(Chart 21; II 1, B, B-2)

The major anchorage in Barbados is off Bridgetown in Carlisle Bay, due north of the fort on Needham Point. It is a relatively poor anchorage because it is open to the rollers from the northwest, and the normal trade-wind sea hooks around Needham Point. When the northwest swell is severe, it is well nigh impossible to land ashore in a dinghy. Anchor off the Boatyard pier (see Chart 21), where the Knowles brothers have opened the Boatyard (Carlisle Bay, Bay Street, St. Michael's, Bridgetown, Barbados). To provide facilities for yachtsmen, they have built a dinghy dock, so you no longer have to land through the surf. They have showers, ice, water, and wholesale drinks, plus an inexpensive and informal bar. Communications are good, and they monitor VHF channels 06, 08, 09, 11, 12, 16, 67, 72, 77, and 78—the call sign is 8 PKM (eight papa kilo mike). They also stock Imray-Iolaire charts and Street guides, and the operation is only a short walk to the center of town.

In years gone by, the Careenage was quite a sight—chock full of vessels of every size and shape. There were always a couple of schooners being unloaded at the pier, water taxis were moving about in every direction, and the harbor police were trying to keep the mayhem under control. During rush hour, one policeman stood in a dinghy ceremoniously directing traffic. To add to the local color, the harbor police wore their picturesque uniforms modeled on the costumes of late eighteenth- or early nineteenth-century British seamen.

Prior to the construction of Deep-Water Harbour, everything was lightered out to ships anchored offshore and passengers were brought ashore in big 30-foot wherries rowed by four men. But the new commercial port ended all this; it is now infinitely more efficient, but nowhere near as picturesque.

Another great attraction in past years was a

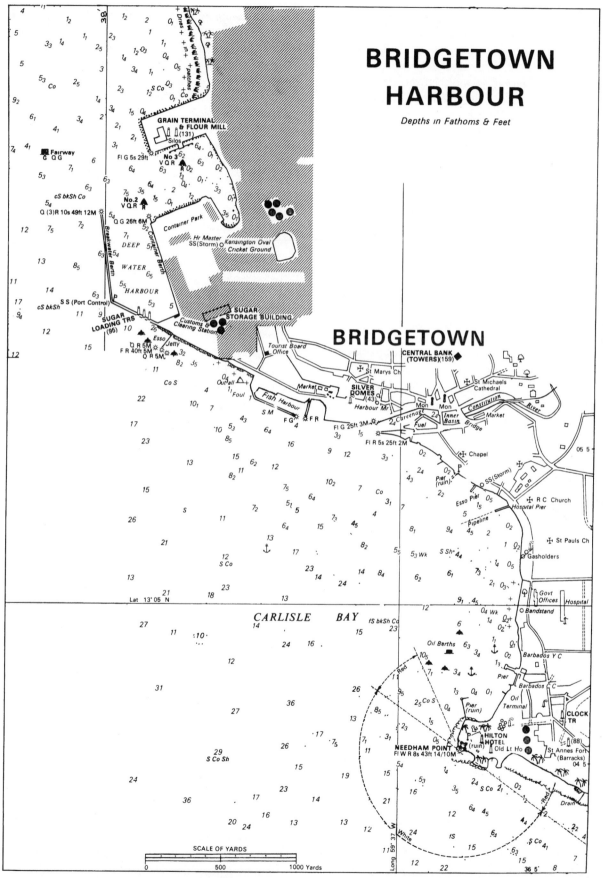

CHART 21 Bridgetown Harbour (Carlisle Bay)

unique screw-lift dock designed and installed by a Scottish engineer sometime in the 1880s. It continued operating, powered by a steam engine, well into the middle of the twentieth century. Finally a diesel engine replaced the steam engine, and the dock stayed in operation until the early 1980s. It was an excellent way to haul, as each section of the dock assembly could be disengaged by a clutch and lowered in such a way that every part of the keel could be worked on without having to move the boat.

This installation was so unique that there is talk now of restoring the old screw-lift dock and using it as a working museum. This would be a great asset to Barbados, as the hauling situation is extremely poor at present. The harbor department does have a 60-tonne Tami lift, which they used to use for hauling yachts (and you could work on your own boat), but the operation is winding down. The area they formerly used as the hauling facility now is occupied by the container terminal. Who knows? Perhaps they will move the Tami lift to another location.

There has been talk for years about building a marina in the Careenage, but it's hard to know whether or not that will happen. The main cargo operation and all of the commercial vessels have been moved to Deep-Water Harbour, and a facility has been built for the fishermen. Now the sportfishermen and the 'day charter boats lie stern-to in the Careenage. It is sometimes possible for visiting yachts to obtain permission from the harbormaster to lie stern-to in empty berths when the berth holders are off being hauled and their slips are empty. Yachtsmen are not allowed to lie alongside in the Careenage.

It's hard to list exactly what's available in Bridgetown, as many things are scattered around the city and are hard to find without a tourist map. I recommend that you go first to the Boatyard, where they will point you in the right direction for docking, hauling (presently limited to about 10 tons), sail repair, or the excellent machine shops throughout the island. International calls may be made via Barbados Radio, which can be contacted through VHF channel 16 or 8269.3 SSB. People wanting to contact yachts through Barbados Radio can dial direct from most areas in the world (telephone: 809-427-5200).

Another good contact is Norman Faria, a local yachtsman and yachting author. In the evenings, you can usually find him having a sundowner at the Barbados Cruising Club bar.

When coming across the Atlantic, sail repairs are always at the top of the list; in some cases, you may need a completely new suit. Hood Offshore Sails (6 Crossroads, St. Philip, Barbados) has built up a strong reputation in the Eastern Caribbean not only for doing excellent repair work but also for making good new sails at a reasonable price. A young Bajan, Roger Edgehill of Edge Sails (Viking, Palm Beach, Hastings, Barbados), deals mainly in sailboard and small-boat sails, but he also does all types of repairs.

Andrew Burke, a young, self-trained Bajan yacht designer designed and built *Bruggadug I* and *Bruggadug II*—32-foot racing boats that have done very well in the Eastern Caribbean racing circuit. *Bruggadug I* also raced and did well in the ARC. He has also designed a number of other successful boats.

Bridgetown is a major transfer point for passengers and cargo. Many freighters stop here, as do most of the cruise ships and airlines. Whatever you may have heard about cargo lost in Trinidad holds true of Barbados as well.

There are a number of good hotels within walking distance of the anchorage, as well as regular bus service to the heart of town. If you are an early riser, for a change of pace try watching the trainers give their horses a workout every morning at dawn at the racetrack.

Many small-boat fittings are available on the island, but it is practically impossible to locate fittings for large boats. Basic marine supplies such as paint are much cheaper here than in the rest of the islands, since there is no duty on any marine supplies. For the most part, you will find supplies here that you were unable to find anywhere else. The major distributors of engines, mechanical equipment, paints, tools, and what-have-you are based on the island, mostly in Bridgetown. It is indeed a pleasure to deal directly with the suppliers.

There are two yacht clubs—the Barbados Yacht Club, north of the Holiday Inn Pier (marked Aquatic Club on some charts), and the Barbados Cruising Club, south of that pier. The Barbados Yacht Club looks like something right out of an Edwardian novel—with large, cool reading rooms; tennis courts; a monumental bar; and just the sort of quiet atmosphere one expects at a well-heeled British club. It was formerly the *Royal* Barbados Yacht Club, and it is still listed as such on charts. The reason for the change, I am told, dates back some years to a time when Prince Philip was paying a visit to Barbados. He had immensely enjoyed the company of Barbados's premier, and discovering that the premier also was a yachtsman, the prince invited him to the Royal Barbados for a drink. The premier replied that he was not a member of the club and furthermore was not permitted to become one. A day or two later, the story goes, the Royal Barbados became just the Barbados Yacht Club. They have loosened up. In the past, they used to feed visiting sailing teams on the beach out front instead of in the clubhouse, but this attitude has changed entirely, and visiting yachtsmen from other clubs are now welcome.

The Barbados Cruising Club seems to be more actively used by yachtsmen. Its friendly bar is nearly always crowded on weekends. During the week, quite a few members stop by for a sundowner. The Bajans are very hospitable and will do their best to solve whatever problems a yachtsman encounters.

The former lack of a dinghy landing used to cause much grief to yachtsmen. Trying to land dinghies in the ground swell was especially trying when rowing ashore all dressed up for a night on the town (the Bajans tend to be rather formal). Many women went ashore in the skimpiest of bikinis, with long dresses, high heels, etc., packed carefully in plastic bags. Once on the beach, they donned their clothes for the big night out. One young woman I know took this a step further. Pointing out how uncomfortable it would be to sit all night in a damp bikini, she made the dinghy trip *au naturel,* with her dress, etc., tied on her head with a bandanna. Needless to say, all this made the damp landing conditions a lot less unpleasant.

When that young woman was on the island, the Cruising Club bar did a land-office business, as the boys sat around waiting for the nightly show. After the woman sailed off to other islands, the bar traffic at the club dropped off substantially.

Now, with the building of the Boatyard dock, these "difficulties" have become nostalgic memories.

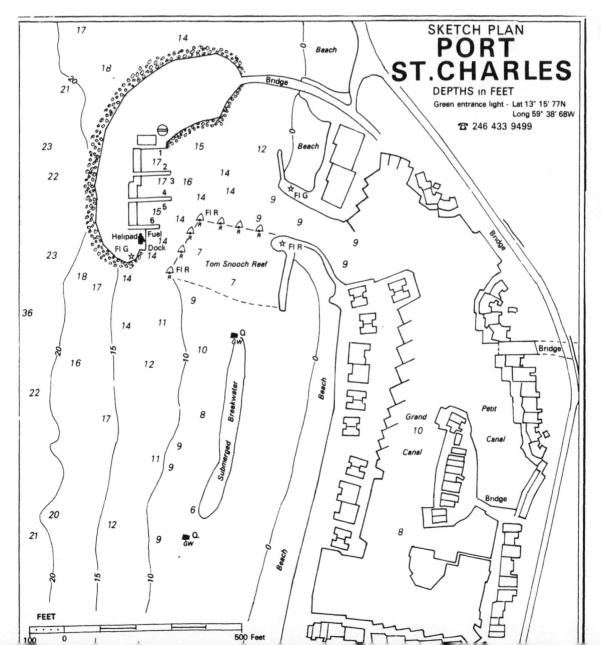

It has been many years since I last visited Barbados. The information that follows is courtesy of Martin Smyth, Boat Designer, Surveyor, Experienced Sailor—two transatlantics and some Fastnet Races. Martin hàs lived on Barbados for many years and knows the island and marine facilities intimately.

If you have real problems contact Martin at Crawford and Messiah Associates, Marine Surveyors, Tel: 246 433 9499; Fax: 246 433 9001 or e-mail tismyth@hotmail.com and hire him as project manager. His mother Trudy, call sign 8P6QM, runs the transatlantic marine mobile net, for licensed Ham Radio Operators (ham) every day on 21.400 every day at 1300 GMT. There is usually a good weather forecast provided for the North Atlantic at 1330 hours (obtained from the Radio France website and from other Ham Radio Operators). Everyone is welcome to listen in— she has a huge listening audience all around the Atlantic and everyone knows her—if anyone (even someone without a Ham License) has an emergency on board, their network is very efficient at providing help or assistance.

In the 1960s and 1970s Barbados was the major landfall for yachts crossing the pond. That changed as the yachting facilities in Antigua and Guadeloupe expanded, plus the difficulties of entering in Barbados, a story too long to present here. However, Barbados may again become a popular landfall for boats crossing the pond as now yachts are requested to enter at Port St. Charles on the North west coast of Barbados. This is a great boon as yachts will approach Barbados via the north coast where there are no off lying dangers. The high land 1099-ft. is five miles south of the northern end of the island. Yachts can still enter at Bridgetown but everyone advises against it.

This is in sharp contrast to the south east coast where the reefs extend a mile and a half off shore, land is low, the current sets on shore. The result is a number of yachts have been lost on the reefs on the southeast corner of Barbados and many have had the living daylights cared out of them when they discovered they were almost on top of the reef.

When approaching the north end of Barbados head for Waypoint A 13 21 N 59 38.5 W and *continue west until the lights on the end of Arawak Jetty lines up with the light on the end of the dock at Pt. St. Charles Marina 167° magnetic.*

The 200-ft. smokestack at Arawak jetty should always be lit with a flashing red light (an international agreement for low flying airplanes!!!), but I am told that often they are out!! This will keep you well clear of Harrison Reefs and the coral heads off Harrison Point.

You will see two clusters of fishing boats anchored off Six Men's and Sherman's pass to the west of these anchored boats and you will be in safe water.

At night, another method of avoiding the shoal, is to continue west until the first cluster of lights on the west coast, Port St. Charles Marina, Almond Beach hotel and Speightstown bear south east, run in on this line of bearing until Port St. Charles bears due east. Then as soon as you are in about 25-ft of water anchor and wait for dawn before trying to enter the marina. Call Port St. Charles on Ch. 77 and report in so customs will not think you are a drug smuggler!!!

DO NOT TRY TO ENTER STRANGE HARBOURS AT NIGHT. The channel buoys at Port St. Charles are hard to pick up due to the shore lights behind them But the immigration and Customs building is well lit and stands out.

Port St Charles is a new 1999 marina with berths for six mega yachts and piers in the inner harbor for residents of the Port St. Charles Residential development.

More information can be had from their web site at www.portstcharles.com

It is not a marina for visiting yachts to base themselves, no showers, Laundromat, marine supply store or food commissary. This is strictly a place to enter customs and immigration and then move on. On a space availability you may be able to stay for a few days to catch your breath after crossing the pond. But don't count on it.

Rodney Roach (Phone: 246 439 0564) lives near Port St. Charles and is planning to provide services for yachtsmen. He is an experienced yachtsman, diver and boat builder who is pretty good at organizing things and since he lives only ¼ mile from Port St. Charles he is a good person to contact if you have problems on arrival.

Being able to enter at Port St. Charles is a great advantage over entering in the commercial harbor of Bridgetown among the commercial vessels and being required to tie up to docks that definitely were not built with yachts in mind. The marina has electricity, water, diesel, sewage discharge, gasoline and telephone available in the berth. It is best to refuel in Port St. Charles as it very to do so in Bridgetown.

Also now from Port St. Charles Customs, you can obtain coast wide clearance and anchor anywhere you want on the lee coast of Barbados. But, from November to April be wary of the ground swell (see Prologue), which can come in any time. It is completely independent of local weather. Rather it is caused by storms in the north Atlantic.

Speightstown (Little Bristol) is ¼ miles from Port St. Charles and provides an interesting anchorage for visiting yachts. The small, quaint town, of about 1000 people, has a beautiful beach and a new jetty, with about 10 fishing boats anchored 200 meters offshore. The anchorage is on a sandy bottom in about 25 ft of water and it is an easy, safe sail of about 10 miles to

Carlisle Bay if a ground swell event announces its pending threat by making the anchorage rolly.

Speightstown has a good supermarket on the beach and easily accessible by dinghy. There are 4 banks, Post Office, a good hardware store, 2 drug stores, doctors and, of course, The Fisherman's Pub with good, cheap food, drink and entertainment on the town beach. This is a pleasant, sleepy town with friendly people. There are no yachting facilities. For diesel and petrol it is strictly a case of jerry cans to the petrol station—a long walk or short taxi ride from the dock.

Diesel, and fresh water can be obtained from the fishing complex harbor in Carlisle Bay. Cooking gas bottles are harder to find. The filling station is some distance outside Bridgetown and expensive by taxi. Rodney Roach (phone: 439-0564) is planning to provide this service for visiting yachts. If you phone Rodney he will collect and deliver your cylinders for a small fee. He collects the cylinder and when he has enough makes the journey to fill up all the cylinders he has—about twice a week—then delivers the full cylinders to the yachts. There are no marine facilities for petrol or kerosene (paraffin). Anybody wanting these has to take a container and go to the nearest petrol station for motor vehicles. There is an one on the beach in Carlisle Bay, just east of the Boatyard.

There is not much changed regarding the anchorage in Bridgetown except that nights ear plugs are useful as extremely loud music floods the anchorage till 0000 in the morning—except on Fridays and Saturdays when it goes on till 0500.

In Carlisle Bay there are two wrecks used by the local divers for diving trips. These wrecks will only be dangerous to deep draft yachts. They can be spotted by the buoys around them used by local dive boats as moorings when conducting dive tours— these moorings are not for visiting yachts.

Getting ashore dry is still a problem. There is no dinghy dock—it is a case of landing through the surf at the Barbados Cruising Club, or Barbados Yacht Club if you have arranged to have a guest card.

There is still TALK of a marina in the Carenage. Talk of restoring the screw lift dock to a working museum and developing the area south of the Carenage with town houses, shops, hotel and perhaps a marina but.............

Hauling facilities have improved—the travelift is now rated at 45 tons, for boats of 7-ft. draft limitation. This can be located on the north east side of the main harbor and is operated by Willies Marine Services; Phone/ Fax:246 425 1060 or via email to his son Mike Hassel at mikie@caribsurf.com

Address: Mike Hassell, Black Rock, St. Michaels. Or, he can also be contacted at —

Phone: 424 4854 or 230 4271 (mobile). It is a do it yourself yard. If you have problems that you cannot solve, Willie will point you in the right direction. If the problems are still unsolvable hire Martin Smyth and if the problem is solvable in Barbados Martin will organize the solution.

Space is limited, they are a hauling facility, not a storage facility. As for parts for the cruising yacht it is not too hot. Willies Marine Services have a small chandlers, Fisherman's corner (north east corner of Carenage) and DI Manufacturing at Guinea, St. John, who will order from the States what they do not have. They will have it shipped down by DHL or FedEx and arrange Customs clearance. It comes in Duty Free as Ships Stores in Transit, but it requires a lot of paper work. Leave that to Fisherman's Corner or DI Manufacturing.

Hoods Sail Loft is now Doyle's and has built up an excellent reputation for good sails at a reasonable price to the extent that they supply almost all of the bare boat fleets in the Caribbean with sails. Business is so good, so there may be a wait on sail repair. Phone: 423 4600; Fax: 423 4499.

Roger Edgehill still does sail repair, but if the surfs up you'll have to go to the surfing beach to find him!!! It is best to contact Roger Edgehill, Viking, Palm Beach, Hastings, Christchurch, Phone: 429 5800

Surfing is good in Barbados it is not Tahiti, but it is good. If anchored in Carlisle Bay, about 1/4 mile east of Needhams Point behind the Defence Forces buildings good surf can often be found. Or, hop on a bus to Bathsheba on the north east coast where you will usually find good surf. International events are sometimes held in "the Soupbowl"—ask the local surfers where that is. If the ground swell is rolling in from the north east there is surfing on Harrisons Reef on the north west corner of the island.

A Bus service covers the island, cheap and is a great way to see the island and meet the locals.

Restaurants vary from cheap local, (but often very good) Bajan food to Cordon Blue cookery (expensive). This is similar regarding the hotels. Some hotels cater to the locals are good and not too expensive.

Barbados is considered south of the hurricane belt, but it has been hit. In October 1800 Rodney arrived with his fleet to resupply only to discover Barbados had been knocked flat by one of the strangest hurricanes in known history. It started near Jamaica then headed south east, passed over St. Lucia destroying that island then on to Barbados.

Yachtsmen crossing the pond arrive after the end of the hurricane season and usually move on well before the beginning of the hurricane season in June.

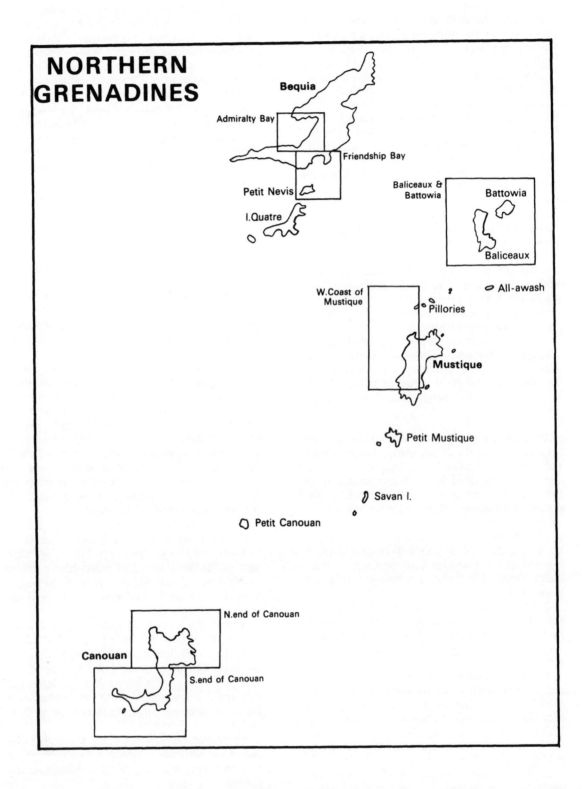

6

Northern Grenadines

(Imray-Iolaire Charts 1, B, B-3, B-30, B-31, B-311)

IMPORTANT NOTE: As this book was being finalized, we discovered that the St. Vincent government was in the process of completely redoing the buoyage system in St. Vincent and the Grenadines. They are replacing missing buoys, and in many cases installing steel piles to mark reefs previously marked by buoys placed so far away from the danger that the mariner often became confused and hit the reef he was trying to avoid. The chartlets in this book have been corrected, but your charts may not have been; in case of discrepancy, rely on the book, not the charts.

I stand by my oft-repeated statement: Do not rely on buoys or lights in Eastern Caribbean waters in the ex-British islands, as they are set up so pilots, ship wreckers, and salvage operators would not starve to death.

The Grenadines comprise a string of small islands stretching 45 miles from Bequia to Ilet de Ronde. They are a varied lot, ranging unpredictably in size and topography. While the Tobago Cays are low and flat, neighboring Union Island soars high into the air. During the popular charter season in the winter, most of the islands are dry and windswept, but in the rainy season their colors change abruptly from dull brown to a bright, lush green. In sailing the Grenadines, the runs are very short; most passages can be made in two hours, and the longest ones never last more than five. There are anchorages virtually everywhere, but these must be negotiated carefully. What distinguishes this area from the rest of the Antilles—and the Virgin Islands in particular—are the vast reaches of shoal water. There is an indescribable thrill in sailing across these banks with only two or three feet of water

below the keel, and in watching from the spreaders as the bottom slips by.

Most of the islands lie along a northeast-southwest axis, allowing a weatherly yacht to lay a course close-hauled going north. This contrasts with the Virgins, where you are either dead before or dead against the wind. There is very little chance of getting becalmed in the low-lying Grenadines. Soon, however, the days of the unspoiled tropical cay will have passed. Many of the islands are undergoing the throes of long-term development ventures.

In 1978, under the direction of the Canadian Hydrographic Office, the government of St. Vincent established lights and buoys throughout the Grenadines. These are marked on the latest British charts. However, it is universally agreed by yachtsmen who are familiar with the area that the installation of the lights, buoys, and ranges is—to say the least—a mixed blessing. The ranges, as will be noted, are often not as marked on the charts and often are poorly placed.

For instance, ranges in the Tobago Cays will tend to put the yachtsman trying to sail into the anchorage right on the rocks. Further, the buoys at Montezuma Shoal and Grand de Coi are virtual booby traps, likely to put yachtsmen right on top of the very dangers they are trying to avoid.

The lights are unreliable and frequently are not working; it sometimes takes months if not years before they are relighted. Needless to say, all this creates a dangerous situation.

Visiting yachtsmen have always been told not to sail at night in this area. Now, with lights and buoys supposedly there to warn the unknowing, some yachtsmen do attempt to sail after dark, and many have gotten into serious trouble. So, despite the buoys and lights that have been installed in the Grenadines, the old rule still applies: *Under no circumstances should you sail in this area at night.* And we can add another rule: *Night or day, treat all buoys with extreme skepticism.*

Bequia

The island of Bequia has been celebrated by sailors for hundreds of years. I have read glowing first-person accounts of Admiralty Bay by officers of the Royal Navy during the Napoleonic Wars. Esteemed by legend and heralded by song, it has always been a fine place to career a ship, muster a crew, or replenish stores. There is a good deal of Yankee blood in the people of Bequia, harking back to the New Bedford whalers who took wives and settled here. In Paget Farm, on the western tip of the island, are descendants of the early French settlers, a group that has remained remarkably separate from the rest of the islanders.

Bequia is the last refuge of the sailing fisherman. Even now, the sail-fishermen greatly outnumber the motor-fishermen. An attitude still prevails here that a motor is an auxiliary to the sail. When the fishermen gather for the sailing races on the major holidays, the level of the competition is as high as you will find anywhere. These people think nothing of sailing down to Grenada in a 17-foot open boat.

Bequia is one of the major yachting centers of the Grenadines, and at any one time, there may be 50 to 60 yachts anchored in Admiralty Bay. Some are visiting yachts, many are semipermanent. Bequia is an extremely attractive island that in a way time has passed by. The only way to get on and off Bequia, as of the summer of 1991, was via the local schooner *Friendship Rose*—which has been doing this run for donkey's years—plus two Norwegian-built steel ferryboats. They leave Bequia about 0645, do the one-hour run to St. Vincent, and leave about 1500, arriving in Bequia about 1600. If you go over for the day, don't miss the boat back, as they all leave at the same time. If you miss it, the next stop is a St. Vincent hotel, where you'll have to wait until the following day.

Possibly by the time you read this, you will be able to fly to Bequia, but I will believe that only when I actually land on Bequia in a plane, and not before.

Needless to say, this lack of transportation has hampered the development of Bequia. To some people, this is deplorable; others feel it preserves the wonderful charm of the island. One thing is certain: The Bequians and the St. Vincentians are two very different peoples, even though both are under the same government. The Bequians, in fact, do not like the St. Vincentians, and they always blame them for any crime committed on Bequia.

That may or may not be fair. Certainly there is crime on Bequia, and neither the local populace nor visiting yachtsmen seem to have much faith in the ability of the St. Vincent police force to do anything about it. This is made clear in the book *Sitting Ducks*, by Betsy Hitz-Holman, the story of the burglary of her boat, the near-killing of her boyfriend, and the difficulties she had afterward with the St. Vincent police and the legal authorities. The book, of course, was not popular on Bequia, and many people have claimed that it is full of falsehoods and libelous statements. However, it is the old story. No one on *any* island wants *anything* derogatory said about his or her island. Throughout my life, I have made my reputation by "telling it like it is." As a result, on every island in the Eastern Caribbean there are some people who intensely dislike what I have written. There are always two sides to every story, and the truth may lie somewhere in between. Betsy Hitz-Holman knew the situation from one side, the Bequians from the other side. Knowing as I do (from firsthand experience) the efficiency (or, rather, the lack thereof) of West Indian police forces, courts, judges, and lawyers, I am inclined to believe much of *Sitting Ducks*, but I suspect that in some aspects, the case may have been overstated.

Yet Bequia is an extremely attractive island, and I hope not too many sailors are scared off by *Sitting Ducks*. I think it's clear that a singlehander or a couple cruising in this and many other parts of the world are vulnerable to marauders. Many people don't like carrying guns—and much of the time they have to be locked up in port anyway. As I have said before, I think the best answer is to have a dog aboard. Even a small dog, as long as it is yappy, will work. Barking of any kind normally will send a would-be burglar rowing off into the night. In all the years I have talked to yachtsmen worldwide, I have never heard of a single boat with a barking dog aboard that has been boarded and burgled.

In any case, there's no doubt that dinghies disappear all the time in Bequia. Of course, Admiralty Bay is open to the west, and I am convinced that about one-third of the missing dinghies are improperly secured and drift off; another third are taken by other "yachtsmen," and the final third are stolen by Bequians or St. Vincentians. Incidentally, the latest ploy is to steal an inflatable dinghy, deflate it, put it and the outboard below, and sail to the next island and sell it.

I have been in the insurance business for more than two decades and have read a lot of reports on stolen dinghies. Not once in my experience has the police department of St. Vincent offered any help in retrieving or searching for the stolen boats. In some cases, they were actually obstructionist when the dinghies were found.

One might argue that the police have better things to do than look for yachties' lost dinghies, but the attitude can be pretty unpleasant nevertheless. I am hopeful that the prime minister of St. Vincent, James ("Son") Mitchell, as a Bequian and a sailor, will do something to improve the situation.

The dingy stealing situation is not as bad in Bequia as it is in other places. But it still exists and further down in the islands, further south in the Grenadines it is even worse. Comments made about the inability and uncooperation of the St. Vincent police department have not changed. This we discovered to our chagrin in 1999.

ADMIRALTY BAY
(Chart 22; II B-30, B-31)
See also notes at the end of this chapter on page 107. A beautiful anchorage and excellent in all normal weather, but an absolute death trap in hurricane season. Witness Hurricane Klaus in November

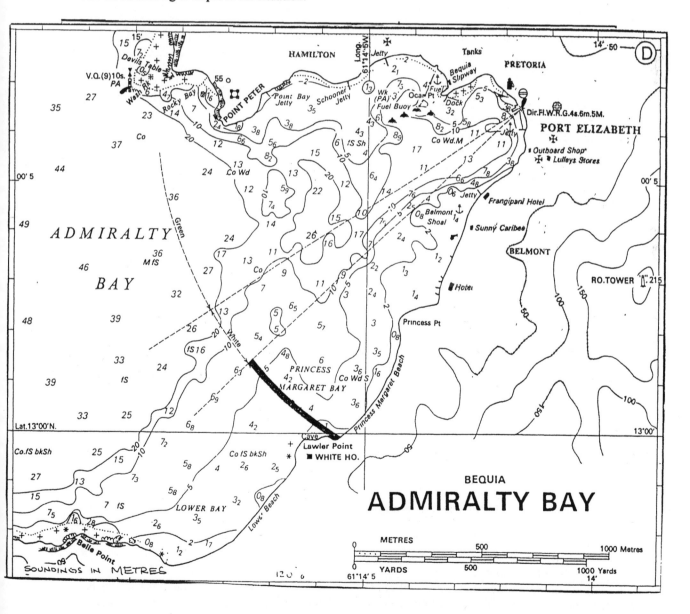

1984, which passed *north* of the Virgin Islands but still sent a swell into Admiralty Bay that put numerous boats on the beach.

Admiralty Bay is the major anchorage and the port of entry for Bequia, and it is easy to enter in daylight, although you should be wary of Wash Rocks, off Devil's Table. Give Devil's Table a good 150-yard berth.

Devil's Table is supposed to be marked by a red lighted can buoy that may or may not be there when you arrive. There is another buoy right in the middle of Admiralty Bay that can be disregarded by the average yacht. Once around Point Peter (Fort Point), you can lay a course for the church in Port Elizabeth (106° magnetic), provided you draw less than nine feet. If you are tacking in, take care to avoid Belmont Shoal, which is foul ground and full of coral heads. If you are approaching from the west, you can set a clear course from West Cay directly to the town dock.

The best anchorage can be had due west of the church. There is deep water quite close to shore, so allow plenty of scope. The hard sand bottom is excellent holding. The anchor may take a moment or two to set, but once it sets, you won't budge. Do not anchor south of the line of boats extending southwest from the church, as these are moored right on the edge of the shoal. Admiralty Bay is a popular spot, and there may be as many as 60 boats at anchor. As always, space is on a first-come basis, which may require anchoring well offshore, leaving you a long row into town. A way of avoiding this problem is to sail right up to shore just north of the church. The bottom drops off so steeply here that it is possible to lie close in, with a stern anchor out, and run up and bury a bow anchor on the beach.

In the past, this arrangement had at least one liability: There was a large bronze bell in front of the church. Now I don't mind a bell calling the faithful to prayer at decent hours, but when every village drunk takes to clanging it at all hours of the night, it gets to be too much. On one Whitsunday weekend, I counted 103 rings in the course of one noisy night and early morning. The next time I hit Admiralty Bay and decide to anchor bow-on to the beach, I will be packing a hacksaw.

In the even more distant past, even if the drunks did not ring the bell at odd hours, the bell was rung at 0600 every day to wake people up in time to catch the 0645 boat to St. Vincent. However, I have been informed by Ian Gale of Bequia Bookshop that the practice has been discontinued.

Since the anchorage off town directly west of the church is becoming very crowded, there are two alternative spots. If you draw five feet or less, there is one right off the Sunny Caribee Hotel, behind Belmont Shoal. This is sometimes good, sometimes bad, depending on whether or not the northwest ground swell is running. Most important, do not approach this anchorage directly from the west but rather from the southwest. Favor the shore side, as the reef and shoal offshore have hailed bareboats by the dozen. It is strictly eyeball navigation, and there is room for only three or four boats. If that many boats are already there, do not attempt to anchor.

There is another anchorage on the north side of the harbor off the now-defunct Bequia Slipway. It is always calm—just a slightly longer dinghy ride to the main dinghy dock in town and the dinghy docks of the Frangipani Hotel and the Whalebone Bar and Restaurant.

Bequia once was one of the major centers of schooner traffic, and was active in owning, crewing, and building them. Right behind where the Frangipani Hotel now stands, the Mitchell family built a 120-foot three-masted schooner, which they launched with only jack iron (rum), rollers, muscle power, and song. Prime Minister "Son" Mitchell, who is also the owner of the Frangipani, used to be glad to show visitors a half model of his father's schooner.

Some years ago, the voices of doom cried that the last of the schooners had been built, that boatbuilding would become a lost art, never to be revived. Nothing could be further from the truth. A young American, Chris Bowman, can probably take credit for part of the present revival of boatbuilding in Bequia, as he built "by eye" (the traditional method) a rather nice, 40-foot gaff-rigged cutter. Then he went to work supervising the construction of a 70-foot traditional schooner for a pop music star. This turned into the beautiful double-topsail gaff schooner *Water Pearl of Bequia*, a classic Bequian cargo schooner built as a yacht. She used to spend the winter season day-chartering out of Marigot, St. Martin, but unfortunately, *Water Pearl of Bequia* is no more. Chris decided to make his dream cruise through the Panama Canal, across the Pacific, and on to Australia. He spent a full two years preparing the boat for the trip and lining up his crew. He had everything beautifully organized, all was well, and it looked like the fulfillment of a lifetime dream. But he made the mistake that all too many yachtsmen have made, and he lost his lovely vessel. I repeat here again: DO NOT ENTER STRANGE HARBORS AT NIGHT.

Chris assumed that the entrance to the Panama Canal would be well buoyed and well lighted, which it is, but there are so many lights that it is very easy to become confused and misinterpret the lights on shore. I have discussed this with numerous yachtsmen. It is common, for example, to mistake the lights of the army base north of the canal entrance for the actual entrance. Chris went high and dry on the beach at 0500. If he had stood off, hove-to, for another hour and a half, until daylight (a schooner like *Water Pearl of Bequia* would heave-to very well), he would be in Australia today cruising around in his boat rather than working ashore as a shipwright. Again: DO NOT ENTER STRANGE HARBORS AT NIGHT. Nor should you try sailing through the Grenadines in the early evening or at night, as that, too, is a guaranteed recipe for disaster.

In the 1980 edition of this book, I mentioned that young Bert Ollivierre of the extensive Ollivierre family (famous as schooner captains, fishermen, whalers, boatbuilders, and smugglers) was building traditional double-enders—referred to locally as two-bow boats—and was talking of modernizing the construction with steam-bent or laminated frames, possibly clinker (lapstrake) construction. This would certainly make the boats much, much lighter, but nothing came of the idea; they are still building their beautiful little two-bowed boats—excellent sailers but certainly not lightweight. They build them in various sizes and race them very competitively; some are working fishermen, others are small versions (13 to 18 feet long) built as pleasure craft. If you are anchored on a weekend in Bequia Harbor, you'll see the two-bowed boats zigzagging back and forth across the harbor, many of them in races sponsored by the Bequia Yacht Club. In fact, everyone in Bequia seems to sail. Now, of course, instead of the old flour-sack sails, they use Dacron sails, plus stainless rigging and bronze fittings.

While anchored in Admiralty Bay, you may notice many boys chasing model yachts to and fro across the harbor. Model-boat racing has been a pastime here for as long as anyone can remember. The kids used to make models of the charter boats that frequent the area, and a feature of big holiday weekends is model-boat races. Each model is attended by its young owner swimming furiously to keep up with it, as the rules provide for one person to adjust sails, rigging, or direction. Those not strong enough to keep up with the boat follow in a dinghy, diving in to make adjustments whenever necessary. Even without the aid of self-steering gear, these model yachts manage to hold a true course and stand up well to the breeze.

To my mind, these models are the best souvenirs that can be brought back from the Caribbean. And it is interesting to note that only in Bequia do the children have the skill and interest to build model yachts that can really perform. No wonder they grow up to be such fine seamen.

To see the next generation of boatbuilders, go to the place where Bequia Slipway used to be, walk across the road, and ask for the model shop. Here you will find beautiful models of the various charter boats that visit the area. More interesting, they also build full models of the traditional Bequia whaleboats, complete with all their whaling gear. It is very interesting to see how, over the years, the quality of these models has improved. Years ago, the models were very crude—now they are extremely skillfully done and not far below the quality of work by top modelmakers in the United States. Needless to say, their prices have also "improved" with the passage of the years.

Lawson Sargeant, who heads the shop, started making fully rigged models of the Bequia whaleboats when he was 16 years old. Now in his thirties, he is still building models and has quite an industry going, employing approximately 16 boys. Marvin Hutchin, one of the boys who worked with him years ago, has set up a rival shop, which is located behind the small supermarket across from the petrol station in the main part of town.

If someone really wanted to help the economy of Bequia (and also yachting, since the modelmakers of today will become the shipwrights of tomorrow), he or she could locate and send books on modelmaking to these enterprising young boys. Books should be sent to: Bequia Model Shop, Bequia, St. Vincent, West Indies. I am sure this would improve the quality of the models even more.

For many years, the economy of Bequia was declining, and yachts did not visit the island too frequently, but now progress has come, and things have changed drastically. More and more yachts are coming in, and the marine economy in Bequia has expanded.

Regarding marine hardware, Missy and Daniel Foulon operate Grenadine Yacht Equipment in the building formerly used by Hodge Taylor's Bequia Chandlery at Bequia Slipway. They started out mainly stocking outboard parts, but they have expanded and now carry a wide variety of general yachting supplies. They also fill gas bottles, so you no longer have to go to St. Vincent for a refill. Their address is Box 79, Bequia (telephone: 809-458-3347; fax: 809-458-3696).

The Bosun's Locker, run by David and Iris de

Lloyd, specializes in stocking anchor chain, rigging, and winches—all duty-free. They can be reached via telephone at 809-458-3246. Their telex number is 7500 CWAGENCYVQ. (People nowadays seldom use telexes, as faxes are so much more efficient.)

Lincoln Simmons, whose sail loft used to be just south of the anchorage by the church, has built a sail loft on the hill overlooking the Frangipani Hotel. King of the sailmakers in the lower Caribbean, Lincoln has been making sails for well more than half a century. He is also the whale butcher on the island, so don't expect him to be there when a whale needs to be dealt with. Lincoln is a storehouse of information about Bequia, and by talking to him and his son Nolly, you can find out everything there is to know about the island. If Lincoln gives you advice, it will be blunt and to the point—take it, even though it may be bitter. Recently I heard that he has a new rival by the name of Allick, but I'll stick with Lincoln.

Bequia Slipway has had a long and varied career, with many owners—the most picturesque of whom was Bill Little, an ex-sergeant who served in the marines from 1939 to 1949. Not only was he in all the Pacific campaigns, but he also was in a company of marines who parachuted into Burma to help General Joe Stilwell retrieve his troops the second time they were kicked out of that country. After he left the marines, Bill became a race-car driver, then a yacht skipper. Thanks to his checkered career, he was an entertaining raconteur and an excellent friend—not someone to be pushed around, as a number of people found out when they tried it. Unfortunately, like many of Bequia's colorful characters, he is no longer on the island. The slipway was sold, then resold. The slipway really slipped, and now it is a disaster area waiting for someone to pick it up and resurrect it.

Getting a shower in Bequia is difficult. You can have one at Mitchell's Guest House in the middle of town, but it's not too cheap and not necessarily the friendliest of operations.

Southwest of the Frangipani Hotel, the Bequia beach is peppered with small restaurants and bars, all ready to take care of the needs of yachtsmen. The Frangipani is not only a hotel but also a mail drop and message center. The Whalebone Bar and Restaurant, adjacent to the hotel, also has a boutique run by Angie and Albert Hinkson, of the old Bequia Macintosh family. There is also Mac's Pizzeria, which sells bread, cakes, cookies, quiche, muffins, pies, and other baked products. Geoff Wallace's Fig Tree Bar is an old standby that goes back donkey's years. Although there have been changes over the years in the Sunny Caribee's management and ownership, the place has been the major hotel in the Admiralty Bay area for more than four decades.

Eating out in Bequia is always an experience. You can find restaurants that cater to all tastes and budgets—from the cheapest to the most expensive, from local fish and fungi menus to five-star eating. Certainly from the outside, one of the most attractive restaurants in the entire Caribbean is the Gingerbread, in a new building built in the traditional West Indian style. It's owned and operated by Pat Mitchell, ex-wife of Prime Minister "Son" Mitchell. Another place worth visiting is Spring Plantation, a restored 200-year-old working plantation with an old sugar mill, a 10-room guest house, and a restaurant. The restaurant management suggests walking from Port Elizabeth to Spring Plantation, but I recommend a taxi—it is only a mile, but you have to go up a mountain and down the other side, and you may work up a heart attack instead of an appetite. The Old Fort Restaurant, overlooking the entrance to the harbor, is certainly an excellent place to sit and watch the sun go down as you look for the green flash. Here you can enjoy twilight drinks and dinner overlooking an empty sea.

One of the newest restaurants is Le Petit Jardin, one street behind the police station. It is run by Owen Belmar, whose father was from Petit Martinique and whose mother was a Bequian. He is a real go-getter who built his own restaurant, landscaped the grounds, and serves a wonderful meal. Belmar is a well-trained chef who cooked at various island resorts and then spent six years as chef with the Johnson & Johnson fleet—most of the time with Dick Sweet, the well-known charter skipper. Sweet is without doubt one of the greatest comedians of all the charter skippers I have met during my three-plus decades in the Caribbean. He is also one of the Caribbean's most competent skippers. As a result, Owen Belmar's restaurant is excellent, with good food served by an enthusiastic and skilled staff in a lovely setting. One sailor has to help another, and it is very pleasant to sit in Le Petit Jardin and discuss the good old days of chartering.

The Frangipani is pretty much the focal point for yachtsmen in Bequia—the complex includes the hotel and bar, the dinghy dock, and Frangipani Yacht Services, which serves as a mail drop and a clearinghouse for yachting information. Their telephone number is 809-458-3244; telex: 7587 FRANGIBQ. Messages can be left here for yachts in the vicinity, and yachts can make calls from here

Northern Grenadines

to other parts of the world.

For women's clothes and accessories, there is the Crab Hole, a nice, simple West Indian boutique right next to the Sunny Caribee. They also sell first-class men's sports shirts—Ian Gale highly recommends it as the place where he buys his.

Ross Lulley is back in business near his old location up on the hill high above the western end of Princess Margaret Beach. He first came to Bequia 37 years ago, when there were practically no roads, and he built his house and shop 300 feet in the air, miles from the nearest harbor. I had always wondered why he did that, since his business involved the sea and fishing, but I discovered the answer some years later: Lulley's shop was equidistant, via backwoods trails, from the fishing communities at Friendship Bay, Paget Farm, and Admiralty Bay. Thus, he was able to draw business from all three communities.

For many years, his shop was a little two-by-four shack jammed full of fishing goodies. Then, as yachting began to expand in the area, Ross branched out into the chandlery business, selling gear at extremely good prices. As the years went by, Lulley's Knife Shop (it was so called because he sold some of the best knives in the world) became known not only throughout the entire Caribbean, but also in Europe and even as far away as the Pacific. Then the shop expanded again, and he installed a big kerosene deep freeze, so he served the coldest beer on the island.

After that, Ross sold the business, but being the kind who can't stay retired, he decided to start up again, selling fishing supplies and some yachtsmen's gear, including Dacron and nylon line at very competitive prices.

To get to Lulley's shop, take a taxi—or take your dinghy around to Lower Bay and land at the northern end of the bay. Here you will find a small path going up the side of the rock with a cave through which you will see the water on the other side. Follow the trails and you will end up at Lulley's with a considerable thirst, which has always been taken care of there by a nice, cold Heineken. I have been told that Armina, Ross's longtime Bequian assistant, is no longer with him—I wonder how he is faring without her. His shop is only open from eight to twelve Monday through Friday mornings. The view from the shop is magnificent, the gear superb, and the conversation always entertaining. On one of my visits, Ross held forth on the subject of the caliber of yachtsmen in Bequia these days. Typically, he has a strong opinion: "I don't call the majority of the present group afloat 'yachtsmen' any longer. 'Waterpeople' is what I call them. I spent one year in Shanghai on the Hwang Pu anchorage back in the forties, and I know waterpeople when I see them."

Unfortunately Ross Lulley has passed away. His famous store on the hill side is no more. But his wife and sons are running a very good shop behind the Anglican Church—the second generation running the shop.

When I first visited Bequia, everything was so primitive that the chickens ate whatever they could find, and the easiest thing to find usually was a batch of fish heads. As a result, the chickens didn't taste like chickens—they tasted like fish! Even when you had bacon and eggs for breakfast in the morning, it tasted like you were eating bacon and fish. The only fresh food available on the island was from the farm of the late Sidney Macintosh on the south side of the island. We all remember him with affection for his wonderful sense of humor. In his hen house was a big sign that read, "Remember, girls, an egg a day keep the butcher away." Those chickens must have been able to read, because they produced an awful lot of eggs.

The Macintosh chicken farm was nearly the most efficient operation on the island, second only to a visiting dentist I once found pulling teeth, forceps in hand, under the large shade tree south of the church. His dental chair was an empty whiskey case; the anesthesia was a shot of rum. He pulled 55 teeth in one day. It turned out that this was the well-known Australian sailor-dentist Bill Howell, who was giving free dental care in exchange for an engine repair. He complained the next day that he had a sore wrist from all the work he had done—and a sore head from all the rum he had drunk while pulling the teeth. The locals had sore heads from the rum anesthetic, and sore jaws where their teeth had been.

The food situation has improved greatly over the years. No longer do you have to go to Kingstown to stock up. Excellent breads of various types are available; there is a good selection of frozen meats; fresh fruit and vegetables can be purchased from the Rastas on the beach; eggs are fresh (and without a fishy taste). Goods vary from one store to another and from one season to another, so you'll probably have to start at the stores by the main dock and then walk along the road, stopping at the small establishments until you get as far as the supermarket near the slipway. By that time you should have found most of your supplies—and you'll want to find a spot to sit and have a cold beer.

In your wanderings for food, make sure you hit Miss Doris's shop right across from the Shell station. Miss Doris's shop has now expanded she now has all sorts of luxury items and caters to the charter yachts. What she doesn't have she most likely will be able to obtain for you. She has a wonderful selection and variety available. She is very helpful and friendly, and you usually can arrange to leave your purchases there while you wander hither and yon. What's more, she will advise you where to go to find what you have been unable to discover on your own.

Ice has always been something of a problem in Bequia. In years gone by, you gave the local schooner captain a sack and he would buy a 100-pound block of ice in Kingstown over on St. Vincent, but by the time he got back to Bequia, it was a 50-pound block of ice. Then the ice plant in Kingstown broke down, and two machines were set up in Bequia that sold ice at astronomical prices. Slowly the situation improved, until now there are a number of places in Bequia that sell both block and cube ice. The availability of block ice is variable, however, as the reliability of the block ice machines has not been great. As of July 1991, block ice was available at Grenadine Yacht Equipment and at the Harpoon Saloon.

Bequia has now become so civilized that the Bequia Bookshop, run by Ian Gale, is one of the best bookstores in the entire Eastern Caribbean. Not only does he stock general titles but also an excellent sailing library, plus the Street guides. He is one of Imray-Iolaire's most efficient chart agents in the Eastern Caribbean and also sells courtesy flags.

Near the western tip of Bequia on the north side is Moon Hole. Inside this cave, which passes directly through the island, one Tom Johnson built a house. But after a rock fell out of the roof of the cave and demolished his four-poster bed—which, fortunately, was unoccupied—he decided he needed a proper, safer house. Now the whole area around Moon Hole has expensive houses built by wealthy individuals who want to get away from it all. They have succeeded, since there is no road (access is by foot, donkey, or boat), no electricity (except what is provided by wind generators), no piped water, and, best of all, no telephones!

There are three good beaches—the one in front of town and two on the south side of the harbor. The easternmost one is called Princess Margaret (formerly Tony Gibbon) Beach; the western one is called Lower Bay. Both beaches are beautiful and frequently deserted. At the western end of Princess Margaret Beach is a cave through the rock that leads to another small beach about 20 feet wide with overhanging cliffs on all sides. Presumably this, too, was a favorite of Princess Margaret.

In Lower Bay on Sundays, there is always a good barbecue/beach party well attended by locals, visiting yachtsmen, and expatriates living on the island; it's a good way to spend Sunday and feed everyone. During the course of the day, there usually are small-boat races off the beach.

On the westernmost beach is a small bar and restaurant called The Reef. When visiting any of these bays in a dinghy, be warned that at certain times of the year, getting ashore in a dinghy is a major operation unless you are very adept at dinghy handling in surf.

In 1985, a young Canadian named Stephen Price, with the aid of Prime Minister "Son" Mitchell, was in the process of collecting bits and pieces of gear and whalebone, plus photos, letters, and the like, to set up a whaling museum in Lower Bay. It never got off the ground, but now Jan Gale of the Bequia Bookshop is on the committee—called the Bequian Heritage Foundation—so I am sure in years to come that there will be a whaling museum in Bequia.

ANSE DE CHEMIN
(II B-30, B-31)
This cove on the west side of the northwestern point of Bequia is seldom visited by yachtsmen. With the wind south of southeast, the anchorage is calm and you'll find three fathoms close to shore. There is good snorkeling, and ashore are the ruins of an old sugar plantation. No road, no people—an old-style, practically undisturbed West Indian anchorage.

PAGET FARM

On the south side of the western end of Bequia, at Paget Farm, there was formerly an anchorage that was usually calm and undisturbed by the ground swell, although there was always a wind that tended to put you onshore. It was the home of one of Bequia's largest fishing fleets, and of course they pulled their boats up on the beach. The people of Paget Farm are descendants of a French group that landed on the island sometime back in history (no one seems to know when). Now I doubt that there is an anchorage here, because the entire reef and beach area has been filled to create an airport. I first heard about plans for an airport in 1960, and now it looks as though it actually will come to be. Flying over the area in May 1991, I noted that the dredging was complete and it only needed to be surfaced. But who knows—with West Indian standards and financing arrangements, it may be 1994 before planes actually start landing. Don't hold your breath.

The airport is finished but very few planes fly in and out of it. The ferry service from Bequia to Kingston is so good and so frequent that it is faster to get on the ferry and go to Kingston than to go to Paget Farm and get an aeroplane to fly to Arnos Vale Airport and taxi to town. A tremendous waste of money that would be better spent on other projects in Bequia.

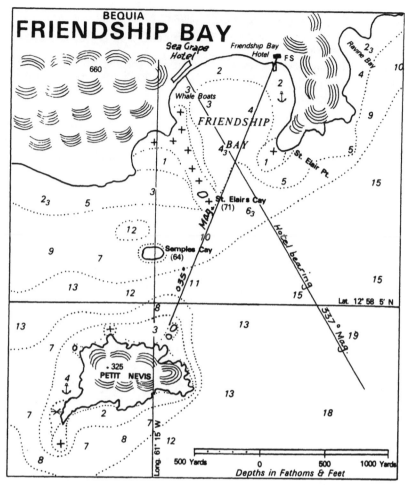

CHART 23 Bequia—Friendship Bay

FRIENDSHIP BAY
(Chart 23; II B-30, B-31)

This part of the island is well worth a visit by boat or taxi from Port Elizabeth. It is easy to enter; merely stay in the middle of the entrance to the harbor, steering 035° magnetic for the Friendship Bay Hotel flagpole or 337° magnetic for the Sea Grape Hotel. Anchor in the eastern corner of the harbor, where you will find the best protection from the ground swell. This is a smooth anchorage for the most part, although it is prone to some turbulent periods. The dock at the Friendship Bay Hotel is for dinghies only. The beach bar is to the west of it. There is good snorkeling on the reef out front, but be aware that the hotel discourages spearfishing. A long, white-sand beach extends from the hotel west to the settlement at Friendship. The beach is lined with pretty manchineel trees whose fruit, which resembles apples, is deadly poisonous.

On the western side of Friendship Bay is a small guest house called the Sea Grape Hotel, run by Sylvester. I am told the food is good and the prices are right; it is an economical place to spend a few days ashore.

At the western end of the beach are the whaleboats—big, heavy craft that weigh as much as a ton each. It's worth rising before dawn some morning to watch the Bequians launch them from the shore; they drag them back up in the evening. A rough way to earn a living. They go out after the humpback whale, a variety that usually travels in pairs, so that when one is caught, the second can be caught also. Often the charter boats will come racing down to watch the whaling boats after the first whale has been taken, making it very difficult to capture the second. The humpback is very fast and sharp of hearing. It is easily frightened, so it is best to stand off while the whalers conduct their business.

Whaling in Bequia is the livelihood of an impoverished people and should be distinguished from the reckless plunder carried out every year by large nations. Only occasionally nowadays is a whale caught out of Bequia, but when it is, the entire animal is used. The oil is sold to the States, the meat is eaten by the poor, and the bones are used to make scrimshaw.

The number of yachts sunk by whales in recent years either reflects an overall increase in the whale population or a new aggressiveness on the part of the mammals. Who knows, someday yachtsmen may end up urging that whaling be increased in order to cull the population. (If nothing else, that statement will instigate plenty of arguments 'round the bar.)

As of 1991, Bequians still were going after whales in the style of Captain Ahab in *Moby Dick*. They use a 30-foot, five-oared, double-ended whaleboat propelled by sail, oar, and paddles—the latter to approach a whale quietly in calm weather. They then strike with a hand-thrown harpoon and experience a Nantucket sleighride. If the hunt is successful, there follows a long, hard pull—towing a 20-ton whale by oar power. It is a slow, grueling occupation.

The Bequians have whaled for hundreds of years. When I first visited the island in 1959, every day during the whaling season (February through June), six whaleboats would be launched at dawn from the beach at Friendship Bay. Now the industry is slowly dying as boats and men retire, although two new boats have been built since 1984, the most recent one by Bequia's most famous harpooner, Athneal Ollivierre. Although he claims to be 60, most people say he is in his late seventies. Nonetheless, he still has the grip of a young man. He swore that 1989 was to be his last year of whaling, but his last year of whaling will probably be like Fred Astaire's last movie—in 1991, he was still at it, although he had caught no whales that year or the year before. When he signs off, an era will have ended.

In 1990, when we were doing a video with Rob and Dee Dubin for *Sailing Quarterly*, we were lucky enough to arrive in Bequia just as the whaling season was starting, and they were having the blessing of the whaleboats. It was a true ecumenical service, with Anglican and Catholic priests and representatives of one or two other denominations. Trust in God and keep your powder dry; get all the religions to bless the boat and hope that one of them has a direct line to God.

PETIT NEVIS

(Chart 23; II B-30, B-31)

This is where the whales caught by the Bequians are brought to be butchered, so whale bones are strewn along the shore. Most of the time, you will find the island deserted, except during weekends and holidays, when the people of Bequia come across to let the good times roll.

There is a good anchorage off the western shore of Petit Nevis, but the bottom falls off so steeply here that you must nearly set your bow ashore before dropping anchor. When the anchor is down, feed out plenty of scope. It is always calm here when it's windy. You can walk over to the windward side, where the beach varies from white sand to loose gravel, depending on the storms that year. This is an excellent picnic spot, and regardless of the condition of the beach, it is always cool, with the trades blowing through the palm trees.

In 1974, there were the beginnings of a great land development scheme on Petit Nevis, but after a few buildings were completed and a few roads started, the scheme fell flat. Too bad for the developers; a break for yachtsmen.

ISLE QUATRE

(II B-30, B-31)

Pretty to look at, but one must be something of a mountain goat to appreciate it. The anchorage is below the house on the northwestern shore in three fathoms of water. The house is perched on a ridge 400 feet above the sea and facing directly into the trades. It must have one of the best views in the entire Caribbean.

The southwestern cove of Isle Quatre can be entered by boats drawing six feet or less—both Ian Cowan of Sun Sail Stevens and John Corbet of *Freya* use this harbor. There is a maximum of a fathom and a half in the cove. The cove is completely reef-encumbered and should be attempted only by an experienced reef navigator under ideal conditions. Both Cowan and Corbet say it is impossible to give detailed sailing directions: Just enter on the eastern side of the cove and feel your way in, *but only under ideal circumstances with good light.* A Sun Sail Stevens charterer tried to get in at 1800, ran aground, knocked his rudder off, and was extremely lucky not to lose the boat.

PIGEON ISLAND
(II B-30, B-31)

Southwest of Bequia, this is little more than a rock sticking out of the water—with no harbor, no beach, and no reason to stop.

Mustique, Baliceaux, and Battowia

MUSTIQUE
(Chart 24; II B-30)

This island has always been a favorite of mine, but the times they are a-changing. Out to windward of the rest of the islands, it was seldom visited by the charter yachts. For many years, the island was owned by the Hazel family of St. Vincent. The first time I visited here, there was a small fishermen's camp on the northwest beach and a small community of farmers barely scratching out an existence.

The fishermen, who formerly camped at Cheltenham, would row their six-oared, double-ended boats down to Grand Bay to shoot their nets at twilight. If there was a yacht around, they would race, and it was quite a sight—12 huge fishermen heaving away and bending the huge, crude West Indian oars. That is all gone now. The fishermen still fish in Grand Bay, but they camp on the beach in the northeast corner and do most of their fishing under power.

All the OWIH (Old West Indies Hands—sailors who have been here 20 years or more) bemoan the fact that the formerly uninhabited islands of Palm, Petit St. Vincent, and Mustique, and semi-inhabited Canouan and Mayreau, are all in the hands of developers. However, one must look at the other side of the coin. In the late 1950s and early 1960s, the inhabitants of the middle Grenadines were practically starving to death, as there was literally nothing for them to do. The islands were too dry to grow anything but sea-island cotton, and the bottom had dropped out of that market. Fish were plentiful, but the economies of St. Vincent and Grenada were in poor shape, which meant that the fishermen could not get a decent price for their fish.

Then the developers arrived: Hazen Richardson and Doug Terman, backed by Mr. Nichols at Petit St. Vincent; and Johnny Caldwell, his wife, Mary, and his two sons on Prune (now Palm) Island. Their efforts were followed by significant developments at the Anchorage on Union Island, Salt Whistle Bay, and Mustique—all of which provided a lot of continuing employment. Most important, remember that the taxes paid by these five establishments in the Grenadines—Mustique, Palm, Petit St. Vincent, Salt Whistle Bay, and the Anchorage—go a long way toward supporting the government of St. Vincent.

One must also admit that these developments have been tastefully done and have destroyed neither the landscape nor the independence of the people.

As for Mustique, the ruins of an old warehouse have become the Cotton House, a splendid restaurant and one of the most magnificently restored buildings in the whole region. Numerous guest cottages around the Cotton House are so well restored that it is hard to tell which ones are original and which are new. A pier has been built, and an airstrip accommodates assorted charter and private planes, as well as LIAT, which flies to St. Vincent, Grenada, Union, and Barbados. Basic supplies can be purchased in the grocery store across the street from Basil's Bar, which is built out over the water near the pier and provides lunch, dinner, and some nightlife.

Mustique takes its name from the French word for mosquito. Although a valiant effort has been made to eliminate this pest, my advice is to get off the beach before sundown—from 1730 to 2000, the mosquitoes are out with a vengeance. Apparently they go to sleep at 2000.

Mustique should be approached cautiously. The offlying Montezuma Shoal has done in any number of ships, including the yacht *Lord Jim,* which might easily have become a total loss had a tug not hauled her off. The shoal bears 311.5° magnetic from the dock at Grand Bay. If you are beating up from Bequia against the easterly trade, under no circumstances should you fall eastward of Range C on Chart 24 until you have passed clearly north of Range B, which bears 136° magnetic on the rocks at the north end of Grand Bay. Staying northeast of Range B, stand in toward shore until east of Range A before working down into Grand Bay.

The best anchorage in Grand Bay is off the new dock. Feel your way in and anchor where the depth suits you. The current here is not particularly strong. It comes and goes at intervals, and frequently during the night you will find yourself

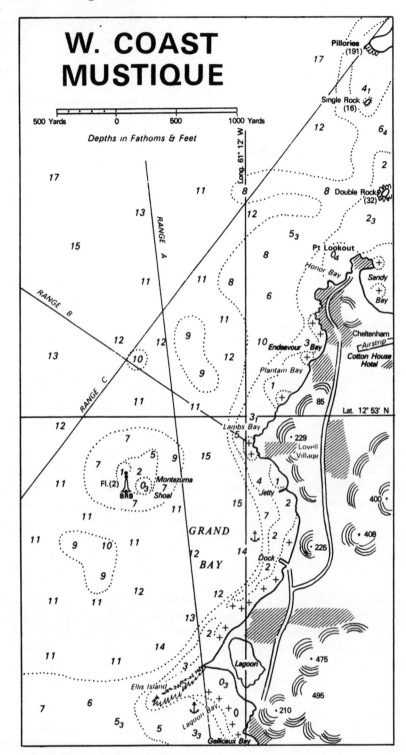

CHART 24 Mustique—West Coast

Range A. SW point of Mustique in line with NE point of Petit Mustique 006°–186° magnetic clears Montezuma Shoal to the E.

Range B. Rocks N end of Grand Bay bearing 136°–316° magnetic clears Montezuma Shoal to the NE.

Range C. Western Pillories in line with N summit of Baliceaux 051°–231° magnetic clears Montezuma Shoal to the W.

rolling for a few hours as the current swings you beam onto the wind, but I have never found it too uncomfortable.

Now that Mustique has become fairly popular with charter yachts, there usually is a cluster of boats anchored in Grand Bay, off the pub built out over the dock. It's just a short row ashore in the dinghy, after which the Cotton House is either a long walk or a short (but expensive) taxi ride away. The manager of the Cotton House, Robert B. Hoflund, who cut his teeth in the Caribbean tourism business at Petit St. Vincent, is doing an excellent job in Mustique. He also stocks Imray-Iolaire charts and Street guides.

A tour of Mustique is certainly worthwhile, but since taxis are fairly expensive, it may be smart to rent one of the little mopeds for the day. Explore the island and admire the beautiful houses, which obviously have been built without regard to expense. Most of them are in the traditional West Indian style.

Amazingly, we discovered in March 1985 that a place called Charlie House was operating a European-style bed-and-breakfast establishment at US$40 per day per couple—not cheap by European standards, but reasonable around here.

It is best to avoid Mustique on Sundays, as a schooner arrives from St. Vincent with a mob of day-trippers hell-bent on a fun-filled day at the beach.

Besides Montezuma Shoal—which I have mentioned and which is difficult to spot even on a clear day—there is a second hazard at Mustique that must be reckoned with. This is the shoal at the southern end of Grand Bay, which extends much farther to the southwest than old charts show. This shoal is growing continually and must be given a wide berth. South of this shoal is a white-sand beach under a steep cliff in Gellicaux Bay, a favorite anchorage of John Corbet of *Freya*. Princess Margaret has a house on the hill above. The southernmost bay, known as Shark Bay, has a rolly anchorage and does not sound too appealing.

Anchoring is not permitted in Mustique. You must pick up a mooring and pay the nightly rental fee. If they are all full, which is possible, you are allowed to anchor but you end up in very deep water on the edge of the shelf. Remember your anchor is trying to drag off the edge of the shelf, leave plenty of rode.

BALICEAUX
(Chart 25; II B-30, B-31)
One and a half miles long and a quarter mile wide,

north-northeast of Mustique, this high, rugged, seldom-visited island is inhabited by transients—fishermen who camp on the beach for weeks or months at a time. In the cove at the southwestern corner of the island is a nice little part-time anchorage. When the ground swell is running, however, this anchorage is impossible; the surf breaks so heavily onshore that even the fishermen cannot launch their boats. But during the spring and summer, it can be a great spot.

As you approach from the south, feel your way up, favoring the eastern shore. The reef to the west is extremely difficult to spot. There is only room enough for one or two boats, so if it is crowded here when you arrive, other anchorages can be found anywhere along the western side of the island, after you have skirted the reef. Once anchored, go ashore and enjoy the view from the top of the hill.

The fishermen here are a hardy lot. Many come down from Bequia for the day only. They leave Paget Farm on the southwestern coast of Bequia early in the morning in their 20-foot boats, beat eight miles out to Baliceaux, arriving before dawn, fish through the early morning, and then reach over to St. Vincent to sell their catch. Late in the day, they beat around the eastern end of Bequia and finish up with a final run down to Paget. This amounts to an 18- or 20-hour day of sailing, fishing, and rowing. It's small wonder that the Bequians are such a lean breed. I have the greatest respect for them.

BATTOWIA
(Chart 25; II B-30, B-31)
As far as I know, Battowia is another island seldom visited by yachtsmen. There is no harbor whatsoever. If the trades are not blowing too hard, an anchorage can be had west of the reefs extending to the west of Church Cay. A Bahamian moor will be required here, since the current runs strongly through the break between Battowia and Baliceaux. I am told by the fishermen that a dinghy landing can be made in the cove on the southeast corner of the island. Here, in the past, small boats would land to drop off and pick up supplies. The island was a sugar island, the only reminder of which is a ruined smokestack at the head of the cove. This is the island where the British detained several thousand Carib tribesmen captured on St. Vincent in the eighteenth century. Now Battowia is uninhabited, but it remains a delightful place to visit when the weather permits.

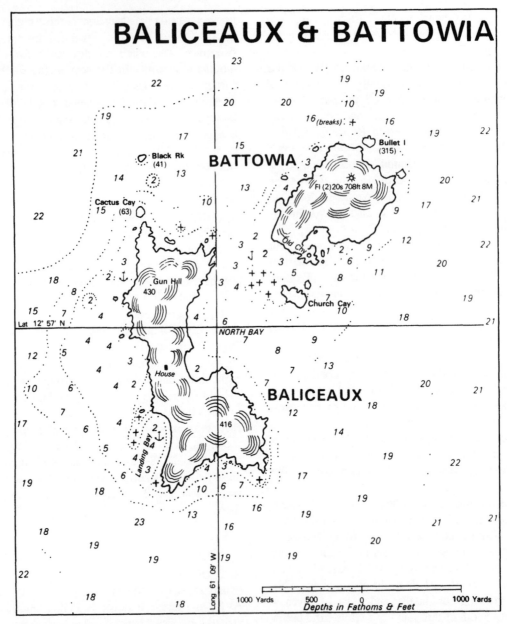

CHART 25   Baliceaux and Battowia

PETIT MUSTIQUE

(II B-31)

A small, steep island south of Mustique with no anchorages and little of interest. As far as I know, it is not visited by yachtsmen.

SAVAN ISLAND

(II B-31)

Well to windward of Petit Canouan. If you are heading south from Mustique, this is a possible overnight anchorage in settled conditions. But the only person I know who has spent the night here is Richard Scott Hughes, a famous charter captain, who stopped here when skippering *Boekanier*, a 65-foot schooner. John Corbet of *Freya* claims that you are likely to rock and roll here so much that your charter party will be seasick in a hurry. He advises making it a day stop; go ashore and have a beach party rather than staying on the boat.

One can anchor in the lee of this island, or between the islands with one anchor on the windward of the two and a second anchor on the reef to leeward. The current runs strongly there, which no doubt accounts for the excellent fishing. No one would suspect that anyone would live on this little pile of rocks, but someone does, and charges visitors for the right to camp or fish. If it is not blowing hard, a north-to-south passage between the islands makes for a spectacular sail. Be sure to have your camera ready on the starboard side as you emerge from the channel: You will see an impressively massive stone arch created by the tides.

PETIT CANOUAN
(II B-31)

Four miles northeast of Canouan, this is steep-to and offers no anchorage possibilities.

Canouan Island

The British island of Canouan is one of the largest in the Grenadines and remains one of the least known and least populated. It offers a variety of good anchorages for visiting yachtsmen. If you are approaching from the south, the westernmost peak of the island, Glossy (or Glassy) Hill, will appear detached from the rest. The narrow, low-lying sand spit that separates it from Taffia Hill is hard to spot from any distance. When approaching from the north, Canouan is the first sizable island after Mustique or Bequia. Its main anchorage is Charlestown Bay.

In the last century, Canouan was a major outpost of the whaling ships. During winters in the 1890s, as many as 20 New Bedford schooner-whalers could be seen anchored in its lee. Although whaling finally died out here in the 1920s, one still encounters scattered remains of whaleboats in the area. (Canouan is covered by Imray-Iolaire Charts B-3, B-31, and B-311, and Charts 26 and 27 in this book.)

Canouan was owned for roughly 100 years by the Snagg family as a private estate. Evidently they made a lot of money from cotton, corn, pigeon peas, and fish. You can see this for yourself by taking the path from the northeast corner of Charlestown Bay across the hill—it's about a 20-minute walk—to the careenage. Here you will find the remains of the old estate buildings, and one of the largest cisterns I have ever seen. It must have held about 40,000 gallons of water. There is also a beautiful old church, one of the biggest I have seen in the Eastern Caribbean outside the towns. The church

was built in the 1860s, completely paid for by the resident Snagg. It has beautiful bronze bells that were cast in England in 1867, but these, sadly, lie on the ground outside the church. The east wall, now bricked in, probably had a stained-glass window. The roof blew off in the 1921 hurricane, and the window probably was blown in at the same time. Repairs were then made to the wall by bricking it in and to the roof by covering it with corrugated iron.

From the look of the buildings and the church, this certainly must have been a prosperous island, even after the slaves were freed in 1838. You can see traces of wide roads with good retaining walls, drainage systems, and other signs of careful planning. Horses were raised and used by the manager, the owner, and his family; oxen were used for plowing and hauling carts. (The only other island in the Caribbean where oxen are found is Marie Galante.) Each laborer had a section of fence to maintain so that the donkeys, goats, and sheep didn't chew up the crops.

There were two whaling fisheries on this island, besides the offshore whaling operation based here. These all died out just prior to World War I. The estate obviously was still relatively prosperous by the 1920s, because the church was repaired after the 1921 hurricane. Unfortunately, the windmill-powered cotton gin went with the hurricane, as did the school, which was in the same area as the Snagg estate. The new school was built down in the main part of town at the southern end of the harbor.

Henry Snagg died in 1924, and then things started going downhill—to the extent that the majority of the estate was sold to the St. Vincent government in the 1930s.

At the present time, the island has only 600 to 700 people, who are supported mainly by money from family members working overseas. As recently as 1980, there were just three vehicles on the island—one tractor, one pickup owned by the Crystal Sands Hotel, and the police Land Rover.

The St. Vincent government has built an airstrip; Island Air comes on schedule, and there are charter flights. The field is unfenced and untended, however, so occasionally planes cannot land until the waiting passengers chase livestock off the runway. I have even seen a dog chasing an airplane landing here. What one doesn't see in these islands!

There is a very nicely designed small hotel, the Crystal Sands, right on the excellent beach at Charlestown. The hotel formerly was run by Mrs. Phileus De Roche. (Her husband originally got into the tourist business as crew on Walter Boudreau's boat *Ramona*, a 112-foot schooner that was

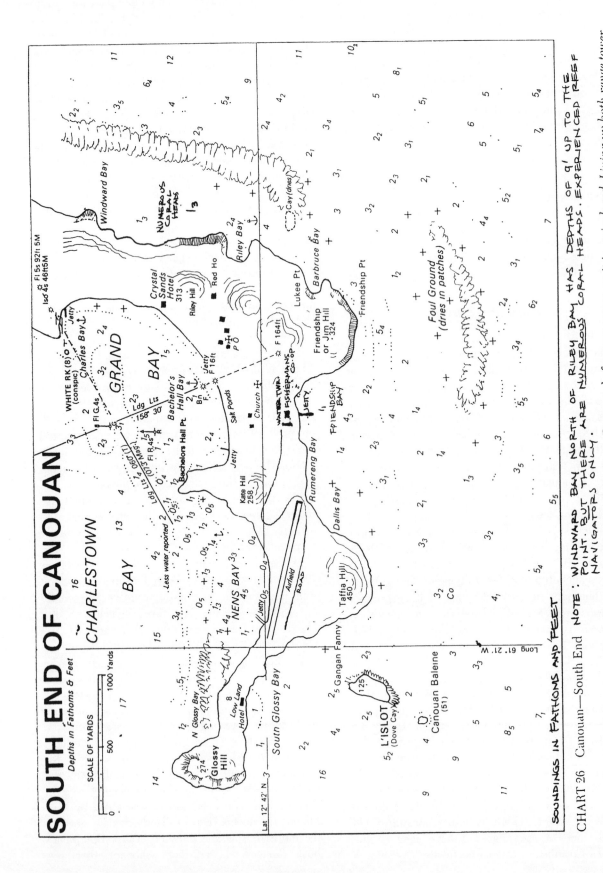

CHART 26 Canouan—South End

Range A. Forward range tower brought to bear 045° magnetic. Note: Disregard aft range tower, as it is misplaced Lining up both range tower (073° magnetic, not the 055° shown on the government chart) places one extremely close to the conspicuous white rock

Northern Grenadines 103

subsequently lost, along with a number of crew, on Bermuda's northeast breakers.) Unfortunately, the Crystal Sands Hotel encountered financial difficulties and was closed in the winter of 1985. Happily, it has all been reorganized, and the hotel is now open for lunch, dinner, and drinks. Another spot for a meal is the Bijou, which you can contact on channel 68 (reservations are necessary).

CHARLESTOWN BAY

(Chart 26; II B-3, B-31)

When entering Charlestown Bay, carefully check Chart 26 in this book, as both the British Admiralty chart and the chart in Julius Wilensky's *Yachtsman's Guide to the Windward Islands* are wrong. The Admiralty chart shows the range in the northeast corner of the harbor bearing 055° magnetic; this range is actually 073° (checked December 1978). This leads to within 20 or 25 yards of the conspicuous white-topped rock in the northeast corner of Charlestown Bay.

The range in the southeast corner of the harbor is listed as 158°30' true (171°30' magnetic), but this was not operating in December 1978 when we were there. The red spar buoy in the middle of the harbor was there.

When approaching Charlestown Bay from the north, sail down the lee coast of Canouan and head for the dock on the south side of the harbor until the conspicuous white rock in the northeast corner bears 070° magnetic. Then come to a course of 100° magnetic, and hold this course until the *forward* range mark bears 045° magnetic. Then run in on this course, disregarding the back range mark entirely. Anchor somewhere in the corner according to your draft.

One can anchor off the Crystal Sands Hotel in 10 feet of water, but the wind loops over the hill, making you lie stern-to the beach. Sometimes it is calm, but if a ground swell is running, it would be most uncomfortable, sometimes dangerous. Make sure when anchoring that you drop the anchor in a patch of sand and not in the grass. If it is blowing hard, you will be well advised to use two anchors out in a "Y" to the northeast.

There is an old wooden dock in the southwest corner of Charlestown Bay, but in the middle of the bay, near the Crystal Sands Hotel, is a large new ferry dock that would be a good place to moor your dinghy while venturing ashore.

NENS BAY

(Chart 26; II B-3, B-31, B-311)

According to the charts, there is a seemingly good anchorage in the bay due north of Taffia Hill, Nens Bay. From an airplane, it also looks like an ideal anchorage. I have visited this spot only once, and I was rocked all night long. The reef on the north side of the bay affords less protection than the charts indicate. There is about three or four feet of water over the reef—enough to let the ground swell from the north come rolling in. For the winter months, therefore, I would have to rule out this spot. Only in the summer, when there is no ground swell and the wind is in the southeast, is this adequate for anything more than daytime stops. The bottom is grass, and the holding is wretched. The night I spent there, I had to dive to the bottom, dig a hole, and bury my anchors before they would hold. The reef appears excellent for snorkeling, and there is an attractive small beach in the cove on the eastern side of the bay. Over the bar at the entrance, the water is eight feet deep, but you must stay within 50 yards of the eastern point as you enter. When the sand beach falls abeam to port, bear off toward the middle of the harbor. There is plenty of water inside the reef; anchor anywhere, but don't plan to spend the night. It is only a short walk west from this anchorage to the new Canouan Beach Hotel complex at South Glossy Bay.

CORBEC BAY

(Sketch Chart 27; II B-3, B-31)

Corbec provides a small anchorage only slightly larger than L'Anse Goyeau. There isn't much of a beach ashore, but again there is good snorkeling. If you want a white-sand beach to walk on, go over a small spit of land to the northern end of Rameau Bay. This beach, although fine for sunning and exploring, is not good for swimming, as it goes from white sand to rock. However, the snorkeling is good.

L'ANSE GOYEAU (GUYAC)

(Sketch Chart 27; II B-3, B-31)

There are a number of other anchorages northwest of Charlestown Harbor, if you'd rather be alone. L'Anse Goyeau is a very attractive small cove with room for just one boat. It's probably best to moor bow-and-stern. The beach ashore is not too good, but the snorkeling is excellent, and you may find small lobsters.

South of Cor Point, the point that forms the southern end of L'Anse Goyeau, you can find a moderately good anchorage if you moor bow-and-stern and on a northwest-southeast axis in Little Bay. There is about 10 feet of water quite close to shore, and everyone can go snorkeling right from the boat, making this a good lunchtime stop.

RAMEAU BAY
(Sketch Chart 27; II B-3, B-31)

This bay is really too exposed for anchoring, but along the shore are a number of very small white-sand beaches, ideal for honeymoon couples landing with a bottle of wine, a picnic lunch, and hopes for an all-over suntan. You are just a short dinghy ride from the anchorage in Charlestown Bay.

SOUTH COAST OF CANOUAN

There is good exploring along the south and southeast coasts of the island (see Imray-Iolaire Chart B-311 and Chart 26 in this book). If the ground swell is not running or if it is not blowing too hard, there is sometimes an anchorage between L'Islot (Dove Cay) and the mainland. Due north of L'Islot is excellent. Sail in and check it out. If it looks calm, drop the hook and enjoy yourself. Farther east, between Taffia and Friendship hills, is another anchorage, but the approach requires careful eyeballing. Post someone in the rigging and stand in cautiously under power or on starboard tack. There is good holding here on a white-sand bottom, excellent swimming, and not too much of a swell unless the wind is from the southeast.

SOUTH GLOSSY BAY (SOUTH GLASSY BAY)
(Chart 26; II B-3, B-31, B-311)

This anchorage varies. I have anchored here, rolled my guts out, stayed for an hour, and picked up my anchor and moved. But the last time we were here, in February 1985, there was only a slight roll and we anchored happily for the afternoon, evening, and following morning.

We also went ashore to the new Canouan Beach Hotel, which finally appears to be making it. It was built a number of years ago but succumbed to the usual problem faced by West Indian projects:

undercapitalization. It went bust three times in a period of a few years, but now it seems to be properly financed and will be a major development in years to come. It has a nice, big dining room, and many cottages under construction. In 1985, a suction dredge was standing by to start dredging the swamp east of the hotel to create a marina with 10 feet of water in it, but as of 1991, nothing had happened. (As everywhere else in the Caribbean, seeing is believing.) The plan is for fuel, water, electricity, and ice to be available, plus a specialty shop that imports French wine, cheese, and cold cuts from Martinique. A boutique is also in the offing. In years to come, this may well become a must stop for charter yachts heading north and south through the Grenadines.

Before you make plans to stop here, however, check on the situation. I have heard (third hand) that the hotel is known as a nice resort that does not cater to yachtsmen. It's no use anchoring, visiting the beach, and smelling good French food—only to discover you can't get in. History may be repeating itself. For many years, the Anchorage Hotel on Union Island was serving wonderful French food to Frenchmen who flew in for the day (a very expensive outing) from Martinique, but when yachtsmen approached, they were told the restaurant was not open to the public—supposedly the 25 or so guests sitting at the bar and in the restaurant were just personal friends of the owner. Such a strange modus operandi.

South Glossy Bay has crystal-clear water, a white-sand bottom, and long stretches of beautiful beach.

EAST COAST OF CANOUAN
(Chart 26; II B-3, B-31)

For the seasoned sailor, deep water can be carried to windward around Friendship Point and a good way north inside the reefs. Boats drawing eight feet have gone up through here. Within the reefs, the current is always running south, and at times too strongly for a person to swim against. You will find complete privacy here, good swimming and snorkeling, and great shelter. A boat drawing five feet or less can easily make its way north all the way to the head of the bay—carefully. Marcy Crow took his *Xantippe*, drawing six feet three inches, all the way to the village at the very end of the basin. A good deal of skill is required for this, however. The deepest water is fairly close to shore off the beaches and at the points of land no more than 30 yards offshore. It is a matter of feeling your way in with a

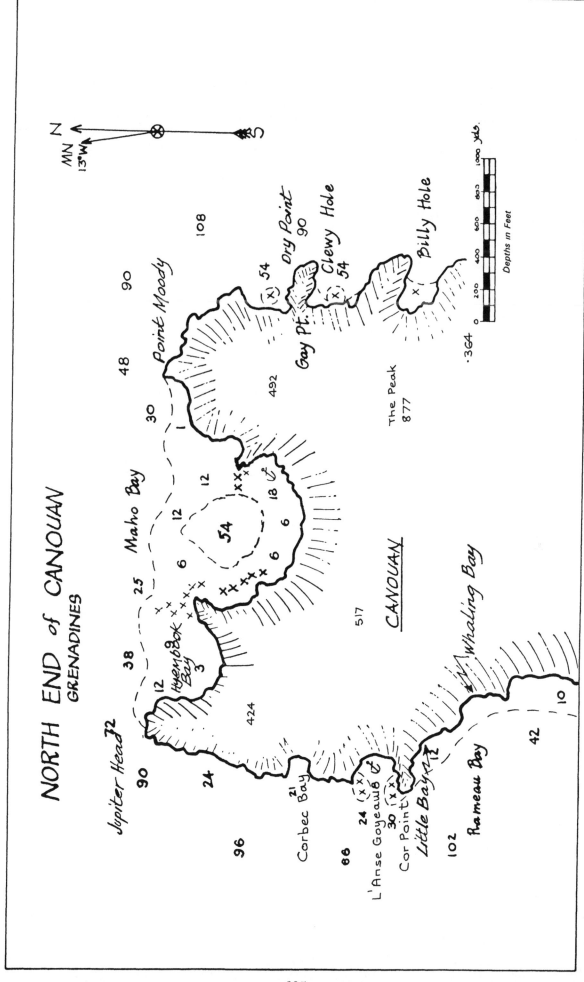

SKETCH CHART 27 Canouan—North End

boathook or with someone leading in a dinghy. When you reach the head of the basin, there is an old church ashore that is worth a look.

In 1999 *Li'l Iolaire* sailed up into Windward Bay—my first visit to this wonderful anchorage. When entering Windward Bay definitely favor the Canouan shore. The deep water is very close to shore. there is plenty of water up to Riley Bay, but remember that the sea is coming in over the top of the reef. There you will discover quite a strong south going current all the time, strongest when the tide is ebbing. The flood tide does not overcome this south going current.

You can sail north as far as Windward Bay with no trouble, as long as you are a good reef pilot. There is 9-foot of water over the sand, but coral heads stick 2 to 3 feet above the sand. It is strictly a case of having a man in the RIGGING and zig zagging through the coral heads. There are too many coral heads to plot on a chart.

This is a superb anchorage as the beaches are soft white sand completely litter free. There is nothing to windward of you but Africa, so there is no garbage floating down from another island. There are no houses, a perfect anchorage for the person who wants to get away from it all.

It is not worth while going north of the north end of Windward Bay then the water gets shallower. Also you are then getting into the area of the ultra exclusive hotel at the north end of Canouan which I do not think appreciates intrusions of itinerant yachtsmen.

I have heard claims that it is possible to enter this basin from the north through a break in the reef, but I tend to discount this as a local boast of derring-do. I have observed the area from the air, and the approach looked quite impossible, although I suppose one or two boats may have done it. I am quite certain that where the charts say three fathoms, you'll find no more than two.

The other bays on the northeast corner of Canouan are not feasible, as they face out into the eastern wind and swell.

NORTH COAST OF CANOUAN
(Sketch Chart 27; II B-3, B-31)
Maho Bay, on the northern end of the island, can be a beautiful summer anchorage when the wind is in the south, but I do not recommend using it in the winter. If you do, rig two anchors and be prepared to move out if the swell makes up. There is a beautiful white-sand beach in the southeast corner of the bay. The best spot to anchor is in the extreme southeast corner, very close inshore. In the past, the cove has been a superb place to get away from the herd, but rumor has it that a new development has been started here. Reports indicate, however, that it will be ecologically responsible, with no high-rises and no disruption of the environment. Time, of course, will tell. Don't hold your breath.

This area is inside the new exclusive ultra expensive resort area—I doubt if they will appreciate yachtsmen anchoring in this cove.

NOTES

ADMIRALTY BAY
(Chart 18; II B-30, B-31)

Admiralty Bay has become very popular with yachtsmen and the harbor is full most of the year. Anchoring is difficult because of the fact that there has been extensive dredging in Bequia harbor all the older charts are wrong as there is much more water than the charts show. Even the chart in this guide may not be correct when you go to anchor. With the dredging even if they haven't dredged where you are anchoring the sand tends to move and fall into the holes. Thus you think the chart shows you are anchoring in 15ft. of water and suddenly you discover you are in 25ft. of water.

There are many reasons why the harbor is so popular. One of the main reasons is the water based facilities. Not only are there water taxis available from early morning to quite late at night, but also there is a water barge that will come along side and pump water into your tanks without you having to go alongside. Fuel—both gasoline and diesel—can also be brought out to your boat. Ice is delivered by various water taxis who specialise in ice delivery. There is one nice girl who comes around with fresh bread every morning. You can call on the radio— Daffodil Laundry—and they will come and pick up your laundry.

On the north side of the harbor there is a miniature industrial park. Mr. Fixit who seems to fix anything, and also a couple of marine supply stores which are very well equipped with Chandlery and a fishing supply store. There is a canvas shop that make dodgers, awnings and covers. There are two sail makers, both of whom are excellent. a look at the local work boats pulled up on shore will show you that there certainly are good carpenters available if you search them out.

Bequia Slipway is back in operation and has a railway—no side tracking—but can haul quite large boats.

For food there is plenty of fresh food available from ladies selling it along side the road and also in the waterfront vegetable market there is excellent produce market dominated by the Rastas.

For supplies, other than fresh fruit and vegetables, there are about four different places in which you can shop. It is just a case of walking and checking the stores. There is one up market store, Doris Fresh Food, that has a tremendous selection of really good meat, wine, cheese and luxury items. What she doesn't have she can obtain on short order. Also, she does yacht provisioning for some of the large charter yachts.

Beside Daffodil Laundry who will pick it up and deliver it back to the boat, there are other various laundry services ashore.

Ross Lulley has passed on to Sailors Val Halla but his widow and off spring operate an excellent store for fishing, diving gear and other bits and pieces in a shop behind the Anglican Church.

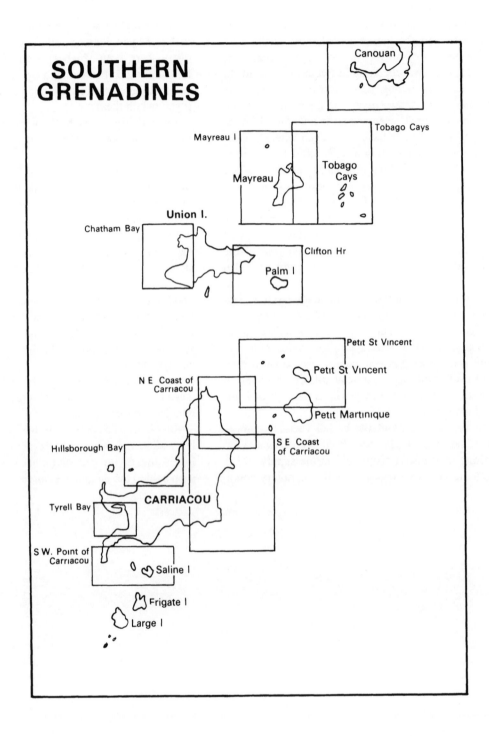

7

Southern Grenadines

(Imray-Iolaire Charts 1, B, B-3, B-31, B-32, B-311)

IMPORTANT: When in the area between the southern end of Canouan and the northern end of Carriacou (including Petit St. Vincent and Petit Martinique), use Imray-Iolaire Chart B-311. Also, do not rely on buoyage lights and ranges in St. Vincent and Grenadines waters.

TOBAGO CAYS

(Chart 29, Sketch Chart 30; II B-3, B-31, B-311)

Please be aware that the Tobago Cays (pronounced "keys") have been designated a national park, and ALL fishing, of every type, is forbidden. Spearfishing, grabbing lobsters with a noose, or even dangling a handline overside—it is all banned. Unfortunately, many foreign yachtsmen (especially French ones) honor this rule in the breach rather than the observance. The only way the St. Vincent government is going to preserve fish and shellfish in the Grenadines is to do what is done in Bonaire—they inspect all the boats, confiscate all spearguns, and keep them in the Customs office until the boat departs. The island of Bonaire is so law-abiding that they will let you keep your guns on board but not your spearguns!

It sounds very drastic, but considering the misbehavior and illegal activity among yachtsmen regarding spearfishing and fishing in the Grenadines, no one could object if the St. Vincent government adopted the same attitude as Bonaire.

If you are a diver and would like to dive and look rather than shoot, you can get on VHF channel 68 and call Dive Anchorage, Grenadines Diver, or Palm Island—any one of the three will arrange to pick you up at your boat. They will arrive with all equipment and will take you to one of the good dive sites in the area.

The Tobago Cays have been without a doubt the most popular, publicized, and photographed cruising attraction in the entire Caribbean. The islands are low, dry, and uninhabited; rimmed with palm trees and white sand; and surrounded by miles of fabulous reefs—the *pièce de résistance* of a Caribbean charter. Now, though, the cays are so overcrowded that they are losing their charm—fast.

First, there's simply the matter of too many boats and too little privacy. I suppose this is inevitable, and it's a familiar lament among yachtsmen almost everywhere these days.

More serious is the garbage problem: As the years go by, the quality of yachtsmen seems not to have kept up with the quantity. People used to be very careful about not polluting the area with trash. (If a few bits and pieces got scattered around, the charter skippers would get together and organize a cleanup—and then have a celebratory party on one of the boats.) For the past few years, the Tobago Cays have begun to resemble a garbage dump, and the problem seems almost insurmountable. Unless *every* visitor learns to carry all trash back to the boat, or unless the St. Vincent government sets up a disposal or collection scheme—which would be an appropriate way to spend some of the income generated by the yachts—the area may well be ruined before too long.

Furthermore, the cays are almost fished out—hence the government's designation of the area as a national park. Years ago, Bequian fishermen started to come down to the cays and camp out on the beach, diving on the reefs to provide lobster for visiting yachts. As the influx of yachts grew, the fishermen spent more and more time in the cays; they even built a permanent house on Petit Rameau. To make things worse, the French from Martinique discovered the cays as a cheap source of fish and lobster and began to buy up everything they could, quickly depleting the supply.

Still, there's no denying the beauty of the Tobago Cays, and if you're lucky or are cruising in the off-season, you'll find a lot of pleasure here. Even though you can't go spearfishing, you're sure to find interesting shelling on the shoals surrounding the cays. Be sure, however, to don a pair of sneakers to protect your feet as you wade about. And, finally, laid-back visitors can have a fine time just lazing about under a deck awning, listening to the water slapping against the hull, or lying ashore in the shade of a palm tree. In the evening, some visitors enjoy having barbecues on the beaches.

The tides run swiftly through the cays, and your movements and activities—especially diving—should be planned accordingly. A swift tide can take you by surprise; every season at least one insurance claim is made for yachts colliding in these narrow straits. If you are approaching a crowded anchorage, you may be wise to drop sail and motor in.

Once into the cays, you may anchor anywhere along the slot between Petit Rameau and Petit Bateau in a full two fathoms. I prefer to moor on the south side of the slot near the shoal that forms the western end of the beach on Petit Bateau. Best to use a Bahamian moor; otherwise, when the tide runs to windward, it will swing your stern into the wind, even when it is blowing 20 knots through the slot. The effect will be to waltz a boat in a 300-foot circle. This can present a problem if there are other boats in the area. Large boats usually anchor to leeward of the cays. If the anchorage within the slot is too crowded, a good anchorage can be had close to shore southwest of Baradal. There is plenty of room here, and no need for a two-anchor rig.

For those who value privacy and wish to be close to a reef, an anchorage can be had close behind Horseshoe Reef. It is cool, breezy, calm, and bugless. If you are planning to stay more than a few hours, two anchors are recommended: a Bahamian moor during the full or new moon if the wind is light; or, during a small moon—neap tides—and heavy weather, use two anchors ahead in a "Y." Given the crowded condition of the cays, I feel that this is now the only place to anchor. It may be a little choppy and certainly will be very windy, but you will be guaranteed privacy and good snorkeling.

The true adventurer in a centerboarder or a bilge-keel boat can anchor behind the reef east of Petit Tabac. A boat drawing three and a half feet can enter the break in the reef at the northwest corner of the island. The depth in behind the reef is about five feet.

Expert divers, and good small-boat handlers who want some exciting diving, should go to the other edge of Horseshoe Reef and to Worlds End Reef. If the weather is not too rough, you can reach them by dinghy via the small-boat pass through Horseshoe Reef (see Charts 28 and 29). You'll need to line up this range very carefully—i.e., the southeast end of Petit Rameau should line up with the cut in the hill that is north of the low area of Mayreau Island. It is easy enough to remember this range when going out, but when you are coming back, tired and wet, it is easy to miss, as you are coming downwind through the surf. And if you miss this pass, you will be swamped. I know this from personal experience, as I became confused coming downwind from Worlds End Reef and was swamped. Luckily, we got through without serious damage.

On this subject, I strongly advise that you trace the profile of this range and take it with you in a plastic bag. Furthermore, I suggest that all cameras and loose gear be packed in waterproof bags and tied down individually or in a bag whenever you are landing a dinghy through surf or passing through surf-surrounded reef areas. Then, if the dinghy capsizes or swamps, the bits and pieces will still be attached to the boat and can be retrieved easily. If everything is lying loose and the boat capsizes, then fins, spears, guns, cameras, face masks, and the rest of your gear will be spread over a wide area and usually will be lost.

Worlds End Reef, east of the Tobago Cays, provides a good anchorage under its lee if it is not blowing too hard. However, this anchorage should be attempted only by yachtsmen who are very experienced and can handle their boats in tight situations. You must be good at eyeball navigation and have plenty of ground tackle. If you want to spend the night at Worlds End Reef, you should be moored on a chain with at least two anchors out—if you started to drag during the night, you'd be in serious trouble, as eyeball navigation simply doesn't work in the dark, even with a full moon.

Approaching the Tobago Cays from either north or south should not be difficult. However, new buoyage and ranges have been installed (see Chart 29), and these do little but confuse the issue; they serve no useful purpose except for a boat that uses engine only. The marked entrance from the west along the top of Mayreau Island is one that a

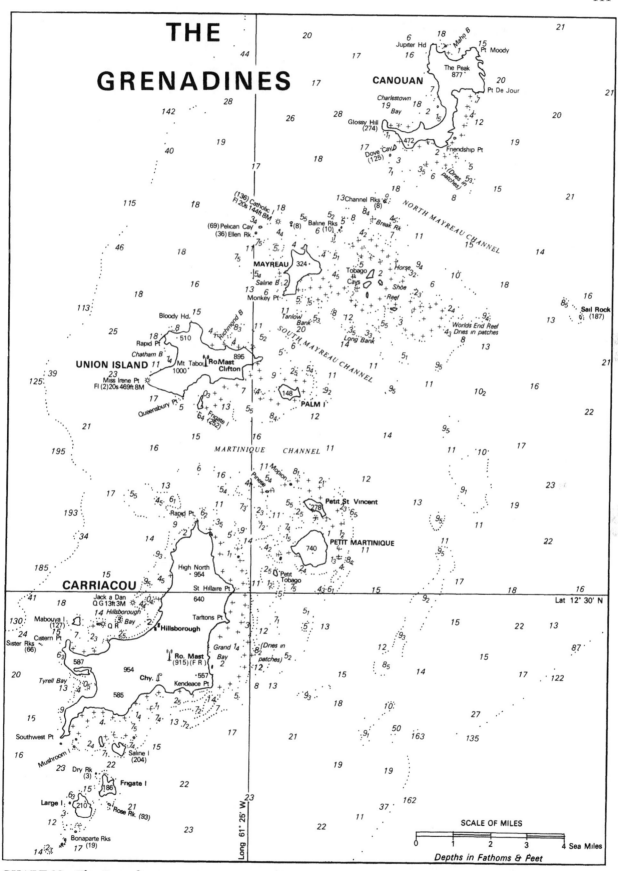

CHART 28   The Grenadines

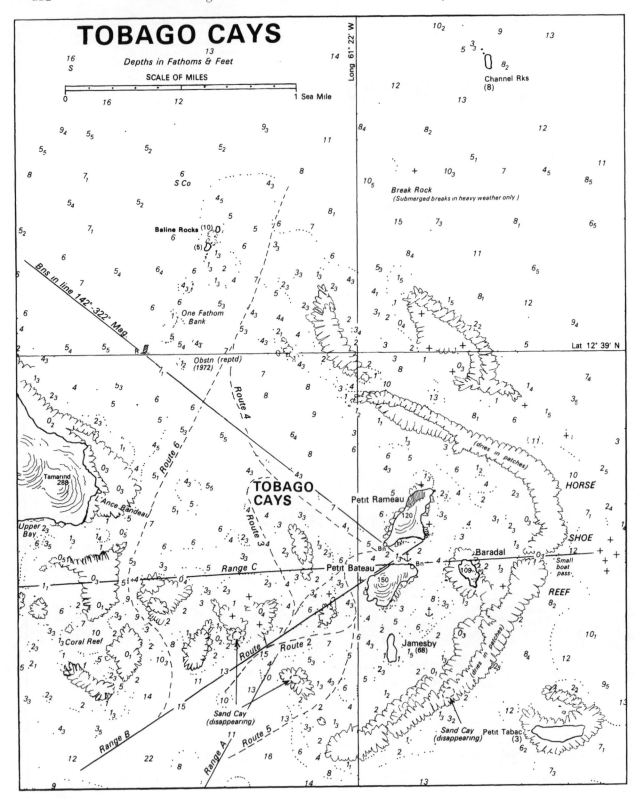

CHART 29   Tobago Cays

Range A.   Middle hill on Palm Island under High North, Carriacou, 043°–223° magnetic leads through S entrance to Tobago Cays.

Range B.   SE point of Petit Rameau in line with NW point of Petit Bateau 071°–251° magnetic leads through S entrance to Tobago Cays.

Range C.   N end of Baradal in line with N end of Petit Bateau in line with S edge of flat land on Mayreau, 100°–280° magnetic, leads through boat pass.

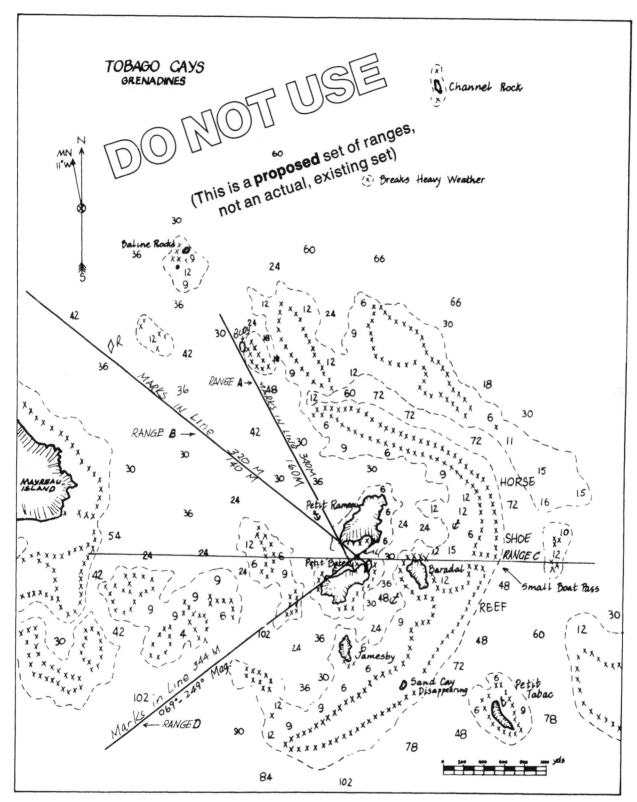

SKETCH CHARTS 30   "Tobago Cays (Proposed Ranges)"

Range A.   (Northern entrance to the cays) Marker on SW end of Petit Rameau (existing mark) in line with mark (to be installed) on N side of Petit Bateau in line with 340°–160° magnetic. Possibly a buoy should be placed as noted on chart to lead clear of reefs NW of the cays.

Range B.   (Western entrance to the cays) Existing range and buoy.

Range C.   (Small–boat pass through outer reefs) Establish marks at N end of Petit Bateau and Baradal—in line to lead through boat pass.

Range D.   (Southern entrance to the cays) Mark on NW corner of Petit Bateau in line with mark on SE corner of Petit Rameau (both marks to be established), 069°–249° magnetic, plus possibly buoy as marked on the chart to keep boats in really deep water instead of having them dodge reefs on Routes 1 and 2 in Chart 29.

sailboat can lay only if the wind is well in the north; this course *cannot* be laid under sail in normal conditions. Below are described some of the approaches that have been used by yachtsmen in this area since time immemorial.

Approaching the Tobago Cays from the North: Coming from the north, you should pass to windward of Baline Rocks, trim sheets, and skirt to leeward of the reefs southeast of Baline Rocks. Take care here, as a number of boats have clipped this reef too close and have bounced off. Luckily, there is an inner and outer reef, and the outer reef breaks most of the swell, so the boats were not badly damaged. Hold a course of approximately 160° magnetic to the southwest tip of Petit Rameau and all will be well.

If, however, you approach the cays from the north but wish to pass through them and on down direct to Palm Island or Petit St. Vincent, it is best to follow Route 6 (all routes are shown on Chart 29 in this chapter). Sail to windward of Baline Rocks and hold a course of around 200° magnetic to the reefs to windward of Mayreau; pass between the reef east of Mayreau and the reef to the east again of that. The channel is narrow but deep; there is no water, port or starboard, but about 40 feet beneath. Continue on this course with a crew member in the rigging, not just on the bowsprit—this is essential, as the channel takes a sharp turn to port and you enter it on a beam reach. Start sheeting in halfway through the channel. At the end, you will be almost hard on the wind, since the axis of the south end of the channel is southeast-northwest. Once clear of the reef to starboard, you can ease sheets and head for Palm Island, Petit St. Vincent, or wherever.

This route is very useful when sailing directly from Bequia or Canouan to Petit St. Vincent and Palm Island, for if you pass to *leeward* of Mayreau, you have to beat back eastward to reach Palm and Petit St. Vincent.

If you are sailing through the cays from south to north and do not intend to stop, pass between the reefs on Range 9 (Chart A in chapter 1), then ease sheets and follow Route 3 northward (Chart 29), joining up with Route 4 and exiting to windward of Baline Rocks.

Approaching the Tobago Cays from the West: If coming under power, no problem—just head for the buoy southwest of Baline Rocks and pick up the newly established range. The course is 139° magnetic, established under the direction of the Canadian experts. This leads directly to the anchorage, in the slot. If, however, you are beating to windward under sail and cannot lay the range, be careful of the nine-foot spot approximately 800 yards south-southwest of Baline Rocks—indeed a case of eyeball navigation.

Approaching the Tobago Cays from the South: When approaching from the south, you should work well to the east until you find Range 9 (Chart A in chapter 1 or Imray-Iolaire Chart B-311). The middle hill on Palm Island should be directly under High North (also known as Mount St. Louis) on Carriacou. This leads between the two disappearing sand islands on Route 1 (Chart 29), and into the Tobago Cays. This is a dead-accurate range that I have used for years. However, as you approach this narrow channel, you can get into trouble if a rain squall blocks out either Palm Island or Carriacou. Thus, a bow range is useful. One that Mike Forshaw has given me (it was given to him in 1938) also leads to the same opening. Put the southeast corner of Petit Rameau just closing with the northwest corner of Petit Bateau and you are set to go through the channel between the two disappearing sand islands. Once through the channel, it is again a case of eyeball navigation, following one of the routes described in Chart 29. One trouble with this range is that unless the wind is well around to the south, it will be impossible to use under sail; you will have to motorsail to use it. Do not attempt to use Route 5 when entering the cays from the south, as there is no range leading to this route; it is an exit route only.

Leaving the Tobago Cays: When leaving the cays to the north, just reverse the entry procedure. For boats heading south, Routes 1 and 5 (Chart 29) are the most popular. Route 5 is most favored for boats heading directly to Petit St. Vincent and passing to windward of Palm Island, since if you use Route 1 when going to Palm, you will throw away a quarter mile of windward ground.

The St. Vincent government has established a buoyage system that I think acts more like a booby-trap arrangement to nail the careless yachtsman. What the government needs to do is establish a buoyage system that would lead boats clear of all dangers. Many yachtsmen feel that range marks should be established in the Tobago Cays as per Sketch Chart 30.

Elsewhere in the Grenadines, Grand de Coi should certainly be marked by a day marker, perch, or what-have-you, directly on top of the reef, which bares at low-water springs. Johnny Caldwell of Palm Island has been volunteering to do this for years, but the St. Vincent government has never accepted his offer.

Montezuma Shoal should also be marked in the

same fashion. I would think that the developers of Mustique would be willing to do it for free.

Union Island Harbor should have a clearly defined entrance range, and, if lighted, should have reliable lights.

If the above were done, perhaps yachtsmen would not be so resentful of the taxes imposed on visiting yachts in the Grenadines.

MAYREAU ISLAND
(Chart 31; II B-3, B-31, B-311)

Mayreau is three miles south of Union, and its peaks should not be confused with those of Union, which are only half as high. Some years ago, the people of Mayreau were living at a bare subsistence level. Today the island appears much more prosperous; the old houses are being fixed up and painted and some new ones have been built. (Tourism certainly has brought some advantages to these small islands.) Saline Bay is a large, open bay on the southwest side of the island, with a dock on its northeast corner. Deep water extends much closer to shore than some of the old charts show. This is a beautiful spot, with a half-mile-long white-sand beach that usually is deserted. Best to spend your time on the beach, as the ground swell hooking around the point makes lying-to a rolly affair.

I've been told that if you tuck up in the northeast corner of the harbor, west of the sand beach, you'll be almost completely out of the swell, which of course is what has created that beautiful beach at the southern end of the bay. For a while there was talk of a restaurant and bar being built in this corner of the bay, but it never came to pass. However, an ex-charter skipper named Denis has built Denis's Hideaway on the hill overlooking the harbor. He serves a good and simple dinner and the view is superb. Here you can watch for the green flash on the western horizon and gam with other yachtsmen. Tie up your dinghy at the jetty in Saline Bay and walk up the hill to the Hideaway.

The one problem in Saline Bay is that Mike Burke's Windjammer Cruises and small motor vessels have been barred from Palm Island and Petit St. Vincent, so now they come to Saline Bay and turn the beach into something like Coney Island. They do leave in the evening, however, so you would have the evening and the early morning to yourselves. Needless to say, the schedules of these boats vary from year to year, and even from month to month. The best thing to do is to call Denis's Hideaway on VHF channel 68, find out the

excursion-boat schedule, and then make your plans regarding Saline Bay.

When departing for the north, give a wide berth to the shoal extending from Grand Col Point. It has a longer reach than some charts give it credit for and thus has dented a surprising number of boats in recent years.

The buoy off Grand Col Point was another Canadian-inspired booby trap, which now happily has been replaced by a post driven into the bottom at the outer edge of the shoal; don't cut it too close. A safe range is discussed in chapter 1.

North of this reef is the submerged wreck of the World War I gunboat *Paruna*. I am indebted to Jol Byerly and Desmond Nicholson for the story of the wrecking of the *Paruna*, a Royal Navy gunboat stationed in the Lower Caribbean during World War I. Royal Navy food not being too tasty, they frequently anchored in Mayreau's southern bay so the crew could go out in small boats to fish. While they were so engaged late one afternoon, a steamer coming out from behind Union Island was spotted and the captain decided to investigate, in spite of the waning daylight. He figured he knew the area well enough to operate at night.

Thus, he weighed anchor, the rudder was put to port, and the ship kicked ahead, making a hard left turn. About the time she had a head of steam up, a hard gust of wind hit, and, having a lot of windage aft, the poor old *Paruna* could not bear off enough to clear the reef. Evidently she hit the bricks going at about eight knots, which took off her whole bottom. She sank on the other side of the reef.

This should be a cautionary tale for anyone who fancies sailing at night; if a Royal Navy gunboat that had been serving in the area for many years didn't make it, you probably won't either.

And even by daylight, pay close attention to the ranges shown on Chart 31 in this chapter for locating the wreck. The current is very strong, so plan your diving expeditions for slack water.

The bay directly east of the wreck is a nice lunchtime spot when the swell is down. The beach is beautiful here, but it definitely is not recommended for overnight stops.

At the north end of Mayreau is one of the most attractive anchorages in the Grenadines—locally called Salt Whistle Bay. The shoal extends south and east from the northern point of the harbor, but there is a full five feet of water south of the reef, and this depth can be carried inside the reef well up into the northeast corner. Proceed slowly, as the bottom comes up gradually. Anchor bow and stern; otherwise, when the wind dies down in the evening,

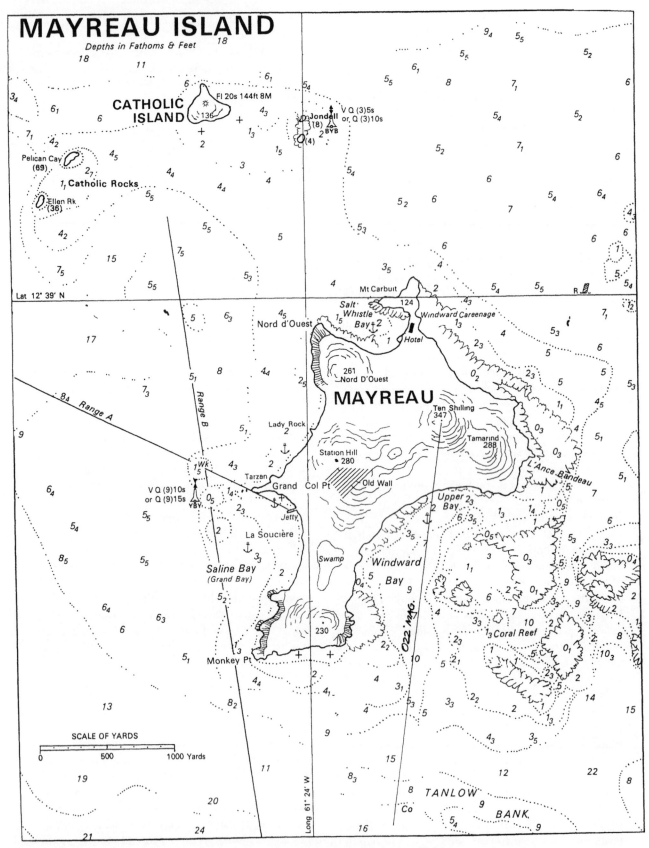

CHART 31 Mayreau Island   SOUNDINGS IN FATHOMS AND FEET

Range A. Cliff of Grand Col Point in line with midpoint of Saline Bay dock leads over wreck.
Range B. Peak of Petit Martinique over western low land of Palm Island leads over wreck.

Note: Use these ranges cautiously and only for finding the wreck; otherwise, you may become one yourself.

Southern Grenadines 117

the swell hooking around the point will throw you beam-to the sea and you will roll badly. Note the condition of the tide: If you sneak too far in and the tide goes out from under you, it may be a few hours of rough bumping before you get out. Beware that the ground swell does not make up while you are inside, as this would make getting out a hazardous proposition. This is a good anchorage in settled weather only.

I estimate that eight is the maximum number of boats for this anchorage, but I have been told that one New Year's Eve there were 22 yachts happily jam-packed in here.

The cove has been beautifully developed by Tom and Undine Potter. I say "beautifully developed" because when you sail into the anchorage and look ashore, you see little or no sign of the cottage-type hotel—the Salt Whistle Bay Hotel—that has been built here; the cottages are all completely hidden in the trees. The only fly in the ointment is a horrible square concrete house at the northernmost point of the bay—which the Potters refer to as "instant disaster." Originally the staff cottage was hidden among the palm trees along with the guest cottages, but it seems that the staff, after quitting time, continued partying until the small hours and were keeping the guests awake. Hence the sudden building of "disaster."

You used to be able to walk across the sandspit and find a lovely beach on the windward side, with sheltered rock pools for warm-water bathing. Unfortunately, whatever garbage yachtsmen don't leave on the islands they apparently throw overboard as they leave, and it all drifts down onto Mayreau's windward beaches, which have become foul with litter and hardly worth the walk anymore.

You can contact the Salt Whistle Bay Hotel on channel 16; they have a small boutique and they can arrange diving and fishing trips.

Mayreau used to be so poor that there was a main catchment and cistern where most people got their water. It was built by a Father Dionne, who, because water was in such short supply, kept the key to the cistern on his person. Father Dionne worked hard to improve the lot of the islanders, but now, with the money that has come in from Palm Island, Petit St. Vincent, and the Anchorage on Union Island, people are better off, and most have their own cisterns. Father Dionne is gone and there no longer is a resident priest.

There is one good anchorage on Mayreau's windward side. On the southeast coast, there is deep water inside the reefs. Sail up inside, round up, and anchor close behind the reef where Chart 31 in this chapter indicates. Use two anchors to keep you off in case the wind dies. A final note on the chart: A one-fathom passage is shown around the eastern point of Mayreau. Looking at it from the hill, it does not seem to exist, but *Brabantine,* with a six-foot draft, succeeded in getting through at high tide.

Through the 1990s there was a tremendous amount of trouble in Mayreau. Boats anchored in Saline Bay and the crews went up the hill to dinner, only to arrive back and discover their boats had been broken into and valuables stolen. Hopefully by the time you read this the problem will have been solved. But check with the bareboat managers, as to the current situation.

CATHOLIC ISLAND
(Chart 31; II B-3, B-31, B-311)
There is nothing to attract yachts to this small island northwest of Mayreau. It is noteworthy only as a hazard for boats working north from Mayreau. Jondell Cays, extending well to the east of Catholic Island, threaten boats beating north against a leeward-setting tide. Low-lying Catholic Rocks to the west are unlighted—no place to investigate after dark.

PALM ISLAND
(Chart 32; II B-3, B-31, B-311)
Formerly called Prune Island, Palm Island was under a long-term lease to John Caldwell. In American folklore, Johnny Appleseed planted apple trees from coast to coast. Here in the islands, it was Coconut John who planted palm trees throughout the Caribbean. For this reason, Prune Island was renamed when John Caldwell took over.

Caldwell had an interesting career. He was married in Australia during World War II, but when the war ended, he found himself in Panama with no means of returning to his wife in Australia. Although he was not a sailor, he bought a small sailboat, and, with more guts than brains, set out for Australia. He got as far as Fiji before wrecking and damned near losing his life. The fiasco resulted in Caldwell's first literary effort, *Desperate Voyage.*

He and his wife moved to Los Angeles, where he received a graduate degree in sociology, after which he set out for Australia in a gaff-rigged Tahiti ketch. The passage was successful and resulted in a second book, *Family at Sea.* He worked in Australia for several years before building his next boat, *Outward Bound.* With his family on board, he sailed westward halfway around the world to the Caribbean, and he has been in the islands ever since.

It has been a long pull for John; his wife, Mary; their sons, John and Roger; and their wives. With nothing but sweat and guts, they have built huge

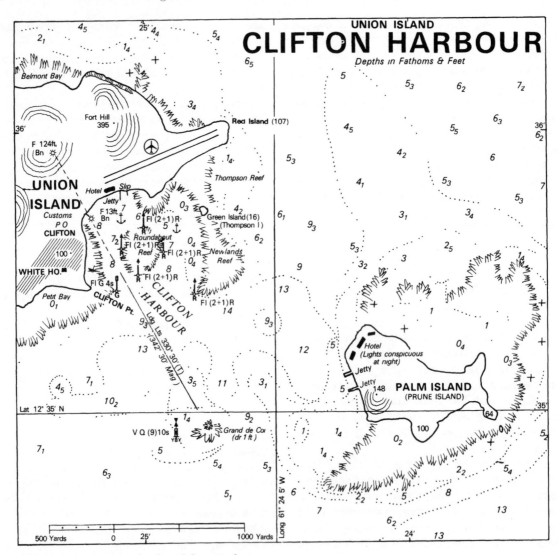

CHART 32 Union Island—Clifton Harbour

cisterns, vacation homes, well-designed rental cottages, a beach bar, restaurant, boutique, and so forth—thus developing a mosquito-infested island into a popular resort that attracts people from all over the world.

As if that weren't enough, John and his sons have, incredibly, salvaged close to 100 boats over the years. At least 10 of them would have been total losses had it not been for the Caldwells. And they have never charged a cent for their efforts. Would there were more people like them around!

Outward Bound was finally replaced by a 41-foot Carib purchased from CSY. With a few other boats, John for a while ran a bareboat operation, but eventually he thought better of it. For years he has dreamed of dredging through to the salt pond and building a marina at Palm, but his project probably will remain in the land of dreams until financial backing can be found.

John's sons and their wives finally decided they had had enough of life in the Grenadines, and they moved to the United States, where both boys embarked on successful careers. However, after a few years in civilization, they decided that the life was not for them, and they have returned to Palm Island. The whole Caldwell clan is once again running Palm Island.

Things are expanding on Palm now—they have

Southern Grenadines

put in a second jetty and a new bar, as the hotel was being inundated with yachties at certain times. A small yacht club has been built specifically for the yachties.

Johnny decided to fix up one of the boats he had salvaged and try his hand at racing. (He solved his engine problems as we did on *Iolaire*—he dropped it overside and made a mooring from it.) Now he has decided that since the very popular Petit St. Vincent Regatta is no more, he will run the Palm Island Regatta over Thanksgiving weekend. It should be great fun, as it will be the first regatta for the Trinidadians in the fall after their long summer layoff. It's always fun to race with the Trinidadians, as they race hard and play hard and are wonderful friends. If you go to the Palm Island Regatta, however, figure on three days of racing and two days of recuperation.

Palm Island can always be reached on VHF channel 16, and their telephone works with a fair degree of regularity. There are parties some nights of the week. Lunch and dinner are always available. There is a dive operation, and you can arrange diving trips in the Grenadines; they will also charge tanks and provide equipment. A boutique, attractively located on the beach and set up by John's daughter-in-law Cindy, is loaded with attractive locally made jewelry, clothes, bikinis, and so forth. This shop also stocks Street guides and Imray-Iolaire charts. A commissary can supply the basics if you run out.

One of the spectacular sights you may see when anchored at Palm is the magnificent sailing vessel *Sea Cloud* running down from Mustique. It is only a 20-mile run from Mustique to Palm, but frequently when the winds are favorable, *Sea Cloud* will set everything to her royals for the trip.

When anchoring at Palm, get as close to shore as possible, let go your anchor, back her down with mizzen or engine, and let out plenty of scope. It is much deeper at Palm Island than the chart shows; you'll find 30 feet right off the docks. Once the anchor is in, it won't drag, but be sure it is well set or you will back right off the shelf into deep water. More than one bareboat skipper has anchored at Palm and gone ashore for a cold drink, only to be told that his boat was heading for Carriacou. Needless to say, this causes instant panic and a hasty pursuit of the runaway boat in a dinghy.

In periods of heavy weather, the anchorage at Palm can be rolly, but it is never dangerous. Just be careful, *and make sure the anchor is set properly.*

The north shore of Palm Island is completely surrounded by reef. There is very little water inside the northeasternmost reef, so you would need a shoal-draft boat drawing less than four feet to penetrate safely inside. (Such a boat, in fact, could circumnavigate most of the island inside the reef.)

By the way, when anchoring off the southwest corner of the island, watch out for the detached coral head 300 yards to the southwest. You can carry a full nine feet between the coral head and the main reef, but keep a sharp lookout for the former.

Grand de Coi is a very dangerous reef approximately one-half mile west of Palm Island. This reef bares at low-water springs, and one would think it would be extremely easy to spot—but unfortunately it is not. Numerous boats have piled up here. The 70-foot schooner *Mollihawk,* after she was sold by the Nicholsons, ran hard aground on Grand de Coi; after a lot of work, she was eventually gotten off. The 70-foot Baltic trader *Annamarie* was not so lucky. She succeeded in running up on Grand de Coi right at the top of the high-water spring tide, and although the motor vessel *Meteor* made a valiant attempt to haul her off, it was not good enough—*Annamarie*'s bones remain on the reef. With great regularity, boats pile up on Grand de Coi and are rescued by John Caldwell and his assistants.

The buoy placed by the Canadians in the early 1980s to mark Grand de Coi was nothing but a booby trap; it was so far away from the reef that you could not figure out where the reef was. Now the buoy (which went adrift) has been replaced by a post on the western side of Grand de Coi—the marking all the local yachtsmen wanted originally. However, the Canadian "experts," who insisted we did not know what we were talking about, installed their own buoy, and more boats hit Grand de Coi after this buoy was installed than before the installation. Definition of "expert": "x" is the unknown quantity, the "spurt" is a drip under pressure. Grand de Coi should be marked by a day marker or a perch on top of the reef.

When heading north or south, follow Ranges 3 and 4 on Chart A in chapter 1. These will allow you to pass safely east or west of Grand de Coi.

When sailing northwest from Petit St. Vincent to Union or Palm in the afternoon with the sun in front of you, it is virtually impossible to see Grand de Coi. In this case, pass between Pinese and Mopion and head for the peak on Frigate Island until you pick up Range 4 or 5 (Chart A in chapter 1 or Imray-Iolaire Chart B-311). Follow Range 5 if

120 *Street's Cruising Guide to the Eastern Caribbean—Martinique to Trinidad*

heading for Palm Island, Range 4 if heading for Union. (Coconut) Johnny Caldwell has gone to Sailors Val Halla to his great reward and Palm Island still operates. But, the Caldwell family no longer has ownership of the island. It was sold to a developer.

UNION ISLAND
(Chart 32; II B-3, B-31, B-311)
As the Grenadines go, Union Island is fairly large. Its population is sparse, with only two small villages, Clifton and Ashton. It is easy to spot from a distance because its rock pinnacles bristle the sky like large spikes. The island is three miles long and two miles across at its broadest.

A beautiful hotel, the Bougainvillea, was built in the northeast corner of Clifton Harbor by André and Simone Beaufrand. They also built a dock, ice plant, slipway, and airport. Now the place has been renamed the Anchorage Hotel and Yacht Club, and it is run by Charlotte Honnart, who is French. The restaurant has a deservedly good reputation for good French and Creole cooking, but unfortunately the bar serves no Heineken—just the local St. Vincent beer, which I consider undrinkable.

The hotel's boutique stocks not only jewelry, bikinis, pareus, and the like, but also the Street guides and Imray-Iolaire charts. Fueling facilities at the Anchorage include water and diesel but no gasoline. You can also get ice and fresh bread. Although there is a laundry service, I would be suspicious of any laundry service in the Grenadines, as water is so scarce it probably is not well rinsed. The sail loft here is run by Gil, a Frenchman who arrived in the Grenadines 10 years ago and stayed. The Anchorage is a good place to pick up fish, as fishermen come into the hotel to have their catch air-freighted off to Martinique—a practice that has helped denude the entire Grenadines of lobster. If I ever see a lobster in these waters, I'll probably die of shock. It has, however, boosted the local economy.

Behind the dock are saltwater pools where you will find lobster, turtles, fish, and even sharks (nurse sharks, not the man-eating kind).

The slipway at Union Island—now defunct—was distinctive in that it was one of the few railways in the Eastern Caribbean that had a proper side-tracking system (Grants in Martinique is the only other one), but, being out in the middle of nowhere, with no infrastructure to support it, the operation never was very successful, and it has now passed to the great beyond.

Behind the hotel is a concrete airstrip, which, while not as hairy as the one at St. Barthélemy, is certainly one whose approach can weaken the knees of even experienced pilots on their first landing attempt there. One of the first planes that tried to come in ended in the harbor, and other accidents have occurred since then. Now the runway has been expanded and the airport is busy from dawn to dusk.

Customs and Immigration can be difficult. There are Customs and Immigration are at the airport.

Garbage is something of a problem, as the only dump is an open pit in town near the post office. Do not leave your garbage at the Anchorage Hotel.

Although there are no marine supplies available in Union, if you ask around, you will discover that CSY usually has a mechanic based at Union who can help out in an emergency with mechanical problems.

Food supplies have improved greatly in the last few years in Union; the supermarkets, although not really "super," do carry the basics—including fresh, hot bread baked every morning.

Union is served by Island Air, from Grenada to St. Lucia; by Martinique Air, running from Martinique and St. Lucia; and by charter organizations from Barbados. Day trips to Union Island and Tobago Cays have become very popular among the French of Martinique. This resulted in what may be one of the most expensive day trips in the world—an early morning flight from Martinique to Union Island (150 miles), then a sail to either Petit St. Vincent or Tobago Cays, arriving back at Palm Island about 1600 or 1700 for a flight back to Martinique. The traffic has become so heavy on this route that the runway is now being extended and altered 15 degrees to the north, which required filling in the land between Union Island and Red Island, plus knocking the top off Red Island. So Red Island is no more. The expansion operation was in full bore when I flew through there in May 1991, and the new landing strip was completed in 1992.

Union Island continues to be a den of thieves as of 1999. *Li'l Iolaire* with the author and his wife on board, had problems in Frigate anchorage. We were boarded by local pirates—there is no space to tell the whole sordid tale but it ended up costing us US$300.00. The police were less than helpful to say the least.

As a result of a big write up, by yours truly, published in the Compass, and a meeting with the Premier, the police department in Union Island have now a VHF (prior to our episode they did not—however, as yet they still have no boat.)

Union Island is pretty much the law of the jungle and is best avoided. Go in, clear with Customs & Immigration and clear out. The situation may have changed by the time you read this, check with the local bare boat managers. They should let you know what the current situation is.

CLIFTON HARBOR
(Chart 32; II B-3, B-311)
In years gone by, the entrance to Clifton Harbor was confusing; when it was buoyed in the early 1980s, the buoys were misplaced, the lights did not work because the fishermen stole the batteries, and in a relatively short time the buoys went adrift and

were not replaced. Now, however, the harbor is properly marked by piles driven into the bottom, with lights at the top; but how long will these lights last??? Do not try to enter Clifton Harbor at night.

When approaching Clifton Harbor, it is easy to spot the outer reef. Round the outer reef close aboard to starboard, sail north toward the gap between Fort Hill and Red Island (eyeball navigation), and round up behind Green Island (also referred to as Thompson Island on some charts and guides). Anchor at a depth suitable for your draft. The bottom is hard sand, and once the anchor is dug in, the holding is extremely good. Make sure you are on the shelf, though, because the bottom drops off very steeply to 35 or 40 feet.

The water here is always calm, while the wind whistles past the anchorage, making it cool and bug-free. Take the dinghy to the hotel dock, where you will be less tormented by small boys than at the main dock. Walk along the shore to town, the post office, and the small supermarket.

Anchorage in the main part of the harbor is not too good, as you'll find 40 or more feet of water, which makes hauling up the anchor a back breaker.

At night, there is supposed to be a range by which to enter Clifton Harbor, but it was not operating the last time I was there; and, in any case, I would not, under any circumstances, enter this harbor at night. Rather, I would anchor in the lee of Palm Island and wait until dawn.

In May 1991, I ascertained that most of the buoys in Clifton Harbor were missing. The range lights were not working, as the range had fallen down and the few buoys that were there had dragged out of position. Thus, they were nothing but booby traps ready to catch the unwary mariner. Unfortunately, the unwary mariner is too often caught, and he ends up on the reef. Ending up on the reef is further complicated here because shipwrecking and piracy seem to be very legitimate occupations on Union Island.

There was one case of a charter yacht ending up on the beach and looking for help. The locals didn't go out to help them get the boat off—they went out, chased the entire crew ashore, and stripped the boat. Complaints to the local police were to no avail—they refused to do anything. By the time the charter company got a crew down to the boat, it was picked as clean as Mother Hubbard's cupboard—a ridiculous situation, as the boat was not hard aground and could have been pulled off by other yachts in the harbor that were willing to help. But the other yachts were chased off by the Union Island shipwreckers.

Ashton, west of Clifton and the main town, has no harbor for boats drawing more than three feet. A path leads up from Ashton or Clifton to Mount Taboi (the Pinnacle), the highest peak on Union. Coming from Clifton, according to John Clegg, the best approach to the peak is from the east, heading for the smaller pinnacle northeast of the main one. From the small one to the summit of the large one, there are two or three routes, and which one is more convenient depends on where the century plants have been growing that year. None should present any problem, but beware the Jack Spaniard wasp, which looks like the North American wasp, only a mite larger. It won't kill you, but it gives one hell of a nasty sting.

FRIGATE ISLAND
(II B-3, B-31, B-311)
This is the small island just off Ashton, at the southern end of Union, and behind it there is a good anchorage indeed. Deep water extends much farther north than some charts indicate. I normally anchor with the high hill on Frigate bearing approximately southeast. It is always sheltered and cool here. There may be some chop, but this is more than made up for by the total seclusion. It is pleasant in the evening to lie back and watch the frigate birds circling lazily around the peak towering above you. The harbor behind the reef is a perfect place for dinghy sailing. The water is shallow and the wind is always good. If the kids capsize, they can stand in the shallows and right the boat.

A marina was started, extensive dredging was done, piers built—but then the whole operation was abandoned—see Sailing Directions on the back of Imray-Iolaire Chart B-311 for latest information.

CHATHAM BAY
(Sketch Chart 33; II B-3, B-31)
The other good anchorage at Union Island—Chatham Bay—was uninhabited until some years ago, when an individual in search of privacy built a small cottage here. He is seldom visited by anyone except a few local fishermen. Inside Chatham Bay, hard gusts have a tendency to blow out of the hills with surprising force. They are not dangerous in themselves, but they may lead you to believe that it is howling outside. Boats have hung back timorously in the harbor for days on end expecting raging gales outside. Finally venturing out, they have found it blowing no more than 10 or 15 knots. Don't be deceived.

From here you can travel to the northeastern tip of Union, where the reef diving and spearfishing are

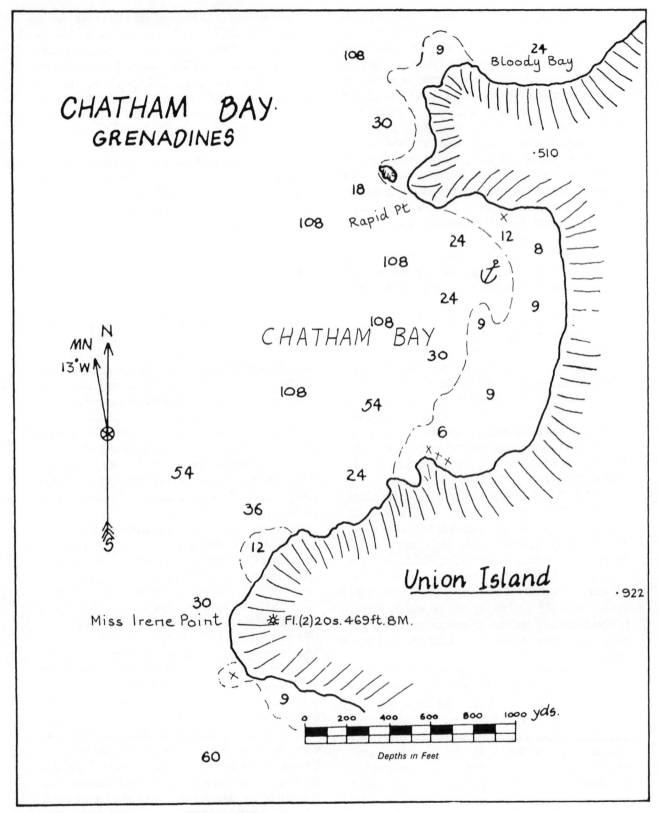

SKETCH CHART 33   Union Island—Chatham Bay

superb. Yachts seldom anchor in the area, but it is good nonetheless. The best place is in the northeast corner in two fathoms. The southeast corner is shoal and exposed to the wind.

Doug Terman and Hazen Richardson served together in the Strategic Air Command. With their mustering-out pay, they bought the 77-foot Crocker-designed schooner *Jacinta* and tried to make their fortune in the charter trade. They did not succeed in that, but they found and fell in love with the uninhabited island of Petit St. Vincent. They managed to buy **it,** and with financial backing they built Petit St. Vincent into the world-famous resort it is today.

Haze and his wife stayed on to run Petit St. Vincent, and Doug went on to become a successful novelist whose books include *First Strike, Free Flight, Shell Game, Enemy Territory* (called *Star Shot* in the UK), and the children's book *By Balloon to the Sahara. Shell Game* is interesting because in it Doug claimed that in the aftermath of the Cuban missile crisis all of the nuclear weapons were not removed—a fact that came to light only in January 1992, many years after Doug wrote his book. *Enemy Territory* features Doug and Haze's schooner *Jacinta* and their long-time mate (and subsequently skipper), the late Tom Clark, founder of Clark Sails of Essex, Connecticut. (Tragically, Tom died very young, of cancer.) The book is a great memorial to Old West Indies Hands (OWIH) who came to the islands in the late 1950s and the 1960s.

They have decided to join forces again, and with backers are planning a multimillion-dollar facility in Chatham Bay similar to that at Petit St. Vincent, including a VHF relay station on the top of Union Island. This is certainly needed, and it will give good VHF coverage to the whole Grenadines. As at Petit St. Vincent, they will do their level best to cater to the needs of the true yachtsman. Needless to say, they won't be catering to those types that Ross Lulley refers to as "waterpeople."

We lose another deserted anchorage, but you cannot stop progress, and if the area is going to be developed, I cannot think of anyone better equipped to do it than Haze and Doug. As of June 1991, however, the plans had not materialized, and Chatham Harbor was still an uninhabited anchorage—probably one of the only good uninhabited anchorages in the entire Caribbean.

Luckily for the sailor the great plans for Chatham Bay have come to naught. Chatham Bay is still a completely deserted bay, but is proving more popular with sailors. Instead of a completely deserted anchorage, you may find four or five boats anchored in the north east corner. But, there is still plenty of room.

Island Dependencies of Union

PINESE and MOPION
(Chart 34; II B-3, B-31, B-311)

These are the two sand cays off Petit St. Vincent Mopion means "crab louse," and the translation of Pinese is "bedbug"; perhaps both are distant relatives of Las Cucarachas ("the cockroaches") off the northeastern tip of Puerto Rico. When passing to leeward of Mopion, be careful of the shoal, since the island is continually extending to the south and southwest, and it is already farther than is shown on the chart. Many yachts have struck this shoal, as several Lloyd's underwriters will attest. There is a channel east of Mopion, known among experienced islands yachtsmen as Crazy Corrigan's Crooked Channel—named after Dave Corrigan of Mariners Inn, St. Vincent. It is perfectly safe for the experienced reef pilot, but there are no ranges whatsoever. I will give the general gist of the directions, but you will have to eyeball it for yourself.

Head a little bit to windward of Mopion until you spot the break in the reef. Enter and head roughly southeast, following the color of the deep water. As Mopion comes abeam, the channel curves to the south, and as you pass Mopion, it curves again to the southwest. Follow the channel around, and, once clear in deep water, head for Petit St. Vincent.

To pass between Pinese and Mopion, pick up the larger island (Mopion), then line up the peak of Petit Martinique on a bearing of 162° magnetic. Follow this bearing. You may have to sail high of the course to compensate for current and leeway. Take out your hand-bearing compass, keep Petit St. Vincent bearing 162° magnetic, and that range will lead you between Pinese and Mopion. Be sure to put a crew member in the bow to do eyeball navigation, as sometimes helmsmen are not steering quite as well as they should be, and people taking bearings on a distant object may not be getting precise readings. When coming from the north, this channel saves about half a mile of windward work, but it should be used only by the brave and skillful, as Pinese breaks water only at low, low water in May, June, and July.

Once you have passed between the reefs, alter course to Petit St. Vincent. The best maneuver is to tack back to the north and work your way eastward to Petit St. Vincent in the lee of the island, as the island will then afford you absolutely smooth water.

PETIT ST. VINCENT
(Chart 34; II B-3, B-31; B-311)

Commonly referred to as PSV, this was formerly a beautiful deserted island, but I am not particularly surprised that it has been built up. It is an attractive island with good anchorages and beaches. The Petit St. Vincent Hotel is spectacular in every respect, right down to the bill that will be tendered you at the end of your stay. Lunch or dinner reservations can be made via VHF channel 16. Ice and fuel are available on the island; water is hard to come by, although in a real emergency, you probably could get some.

PSV has always catered to the yachtsman, helping out in emergencies, and throwing excellent weekly jump-ups during the winter charter season. The hotel used to host the four-day PSV Thanksgiving Regatta, which featured good racing and good parties, but I guess Haze Richardson decided he was getting old and couldn't keep up with the Trinidadians racing all day and partying all night. So the regatta has now been moved to Palm Island. Johnny Caldwell is much older than Haze, but he claims he is young at heart and can endure the pace of the frenetic four days.

Unfortunately, the free showers the Petit St. Vincent Hotel used to offer visiting sailors are no longer available because too many so-called yachtsmen aren't. But the fruit drinks sold on the hotel terrace, with or without booze, are still terrific, and the view is likewise.

PSV is part of St. Vincent. If you are headed north from Petit Martinique or Carriacou, you are supposed to clear through Clifton Harbour on Union Island before anchoring in Petit St. Vincent. Considering the number of yachts that now visit PSV, it would make great sense to designate it as a port of entry.

At one point, Customs officers from Union used to raid PSV and demand that any yachts that hadn't cleared properly sail over to Union in the dark to enter. There isn't an operating Customs launch at the moment, though, so there's little chance of being nabbed. (If Haze Richardson needs a policeman on PSV these days, he has to provide transportation!)

Furthermore, as mentioned earlier, it seems likely that even if a yacht hasn't cleared properly, it won't be jumped on by Customs (as long as it's doing nothing illegal) if the skipper says he has gone into a harbor of refuge, i.e., couldn't reach a clearance port before dark.

Fishermen from St. Vincent and Bequia camp at the western edge of the beach below the Petit St. Vincent Hotel. They are *not* employees of the hotel or in any way connected with it. Many of them are the finest old-time Bequian fishermen— hardworking, honest, and helpful—who are a pleasure to meet, talk to, and do business with. Others, unfortunately, of the younger generation are rough, tough, broke, and out to get everything they can. That could include your dinghy. The fishermen who camp on the PSV beach always maintain that dinghies are stolen by smugglers from Petit Martinique; the Petit Martinicans insist that the dinghies are stolen by the Bequian fishermen. Either way, lock your dinghy to the mother ship or to the dock.

The shoreline of PSV is a string of beaches, separated one from another by intermittent outcroppings of rock. It is possible to walk around the rocky points, but if you do it, I suggest that you wear sneakers unless your feet are more leathery than most. The shelling on the rocks is unusually bountiful; diving expeditions can be made to the reefs windward of the island; small boats can be rented from the hotel.

The normal anchorage is off the south coast. The larger boats favor a location due south or slightly east of due south of the highest peak on the western end of the island. Smaller boats can tack farther east between the reef and the island, ending up at anchor south of the saddle formed by the two hills. The bottom is hard sand and good holding. The current reverses along here, so I recommend a Bahamian moor, especially when the anchorage becomes crowded. Since the completion of the new dock, the shoals along the shore have been growing and shifting, so *proceed with caution*. When leaving the anchorage, boats drawing eight feet or less can pass to windward of the shoal before turning to the south and west. This sometimes is an easier way out than threading downwind through a crowded anchorage. (In March 1985, we bounced going out with *Iolaire*, drawing seven feet six inches. So the channel has shoaled a bit.)

The chart shows a ragged sort of channel through the reef between PSV and Petit Martinique. Some of the sailing workboats use this channel, but you would have to be one hell of a seaman to make it through, and I strongly urge newcomers not to use it. The first time I saw a boat in this channel with seas breaking all around, I thought I was watching the preliminary maneuvers of an elaborate suicide.

Haze Richardson of PSV ascertained from the

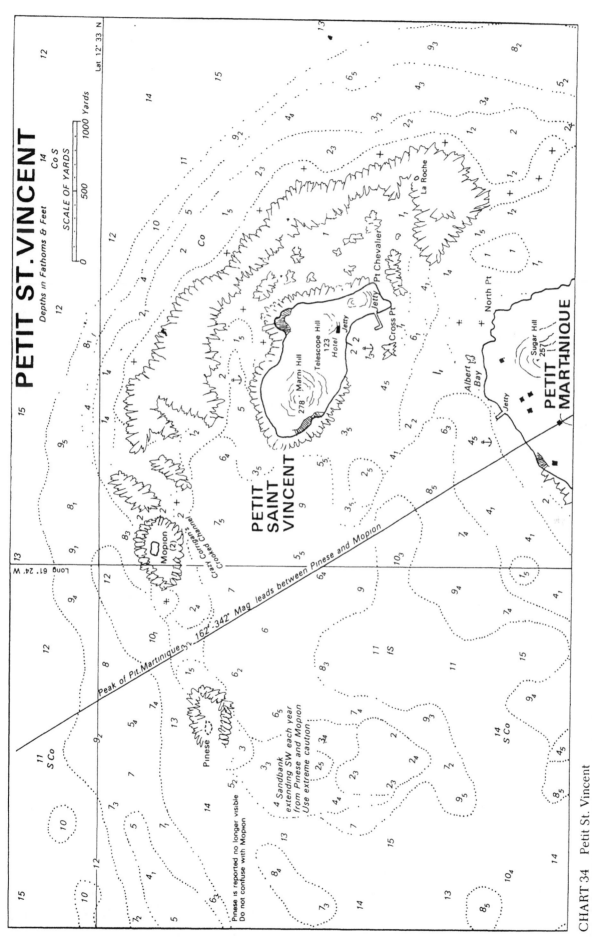

CHART 34 Petit St. Vincent
SOUNDINGS IN FATHOMS AND FEET
NOTE: FUEL AVAILABLE AT PETIT MARTINIQUE JETTY

local fishermen how they manage to thread their way through these reefs going downwind: "The highest land on Union, the Pinnacle, is sighted through the lowland of PSV. Stay on this range until the southeast corner of Carriacou comes out from behind Petit Martinique. Then take a short tack to the east, eyeballing it to find a narrow gap between the reefs." Sailors who use this channel are either good or aground—there is no room for error.

Some boats in search of privacy anchor north of the island or else work their way along the south coast through the reef to an anchorage east of the island.

Island Dependencies of Carriacou

PETIT TOBAGO and FOTA
(II B-3, B-31, B-311)

No anchorage here and little of interest except to the geologist, although in calm weather there is a marginal anchorage off Fota's lee shore. The islands do provide a number of helpful ranges, which are shown on Chart A in chapter 1.

PETIT MARTINIQUE
(Charts 28, 34; II B-3, B-31, B-311)

If you visit this dry, windswept island, you will notice rows of houses like the wooden saltbox houses of Nantucket Island in Massachusetts. Back in the old days, the locals must have learned house construction from New England whaleboat crews. High in the hills on the northern tip of the island is the Catholic church, whence the view is stupendous.

The islanders make a living by going to sea for legitimate trade or illicit smuggling. At times, the Customs inspector comes over from Carriacou, but his visits are always well advertised, and the people have time to put their island in order. I suspect that if the government chose seriously to crack down, Petit Martinique would soon be uninhabited. Basically, the people of Petit Martinique are hardworking and honest, with a strong streak of independence.

An interesting story is told about Petit Martinique smugglers of the past; perhaps, like many good yarns, it has very little to do with what actually happened, but it has been repeated so often that most people now take it for the truth.

It concerns a Petit Martinique smuggler who killed a rival smuggler from Venezuela who was poaching on his patch. The Grenadian government sent the chief of police to investigate the murder, and after sorting things out a bit, the chief ordered one of his sergeants to arrest the Petit Martinican.

"I am sorry, I am not going," replied the sergeant.

"Then I am holding you for direct disobedience," replied the chief, to which the sergeant responded, "Sir, I have just resigned from the force."

After a lot of shouting, everyone returned to Grenada; months later, the chief went himself to make the arrest. Arriving by boat off the island about four in the afternoon, he noticed that every soul on the island was assembled on the beach near the burial ground, dressed for a funeral. As the anchor went down, a man came swimming out from shore and said, "Oh, commissioner, sir, please hurry ashore immediately."

"I don't want to interrupt a funeral. I'm here on official business," he said.

"But, sir, we don't like to bury someone after dark."

"Well, who died?" asked the mystified chief.

"No one, yet," the messenger replied. "It's your funeral; the coffin is ready and the grave is dug. But please hurry, because it will be dark soon."

The chief wisely decided to up anchor and go back to Grenada; history does not record what happened to the smuggler from Petit Martinique who killed the smuggler from Venezuela.

Grenada's Gairy administration at one point tried to do in the smugglers of Petit Martinique and Carriacou by drastically reducing the duty on liquor, hoping to make smuggling unprofitable. That didn't work—it just reduced the profits and changed the smuggling products. Instead of rum, whiskey, and gin picked up in St. Barthélemy and smuggled into Grenada, they went only as far as Martinique and loaded up on good Dutch Heineken beer (as opposed to second-rate St. Lucian and Trinidadian Heineken beer) and smuggled that. When the exchange rate is favorable (when things are cheaper in Martinique than in Grenada), they also load up with various household items and take them to Carriacou. Many imported French items are much cheaper in Carriacou than they are in Grenada. While heading north, they smuggle milk from Grenada into St. Vincent. The previous St. Vincent government established a dairy and made it illegal to import milk, but the dairy doesn't produce a sufficient quantity, so the smugglers provide it.

Southern Grenadines

Good smuggling stories abound. Bill Stevens of Stevens Yachts, a very active fisherman, points out that it is easy to tell Petit Martinican, Carriacouan, and Venezuelan rum smugglers from true fishing boats: Just look at the railcap. If the railcap is clean and unscarred, it is a rum smuggler; if it has gouges dug in by fishing lines, it is a fishing boat.

See also the Epilogue at the end of this guide.

Bill tells another story. When he first arrived in Grenada, he and his wife, Barbara, ran a small hardware store that specialized in supplying nets, hooks. and lines to the fishermen. Bill was often away up on the north end of the island, where he made friends with a Catholic pnest. Bill dropped by one afternoon about five oclock, and the good father offered Bill a glass of Scotch.

While the priest xwas in the kitchen getting glasses and ice, Bill went to the liquor cabinet, pulled out a bottle of Scotch, and noticed that it bore no Grenada tax stamp.

He said, "Father, I am glad to see that even the priests buy their booze from the smugglers."

"No, Bill," the priest replied, "you are mistaken. I am a poor priest in a poor parish. The farmers bring me produce; the butcher drops off meat—beef or goat; the fishermen drop off fish; and, needless to say, my parishioners who are smugglers keep me well supplied with beer and booze. When they bring it to me, I can hardly ask them to go into town and pay the duty on it before I accept it!"

Petit Martinique is, as you might expect, an excellent place to buy liquor at the right price. It is also the place to buy a fiberglass dinghy that rows well; again, the price is right. Linus Belmar, who learned to work with fiberglass in various boatbuilding companies in England, has returned to Petit Martinique and set up a shop making splendid dinghies, using as a mold the standard Grenadines rowing boat.

Neither the People's Revolutionary Army (PRA) nor the People's Revolutionary Government (PRG) made much of an impression on Petit Martinique— the Petit Martinican is an out-and-out capitalist. The PRA officially ran the island, but I am told they always left before dark. Apparently the PRA teacher was singularly unsuccessful in trying to convince the children of Petit Martinique that communism was great. But, with European financing, the PRG built a generator on Petit Martinique. The island residents had had plenty of money, but they had never before had electric power. Once power arrived, instant civilization followed—everyone immediately installed lights, refrigerators, TV sets, VCRs the works. Now the island is lit up like a neon sign.

You can find a good daytime anchorage—as long as the ground swell is down—due west of a small jetty at the northwest corner of the island. From here to Petit St. Vincent is only a short hop, but watch out for the shoal marked 1½ fathoms between the two islands. I sailed across it in *Iolaire* some years ago—heeled over and drawing no more than six feet—and I touched repeatedly. I advise sailing around this spot altogether.

At Petit Martinique now one can obtain fuel and I am told the best prices in the Caribbean. Also, needless to say, beer and booze is available at extremely good prices and on the beach in Petit Martinique one can find an extremely nice restaurant with wonderful palm shaded gardens. PALMS

If anchored at PSV one can call the restaurant on the VHF, they will send a dinghy to pick you up for dinner and deliver you back after you have finished at no extra charge.

Carriacou

This is the most populated island in the Grenadines. At first, one wonders how the inhabitants support themselves, much less maintain so many respectable homes. As it turns out, several generations of Carriacouans have made their living by going to sea or to the oilfields of Venezuela and Aruba. They stay away for many years, sending money home to their families; eventually they return home themselves to marry in middle age and raise a family.

An alternate source of income for many years used to be the smuggling trade, as on Petit Martinique, which was carried out with surprisingly little government interference. It was argued that as long as the government did not intervene, a sizable part of the population was kept off the public dole.

In Tyrell Bay, it used to be a common occurrence at night to hear a sloop working its way into the harbor with no running lights. It would anchor silently close to shore and the headsails would come down, but the main would be left sheeted flat—the marine equivalent of the idling engine of a getaway car. You could hear the motors of unlighted cars and the slapping of dinghies shuttling back and forth from sloop to shore. After 15 minutes or so, the sloop would haul anchor and sail off around Cistern Point to Hillsborough, there to be found the next morning, anchored docilely off town, legally entering a regular cargo.

TYRELL BAY (HARVEY VALE BAY)
(Chart 35; II B-3, B-32)
This is the customary anchorage for boats coming to Carriacou from the south, and it is excellent in all weathers. Plenty of breeze and good holding over a white-sand bottom. The US chart is incorrect: The shoal in the middle of the harbor marked 1½ fathoms is actually shallower. *Iolaire*, drawing seven feet six inches, brushed it, as have others with even

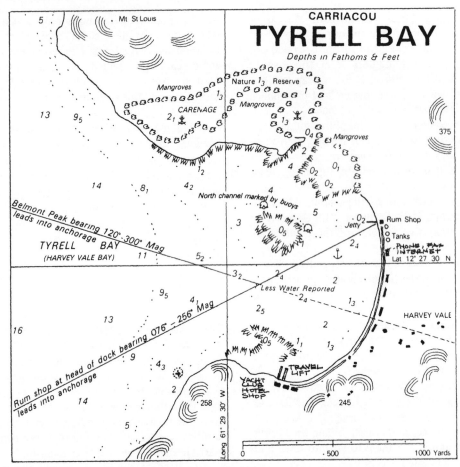

CHART 35 Carriacou—Tyrell Bay · BOUYAGE UNRELIABLE · SOUNDINGS IN FATHOMS AND FEET

less draft. The spot is seen easily in good light, and it is safe and advisable to steer north or south of it. The north side probably is the better route if coming around the northern side of the reef; proper buoys were installed north of the reef in 1991, and they should last for many years. One can come in north of the reef by lining up Belmont Peak (the hill behind Tyrell Bay) on a bearing of 120° magnetic. As you tack in along the north shore, watch out for the shoal in the corner of the harbor near the entrance to the carenage. Similarly, if you tack in along the south shore, you must watch for rocks 200 yards offshore below the cliff. Since the slipway has been built, shoaling has been reported in the southern half of the bay, so proceed with caution.

The rum shop at the head of the dock north of the tanks is a little hard to spot because of the growth of trees and the buildup in the area, but if you come in on a line of bearing 076° magnetic on the head of the dock, all should be well. See also the Epilogue at the end of this guide.

If you must enter at night, which I do not advise, the rum shop usually is lighted by a kerosene lamp until late. Most nights it is easy to spot the open-air theater south of the rum shop. If this is brought to bear at 085° magnetic, you will also pass clear. The best anchorage is off the dock or south of it. Do not go farther inshore than the end of the dock or you will run aground.

An interesting diversion is to sail a dinghy into the carenage, where the old, wrecked schooners lie. The mangroves are alive with birds that will flit close around you, and you can tie up in total solitude—but do not anchor. The whole carenage mangrove area has been declared a national park, and anchoring is forbidden (except, of course, when

Southern Grenadines

hurricanes are approaching). Fishing is banned, as is the taking of oysters. Besides, the oysters are not safe to eat—a couple of cases of hepatitis have been traced back to this patch of mangroves. Having experienced mean bouts of hepatitis twice, I strongly advise against sampling the oysters here.

A 50 ton travelift has now been established at Tyrell Bay Yacht Haulout. There is a good fuel dock, water, phone and fax: 473 443 8175.

Right next to the Tyrell Yacht Haulout is Carriacou Yacht Club with accommodation, restaurant, mini-market, laundry, internet café, showers etc. Phone/Fax: 473 443 6292.

Ashore you will of course find the inevitable couple of rum shops, plus a small "unsuper" market and numerous small bars and restaurants. A walk up to the top of the hill is very worthwhile for a splendid view of the south coast of Carriacou—including Saline Island, White Island, and One Tree

Bill Pringle and Mike Forshaw have open a marine supply store to supply the needs of the mariner phone 443 6992fax 4438092

L'ESTERRE BAY
(II, B-3, B-31)

This lies south of Sandy Island, southwest of Hillsborough. it is shallow, and the wind tends to sweep in from the north. All but the shallowest-draft boats must anchor far from shore. I can recommend it for daytime use only.

SANDY ISLAND
(Chart 36; II B-3, B-31)

Sandy island is owned and protected from development by the government of Carriacou. The people of Hillsborough frequent the island on weekends and holidays, and charter boats often anchor off its southwestern corner, their parties going ashore for lunch and snorkeling. Spearfishing is prohibited. This is a good and justifiably popular daytime anchorage.

In recent years, more and more boats have been spending the night in this rather exposed anchorage. Since you are sheltered by Carriacou 1½ miles to the east, the sea can't get too rough, but the wind can whistle across Hillsborough Bay. If you are going to spend the night, make sure you are well and truly anchored—probably two anchors set in a "Y" to the east would be best.

HILLSBOROUGH
(Chart 36; II B-3, B-31, B-32, B-311)

The principal town on Carriacou. The interisland schooners can be seen offloading cargo from a dock at the eastern end of town.

Carriacou was for many years opposition territory for the ruling Gairy government in Grenada, so zero money was spent here. The Bishop government wasn't much better. The dock collapsed, the airport terminal rotted, and the telephone system became practically nonexistent, as did the cable service. Carriacou was basically incommunicado. The roads, once adequate, deteriorated very badly. The piped water system in Hillsborough was allowed to rust, leaving only the catchment area and the cisterns as they were 20 years earlier. (Even if the population of an island stays the same, or perhaps decreases, as here, the water consumption per capita rises drastically as the people become more "civilized". The West Indian who in the 1950s kept immaculately clean using a bucket of water now usually has built a shower and uses 20 gallons of water to do the same operation.)

The 1985 Grenada government was headed by Herbert Blaize, who was from Carriacou, and that regime tried to rectify the 15 years of neglect of Carriacou—the dock was rebuilt, a new airport terminal was erected, and a telephone system was installed that was as modern as any in the world. (The instruments were made in Ireland, and some swear the bell has an Irish lilt!) The new dock has a dinghy landing on the south side, but because of the surge, be sure to have a stern anchor to hold the dinghy off if you leave it there.

Customs and the post office are at the head of the dock, and Immigration is across the street. If they are closed and you really want to clear after hours, swing into the nearest rum shop and they will send you off in the proper direction.

In January 1990, we ran into the craziest situation here that I have ever encountered. Since it is absolutely illegal to dump any plastic at sea, and since we do not want to pollute the sea or the beautiful anchorages in the Grenadines, we had been carrying our garbage throughout our Grenadine cruise. Thus, we arrived in Carriacou with three rather fragrant trash bags and carried them ashore in Hillsborough. When we went to check in the Customs officer told us we were not allowed to take the bags ashore and dump them in any of the garbage bins. The street was line with 55-gallon barrels, each of which bore a sign saying,

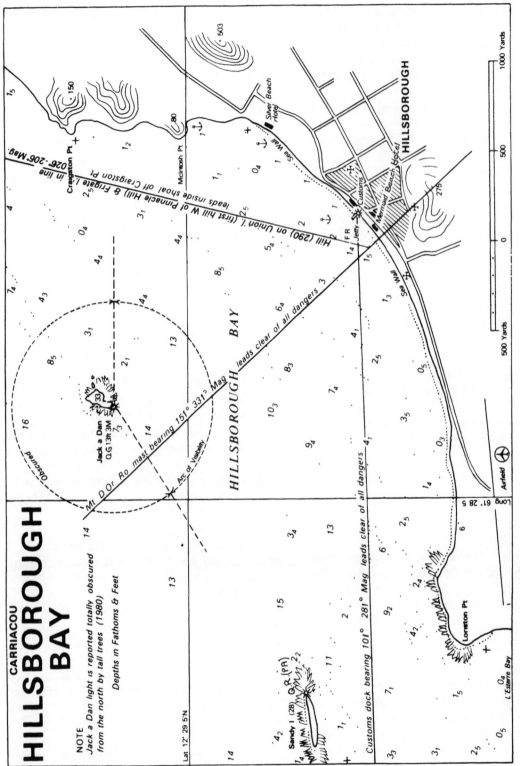

CHART 36 Carriacou—Hillsborough Bay

Range 1. Course 151°–331° magnetic on Cable and Wireless tower leads clear of all dangers.
Range 2. Course 101°–281° magnetic on Customs dock leads clear of all dangers.
Range 3. Hill on Frigate Island in line with 290-foot hill on Union (hill is W of the Pinnacle, which is highest on Union, 741 feet) leads clear inside shoal spot (4 feet) inside Jack a Dan, 026°–206° magnetic (see Chart A, Range 18, in chapter 1).

"Keep Carriacou Clean," but I guess they should also have said, "But Pollute the Ocean."

The official insisted that we could take the garbage ashore only if we hired a van for EC$10 or EC$15 to drive us out to the dump to deposit our trash there. Needless to say, I was not about to spend that kind of money to get rid of the garbage, so we put it back in the dinghy, waited until the Customs office closed, then smuggled the bags ashore to the empty barrels. As we put the bags in, I reflected that it would certainly be newsworthy if the Caribbean's best-known yachting author got thrown in jail for smuggling trash ashore in Carriacou. I certainly hope this crazy situation will be rectified by the time you read this.

Shopping in Carriacou has improved dramatically over the years. The rum smugglers discovered that they could also make money smuggling all sorts of duty-free goodies in from St. Martin—at a far lower cost than buying the goods in St. Georges on Grenada, paying duty and VAT, and transporting them up to Carriacou. Smuggling has always been a way of life on Carriacou, and no change of government—even the communist People's Revolutionary Government—has been able to alter the situation, so it is unlikely to be any different during our lifetime.

Except for frozen and chilled items, the food-shopping situation is much better than it was in the past, and some people maintain that it is better in Hillsborough than in St. Georges. This has been brought about by two factors. First, the fishermen have discovered that it is more profitable to sell fish in Martinique than in Grenada. Once they sell their fish in Martinique, they load the boat with French dry goods and bring them back to Carriacou. Second, the National Marketing and Import Board has been completely refurbished and has fresh vegetables and fruit from the north end of Grenada. Thursday is the best day to shop.

The Mermaid Tavern, a traditional yachtsman's stop for more than 20 years, briefly became the Mermaid Beach Hotel, but it has now closed. Every month a new rumor surfaces that someone has bought it and it will reopen. As usual, seeing is believing.

The Silver Beach Hotel, a cottage-type establishment with an open-air dining room, located east of town, has received a facelift and interior renovation. Various small guest houses, boardinghouses, and small restaurants open and close in Carriacou with too great a frequency to report here, so just wander up and down the streets

of Hillsborough, take a look, and find one that appeals.

The Carriacou Historical Society operates a mini-museum. Amazingly, despite the island's small size and the arid climate, there is also a botanical garden in Hillsborough, within walking distance of the jetty.

Across the street is an ice plant of uncertain heritage. I have never been able to find out who built it or when, but periodically some clever and industrious soul takes it upon himself to overhaul the machinery and get it operating. To everyone's amazement, the plant then actually makes ice. This goes on for a year or so, until the ancient plant breaks down, no one can repair it, and it lies doggo for a while—sometimes years—before another genius comes along to resurrect the beast. Presently, the beast is alive and well, producing ice. I wouldn't hazard a guess as to what the situation will be when you arrive in Carriacou.

A taxi will take you around the island, and a trip up to the hospital is a must, as that gives a fantastic view of Hillsborough Bay. It's a wonderful place for a hospital—cool and airy, with no need for air-conditioning. Then take the taxi down the windward side, where you'll find commercial schooners and small sloops being repaired on the beach.

Francis Brinkley, who knows Carriacou intimately, feels that a stop at Belair or Doctor's House or Camp Mashie (three names for the same place) would be a better spot for a visit. The view there is panoramic instead of just Hillsborough Bay: north to the Grenadines, south to Grenada, and also Hillsborough. In the same area are the ruins of an 1809 great house, sugar mill, tower, etc. In recent history, it was the PRA headquarters.

Despite what has been written to the contrary, schooner and sloop building has not died out in Carriacou. One continually reads articles by misinformed individuals stating that boatbuilding is dying out (or has already done so) because the young men are unwilling to work and are not learning the trade. Well, we were over at the windward side in March 1985, on what was supposed to be a legal holiday, and we saw at least a dozen shipwrights ranging in age from 12 or 14 years right up to 25 years hard at work building and repairing boats. We returned there in January 1990, while doing a video with *Sailing Quarterly*. Again we arrived on a holiday, again we found people hard at work on local sloops and schooners. The death of Carriacou sloop and schooner building certainly was announced prematurely. (Reminds me of the three times I have arrived home to read my own obituary because the Coast Guard had reported that the boats I was on were missing at sea with all hands.)

It is interesting to see the changes that have taken place in the Carriacou sloops over the years as the Carriacouans race, crew on yachts, and salvage the remains of wrecked yachts. The good Carriacouan fishing boats, trading schooners, and smugglers now sport stainless-steel rigging, Barient winches salvaged from wrecks, and Dacron sails—recut throwaways from yachts. The lines of the boats have changed drastically during the same period. They have become much more yachtlike—narrower, deeper, and better constructed and finished. Many builders are switching from gaff- to jib-headed rig, but they have not yet gone to outside ballast, as that would make it impossible to careen their boats the way they presently do.

Before the roads of Carriacou fell apart due to lack of maintenance over 15 years or so of neglectful government, they were well above the norm for this part of the world. They date back to the days when the British and the French were squaring off for control of the islands. The British ruled the sea around Carriacou and the French the land, so the French built roads to give their ground forces mobility against the British fleet wherever it tried to land. If the British fleet, thwarted at one landing, decided to haul up and sail down to the next inlet, the French would simply hitch up their cannon and follow them overland. So it went for many years, until an elaborate set of roadways crisscrossed the island.

The first weekend in August, known as August Monday, is one of the big weekends of the year in Carriacou. Many yachts come from Grenada to watch the workboat race in Hillsborough, and the island is filled with people. A good chartering idea is to take a boat through the Grenadines in late July, timing your arrival in Hillsborough for August Monday—races start Sunday afternoon. The spectacle of some 40 Grenadine workboats vying for cash prizes is really stunning.

The anchorage in Hillsborough tends to be rolly; in the winter it can be all but impossible. The usual anchorage west of the dock is not the best— northeast of the dock is far better. Work your way as far northeast as your draft will permit, and anchor tucked in as close to shore as possible. Boats drawing seven feet will have to anchor outside the shoal off the small hotel. Those drawing six feet or less can sneak in behind the shoal and anchor close to shore. The channel leading into a natural basin east of the shoal is best approached from the north—an eyeball proposition. The sand bottom is good holding in front of the hotel.

Northeast of Hillsborough you'll see an old dried-out streambed running down into the harbor at McIntosh Point. This forms quite a nice little cove and actually is the quietest anchorage in all of Hillsborough Harbor, but it is limited to boats drawing 5 1/2 feet or less. Deeper draft may be squeezed in, but at low-water springs you probably would be touching bottom.

If the ground swell is rolling in, or if the wind is well in the north, be careful. It is easy to drag, and the swell sets you onshore. That is how I came close to losing *Iolaire* here many years ago. The wind was well in the north, blowing hard, and a fair-size sea was rolling in. I thought the anchor, my trusty old Herreshoff fisherman, was well set, but we suddenly found ourselves drifting back onto the beach. By backing the mizzen to port and the staysail to starboard and cutting the rode, we managed to fall off, gather way, and get out just as we bounced off the bottom. It turned out that the anchor had landed in a rusty old ham can; the tip pierced the tin partway, but the bulk of the can had prevented the fluke from fully burying. *Moral:* Be *sure* your anchor is set. Wishful thinking won't do it.

As I have stated many times, never enter a strange harbor at night. However, if you decide to be foolish and do so here, remember that the Jack a Dan light is obscured from the north. If you come from the north or northwest, bring the Cable and Wireless relay tower (a tower with two bright red lights) to bear on 151° magnetic, which will lead right into Hillsborough Harbor, clear of all dangers (see Chart 36). This radio mast (located on Mount D'Or) forms a very good point of reference in general. It is clearly marked on Imray-Iolaire Charts B-31 and B-32, and it makes a good landmark when you approach from the south.

Incidentally, don't forget that the Cable and Wireless tower is lower than Chapeau Carré Mountain and therefore will appear and disappear as you sail up the west coast of Carriacou.

When approaching Hillsborough from the southwest, round Cistern Point and short-tack up between Mabouya Island and Cistern Point, and between Sandy Island and Loriston Point. Just be careful not to sail too far into L'Esterre Bay, which is quite shallow. Staying inside Mabouya and Sandy islands keeps you out of the swell. If you are powering in, a bearing of 101° magnetic on the town dock will keep you in deep water all the way.

If you are approaching from the north, sail right on down the coast of Carriacou, as there are no dangers except for the four-foot spot between

Southern Grenadines

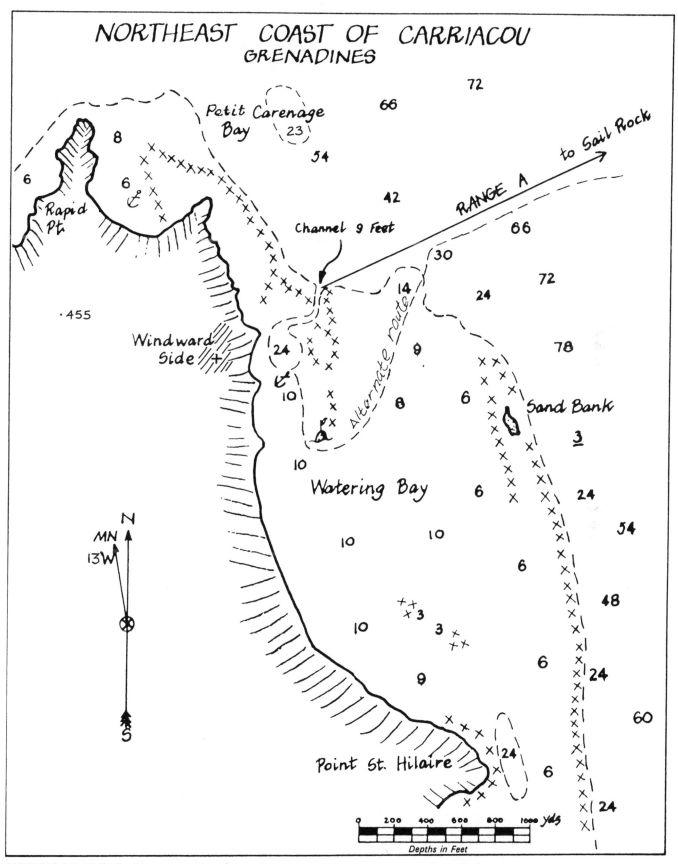

SKETCH CHART 37   Carriacou—Northeast Coast

Range A.   Sail Rock three fingers open to NW of Petit St. Vincent leads to channel into Windward Side, Carriacou.

Craigston Point and Jack a Dan. This spot is easy to avoid if you get on the range shown on Chart 36.

The coast of Carriacou north of Hillsborough offers no overnight anchorages. There are, however, one or two places where you might put in for lunch and a swim, and some spectacular beaches. Standing north from Hillsborough, don't forget the four-foot spot inside Jack a Dan.

PETIT CARENAGE BAY

(Sketch Chart 37; II B-3, B-31, B-311)

Due east of Rapid Point (locally referred to as Gun Point) is a cove called Petit Carenage Bay, where there is an anchorage for shoal-draft boats behind the reef, and a good beach. It is best suited for multihulls, centerboarders, or shoal-draft motorsailers.

WATERING BAY and GRAND BAY

(Sketch Charts 37, 38; II B-3, B-31)

On the east coast of Carriacou, locally known as Windward Side, is Watering Bay, still called Bay à l'Eau. The entrance to the bay is slightly intricate and should be made when the sun is directly overhead. If you are lucky, you can follow one of the local sloops that frequent the area. When coming from the north, proceed until Sail Rock is three fingers open on the northwest corner of Petit St. Vincent. (West Indians say two fingers, but their hands are bigger.) Then turn west on this range, 250° magnetic, until Fota joins Petit Martinique. When these two join, you should be close to the channel entrance; put a person in the rigging to con you into the channel, which first heads south, then west, into the basin.

Or else you can sail south along the outside of the reef, heading for the stone marker at its south end. Leave it to starboard and sail north into the anchorage (see Sketch Chart 37).

This is where you'll often find sloops under construction—confirming that boatbuilding is very much alive in Carriacou.

You can then head south, leaving the marker to port, and sail through Grand Bay, exiting Windward Side at Kendeance Point (see Sketch Chart 38). The best water is near shore, but you will have to eyeball it yourself. On the chart there appears to be a break in the reef off Jew Bay, but I have tried twice to enter through here with no success. If you are entering at Kendeance Point, proceed carefully with

a crew member aloft and you should have no problem. The channel is narrow, deep, and easily spotted by the breakers on the reef to windward. Because the wind and current will be setting you to leeward, hold high and stay as close to the weather side of the channel as the color of the water will permit. Inside, it is calm and secluded. You can sail in a rail-down breeze against no more than a light chop. Anchor close to the reef and stay there for days undisturbed by traffic of any sort, just as Jim Squire of the 55-foot schooner *Te Hongi* frequently used to do.

SALINE ISLAND

(Sketch Chart 39; II B-3, B-31, B-32)

Just south of Carriacou lies Saline Island, seldom visited by yachts and one of my favorite islands in the Caribbean. It is possible to anchor between Saline and the reef to the north, but the tide runs a solid three knots down this channel, requiring a heavy anchor and a Bahamian moor. Inside the cove on the north side of the island, however, is a superb anchorage for shoal-draft boats. The southeastern portion of the bay is completely out of the tide. The shelf is one fathom, dropping off steeply at the northwest corner of the harbor near the old lime kiln. Good holding can be found by nosing right up to the shoal, dropping a bow anchor onto it, and setting a stern anchor to hold you off. With the kiln bearing southwest, you will find yourself out of the tide in three fathoms of water. Exercise caution in making your approach, as the bottom shoals from two fathoms to one fathom within 30 feet. The western tip of the island drops off so steeply that you can dive from the beach straight down into the sea. The snorkeling on the southwest corner is as fine as anywhere in the Caribbean. Stay close to shore and make allowance for the tides; once you are caught by the current off Saline Island, there is no swimming back to shore.

In summer, be prepared to be completely engulfed by mosquitoes as soon as the sun goes down.

WHITE ISLAND

(Sketch Chart 39; II B-3, B-31, B-32)

Looking out from the hills of Carriacou (from the French restaurant above Tyrell Bay), I spotted what appears to be a very nice beach on the western side of White Island and an anchorage off the beach on

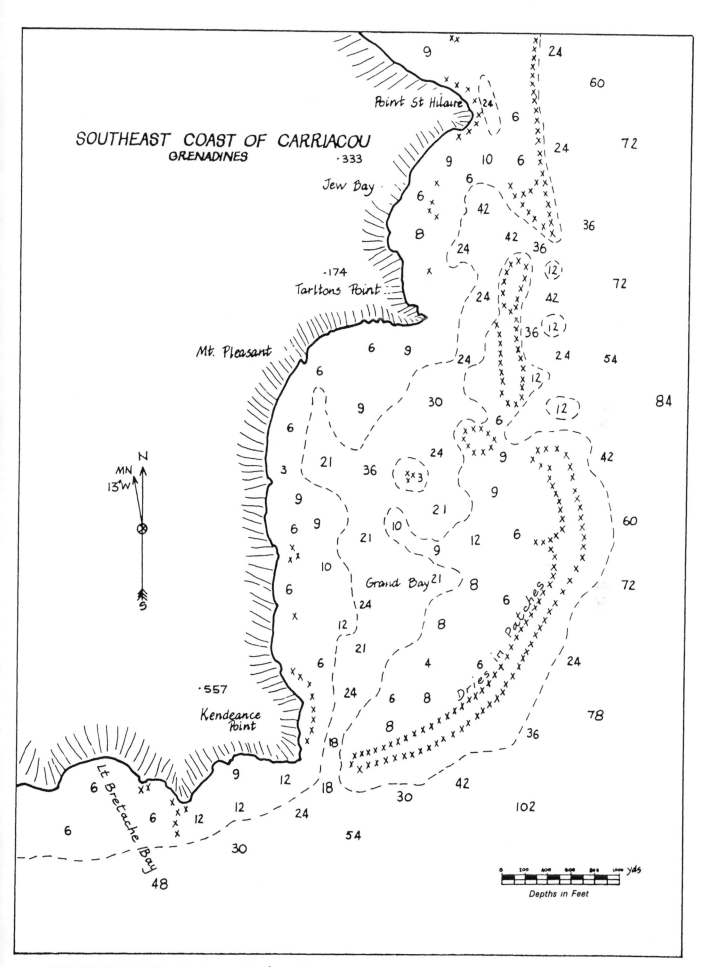

SKETCH CHART 38   Carriacou—Southeast Coast

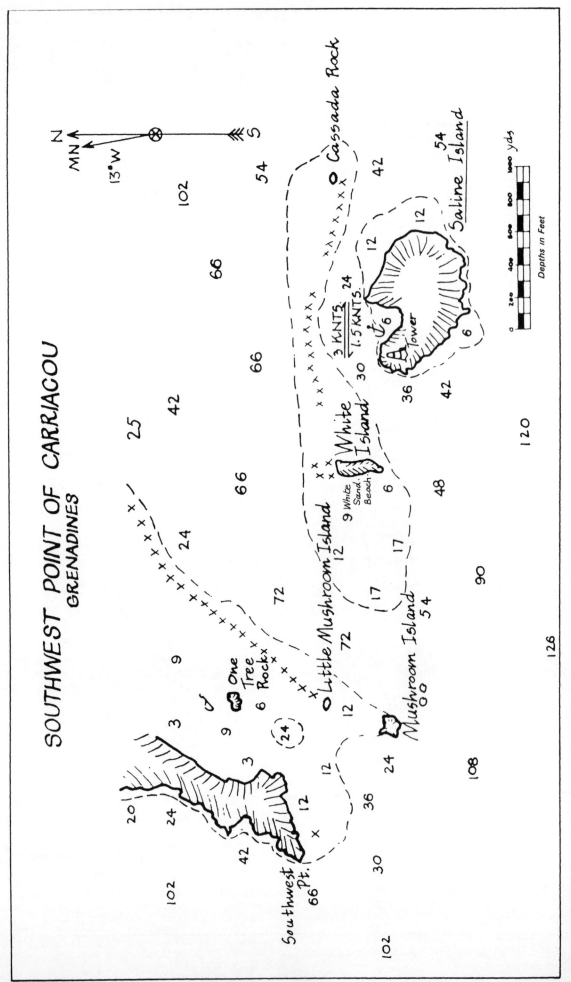

SKETCH CHART 39 Carriacou—Southwest Point

the northwest corner of the island. I have not visited this anchorage, but it looked intriguing. That day, it was blowing a good 25 to 30 knots, yet the water appeared calm behind the island.

Subsequently I discussed this anchorage with Gordon Stout, who spent many years exploring the Grenadines on his little 40-foot motorsailer *Quest* and then his 51-foot fiberglass clipper ketch *Shango*. He stated that this is an excellent anchorage, and he has used it frequently to avoid the charter boats, but eyeball navigation is definitely required. Approach the island from the west.

ONE TREE ROCK

(Sketch Chart 39; II B-3, B-32)

If you are beating up the windward side of Carriacou from the south, a good anchorage may be had inside the reef extending northeast from Little Mushroom Island. Enter to the west of Mushroom and anchor behind One Tree Rock. This is a wonderful spot. Approach Mushroom Island from the south, keeping Little Mushroom and One Tree Rock on the starboard hand; round up north of One Tree and anchor in 1 1/2 fathoms over white sand. The many coral heads to windward break the worst of the swell and are a good area for spearfishing. In one hour, we took 10 fish and three lobsters. The times I have stopped there have been during the summer in calm weather, but the Bequia fishermen tell me that even in winter it never gets too rough through here. The only problem they speak of is the winter swell that pours over the reef and pours out again through the southern entrance, setting up a stiff current that could give a swimmer quite a scare. Incidentally, a boat drawing four or five feet of water can sail up inside the reef to Manchioneel Bay and get away from the heavy swells.

FRIGATE ISLAND

(II B-3, B-32)

This is one of two islands so named in the Grenadines, the other being just south of Union Island. Strong currents and narrow beaches are its drawbacks. Some have found it convenient to anchor off the western shore of Frigate. From here the dinghy can be taken around the northwestern tip and into the bay on the north. The bay is extremely shoal, however, and should not be entered except by dinghy, the chart notwithstanding.

There is good shelter in the southeast corner of the bay, but I cannot recommend this. Even a very shallow-draft boat (three feet maximum) would have a rough time of it.

LARGE ISLAND

(II B-3, B-32)

The chart shows an anchorage in the northwest corner of this island, but the beach facing it is not particularly good. There is an abandoned estate ashore, but a strong current makes the approach difficult.

BONAPARTE ROCKS

(II B-3, B-32)

This is the small pile of rocks south of Large Island. I have never heard of anyone making a landing here, and I can't imagine anyone wanting to. The tide rips by them at four knots at times. They are best avoided.

ILE DE RONDE and ILE DE CAILLE

(Chart 40; II B-3, B-32)

From Grenada north to Carriacou is 38 miles; if the current is running to leeward and the wind is in the north, this can be one of the longest beats you will encounter coming from the south. Many people break up the trip by stopping off at Ile de Ronde. The island is particularly vulnerable to a northwest ground swell, but in settled weather you couldn't find a better lunch spot. The fishermen keep their boats on the beach on the southwest shore. Here, if you sail in close and anchor on the edge of the shelf, you will find a passable anchorage. The tide runs swiftly, and it is likely to be a bit rough, but the great attraction is a really beautiful beach.

A path, marked on Chart 40, leads past the lake (a pond in the dry season) to the beach and reef on the windward side. From this anchorage you can also visit Ile de Caille, the tiny island south of Ile de Ronde made famous by Frederic ("Fritz") Fenger's *Alone in the Caribbean*. Whale Bay on Ile de Caille is recommended only for dinghy trips in calm weather.

Corn Store Bay in the northwest corner of Ile de Ronde is perfectly adequate in settled weather. However, a ground swell can force your stern

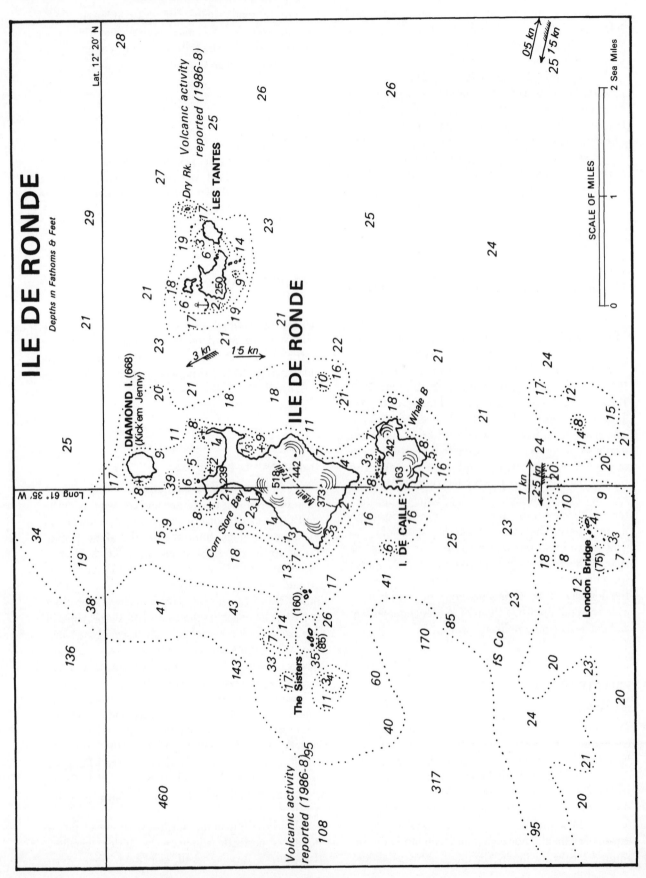

CHART 40 Ile de Ronde

Southern Grenadines

ashore. Two boats have been lost here in this way. If you elect to spend the night here, be certain to use a Bahamian moor. Feel your way in with the leadline and anchor off the little beach in three fathoms, with the hut bearing northeast. The snorkeling is fairly good, and with any luck you should be able to spear a few pan fish for lunch. The cove on the north shore of the island may be visited by dinghy. The swimming and snorkeling are good here, but I would not recommend taking the boat inside unless you are very adept at reef navigation and your boat draws no more than three feet. As it stands now, the reef does not afford enough protection from the sea; no doubt some enterprising developer will soon arrive on the scene to remedy this.

THE SISTERS
(Chart 40; II B-3, B-32)
The Sisters are a group of isolated rocks that lie approximately half a mile west of Ile de Ronde. About 600 yards west by south of the westernmost Sister is a shoal spot that is GROWING. When last sounded by the Royal Navy, the shoal was under 22 feet of water, but don't count on that. It is a volcanic peak that began rising out of the sea sometime in the late 1970s—it was very active during the period from 1986 to 1988, and even now boats occasionally report smoke or steam coming out of the water.

A few years ago, I received a letter from a sailing volcanologist who said that at the rate it is growing, it could break water sometime in the mid-1990s.

If you see smoke coming out of the water, stay away from it. In fact, I advise avoiding this area in any case, as the volcano pinnacle rising out of deep water undoubtedly could cause the sea above it to be quite rough.

LONDON BRIDGE
(Chart 40; II B-3, B-32)
This small island is about 1½ miles south of Ile de Caille and noteworthy only for the hole that the sea has washing through it. The rock formation is fascinating and picturesque—a good view to bolster your photo album.

DIAMOND ISLAND (KICK 'EM JENNY)
(CHART 40; II B-3, B-32)
The etymology of this island's nickname is a mystery; It is probably some untraceable corruption of a French place name. There is no landing here at all. A strong current north of the island frequently sets up in the direction against the wind and kicks up quite a chop. It should also be noted that the shelf drops off steeply from 25 to well over 100 fathoms.

In sailing between Diamond Island and Carriacou, always hold well high of the course. Although it is only a six-mile run, it can get very rough at times. Flying over this area is a real eye-opener. Tide rips can be seen cropping up in every sort of unpredictable place. If possible, carry the dinghy on deck to avoid a swamping. If the current is setting you to windward, you will have no trouble laying the course, but it will be rough going. A set to leeward will give smoother water, but then you'll need to do some tacking.

LES TANTES
(Chart 40; II B-3, B-32)
To windward of Diamond Island and Ile de Ronde, Les Tantes is a series of uninhabited islands. A rough anchorage can be had off their western shore, but I recommend it only for the adventurous. The swell and a stiff current are invariably a problem. Transient fishermen camp on these islands from time to time; otherwise they are deserted. Volcanic activity was also reported in this area between 1986 and 1988.

PETIT MARTINIQUE
(Charts 28, 34; II B-3, B-31, B-311)
As of the year 2000 Petit Martinique still continues to thrive. smuggling is still a major occupation, but it is good honest smuggling; beer, booze; cigarettes; TV's' drugs you can forget about they don't deal in that.

The coastguard established a base on the island, but the Petit Martinicans made it clear to them that they should go and chase the drug smugglers and not the local rum smugglers. If they tried to chase the local rum smugglers the coast guard would have their boat sabotaged in very short order.

The Petit Martinicans are now in the racing scene with a vengeance. They have their own local class, where it appears the only rule is a maximum length of 18-feet. Other than that the sky is the limit. Plenty of sail area, tall masts, three men on a trapeze, open stern - real fliers. They can be seen racing in most of the local regattas in Grenada and the Grenadines.

One can find a very nice restaurant. P.A.L.M.S......, in a wonderfully planted landscaped garden. You don't have to be actually in Petit Martinique to take advantage of the restaurant. Anchor over in Petit St. Vincent, give them a call on the radio and they will send the boat over to pick you up. They take you over to the restaurant, have yourself a good fee, have your drinks and not have to worry about running your own dinghy back. They will then deliver you back to your boat.

TYRELL BAY (HARVEY VALE BAY)
(Charts 28, 34; II B-3, B-31, B-311)
The Slipway never really got going and died a natural death. The latest operation is a travelift capable of hauling boats drawing u to 8-feet. To date (April 2000) marine supplies are a problem. It is a case of arriving with your boat and all the bits and pieces you need for your haul.

Bill Pringle and Mike Foreshaw—the latter a retired St. Georges Harbour Pilot—as of November 2000, are setting up a Marine Supply store to supply the needs of yachts hauling in Cariacou. 443 6993 FAX 8092

Right next to the slipway is Carriacou Yacht Club with a very nice little hotel with bar, restaurant, small commissary store, fax, phone, email-the works.

You will also find, up at the other end of the harbor, near the oil tanks, a small Artists Studio, bar, cyber café, fax, phone and email. Between the two above mentioned establishments, one will find various hotels, bars restaurants, and grocery stores.

At one point it was alleged that shopping in Cariacou was better than it was in Grenada. This was possibly true, in the days of the PRA but definitely it is no longer true today.

8

Grenada

(Imray-Iolaire Charts 1, B, B-3, B-32)

Formerly a British colony but independent since 1974, Grenada is a large, lush, populous island of about 90,000 people. Situated roughly 460 miles southeast of San Juan and 90 miles north of Trinidad, it is 18 miles long and 8 miles wide. A mountain range extends almost the entire length of

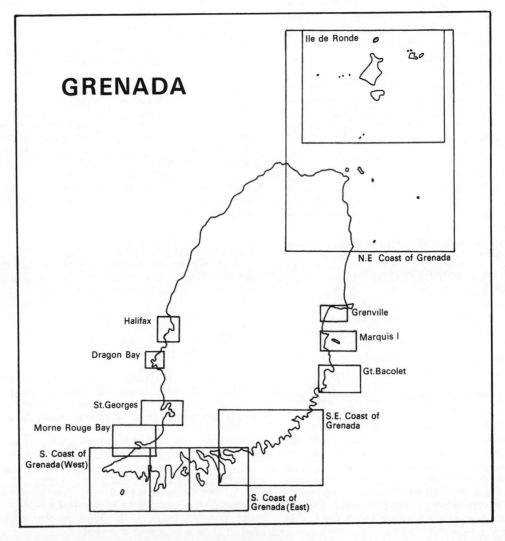

the island, and there is enough rain to make most of Grenada verdant throughout the year. However, because the north and southwest ends are low, the island basically has three climates: The rainfall in the mountains is double that of the town of St. Georges, while out toward Point Salines, Prickly Bay (Anse aux Epines), and Mount Hartman, the rainfall is half that of St. Georges. This makes the south coast hard on farmers but wonderful for vacationers and yachtsmen.

Grenada was settled originally by the French and then taken over by the British during the eighteenth-century colonial wars, when spices had become as valuable as gold. The value the British assigned to this trade can be judged by the number of old forts still visible on the island. Fort George stands today as it did in the early eighteenth century. A small fort on the top of the hill to the north of town reputedly was once connected to Fort George by a tunnel. On the hills east of town are Fort Frederic, Fort Lucas, and Fort Dalfas, with their large parade grounds out front. Dalfas has been a prison for many years. Fort Jeudy, on the south coast, was built to protect the entrance to Port Egmont.

A French colonial influence persists in the commercial habits of the island, in that everything revolves around the capital, St. Georges. Produce grown throughout the island is shipped to the market at St. Georges, where it is sold, loaded into carts, and trundled back out to the countryside. The market itself—which is quite a spectacle—is open six days a week. (Best days to go are Wednesday and Saturday.)

On any Saturday during the year, a profusion of cargo schooners and bright-red sloops can be seen lying peacefully at the waterfront, set off against the green hillsides, whose slopes are zigzagged by the narrow tracings of roadways. The market is piled high with wonderful collections of fresh fruits and vegetables, trussed-up chickens and hens, and squealing pigs and goats. Through this organized chaos scamper hordes of small children. Brightly uniformed policemen gesticulate smartly to unsnarl the traffic through town. In decades past, much of this traffic used to be squadrons of colorful trucks, their sides emblazoned with eyecatching slogans: "Trust No Friend," "Fool's Paradise," "Happy Home."

These "mammy buses," as they are called, were big banana trucks converted to carry passengers when they weren't carting bananas. During the days of Maurice Bishop's People's Revolutionary Government (PRG), however, most were replaced by minibuses, which are less colorful (though they still bear slogans) but much more efficient. They run many routes until almost midnight.

It's no problem to tour the island by rented car or taxi. The taxi drivers are courteous and honest, but it is best to check out the fares beforehand, particularly for long trips. There are many taxi drivers who are favorites of yachtsmen, but one old faithful is Wilfred Lewis. If you are interested in the flora and fauna, call Wilfred (telephone: 2743), who has a thorough knowledge of all the best places to visit in the botanical garden, spice estates, and rain forest.

An interesting one-day schedule is to tour the island in the morning, then stop in the island's northeast corner for an excellent two-hour West Indian lunch at Betty Mascal's Plantation Morne Fendue restaurant, La Belle Creole, St. Patricks (telephone: 9330). Then, before going home, swim and sunbathe at one of the beaches at the north end of the island.

For many years Grenada was one of the wealthiest islands in the Eastern Caribbean. Examination of the *British West Indian Yearbook*— compiled by the British government throughout the nineteenth century and up to recent years—shows that Grenada had a favorable balance of trade and profit year in and year out (with the exception of an occasional bad year) from 1820 until 1955, when the island was devastated by a hurricane. It was the only island in the Eastern Caribbean that could boast this economic distinction. The bases of its economy have long been cocoa, nutmeg, and other spices—hence its label, "the Spice Island."

Historically, Grenada has had the largest collection of small landowners of any of the islands in the Eastern Caribbean. Cocoa, nutmeg, and bananas are crops that small farmers with just three or four acres could cultivate and from which they could make a decent living. There were also large estates, of course, but most of the land was owned by Grenadian farmers. Unlike the inhabitants of other West Indian islands, the Grenadians do not feel that they have been victimized over the years by the big sugar planter or the banana producer— which affects markedly their attitude toward nonlocals.

Visiting yachtsmen are often surprised to discover that the day laborer varnishing his brightwork or painting his topsides owns his own plot of land, or sometimes three or four acres. And those men constitute what is probably the best labor pool available in the entire Eastern Caribbean.

A word of warning, though: While many of these

workmen are excellent, a few are terrible and should be avoided at all costs. Some of the worst are among the most enterprising, so do not hire the first person who comes along. When at the Grenada Yacht Club, check with the local yachtsmen before hiring anyone. At Spice Island Marine Services and Grenada Yacht Services (GYS), be sure to check with the office before lining up a worker. This is extremely important, as both yards have some laborers hanging about whom they certainly would not recommend.

For all its historical prosperity, Grenada has suffered hard times in recent decades. Political disasters have been bad enough, but the first blow fell in 1955, when Hurricane Janet completely flattened the island. England sent massive aid to support the rebuilding, and anyone who could wield a hammer was pressed into service. (These days, the worst insult you can lay on a Grenadian carpenter is to say, "You're nuttin' but a Janet carpenter, mon.") The British government awarded large disaster-relief loans to farmers and estate owners to help restore their nutmeg and cocoa crops, but a cocoa tree takes about seven years to mature, and a nutmeg tree takes seven to 10 years to bear and 15 years to produce—so it has been a long pull for the farmers. Still, they have a lot going for them. Anything can be made to grow in Grenada, including, nowadays, onions and Irish potatoes—two crops that used to be imported because the agricultural "experts" maintained they would not make it in the tropics.

Tourism began to take hold in the early 1960s, and by the early 1970s, Grenada had a rapidly expanding industry. The island had also become the center of yachting in the Southern Caribbean.

Then came the disastrous political troubles that reversed all of the economic gains of the 1970s. I don't want to dwell too long on politics in this cruising guide, but if Grenada resumes its place as a yachting capital, as I feel sure it will, it's important that yachtsmen have some historical perspective on what's been happening there.

The US intervention in Grenada in October 1983 was merely the culmination of 30 years of political turmoil that began in the 1950s, when a young labor leader named E.M. Gairy returned from Aruba and founded GULP (Grenada United Labor Party). He organized the agricultural workers for the first time and was elected premier. Then began a period of such unbridled free-spending—known as the era of Squandermania—that the British actually sent in a frigate, landed troops, removed Gairy, and installed the opposition. This happened twice, in fact, and

each time Gairy got himself reelected, the second time in 1969. For a fictionalized picture of this period, read Alec Waugh's 1956 novel *Island in the Sun*, or see the 1957 film of the same name, which starred Harry Belafonte. It is the thinly disguised story of Gairy and Grenada. Another novel depicting the rise of Gairy is the excellent book *Ruler in Haroona*, available in paperback at the Sea Change Bookstore in St. Georges, underneath the Nutmeg Cafe (which also stocks Street guides and Imray-Iolaire charts).

Although a period of economic prosperity followed, Gairy established a tyrannical one-man rule, enforced by the much-feared "Mongoose Gang," which many have compared to Haiti's Tonton Macoute. Law and order broke down and crime and violence were rife.

In 1973, Gairy won yet another suspicious election, and he took that as a mandate to lead Grenada to independence. A general strike followed, during which, on Bloody Monday, Gairy sent out his goons armed with 303 Enfield rifles—which, fortunately, most of them didn't know how to use. They did, however, kill Rupert Bishop, father of Maurice Bishop, who later became the leader of the People's Revolutionary Government (PRG).

Although most Grenadians didn't want independence (at least under Gairy), the British in 1974 acted on Gairy's wishes—they removed Grenada from Associate State status and gave it independence. This put an intolerable burden on the island—as it did on all the other former colonies that had dropped out of the British West Indies Federation to become independent. (Now, all the former British islands except Montserrat, the British Virgin Islands, and Anguilla are independent.)

Even in pre-independence days, the islands, encumbered with top-heavy bureaucracies, could barely make ends meet. Now, with missions to the United Nations, London, Ottawa, Washington, and other capitals, plus the burden of raising and equipping defense forces, the barriers to solvency seem insurmountable.

Furthermore, there are only so many educated people in the islands, and when a lot of them go off to the foreign service, there aren't enough left at home to operate government and business. Inevitably, some of those jobs are going to be filled by people who are partially or altogether unqualified.

After Grenadian independence in 1974 came another election, well managed by the Gairy government to retain his hold on the office. But after a few more years, Gairy's ego and the oppression and confusion of his rule became so overwhelming that many Grenadians—including businessmen as well as politicians—decided something had to be done.

On March 13, 1979, an almost bloodless coup—extremely well organized by the New Jewel Movement and led by Messrs. Bishop, Radix, and Cord—overthrew the Gairy dictatorship. It was so neatly done that tourists wandered through the streets taking photographs of the revolution as it progressed. On the morning of the coup, everyone was most impressed by Maurice Bishop's speech broadcast over Radio Montserrat. He stated that the people were justified in overthrowing the Gairy government and that the new government felt that foreigners were welcome on the island, that they had a right to stay on the island, and that their property would be protected. The next morning, the newly created People's Revolutionary Government flew the American ambassador and the British and Canadian high commissioners to Grenada from Barbados. Officials of the new regime took them on a tour of the island to prove that all was calm, and they requested these representatives to assure Grenada that their respective governments would not support ex-Premier Gairy, who had appealed to them and to the United Nations for money and matériel to invade the island and rout the PRG.

Within 24 hours, the British and Canadian governments gave their assurances. However, the American government took a full 10 days to do this. Although the United States did not flatly turn down the new regime's request for arms and aid funds, it certainly put off the PRG. Nor did the newly appointed US ambassador distinguish herself by her understanding of and dealings with the new government.

The Cubans saw the opportunity, jumped into the breach, and supplied arms, ammunition, and instructors to turn the ragtag group of instant revolutionaries into a proper army. Cuba supplied medical aid in the form of doctors, equipment, and money for the hospital, all of which were sorely needed. Most important of all to the average Grenadian, Cuba promised to build a jetport to make possible night landings on the island—something every Grenadian had been dreaming about for the previous 15 years.

When Bishop's group took over, most of us didn't know whether they were communists, socialists, or something else. And for a while, things definitely improved. The Mongoose Gang was locked up, crime was curbed, and thieving in Grenada's harbors was nearly eliminated.

But the People's Revolutionary Government (and its defense wing, the People's Revolutionary Army) turned out to be working not for the Grenadian people but rather for the cause of communism, and improvements in law and order were offset by suppression of individual freedoms. Those who opposed the administration ended up in prison—referred to as Mr. Bishop's Reeducation University. A power struggle developed between Cord, the radical, and Bishop, the moderate. The island was flooded with Cubans, who not only built the promised airfield at Point Salines but also dredged a 20-foot channel into Port Egmont so they could off-load heavy equipment directly onto the military base.

The base was not for launching rockets at Washington (what's the point, when Cuba is closer?), but to build an army that could immediately go to the support of a communist revolt or coup on any of the neighboring islands.

Nor was the airfield a military installation, as President Ronald Reagan claimed in his verbal attacks on Grenada. (He was singularly ill-advised by his advisers.) The airfield was certainly not military, since all of the fuel tanks were above ground. On the other hand, it *was* a perfect staging and refueling point for any Cuban or Soviet planes that might have had business in the area. Remember the Soviet plane loaded with arms that was seized in Brazil? Had the Grenada runway been completed at the time, that plane almost certainly would have refueled in Grenada and not have been seized in Brazil. So, to that extent, the airfield had military value.

In October 1983, the feud between Cord and Bishop finally boiled over, and there was a bloody massacre at Fort George, where Bishop and an unknown number of his supporters were murdered. A general curfew rang out, and there was allegedly a list of some 5,000 people—out of a population of 90,000!—to be eliminated.

That is when Governor General Scoon and the heads of other Caribbean states asked the United States to intervene. (The United States dodged the stigma of aggression by calling the action, if you can believe it, a "vertical insertion"; the Grenadians refer to it simply as the "rescue," or the "intervention.") The intervention used massive numbers of men and massive firepower, and it was accomplished quickly despite incredibly bad planning and lack of information. The CIA had complete intelligence about the island, the Cubans, and their gun emplacements, and various people had been contacted and were ready to advise the liberating forces about the lay of the land, but as a result of massive communications blunders, little of this help reached the American military. Helicopters were even flying around without maps of the island!

Nonetheless, the troops behaved magnificently during the liberation, and they continued to do so after the island was secured. They remained until April 1985, and many Grenadians were sorry to see them go then, being firmly convinced that hard-core PRA types (with buried guns) will make trouble again sooner or later.

The performance of the US State Department and AID (Agency for International Development) officers is another story. So unimpressive was their record that for the first time in my life, I was embarrassed to be an American.

First of all, the US government employees on the island drew *combat pay* for a long time after the liberation. They rented the most expensive homes, paid considerably above the market price, then stored the indigenous furniture at government expense and had all their fancy American amenities flown down from the States. At the same time, the Grenadian government couldn't get AID to furnish a few secondhand trucks to carry water to parts of the island that had gone dry!

At one point, I met an officer of the OAS (Organization of American States) who, after spending a few months checking the yachting scene on Antigua, had come to Grenada to see what could be done to reestablish yachting there. (I admit that he got off on the wrong foot with me by saying he'd never heard of this guide or the Imray-Iolaire charts.) His chief concern seemed to be how he could buoy the beaches so that water-skiing boats would not interfere with swimmers! I fear I ruffled his feathers by pointing out that there weren't more than three water-skiing boats in all of Grenada— and that two of them probably were broken down. So much for misdirected aid.

A US embassy has been established in St. Georges, complete with ambassador and staff, but they don't issue passports or visas. You have to go to Barbados for those. What does the embassy do? I met the ambassador at a party at Spice Island several months after the invasion, and he told me in no uncertain terms that he worked from nine to five and that he didn't care how long I had lived on the island—he was not interested in talking about Grenada with me unless I made an appointment to see him in his office. Our dedicated diplomats at work.

In general, although great goodwill and enthusiasm accompanied Uncle Sam's establishment of a massive aid program to repair battle damage and restore basic services, most local people feel that the amount of money spent constructively in Grenada bears little relation to the stated total amount of the aid program.

Nevertheless, things finally started moving ahead under the interim government. Then an election was called in 1985, and it was won by Herbert Blaize, who was put up by a coalition assembled for the sole purpose of ensuring that E.M. Gairy did not get reelected. That government—which was somewhat hamstrung by the fact that it was a coalition—stayed in place until 1990, when Blaize died. In any country, coalition governments seldom achieve anything of importance; in the West Indies, they achieve very little. Some excellent development schemes were proposed by outsiders willing to invest large quantities of money, but the projects died because Grenadian officials were unwilling to make decisions.

One of the biggest problems in Grenada (and, in fact, in all of the West Indian islands) is that the government is run by political theoreticians— politicians who have never run successful businesses. They cannot comprehend business and the need to make prompt decisions to encourage capital investment. For example, take the marine scene. In the heyday of yachting in Grenada, the early 1970s, some of us sat down and figured out that between Grenada Yacht Services, Stevens Yachts, Spice Island Boatyard (now Spice Island Marine Services), and the charter fleet—the yachting business directly employed (not counting taxi drivers, laundry women, etc.) roughly 50 percent of the total workers in the island hotel industry. When you consider that the yachting industry pays wages considerably higher than hotels—in cold cash coming onto the island—the yachting industry at that time probably generated two-thirds to three-fourths of all the cold cash paid to labor in the hotel industry. The government was jumping up and down and doing backflips to help the hotels, but it would do nothing for the yachting industry, claiming that yachtsmen contributed nothing to the economy of the island.

This is a war cry throughout the Eastern Caribbean islands: The politicians insist that yachts contribute nothing to the economies of their islands, which is absolutely NOT true. This is well supported by the fact that in St. Thomas the tax department (which evidently did not believe what the politicians were saying) did a survey of where their tax dollars were raised, and they came to the conclusion that charter yachting (general yachting was not included) produced 18 cents out of every dollar raised in taxes in St. Thomas. If you threw in general yachting, it would have gone up to 22 or 23 cents. The survey showed that charter yachting was one of the largest single sources of tax revenue on St. Thomas.

Now that Grenada has a VAT (value-added tax) on virtually everything, I am sure that if yachting were to get rolling again in Grenada, it would be one of the largest (if not the largest) sources of tax revenue for the government.

Unfortunately, yachting still has never gotten back on its feet here. When the island was "liberated" in October 1983, Grenada Yacht Services was (as is said locally) "in a state of disrepair." If the government had actively encouraged the sale of GYS, I am sure the operation would have been sold and completely rebuilt many years ago.

The most recent proposal to rebuild GYS and develop the whole Lagoon was a particularly grandiose one, and it died on the vine after taking three years to stem local opposition and obtain all the government approvals. The plans included knocking down the Islander Hotel, the forced sale of all land on the hill above GYS, the purchase and bulkheading of the entire Lagoon to create a 300-boat marina, the complete revamping of the present GYS site as an upscale marina catering to megayachts. Plans also included the construction of a 300-ton synchro-lift on the eastern side of the harbor, complete with side-tracking transfer facilities.

Why can't developers propose a less ambitious and more realistic project? To fill the bill, GYS needs a good marine store, a strong charter organization, and a powerful communications setup (both SSB and VHF), with a relay tower in the mountains. It must have carpentry, fiberglass, paint, machine, engine, refrigeration, electric, and electronic shops; and it has to have really good hauling facilities, with adequate side-tracking capacity so there won't be any waiting in line to get hauled. In short, new owners will have a tall order, and a great responsibility to yachting in Grenada.

What the government of Grenada should have done—and could still do—is advertise Grenada Yacht Services for sale in the major European yachting publications: English, French, Italian, German, Swiss. (More and more Swiss boats are coming to the Caribbean, and the Swiss always have money!)

If a legitimate proposal comes through, the government should lean on the present owners of GYS and persuade them to sell at a reasonable price, as the purchaser basically would be buying only the lease and the property.

I say this because, apart from the main building, which needs massive repairs, the other buildings should be bulldozed and completely rebuilt. And the docks are worthless, with decking in such bad shape that it is said the only safe way for a fat man to walk on them is to wear snowshoes or skis!

It's the same story with the lift dock. It needs a complete survey by a competent engineer familiar with that type of machinery.

Just putting in the hauling facility—instead of spending money on acquiring hotels—would ensure the profitability of the operation. A project of this size could be financed; the grandiose projects are too enormous to obtain adequate financing and all of the necessary government permits.

Similar problems are occurring in Grenada's hotel industry: It's taking two and three years to obtain permission to build hotels. In many cases, at the end of a year of struggling with the government, the investors have said to hell with it, packed their bags, and gone to other West Indian islands to build their hotels. Needless to say, this means a tremendous number of employment opportunities lost to Grenada.

St. Georges Harbour is slowly being expanded, partly to cope with the increased freight traffic caused by Grenada's reawakening economy and partly to attract more cruise-ship business. The harbor department proposes widening the existing channel into the Lagoon to create a cruise-ship berth in front of the Grenada Yacht Club. This would be a mixed blessing, for although it would increase the number of cruise-ship visits, the widening of the channel might very well allow the winter ground swell to get into the Lagoon, thus destroying it as a totally secure anchorage. The loss of the potential yachting industry is too big a price to pay for a few more cruise-ship customers—who don't spend that much money in Grenada anyway.

My suggestion is to let the cruise ships continue to anchor off, but provide big, power-driven catamarans that could carry 250 passengers at once instead of taking the passengers ashore in little launches. This plan would cater to the cruise-ship business but would cost a lot less than building a cruise-ship berth in the Lagoon, and it wouldn't destroy the Lagoon as a yacht haven.

With a thriving hotel and tourist business, a reestablished yachting industry, and revitalized agriculture, Grenada could again become the Caribbean's wealthiest as well as one of its most beautiful islands.

One last note that indicates how a lot of Grenadians felt about their governments in recent years is the fact that somewhere around 50,000 of them left the island during the 10-year period following independence. As the saying goes, they voted with their feet. Among those who left were a tremendous number of well-trained and competent crew and shipyard workers. You will run into Grenadian boat boys in Antigua, Tortola, Miami, and even Newport (but only in the summer—they don't like the cold weather any more than the birds do). Almost to a man, the Grenadians who worked on boats were opposed to both the Gairy and Bishop governments.

Iolaire, incidentally, emerged from the intervention in Grenada almost unscathed—but she was lucky! She was moored at the end of the GYS dock in St. Georges, and during the attack, a rocket ripped a six-foot hole in the dock only 20 feet away from her starboard side; machine-gun bullets and shrapnel stitched holes in the dock behind her and up along her port side. (Meanwhile, the Street family's two houses, which had been occupied for three and a half years by the Grenadian military, were blown to smithereens by Uncle Sam's helicopters.)

After the liberation, we took *Iolaire* to St. Thomas on a fast starboard-tack sail, and not until we were in Tortola, smoothing over the dings in her topsides, did we discover that a piece of shrapnel had gone clear through the hull on the starboard side and lodged behind the icebox. Someday I'll buy a Purple Heart from a hock shop and mount it on the bulkhead!

We hope the yachts will be coming back to Grenada. Indeed, this is probably inevitable. From a yachtsman's standpoint, the island is almost ideal. Back in 1839, it was described in the old British Sailing Directions as "the loveliest of our islands in the West Indies." Little has happened in the last 150 years to change that view. I have sailed in the Eastern Caribbean for some 30 years now, and Grenada still is tops.

In St. Georges you have a safe, secure anchorage in the Lagoon within dinghy distance of produce markets, supermarkets, fish markets, telephone, cable offices, banks, and marine and general hardware stores. The south coast of Grenada has a beautiful cruising climate and anchorages literally too numerous to mention. In short, if you miss Grenada, you are missing the best part of a Caribbean cruise.

You'll find Customs and Immigration for Grenada at Prickly Bay (Anse aux Epines), Grenville, and St. Georges. In the latter, tie up at the Grenada Yacht Club dock or anchor, hoist your "Q" flag, and send the skipper ashore to clear. At Prickly Bay, follow the normal "Q"-flag, skipper-only-ashore routine.

Through a generous grant, **the buoyage of Grenada has been changed to the IALA system B—i.e., the US system of red/right/returning**.

The harbor department has on its staff Mike Forshaw, a surveyor recognized by the leading Lloyd's underwriters, a good yachtsman, and the former hauling boss at GYS.

Thanks to much hard work, the buoyage and lighting system of Grenada and the Grenadines has been vastly improved. The buoyage and light system as of July 1991 is shown on the charts and sketch charts in this book. However, remember that in all the islands the harbor pilots are stuck for funds, and there is NOWHERE in the Eastern Caribbean (with the possible exception of the French islands of Martinique and Guadeloupe) where the lighting and buoyage system can be relied upon. Thus, once again: DO NOT ENTER STRANGE HARBORS AT NIGHT.

ST. GEORGES HARBOR
Chart 41: II B-3, B-32)
(SEE UPDATES TO 2001 ON PAGES 169-170)
There is no problem in entering here. The ranges in the outer harbor are for large ships, and you can disregard them. There is plenty of water all the way in. If you arrive at night, it is best to anchor in the northeast corner of the Carenage. The range lights shown on the chart may not be working, but there are no hazards, and you should have no trouble entering if you pay attention to the charts. *All buoy lights, however, must be regarded as unreliable.* The "official" yacht anchorage is in the northeast corner, beyond a line drawn between the firehouse and the Texaco agency (dotted line, Chart 41). Stay well up in the northeast corner to be clear of the maneuvering big ships. It is best to drop anchor in the shallows and then pay out into deeper water. The center of the harbor is 60 feet deep over a poor-holding mud bottom. Yachts are not permitted to go alongside the main wharf unless they have made previous arrangements with the harbormaster. It is reserved for large vessels. (Many of these tie up stern-to, with the wind holding them off.) It goes without saying that you should anchor clear of the fairway, but I have more than once seen yachts

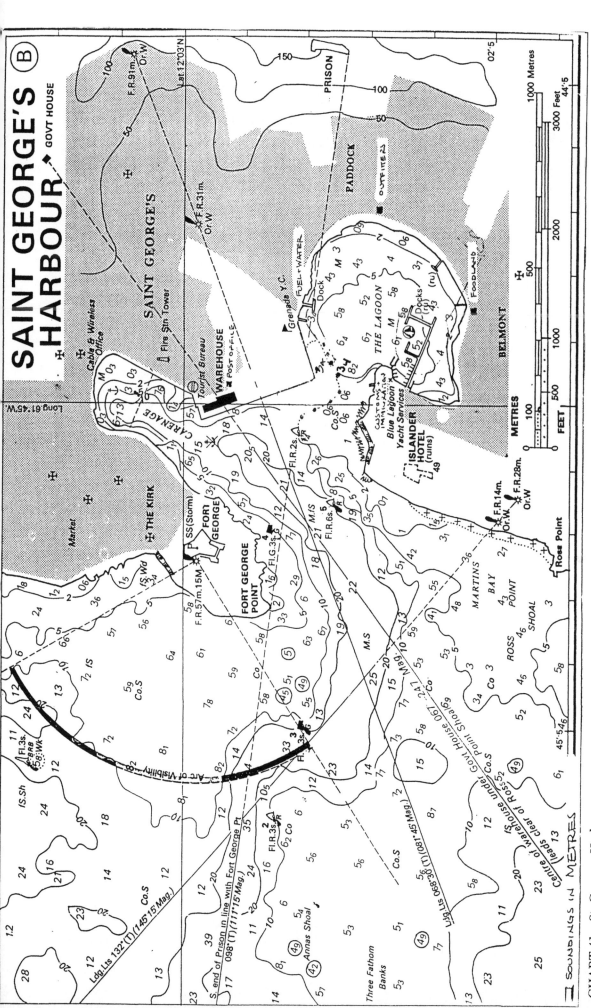

CHART 41 St. Georges Harbour

Range A. Two red lights ashore in line leads E of Anna's Shoal, 145°–325° magnetic.
Range B. Two red-orange lights in line leads along harbor channel, 081.5°–261.5° magnetic.
Range C. SE corner warehouse under Government House leads clear of Ross Point Shoal, 065°–245° magnetic.

Note: *Buoy lights are totally unreliable; some posts marking the channel have been knocked down and have not been replaced.*

148   *Street's Cruising Guide to the Eastern Caribbean—Martinique to Trinidad*

anchored at the mouth of the harbor right smack in the middle of the commercial channel.

St. Georges Harbour still looks a bit like a battlefield. In May 1986, three steel freighters in the harbor were one step away from sinking, and five or six fishing trawlers were sitting there unused. Inevitably, someone would forget to pump the bilges and the boats would go glug-glug, necessitating a salvage operation. By May 1991, little had changed. The Lagoon has various wrecks, the most conspicuous of which is the *Aurora Borealis,* a 185-foot wooden World War II army freight boat, sunk right next to Grenada Yacht Services. Needless to say, as long as its main harbor is littered with wrecks, Grenada will have trouble becoming a yachting center again.

There is always a great deal of activity in the Carenage, with water taxis and fishing boats shuttling back and forth all day long. These water taxis (bumboats) are the most economical way of getting from one side of the harbor to the other. They will also pick you up at Food Fair or Foodland, where you can load all your groceries directly into the water taxi and be rowed right to your boat. It certainly is a lot more pleasant to climb in a bumboat, sit with a beer in one hand and a book in the other, and have a leisurely ride back to the yacht club or your boat moored in the Lagoon than it is to bounce over the rough roads and fight traffic jams in a taxi and then have to carry your groceries down a long dock! The only problem is that getting a water taxi into town from the yacht club, the Lagoon, or GYS can be difficult. It is beyond my comprehension why, over the last 20 years, GYS has not made a deal with a boatman to be there at, say, 0900 and 1300, when people are likely to want to go into town.

Food Fair used to be one of the best places in the whole area to stock up for a cruise. The variety was superb and the management was willing to get what they didn't have if you asked for it. With the difficult times, however, Food Fair understandably declined, so that it stocked just the basics. In 1989, however, things picked up, foodwise. A new organization, Foodland, has built a beautiful supermarket on the south side of the Lagoon, complete with dinghy landing. Plus they have another small store on the roundabout on the road to Prickly Bay (Anse aux Epines). Spurred by the competition, Food Fair and Buy-Rite have pulled up their socks. After having sailed through the islands in January 1990, I would say that, with the exception of the French islands, Grenada now has the best food shopping in the Eastern Caribbean south of the Virgins. St. Martin may be cheaper for meats and prepared foods, but Grenada wins six ways to Sunday on fresh produce.

Access to the Lagoon—the recess south of the Carenage—is via a narrow channel. No more than 12 feet can be carried through here at high water. Originally the channel into the Lagoon was marked by a row of posts along each side. Over the years, however, boats have run into the posts and knocked them down or bent them over, and they have not been replaced. So only half the posts are there. Be sure you line up the remaining ones and stay exactly in the center of the channel. In December 1978, the trimaran *Tri-Star* was coming down the edge of the channel and impaled herself on one of the bent-over poles, which went through her center hull and emerged in the main cabin. Luckily, she had enough buoyancy to float on her outer hulls. Now the channel is clearly marked by buoys, but the broken-off posts are still there on the edges. Make damned sure you stay absolutely in the middle. Also, remember that the Caribbean's water is lower in May, June, and July. Deep-draft boats are advised to check the depth of the channel by leadline from the dinghy before entering.

It is possible, although not recommended, to sail through this channel; the axis is 150° magnetic. If you decide to anchor off the dock near GYS, bear in mind that the bottom is the softest mud and poor holding. This is the place to use your heaviest anchor and plenty of chain. The advantage of lying in the Lagoon is the easy access to town and the fact that you are out of the way of the heavy commercial traffic. However, it does tend to be muggy at night, and the water is too foul for swimming.

If you are anchored in the Lagoon and want to swim, jump in the dinghy and go across to the flats southwest of the main channel, where two or three feet can be carried. Anchor the dinghy right off the statue under the Islander Hotel. Here you will find clear water and a great place for a wake-up or end-of-the-day swim.

The best dinghy landings in town are off Food Fair, the Nutmeg Restaurant, and the post office. The latter offers ready access to Rudolf's restaurant and bar—but leave a stern anchor out to hold your dinghy off or it will try to bash itself to pieces against the seawall. Or else tie your dinghy to the small dock at the Turtle Back restaurant.

Fuel, water, and electricity are available alongside the GYS dock. Cube ice is available at Claud's Marine Store, while Basil St. John, who lives across the street from GYS, supplies block ice and is also a refrigerator repairman.

At the southeast corner of the Lagoon you'll find

Lincoln Ross, who specializes in ironwork; it may not look polished and smooth when he's finished, but his work is strong and the price is usually right.

On the north side of the Lagoon is the Grenada Yacht Club, a long-established and most hospitable organization that has entertained yachtsmen from all over the world. The frequency with which it is visited by yachtsmen in proportion to its size puts it in the same league as the Island Sailing Club at Cowes. After the hiatus during the political troubles, yachtsmen started returning here, and the club was extensively redecorated in 1992.

The bar of the Grenada Yacht Club overlooks the harbor and is one of the most pleasant places in the world to enjoy a sundowner. Because you sit looking west, toward the setting sun, you have a wonderful perch to see the green flash. For half of the year, the sun sets in the slot between Fort George and the Islander Hotel. The green flash (a phenomenon reported on at some length in *Cruising World*, in August 1982 and July 1983, and in *Yachting*, in August 1986) is sometimes seen just as the upper limb of the sun goes under the horizon—if you have a crystal-clear sky with no haze on the horizon. The old saying goes that if you have not seen the green flash, you have not met your true love. The club has showers and a phone that are available to members and visiting yachtsmen.

There is also a small hand-powered slip capable of hauling boats to about 35 feet. This provides probably the cheapest hauling in the Eastern Caribbean. Visiting yachtsmen are given guest privileges for two weeks. After that, they need to take out temporary membership, which is still one of the best bargains in the yachting world.

The club sponsors fleets of Lasers and Mirror dinghies, which provide excellent training for up-and-coming yachtsmen. The club also conducts races for larger boats. The two main regattas are the Carl Schuster Memorial Race and the Round Grenada Race, which take place during the first weekend in February; and the Easter Regatta, which comprises a race from Trinidad to Grenada, small-boat racing in St. Georges, and a race to the south coast for the larger boats. During these regattas, the club is besieged by, among others, the fun-loving, hard-drinking, competitive Trinidadians, who race all day and party all night.

The Trinidad-Grenada Race and the Easter Regatta combine with either the Trinidad or Barbados three-day Race Week—they alternate years—to form the Southern Caribbean Ocean Racing Circuit. Unlike the regattas in the northern end of the Caribbean, this circuit has very low entry fees and lots of free parties. The racing is good, and tough, and while the races admittedly are not run with the expertise of the northern regattas, they are still a lot of fun, especially for the cruising division. It's a circuit worth taking in.

One of the nicest things about the Grenada Yacht Club is the fact that both the starting and finishing lines are ranges from the clubhouse; thus, a spectator can see the entire small-boat course and the start and finish of every cruising race right from a bar stool.

Although St. Georges still offers such amenities as well as basic facilities, it has a long way to go to become the preeminent yachting center it used to be. Let's hope new ownership will take over Grenada Yacht Services and spearhead the revival, and in turn do great things for yachting in Grenada.

Yachting had a tremendous amount to do with the healthy economy of Grenada in the 1970s, and it could go a long way toward rejuvenating that economy if private money and government assistance were forthcoming. Is anyone out there listening?

GRAND ANSE
(II B-32)

If you tire of the Lagoon, it is possible to find a good anchorage fairly near town at Grand Anse. This is very good in the summer and somewhat variable in the winter, when the ground swell is up. At such times, the best solution is to anchor bow-and-stern, or stern-to or bow-to the swell, whichever way your boat rides best. If you are approaching from St. Georges, steer a course of about 250° magnetic from the harbor reef, which is marked by a buoy at the southeast corner of the harbor. This course will clear the shoal off Ross Point, after which a course may be steered farther inshore, although you must be very careful of Dathan Shoal north of the Silver Sands Hotel, a three-story white building with porches on all levels. The shoal is about 350 yards offshore. The beach at Grand Anse is a full mile long, lined with hotels and palm trees, and some consider it one of the most magnificent beaches anywhere.

The most popular anchorage seems to be between the Silver Sands and Grenada Beach hotels. (Be careful of the shoals to the west of the Aquatic Club.) You would do well to dive down to inspect the set of your anchor, as it is all too easy to wrap a rode on a coral head here. During the winter, there is always a good deal of activity on the beach. Small boats may be rented from Grenada Water Sports, near the Grenada Beach Hotel.

Whether or not you will be allowed to anchor off this beach is problematical—a war is raging among the yachtsmen, the Hotel Association, and the Park Department. The Park Department, with great justification, points out that if boats anchor amid the coral, they will do damage to the coral that will take hundreds of years to repair. This problem could be solved easily, however, by buoying the coral areas so that yachts would anchor on the white-sand-bottom areas in the center of Grand Anse beach, outside of the coral.

However, the Hotel Association feels that yachts are polluting the beach at Grand Anse, although nothing could be further from the truth. The pollution at Grand Anse is caused not by the yachts but by a variety of factors. First of all, the so-called St. John's River (basically nothing but a dry gut) leads down from the hillside east of Ross Point in an area that is heavily built up with third-rate houses, most of which either have third-rate septic tanks or outhouses with no septic tank. Also, the hills behind Grand Anse beach are loaded with houses of similar ilk. The result is that every time it rains, sewage washes down the hillside and into the bay off Grand Anse. Further, the hotels have expanded to such an extent that their septic tanks (which are built in low, swampy ground and thus are singularly inefficient) overflow into the bay. Between the small private homes and the hotels, the sewage from a couple of thousand people pours each day into the Grand Anse beach area—yet the Hotel Association has the gall to accuse six or eight anchored yachts of polluting the harbor. Let's get the record straight.

A similar situation exists in Tortola, where yachts have been accused of polluting Wickham's Cay—when in fact the runoff of outhouses and the bad septic tanks on the surrounding land are doing the damage. Then there is New York City, where state politicians accuse yachts of polluting the harbor, yet they allow the World Trade Center—which has thousands of people in it every day—to flush its sewage right into the harbor. The amount of sewage produced by the World Trade Center is more than the amount produced by ALL of the yachts in the state of New York!

Thus, in Grenada, the yachtsman is a handy whipping boy used by the politicians and the Hotel Association to divert attention from the grossly inadequate sewage facilities in the area. What the Grand Anse regulations will be when you arrive in Grenada, I don't know. Check locally and proceed accordingly. Also check as to whether or not you are allowed to anchor off Grand Anse.

MORNE ROUGE BAY

(Sketch Chart 42; II B-32)

This is west of Grand Anse and south of Long (or Quarantine) Point, and, draft permitting, is a far superior anchorage to Grand Anse. Feel your way in carefully and anchor in the mouth of the bay. Well offshore, the bottom rises abruptly from five fathoms to one and a half fathoms and then to one fathom. The bottom is hard sand with patches of grass. Shoal-draft boats can work their way in farther using the leadline or sounding pole. Long Point Shoal offers a good deal of protection from the ground swell hooking in from the west around Long Point. Normally a yawl with its mizzen up will lie stern-to the swell; she will hobbyhorse gently rather than pitch wildly.

The bays between here and Point Salines can be regarded only as lunch stops. There are several beaches along this stretch, but all of them are exposed to the northerly swell—good in calm weather only. When heading westward from Grand Anse to Point Salines, avoid the shoal extending northwest of Long Point. You can pass inside the shoal by placing the southeast corner of the warehouse on the dock at St. Georges Harbour under Government House (Sketch Chart 42, Range A, course 062° magnetic). Or you can pass outside by placing the northeast corner of the same warehouse under Government House (Sketch Chart 42, Range B, course 069° magnetic).

Before the Cubans built the runway on Point Salines, yachts sailing out of St. Georges could be becalmed under the point, then be knocked flat by the wind on the south coast; it blows unobstructed all the way from Africa. The lighthouse and hill that used to be on the point were removed when the runway was built, though, so now the wind whistles across the runway and gives you a pretty good idea ahead of time whether or not you should tie in a reef for the beat up the south coast. If you have any doubt, reef.

Don't approach the point too closely, because when they leveled the hill, some large chunks of it fell into the sea; no close-inshore surveys have been done, so watch out.

South Coast

About 150 yards southeast of Point Salines and unmarked by the chart is a rock with six feet of water over it. I discovered this one the hard way during the Easter Regatta in 1973. *Iolaire* received

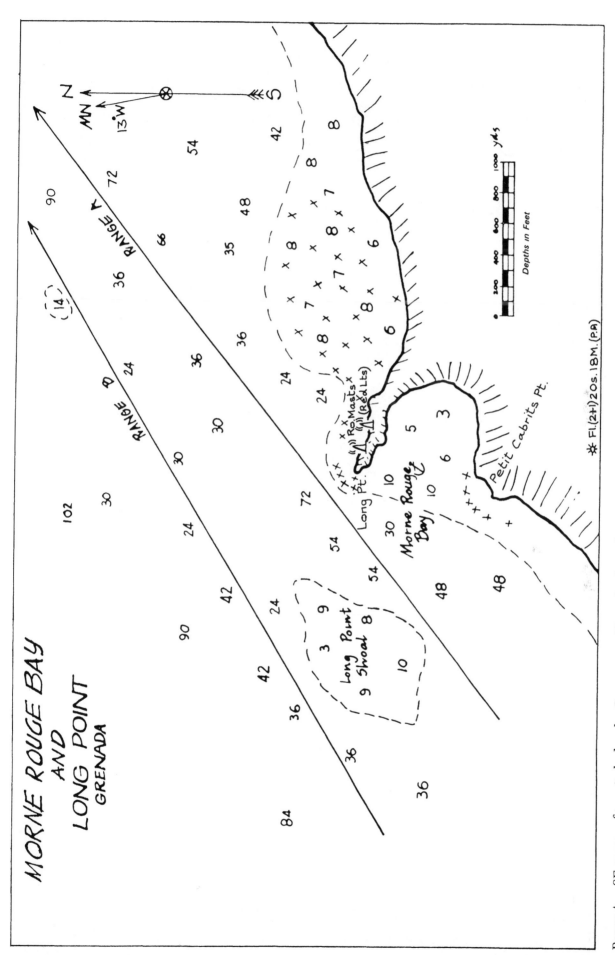

Range A. SE corner of transit shed under Government House leads inside Long Point Shoal, 062°–242° magnetic.
Range B. NE corner of transit shed under Government House leads NW of Long Point Shoal, 069°–249° magnetic.

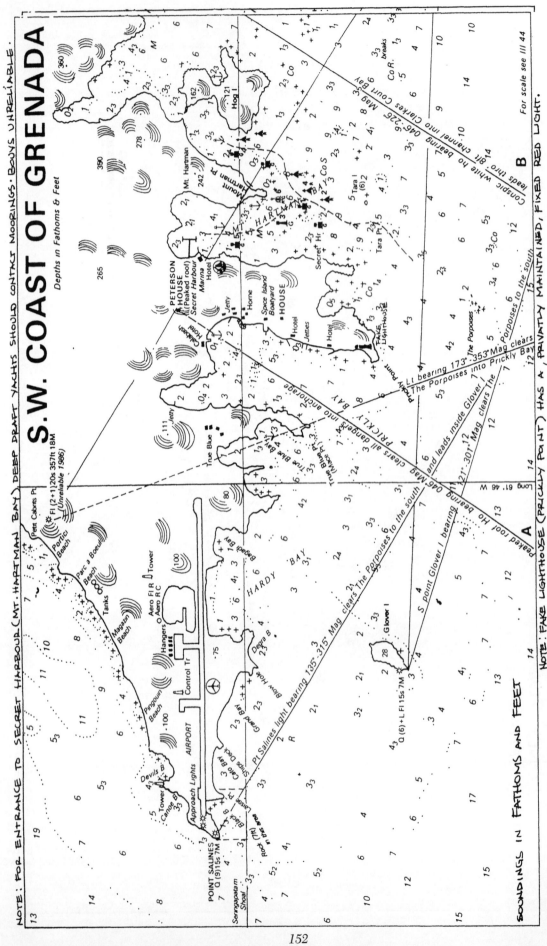

CHART 43 Grenada—Southwest Coast (A)

a good thwack, although *Rosemary V.* following directly behind, passed by safely. It could be that we knocked the top of it off, but I mention it just the same.

Glover Island, south of Point Salines, is seldom visited, except as a lunch stop in its lee. From here you can row ashore and explore the ruins of a Norwegian whaling station.

Hardy Bay used to be an attractive part-time anchorage, but the airport construction filled it in, and it is no longer of much use.

TRUE BLUE BAY
(Chart 43; II B-32)

The water is not very clear here, and it shoals at the head. A protected anchorage can be had northwest of True Blue Point (Mace Point) on the eastern side of the bay. The bay is easily spotted from seaward by a flagpole on the point and by several buildings that were erected for an exposition in 1969. When entering, be careful of the reef off the western corner of the bay.

A bar and restaurant has opened up in True Blue Bay, catering for the yachtsman, making this harbor more frequented by yachts than in the past.

PRICKLY BAY (ANSE AUX EPINES)
(Charts 43, 44; II B-32)

East of True Blue Bay, Prickly Bay (or Anse aux Epines in French) is the most popular anchorage on Grenada's south coast. This is the home of the Calabash Hotel, the Horseshoe Bay Hotel (12° north), and Spice Island Marine Services (formerly the Spice Island Boatyard). At the head of the bay is a beautiful white-sand beach. The best anchorage is in the northeast corner. The bay may be rolly during the winter, with the swell hooking around the point and piling up into the harbor. This is not a dangerous situation, only an inconvenience. Once you have cleared to windward of the shoals east of True Blue Point, bring the peaked-roof house (Chart 43) to bear at 046° magnetic, which will take you clear to windward of the reefs west of Spice Island Marine Services. The harbor is a four-mile drive from St. George's. Taxis can be found at Spice Island.

Spice Island Marine Services had its origins in the mid-1960s, when Peter Spronk started his career as a catamaran designer/builder and convinced Gordon Braithwaite, who owned the Anse aux Epines estate and was starting a residential development, that it would be nice to have a catamaran. To build one, said Peter, you had to have a building; so, after the building was finished, Peter decided he wanted to haul his own boat, so he built a small railway. Others came and asked to be hauled; one thing led to another and the place

slowly grew. *Blue Crane,* Peter's first catamaran, was launched, and then Bill Stevens of Stevens Yachts took over the establishment and started building the Spice Island Boatyard. It was later sold to John Blunt, who, building on the basically good structures and ideas of Bill Stevens, and aided by Dodd Gorman and Adrian Voleny, created what I have previously described as "the prettiest little boatyard in the Caribbean."

Needless to say, with the Gairy troubles, followed by four years under the People's Revolutionary Government, everything went to hell in a handbasket. Then, in 1985, Glen Evans. Jr. (known throughout the Caribbean as "junior"), and backers bought the yard. Junior, his wife, and his younger brother Champie undertook a massive rebuild of the yard and its structures. They abandoned the old railway, installed a 35-ton Travelift, built an excellent restaurant, continued the superb laundry service, and, in short, really got things rolling.

However, after a few years, Junior (who is a topnotch sailor and at one time was the world's youngest certified Boeing 707 flight captain) decided to go back to Singapore Airlines—flying planes was easier than battling with yachtsmen. His brother Champie and his sister Michelle continue to run the yard for many years, but have now given up. Cyrus and Annabelle have continued to run the yard, with more charm than efficiency. The local joke is "you can't complain about the management of Spice Island there IS NOT MANAGEMENT!!!

But while the yard may not be too efficient, they make up for it in friendliness. The management and staff are without doubt the friendliest and most cooperative people you can find in any boat yard anywhere.

The government of Grenada gave the Spice Island operation a 10-year duty-free exemption on the importation of paint and sailcloth—which we all hoped would lead to the creation of a first-rate marine supply store and a good sail loft under the care of Johnny Phillips, who has developed a good reputation as a sailmaker. Unfortunately, things have not turned out that way—the marine supply store is adequate (and stocks Street guides and Imray-Iolaire charts) and the sail-repair operation is still functioning.

Spice Island is a nice, clean, attractive boatyard, and still the prettiest in the Eastern Caribbean, but, as with a tremendous number of marinas in this area, the owners claim they are losing money. But they have to realize that they lose money via reversible routes: For example, neither electricity nor water is metered at the yard, and their method of operating showers costs them money and antagonizes customers. As I mentioned in chapter 3, all marinas should follow the lead of John Ackland, of Tortola's Village Cay Marina, and install token-

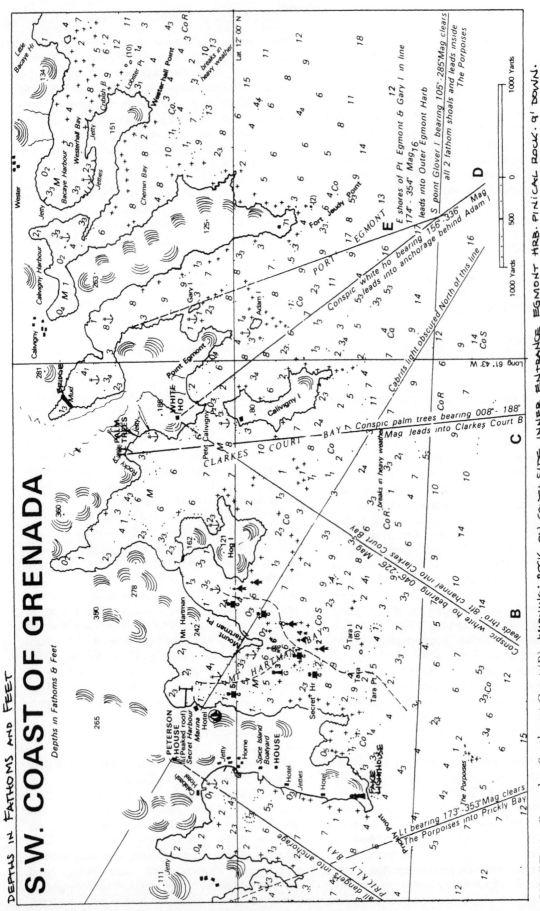

CHART 44 Grenada—Southwest Coast (B)

Range C. Conspicuous palm trees bearing 008°–188° magnetic leads into Clarkes Court Bay.
Range D. Conspicuous white house bearing 156°–336° leads into anchorage behind Adam Island.
Range E. E shores of Point Egmont and Gary Island in line 174°–354° magnetic leads into outer Egmont Harbour. Follow range until Fort Jeudy Point is abeam to starboard, then head up. Follow E side of harbor to avoid reefs S of Gary Island. Stand off and anchor in inner or outer Egmont Harbour.

operated showers. If every marina that has problems with water would install these devices, life would be considerably more pleasant for all yachtsmen.

The most ridiculous aspect of the water situation at Spice Island is that they charge 20 cents (EC) a gallon at the end of the dock, where there's a meter, but people lying alongside and the yard employees have access to unmetered water, and they leave hoses running all day long and waste thousands of gallons.

Regarding electricity, if meters were installed, they would pay for themselves in short order—and after that, it's profit. As it is now, small boats that use minimal electricity are being overcharged, and large boats are being undercharged.

Unfortunately, it's very difficult to get anyone in the Eastern Caribbean to change their methods. The above suggestions were offered to Spice Island Marine Services in 1989, but so far nothing has happened. They claim it all costs money and they don't have the Funds. I say, go borrow it. They are like the guy who staggers into the emergency ward bleeding to death from three large knife wounds. He refuses to let the doctor sew up the wounds because it costs too much, so he staggers out onto the street to die. Spice Island is bleeding to death via the overuse of electricity and water (including showers).

In 1991, Alan Hooper was running the Go Vacations charter fleet here. Alan found himself in a strange position: Go Vacations was in the process of going belly-up because all of its divisions—except Alan's—were losing money. His operation turned in a nice profit, but who knows what the future holds.

Shirley Hooper has created an excellent commissary, which provides the basic needs of boats anchored in Prickly Bay.

Unfortunately, one feature that does not exist in Prickly Bay is a good, reliable bus service to town. Most of the time, it is a case of walking a mile up to the road junction and picking up a ride from there. Slightly inconvenient. The people at Spice Island claim it is impossible to organize bus transportation to and from town. But many people consider that this just means no one is trying very hard to do it. After all, the buses come to the traffic circle a mile away from the yard and then turn around. Is it really impossible to have one driver go an extra mile, perhaps twice a day, to pick up a half-dozen fares?

Within walking distance of the boatyard is the Red Crab, a delightful anachronism. Who would expect to find an English-style pub run on English hours by a Czechoslovakian ex-British Spitfire pilot in Grenada? Unfortunately, Julian Pianachez, who built the Red Crab, is no longer with us, but his pub

is. (One time, I was walking barefoot down the blacktop road at noon, headed for the Red Crab, when I passed two boat boys sitting under a tree drinking beer. One shook his head, looked at the other, and said, "The Skip may look like a white man, but he sure got black man's feet!")

Situated at the head of the bay, the Calabash Hotel has beautiful grounds, a beach bar that is most hospitable, and sailboards and Sunfish for rent on the beach; arrangements can be made for dinner ashore. It is only a short walk through the Calabash grounds to the Red Crab.

South of Spice Island Marine Services is the Horseshoe Bay Hotel, an extremely attractive small hostelry built by John and Aggie Yarwood. It was taken over by the government of Grenada in the PRA days, and the government continued to own it for a number of years after the liberation. Now it has been sold off to a private business/individual and again is in operation. It definitely is worth visiting there, having a drink, and ascertaining whether or not you wish to stay for dinner.

The Porpoises are a group of awash rocks three-quarters of a mile south-southeast of Prickly Point. There is deep water all around them, except that 40 yards north of the easternmost Porpoise is a rock only six feet under. Although the chart didn't mark it, Bill Stevens of Stevens Yachts discovered this one by bouncing hard off it in a Hughes 38.

A buoy was established southeast of The Porpoises. It was a south cardinal buoy, but did not last long—It soon went adrift and was not replaced. You can pass either north or south of The Porpoises—just do not sail close aboard either side of them. Frequent hurricanes passing north of the island have caused the Porpoise buoy to go adrift. The likelihood of a reliable replacement is rather minimal.

MOUNT HARTMAN BAY (SECRET HARBOR)
(Charts 43, 44; II B-32)

To enter this harbor in years gone by required a fair amount of reef dodging, and one had to be extremely careful. It also required a correct chart, as both the British and American charts showed Tara Island as an underwater reef, and the reef to the east of it as an island. If you didn't realize that the charts were wrong, you could become very confused. (The Imray-Iolaire chart is correct.)

In 1963, Hurricane Flora passed north of the island, creating a ground swell that changed the entrance to Mount Hartman Bay. The island washed away and the reef to the west was created. Called Tara Island by the locals, it has now built up to about six feet in height. No more than a heap of slab coral, it teems with sea life and appears to be growing all the time. The water is shallow, and a strong current sweeps by it in such a way that there is no convenient lee in which to make a dinghy approach. If you go ashore, wear sneakers and take along two light dinghy anchors—one to hold the stern off and the other to bury ashore.

Most charts (and some guidebooks) have incorrect information about this area, so be very careful. Do not rely on any bearings taken from the chart unless you are using Imray-Iolaire Chart B-32 or this book.

The Moorings charter firm has established a large base here, purchasing the Secret Harbour Hotel and building a 50-boat marina. Needless to say, they did not want bareboats bouncing off the reefs, so the whole area between Prickly Point and Hog Island has now been buoyed. Entrance is now quite easy; as you beat up the coast, you will find a mark off Tara Point, and you continue on to the mark off Tara Island. Most boats can pass anywhere between the two buoys, but deep-draft boats should hug the Tara Island buoy and stay in deep water, because if the ground swell is running, you could easily bottom out on the two-fathom spot west of Tara Island. If the Moorings maintains its buoyage system, you'll have no problem taking bearings—you'll just follow the buoys.

The Moorings operation is managed by David Baglow, who started his career in the Eastern Caribbean working for Cable and Wireless. He has been a sailor all his life and eventually drifted into the charter business—first in the Eastern Caribbean, then in the Pacific, and now back here. He is also battling the shower dilemma—perhaps he will see the wisdom of installing token-operated showers as has been done at Village Cay Marina in Tortola. One problem he has encountered is that the crews of boats moored up at Hog Island come down to Secret Harbour to collect water in jugs and use the excellent and clean showers at the Moorings. Needless to say, he feels that the Moorings charter guests and the boats paying dock rent should have access to free showers, but how to do it without going broke in the process?

The anchorage is good anywhere in Mount Hartman Bay; one that is guaranteed to be cool and bug-free is behind the low saddle at the southern base of Mount Hartman. The easterly breeze sweeping through this notch in the land is most refreshing. High on a hill on the western side of the harbor stands the Secret Harbour Hotel, which was built back in the early 1970s by Bill and Barbara Stevens. Its architecture is among the most attractive in the area. (It is interesting to note that the three most tastefully designed hotels in Grenada—Secret Harbour, Horseshoe Bay, and the Calabash—all were built without the aid of architects. I ended my university career as president of a fraternity that consisted of 29 architects, a philosophy major, and myself—a history major. I love to needle my architect friends by stating—in light of what I have seen in the Eastern Caribbean—that an architecture degree is merely a license to charge a hell of a lot of money for the plan of a bad building.)

East of Mount Hartman Bay is an unnamed anchorage behind Hog Island, which is one of the finest spots on the south coast of Grenada. To get there from Mount Hartman Bay, you have only to swing around the reef off Mount Hartman Point along a wide semicircle. The shoals extending west of Hog Island must be eyeballed. You can anchor anywhere in the basin between the island and the mainland. I prefer a spot west of the north hill on Hog. There is a dinghy passage into Clarkes Court Bay between the island and the mainland, and it is possible to take a boat through here, but I hesitate to recommend it. For shoal-draft boats, here are the directions: Coming from the west, approach the gap favoring the starboard side of the channel; as you approach the point on Hog Island, veer to the left on 010° magnetic for a distance of 40 yards; then veer right and you are through. The controlling depth is five feet and the channel is 30 feet wide at its narrowest.

The inner entrance to the Hog Island anchorage is now buoyed. If you are approaching the anchorage from seaward, you can eyeball it by taking bearings on Mount Hartman Point. When coming from the east, stay well offshore in the blue area of the Imray-Iolaire chart, bring Mount Hartman to a bearing of approximately· 350° magnetic. Continue on this line of bearing until you spot the reef on your starboard hand, but keep an eye out for the shoal water to port with the two-fathom spot, which can break in heavy weather. Continue until you pick up the four buoys leading into the inner anchorage of Hog Island. If approaching from the south or west, leave Tara Island to starboard, follow· the buoys into Secret Harbour, then swing off to starboard, leaving the red and green buoys to port and heading for the green buoy. Make sure on your inboard tack that you don't pile up on the reef between the two buoys.

The buoying of Mount Hartman Bay/Secret Harbour and Hog Island certainly has made sailing

Grenada 157

into these harbors much easier, BUT it still is a case of eyeball navigation. Do not attempt it in poor light or you could very easily find yourself hard aground.

The buoys are privately maintained and the buoy system is not overly reliable.

SEE ALSO UPDATES FOR HOG ISLAND ON PAGE 170.

CLARKES COURT BAY

(Chart 44; II B-32)

This large harbor contains many coves and is one of the loveliest bays on Grenada's south coast. Other bays may have better anchorages, but not one has so many in a single, sheltered bay. Twenty boats could anchor inside Clarkes Court Bay and still not feel crowded.

I fell in love with this bay early on in my visits to Grenada. In 1963, I bought a house and some land overlooking the bay. I expanded the house and built another for my in-laws, largely in anticipation of the development of a marina and boatyard in the harbor. This would enable me to have the yachtsman's dream: a house high on a ridge, cool and bug-free, from which to look down on my boat, moored stern-to the beach. Our view to the east was all the way to Westerhall Point, to the west as far as Point Salines. Our nearest neighbor was half a mile away.

Alas, so much for a sailor's dream. The People's Revolutionary Government decided that our domain, with its commanding position over the coastline, would be a perfect spot for a military base. So they took over the whole point, walked into our house, and at gunpoint chased out our maid and gardener, allowing them to remove nothing from the house. The maid cleverly grabbed most of my charts (crammed with necessary navigational notes), and later we got Mr. Bishop to order the army to relinquish our double bed, which is now in Glandore, Ireland, and a prized etching of Star boats racing. Otherwise, everything in both houses was burned or used up. No one in the family was ever allowed to visit the place again.

The PRG partially compensated us for the houses; better still, they never transferred the titles of the houses in the register. So, although the US helicopters that blasted the houses left us with only two concrete slabs, we still own seven acres, hold the deeds, and pay the taxes. Someday we hope to rebuild. Certainly Calivigny Island and the neighboring point would make a fantastic site for a development. We'll wait and see what happens.

Calivigny Island forms the eastern side of Clarkes Court Bay, and one of the best anchorages in the area is between it and the mainland. You can sail right up to the shoal, throw your anchor on top, and back off. You will need to use a stern anchor overnight, when the wind has died down and when the current has a tendency to swing you around. It is best to use a heavy anchor, as the bottom is grass.

In the center of the harbor, directly south of Rocky Point, is a large shoal spot with about one foot of water over it. Because this is extremely difficult to make out, I strongly advise against going to the head of the bay unless the light is perfect.

There is another good anchorage in an area I have come to call Saga Cove, on the eastern shore of Hog Island. *Saga*, owned by Harry Disharoon, frequently anchored here, and he considered it one of the best anchorages in Grenada. Good swimming and snorkeling can be had, and as this is on the lee side of the harbor, there is always a good breeze over calm water.

When entering Clarkes Court Bay, beware of the shoals, whose depths are significantly less than shown on the government charts. You have to eyeball the route in good light. It is possible to sail to windward across the shoals southeast of Hog. Range B on Chart 43, course 046° magnetic, will carry seven feet—but no more—safely over the shoals. Certainly the safest way to enter is to stand eastward, taking care to avoid the two-fathom shoal south by east of the hill on Hog. This frequently breaks in heavy weather. Continue east until Stevens Beach bears 008° magnetic (Range C). The beach may be identified by a line of palm trees, a cliff on either end, and a small stone dock in the center.

When anchored in either Hog Island anchorage or Clarkes Court Bay, the easiest way to get to town is to take the dinghy to the head of the harbor, tie up to the dock, put out a stern anchor to hold the dinghy off, and walk to the road, where you will find a couple of friendly rum shops and the stop for the bus to town. Also, at a typical West Indian rum shop, you usually can buy such basic supplies as flour, sugar, eggs, a few canned goods, and sometimes fruit.

SEE ALSO UPDATES ON PAGE 170.

Five feet can be carried between Petit Calivigny and Calivigny Island. You have to stay 50 feet off the Point Egmont shore and feel your way along with a sounding pole. You can spot the channel by heading about 50 yards north of the point south of the conspicuous white house. As you approach shore, start curving to the south, following the shoreline around the point. Once around, head north, east, and then south to the Adam Island anchorage. It is advisable to test this route beforehand from a dinghy. Even so, you will save time over the long beat around to Adam Island.

ADAM ISLAND

(Chart 44; II B-32)

The anchorage behind this island is a good deal better than the government chart indicates. The chart does not reflect the extent to which the small reef south of the island hooks to the west. If you tuck behind—northwest of—this reef, you will be sheltered at all times. From my house on Point Egmont, I never saw it rough behind the reef. To enter from seaward, place the white house marked on Chart 44 on a bearing of 336° magnetic (Range D). Put a person aloft and watch your course carefully, as there is very little room for error through here. Follow this bearing and round up immediately after passing the west reef; beach in and anchor when the house on Adam Island bears southeast and the west reef closes with the southern end of Calivigny Island. Between Adam Island and the mainland, there is a dinghy passage with 18 inches of water.

GARY ISLAND

(Chart 44; II B-32)

There is a good shoal-draft anchorage behind this island that will carry no more than four feet. A deeper daytime anchorage (two fathoms) can be found immediately south of Gary Island. It is well sheltered from normal trade-wind weather but open to winds from the south.

POINT EGMONT

(Chart 44; II B-32)

The inner harbor here is the most protected harbor on the south coast of Grenada. Almost landlocked, it is surrounded by high hills on all sides. Even in the most violent hurricane, I cannot imagine a boat's incurring damage in Egmont Harbor. The entrance is simple as long as you proceed when the sun is high. Steer east offshore until the eastern end of Gary Island is in line with the eastern side of Point Egmont (Range E, 354° magnetic). Bear off, favoring the right-hand side, and continue in a northerly direction into the harbor. The wind hooking around Fort Jeudy Point is likely to put you dead before it. As you approach the head of the harbor, watch out for the shoal along the western side and for an unmarked shoal north of the anchor. symbol on Chart 44. Both can be hazardous.

The inner basin and channel were always thought to be steep-to on both sides, and so they are—if you draw less than nine feet of water. But there is a rock with a bare nine feet over it on the south side of the entrance to Port Egmont's inner harbor—we know this for sure, as Mike Jarrold's *Lily Maid,* a beautiful 1904 British-built cutter, bounced off it in the winter of 1978. With this exception, there is a minimum of 12 feet through this channel.

As mentioned earlier, the Cubans dredged Egmont's inner-harbor channel to 20 feet, presumably so they could off-load military equipment onto the base in secrecy. They planned to put their dock in the southern bight of the inner harbor, but evidently they hadn't read the Street guide, or they would have known about the rocks that *Lily Maid* hit. As it was, they were unable to dredge over to the south side because there was too much rock. Egmont is now deeper than before, but still an excellent hurricane harbor.

Correction: The Cubans attempted to dredge a 20-foot channel into the harbor but somebody did not read this guide and discovered the 9-foot rock under the loose sand. They gave up.

To facilitate land development in the area a bridge has been built across the head of the harbor.

You can anchor anywhere in the inner harbor. It is so sheltered that there will be very little strain on the rode. The swimming and fishing are excellent and the seclusion is perfect.

When you leave, the wind will be dead against you, so it probably is advisable to motor out and set sail under the lee of Fort Jeudy Point. As you depart, stay east of Range D (Chart 44) until Prickly Point separates from the southern tip of Calivigny Island. This will keep you from bearing off onto the shoals south of Adam Island.

CALIVIGNY HARBOR

(Chart 44; II B-32)

The next harbor east of Point Egmont, this is not to be confused with Calivigny Island. The old Sailing Directions speak highly of this harbor, inasmuch as the square-riggers could sail in without having to anchor first and warp their way up to the anchorage at its head. The outer entrance, to Chemin Bay, is very narrow. The shoals extending southwest of Westerhall Point are shallower than the government charts indicate. Stand right on up the harbor, keeping to the middle. You may anchor anywhere within the inner harbor. Some boats prefer to drop a stern anchor and sail up to the sand spit, which is very steep-to. You can jump ashore and tie a line to a bush or bury a hook in the sand. There is abundant fishing among the mangroves on the western side, and there's a good dock on the

Westerhall side of the harbor. Westerhall Point is a large, private development put together by Beres Wilcox. The houses are expensive and beautifully landscaped in this rather nice preplanned community, which is on the main road from St. Georges. 30 minutes away by car. The guard at the entrance probably will allow you to use the phone to call a cab.

The western half of Calivigny Harbor has shoaled drastically. (See the newest corrected Imray-Iolaire charts dated after October 1985.) In the eighteenth and nineteenth centuries, this arm of the harbor was the main port for the island of Grenada; it has shoaled up so much over the years that only a dinghy can get in now.

BACAYE HARBOR/WESTERHALL HARBOR
(Chart 44; II B-32)

North of Westerhall Point, Bacaye is an excellent anchorage, although it is seldom used because of the gross inaccuracy of the government charts. The deepwater passage shown between Lobster Point and the small island east of it has shoaled. The two- and three-fathom spots noted farther southeast have become shallower. The three-fathom spot breaks in heavy weather, and the two-fathom spot has no more than eight or nine feet and breaks continually in heavy weather. Give both spots a very wide berth.

Access to the harbor is through Westerhall Bay along an east-west axis; don't enter after 1300 or the sun will be in your eyes. The depth sounder will not substitute for careful eyeballing, since the reefs are steep-to and would not show up on the dial before you were hard on them. The best anchorage is in the cove on the south side of the harbor in nine or ten feet of water. The bottom is soft mud, so be sure to use a good, heavy anchor.

The best time to depart is after noon—and go out under power. At 0900, the sun will be directly on your line of bearing, making an exit difficult if not impossible. Many years ago, I ran aground in four feet of water trying to tack out in the early morning, having misjudged the end of the reef on the north side of the harbor. No damage was done, thanks to a full-length lead keel; with the aid of a strong anchor windlass, I managed to kedge off.

Just west of Little Bacoklet. It is a small cove which provides a good anchorage for one boat as long as the wind is east or north of east.

Southeast Coast

ST. DAVID'S HARBOR
(Chart 45; II B-32)

Grenada Marine in St. David's Harbor— telephone 473 443 1667; fax 473 443 1668; email info@grenadamarine.com is the newest hauling facility in Grenada. It was created by Jason who is a young Grenadian "go getter" who created a very profitable fish wholesale business buying fish from the local fishing boats, and shipping it off airfreight immediately to other areas.

The travelift is an extra wide travelift to facilitate the hauling of multihulls. He has established a bar, restaurant, showers, storage area for boats. The operation commenced in the closing months of 1999 and it will be interesting to see how the operation develops.

Budget Marine is scheduled to move in and establish a marine supply store also.

As of Spring 2000 the operation showed signs of real success. the only problem is the access road is so bad that taxi drivers recommend people visit via boat rather than taxi. This problem certainly should be surmounted in the years to come.

When entering the harbour keep south along the bearing of 070° on St. David's Point. Keep heading east until the western most building of the hauling facilities bears due north magnetic. Running on this line of bearing and anchor at a suitable depth—it is best to anchor bow and stern facing into the swell, which always seems to hook around St. David's Point.

LA SAGESSE BAY
(Chart 45; II B-32)

The only anchorage is in the eastern half of the bay, west of Marquis Point. A beautiful white beach always has some surf on it. The bay is easily identified by an old estate house on the northeast corner of the beach. This is a popular spot with Grenadians on weekends, and it is a good lunch stop for the visiting yachtsman, but in the past I have not regarded it as suitable for overnight use. Now, having visited La Sagesse a number of times since this book was first published in the 1970s, and having discussed the harbor with other yachtsmen— some of whom spent the night—I have reached the conclusion that La Sagesse does make a viable overnight stop, except when the wind is well around to the southeast and blowing hard.

Even if it is not blowing hard, the swell does hook around the point—not to the extent that it makes the anchorage dangerous, but it can be rocky and rolly. When the wind dies down at night, you will be lying beam-to the swell. Thus, if anchoring overnight, I advise that you moor bow-and-stern facing into the swell; then you should have a good night's sleep.

This stop is especially viable now, because the estate house has been restored and opened up as a very good restaurant. Now you can anchor in La Sagesse Bay, go ashore to a wonderful old Grenadian manor house, and enjoy a true Grenadian meal.

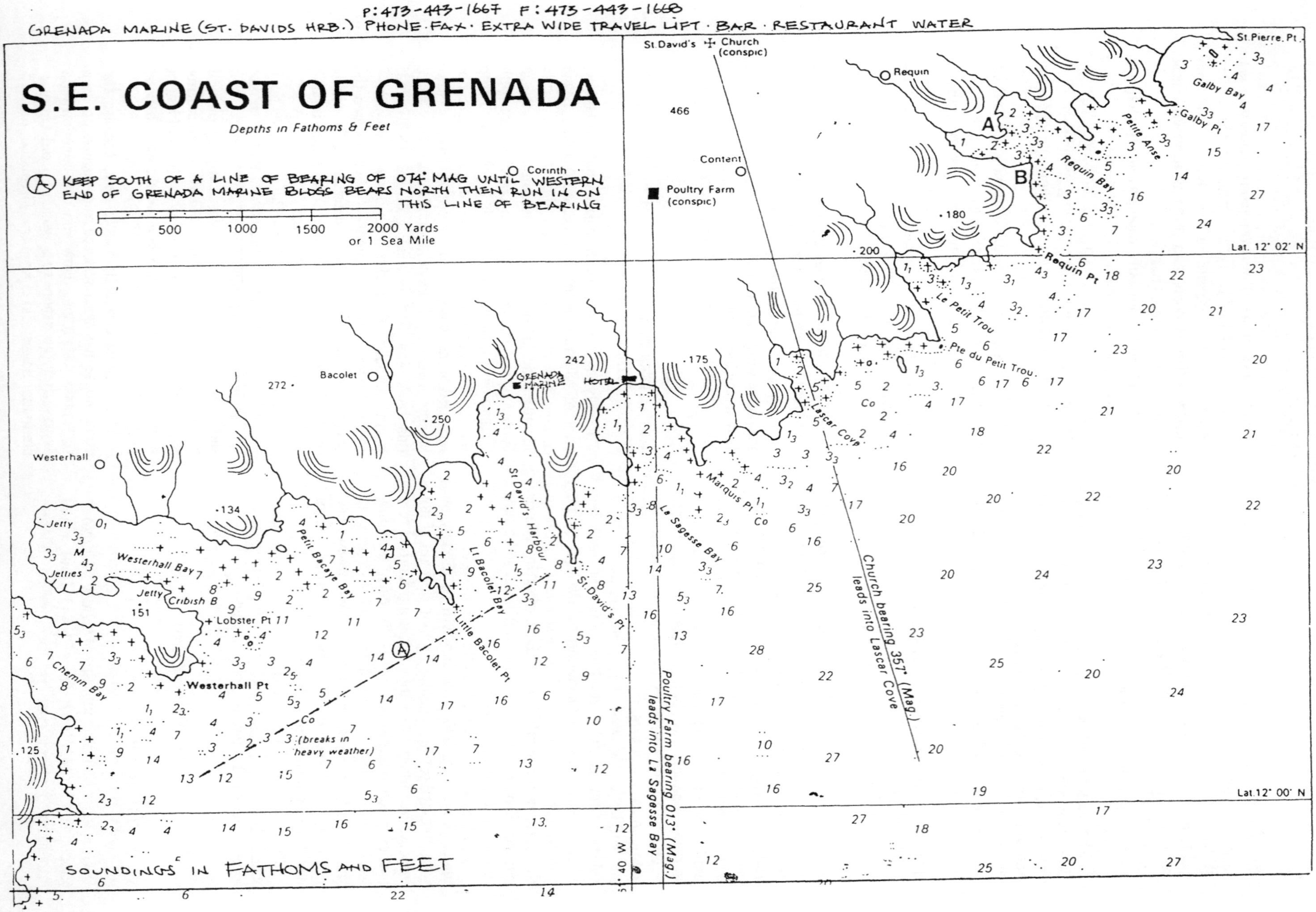

GRENADA MARINE (ST. DAVIDS HRB.) P:473-443-1667 F:473-443-1660
(ST. DAVIDS HRB.) PHONE. FAX. EXTRA WIDE TRAVEL LIFT. BAR. RESTAURANT. WATER.

S.E. COAST OF GRENADA

Depths in Fathoms & Feet

Ⓧ KEEP SOUTH OF A LINE OF BEARING OF 074° MAG UNTIL WESTERN
END OF GRENADA MARINE BUDGE BEARS NORTH THEN RUN IN ON
THIS LINE OF BEARING

○ Corinth

2000 Yards
or 1 Sea Mile

0   500   1000   1500

St Pierre Pt.

Galby Bay   4   4   17
3   3³   4
3   Galby Pt   33   15
3   27
3³   33   24
Petite Anse   3³   14
5   16
Requin Bay   3³   7
Requin Pt 18   6
Requin ○   A³ 3
A   2   B   4   180
1   2   3³   3³

Lat 12° 02' N
23
20
21
21
22   22
20
23   20
21   23

St David's ⊹ Church (conspic)

○ Content

■ Poultry Farm (conspic)

.466

Church bearing 357° (Mag.)
leads into Lascar Cove

Poultry Farm bearing 013° (Mag.)
leads into La Sagesse Bay

Le Petit Trou
Pte du Petit Trou.
Lascar Cove
Marquis Pt.
La Sagesse Bay
.175
HOTEL 242
GRENADA MARINE
.250
St David's Harbour
St David's Pt
Lt Bacolet Bay
Little Bacolet Pt

Lat 12° 00' N
61° 40' W

○ Bacolet

.272
.134
○
Petit Bacaye Bay
Westerhall Pt
Lobster Pt
Jetty Cribish B
.151
○ Westerhall
Jetty
Jetties
Chemin Bay
.125

Ⓐ (breaks in heavy weather)

SOUNDINGS IN FATHOMS AND FEET

CHART 45   Grenada—Southeast Coast

Grenada 161

Further, the establishment of the Moorings fleet in Secret Harbor provides a good opportunity for charterers: If your boat has any windward ability at all, a good way to get to Carriacou would be to leave Secret Harbor, make the short beat to La Sagesse, and stop there for a swim and dinner. Early in the morning, you can head off from La Sagesse, which will mean only four miles of windward work before turning the corner. After rounding the corner, the course to Carriacou (with a good boat) would be about 035° magnetic, even allowing for the lee set of the current. This should be a fast, cracked-sheets, 27-mile close reach—versus as much as 32 miles dead to windward all the way from Point Salines. By leaving for Carriacou from these harbors on the east coast, you are eight or more miles to windward of Point Salines and 12 miles closer to Carriacou. This all but eliminates the long beat up the lee coast of Grenada and a hard beat from David Point (Tangle Angle), Grenada, to Cistern Point, Carriacou. David Point to Carriacou is a straight-line distance of 15 miles, always hard on the wind. Very seldom can you lay the course so it is a dead beat; thus, the sailing distance is 20 to 25 miles, with a total distance of probably 45 miles up Grenada's lee coast from Point Salines, all hard on the wind, versus 27 miles from La Sagesse or Petit Trou.

The chances of doing all this are improved if you pass the northern end of Grenada early on the weathergoing tide. (*Street's Transatlantic Crossing Guide and Introduction* to *the Caribbean,* chapter 6, has further information on calculating the tides.)

LASCAR COVE
(Chart 45; II B-32)

This heretofore-unnamed cove was sounded by Bill Gould and myself aboard his *Lascar*—hence the name. It is a beautiful spot, located between Marquis Point and Pointe du Petit Trou, with a small, first-rate anchorage in its northeast corner. There is a slight roll in the northwest corner, where a small stream enters. The cove is difficult to spot from seaward. As you work your way eastward, a small white building that looks like a church and is marked on the British chart as a courthouse will come into view. Bring this to bear at 357° magnetic and it will lead you directly to Lascar Cove. Enter in good light, as the reefs impinge closely from either side. The opening is no more than 100 yards. Once inside, head for the beach in the northeast arm of the bay and anchor off in two fathoms. Stay to the west of the reef on the starboard side. Another reef projecting southward breaks tile harbor into eastern and western halves. There is enough room to round up and anchor, but I would advise using a Bahamian

moor, especially if there is more than one boat inside. Tile diving and fishing are very good in here.

In December 1977, I talked to a Dutch couple who had sailed across the Atlantic with their small baby, stopped in Barbados. and then cruised onto Grenada. After reading the 1974 edition of my *Cruising Guide to the Eastern Caribbean,* they decided to anchor in Lascar Cove. As soon as the anchor went down, a man came out in a rowboat, welcomed them to the harbor, and said they were only the third yacht ever to stop in Lascar Cove.

"What can we do to help you?" local people asked the couple. "Could we look after the baby while you explore ashore?" The couple stayed in the cove for three or four days, and during this time the local people brought them fruit, vegetables, fish, and lobster. They couldn't speak highly enough of the cove, the fishing, and the marvelous people. This is how yachting used to be 30 years ago, and it's heartwarming to think that experiences like this still occur.

PETIT TROU
(Chart 45; II B-32)

There is a pretty, deserted beach here, but the shelter is not good, so I can recommend it only for daytime use in settled weather.

Correction: We visited this harbor in *Li'l Iolaire,* both in November 1998 and November 1999 and discovered excellent shelter and a very attractive harbor. It is completely sheltered unless the wind is well into the south.

REQUIN BAY
(Chart 45; II B-32)

This bay can be hard to make out; a pair of rock arches marks the next bay east of it, from which you should count back one bay to Requin. Once Requin has been identified, stand to the northeast until point A appears from behind point B (Chart 45). Bear off to a course of roughly 335° magnetic, which leads up to the white-sand beach on the northeast arm of the bay. This is a dogleg channel requiring eyeball navigation. The reef extends from the eastern point of the bay farther than the chart shows. Once you have cleared the eastern reef on starboard tack, head up until you are past the other reef on your port side. Then bear off and run down into the western arm of the bay. The best anchorage is south of point A, since the bottom becomes grassy and the holding is poor farther west. Eight feet may be carried all the way to the dock on this western

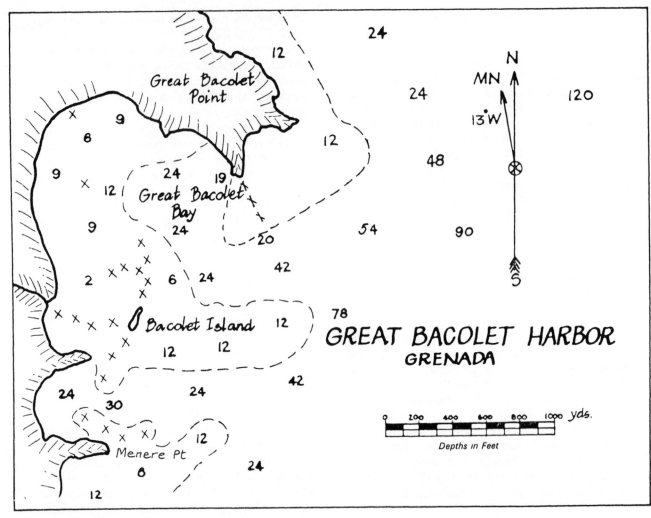

SKETCH CHART 46 Great Bacolet Harbor

arm. The eastern arm has a slight roll most of the time. There is a fine beach ashore where the Little Requin River empties, but it's the old story of the good beach that seldom gives a good anchorage. Beware of the turtle nets as you enter. They are used all along the southeast coast of Grenada. Their buoys are almost flush with the water, set wide apart, and difficult to spot.

Between Requin Bay and Marquis Island, there are a number of bays that I have not investigated but that seem to have possibilities. La Tante Bay has a good beach but poor shelter. The bays to either side of Menere Point look promising. Behind Crochu Point looks very good indeed. Great Bacolet Bay (Sketch Chart 46) is probably not a good anchorage, but it has a beautiful beach.

MARQUIS ISLAND

(Sketch Chart 47; II B-32)

Anchorages may be had behind the island or between the western tip of the island and the mainland. The former is the more protected, although a Bahamian moor is required, as the wind looping over the top of Marquis will waltz you in every direction. It is not a particularly good shelter.

GRENVILLE HARBOUR

(Chart 48; II B-32)

The only port of entry on Grenada's east coast, Grenville is the island's second-largest town. Food supplies are available, but in nowhere near the abundance found in St. Georges. The windward reef affords total shelter, while the wind blows in to

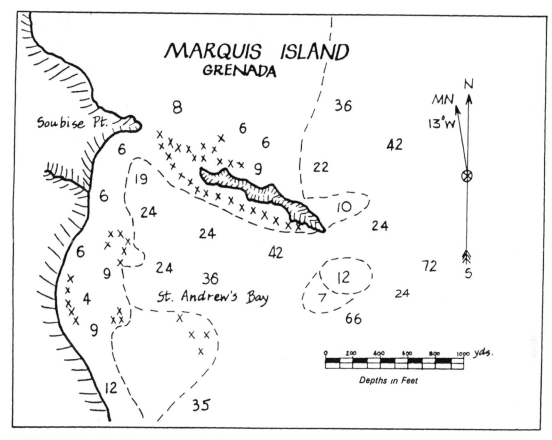

SKETCH CHART 47   Marquis Island

make the place cool. Ashore you'll find two beautiful old churches and an altogether pleasant atmosphere.

The town is best visited on Fridays or Saturdays. The small sloops from Carriacou come down on Friday nights for the Saturday market, while the schooners come in from Trinidad the same afternoon. The harbor is crowded with local vessels whose crews spend the night making merry. In the morning, they all leave.

The departure of a West Indian cargo vessel has to be seen to be believed. A large crew and a heavy cargo, complete with deckload, put the vessel right down on her marks. Yes, they do have Plimsoll marks, but whoever places them has an optimistic view of the weather: They are just below the sheerline. On top of the deckload, a few goats and chickens will be tethered, and you will notice a number of the crew's girlfriends going along for the ride—plus occasionally passengers as well. Sails go up slowly—first the main, then the fore, amid the squealing of blocks (no West Indian seaman would dream of greasing a block). Then the anchor chain comes in. Usually the windlass won't work, so a tackle is hitched to a chain, which is always old, rusty, and corroded. The anchor comes home accompanied by much shouting, groaning, and singing. Headsails are hoisted, backed, and sheeted home (again amid shouting, confusion, and contrary orders) while the schooner threads her way among the vessels in the harbor—seldom, if ever, fouling another boat. As she leaves the harbor, you will notice one person standing quietly at the wheel, saying nothing, observing all, handling the boat beautifully, and completely ignoring the antics of the rest of the crew. He is the skipper. Photographs of a West Indian schooner leaving port miss the best part. Only a video camera could catch the true flavor of the show.

Grenville Harbour is sheltered, but its entrance and exit are not easy. The buoys and range marks have always been unreliable. The last time I was there, about 20 years ago, there were no range marks, and the two outer buoys were missing. We were informed that "De range mark fall down, de buoy is sunk and we is negotiating for replacement."

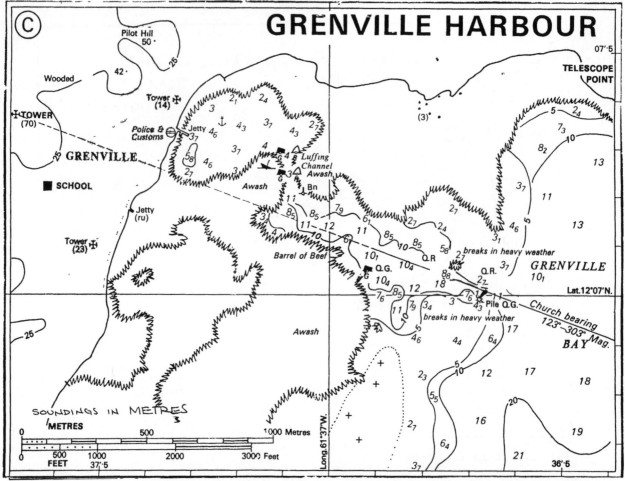

CHART 48   Grenville Harbour   Range marks have been reestablished, but the range on church probably easier to pick out. Barrel of Beef not properly marked, favor north side of range when passing Barrel of Beef.

In the old days, pilotage was cheap—about one bottle of rum. Today, who knows? But the problems still exist, despite a large amount of money having been spent on buoying the entrance to Grenville Harbour. The outer buoys are so exposed that they are continually breaking their chains and going adrift. As a result, the government is trying to raise enough money to construct pilings/pylons to mark the outer channel entrance.

As you can see on Chart 48, the inner harbor has either plenty of water or none at all. In the outer approaches, it is important to remember the chart notation, "Breaks in heavy weather," on the two-fathom shoals on either side of the entrance channel, leaving only a narrow gap of deep water with no breaking crests.

The latest information I have received—August 1991—was that the outer buoys on the starboard side of the entrance have gone adrift. On the south (port) side of the outer channel, the green buoy has been replaced by a steel piling with a platform and a green light on top. The next buoy—the Barrel of Beef buoy—may or may not be there when you arrive, but the inner buoys (red on the starboard side, green on port) should be there. The southernmost beacon at the entrance to Luffing Channel is a piling with a triangular day shape. The range marks have fallen down and will not be replaced in the foreseeable future. Everything has all grown up, so the old building that used to be a landmark is no more, and the huge, green shade tree *(Ficus benjamina)* has died.

If you are entering on your own, stay outside the line drawn from Great Bacolet Point to Telescope Point until the south end of town bears approximately 300° magnetic. Swing downwind, pick up the old church steeple, put that on a bearing of 303° magnetic, send a crew member into the rigging, and search for the green piling that marks the south side of the channel.

Once past the outer port-side channel marker, alter course slightly to starboard to pass the 1 1/2-

Grenada 165

fathom spot (Barrel of Beef) to port. (Note: Local sailors also refer to the eastern group of rocks flanking Luffing Channel as Barrel of Beef, so be sure not to confuse the two.)

As you approach Luffing Channel, marked by the red piling with the triangular day shape on top, come around to a course of about due north magnetic, shoot through the channel, round up, anchor, and pour the skipper and pilot (who should have been standing in the spreaders) a stiff drink. Then worry about clearing.

Do not attempt to enter Grenville Harbour after 1400, as you will be heading into the sun and then will not be able to spot the shoal water. For similar reasons, do not attempt to leave the harbor before 1100.

In May 1986, the US Navy "Seals" had some fun here and created a hell of a bang. The fishermen loved it, because the harbor was littered with dead and stunned fish; the schooner skippers loved it because Luffing Channel is now considerably wider and slightly deeper.

Sailing out of Luffing Channel can be extremely difficult without a very competent crew, so it's advisable to motor out. Keeping the range in line over the stern while tending sheets and short-tacking is a complicated procedure, especially at the outer end of the channel, where the gaps in the reefs are no more than 70 to 100 yards wide. If your engine is out, it is easy to arrange for a tow.

Between Grenville and Bedford Point, there are no harbors, and none on the northeast coast of Grenada. When proceeding northward, beware of the shoal west of Range E (Chart 49), which breaks in heavy weather. If the ground swell is down, a good anchorage can be had in the lee of Sandy Island or Levera Island.

SANDY ISLAND

(Chart 49; II B-32)

One may anchor due west of the house on Sandy Island in two fathoms. The tide is very strong here, requiring a Bahamian moor. The wind will be from the east, while the tide will be setting northwest-southeast, which is the axis to which your boat should lie. Make sure that both anchors are set securely. The snorkeling is good on the reefs west of Sandy Island, as is the shelling on the reef extending from the southern tip. The lovely sand beaches are seldom visited.

GREEN ISLAND

(Chart 49; II B-32)

The best anchorage due west of the hill is made difficult by 40- to 60-foot depths and a very strong reversing tide. A Bahamian moor will be necessary, with about 275 feet on each rode. If you are willing to make this effort, you can enjoy some beautiful beaches and good snorkeling off the south coast.

LEVERA ISLAND (SUGAR LOAF)

(Chart 49; II B-32)

To the west of Sandy and Green islands lies Levera Island, called Sugar Loaf by the locals. The best anchorage is roughly west of Sugar Loaf Peak. Here the water is not particularly deep, but the tide is extremely strong and will reverse itself east and west. Anchor accordingly. This is the best of the small-island anchorages and usually has the least amount of swell. Care must be taken in entering from the west, as the 1 3/4-fathom shoal has grown ever shallower over the years. Entering or leaving, you have to eyeball the deep water. The tide runs anywhere from one to three knots, and you'll need to take this into account when planning any swimming expeditions.

Sailing the north and west coasts of Grenada, you will see countless miles of sand beaches off which there are practically no anchorages. It can be a frustrating experience, yet there really is no point in putting in to shore unless you want to turn your insides out. It is, at least, fairly easy sailing along these shorelines, with few offlying hazards. The only danger on the north coast is the seven-foot shoal located six-tenths of a mile west of Levera at 305° magnetic. The shoal probably is more shoal than the charted depth, and it breaks continually in heavy weather. David Point—locally called Tangle Angle—can be rounded close aboard. The west coast of Grenada presents no difficulties. The shore is steep-to, the water very deep, and the winds usually from the east.

HALIFAX HARBOR

(Sketch Chart 50; II B-32)

This is the only proper harbor north of St. Georges on the west coast of Grenada. Known locally as Black Bay, it used to be spotted by the buildings on the Perseverance estate, set well back in the hills. But the Perseverance estate, like many others, was

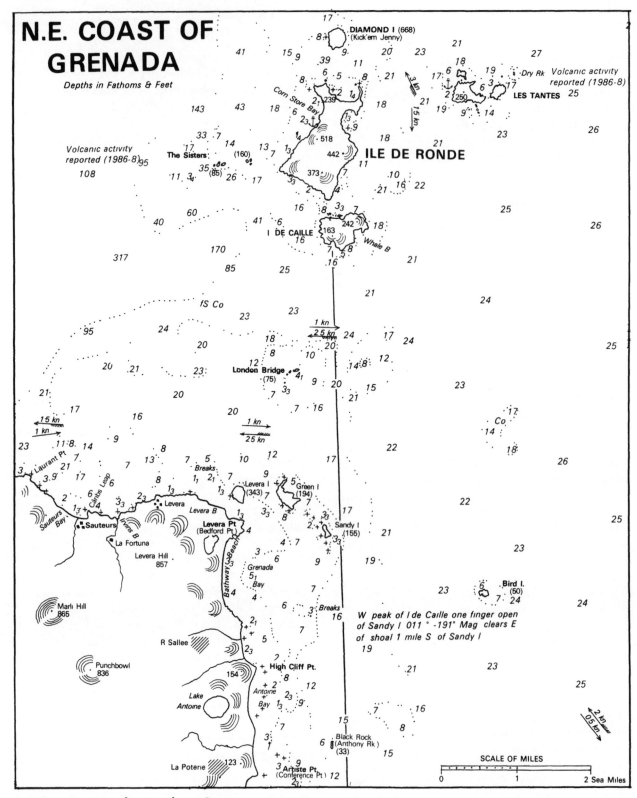

CHART 49 Grenada—Northeast Coast

Range E. Stay outside a line drawn from the high land of Ile de Caille along the E coast of Sandy Island to Black Rock (Anthony Rock), 011°–191° magnetic. This will clear the shoal SSW of Sandy Island.

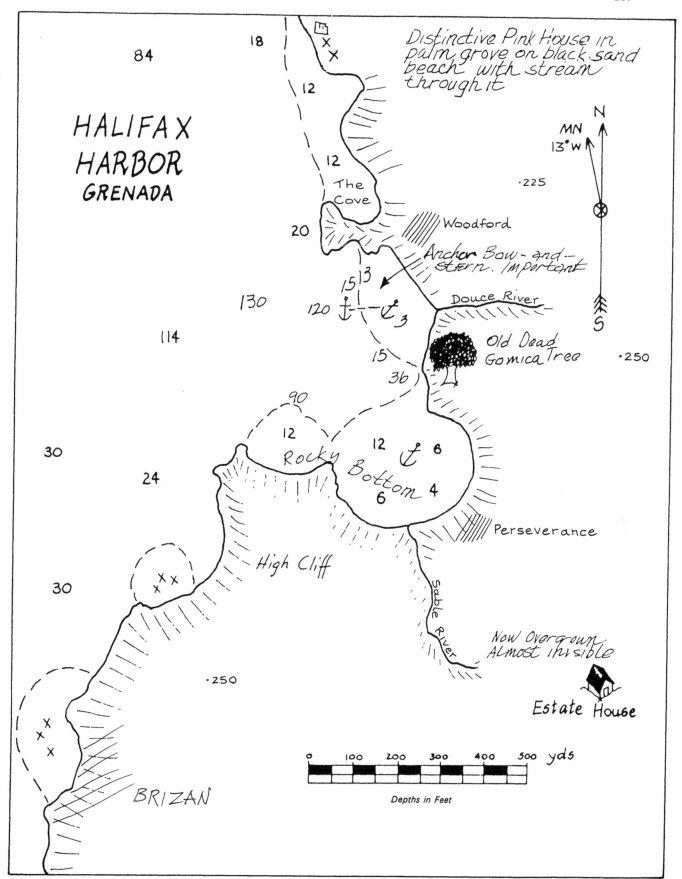

SKETCH CHART 50   Halifax Harbor

168   *Street's Cruising Guide to the Eastern Caribbean—Martinique to Trinidad*

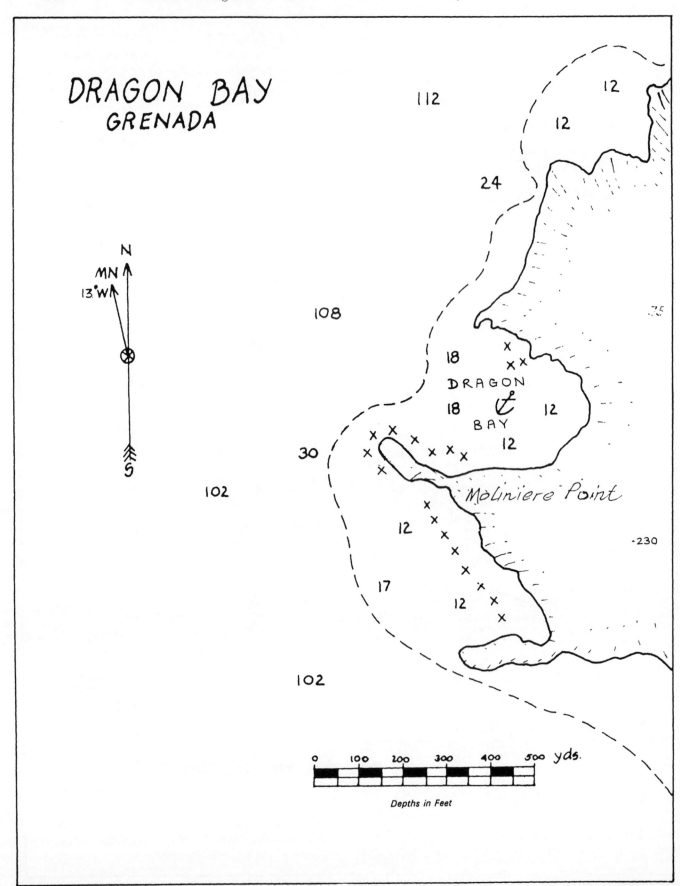

SKETCH CHART 51   Dragon Bay

Grenada 169

semi-abandoned during the political troubles on the island and became largely overgrown and barely visible through the trees. If the estate is renovated and the foliage cut back, it can again serve as the sailor's landmark for Halifax Harbor.

Another landmark in the region of Halifax Harbor is a square pink concrete house right down at the water's edge, south of which is a grove of palm trees and a black-sand beach with a stream running through it. Roughly a quarter of a mile south of this beach is Halifax Harbor. When heading north, if you see this landmark, you will know you have gone past Halifax and can turn around and go back.

One fair anchorage is in the southeast corner, with Perseverance bearing southeast. This part of the harbor is rolly in any sort of swell. Feel your way in to a suitable depth and drop anchor in soft mud. Make sure you anchor bow-and-stern, as the wind dies at night and you will swing around, beam-to the sea, and roll your guts out. Do not anchor off the southwest corner of the harbor, as that area is very rocky and you are guaranteed to foul your anchor.

Most of the time, the best anchorage is in the northeast corner of the harbor. (The government charts are not reliable here; see Sketch Chart 50.) The bottom comes up quickly from really deep water to two fathoms and then shoals to three feet. This three-foot shelf extends about 200 yards offshore.

Drop a stern anchor with 40 feet of line; as soon as you feel the anchor set, feed out line until you get to the three-foot shelf. Then walk or row the anchor well onto this shelf and set it hard. Don't attempt to lie to a single anchor.

I think this harbor is a bit overrated, because the swell can at times make it almost untenable. But when it's good, it's very good. An interesting exploration, especially for photographers, is a dinghy ride up the coast around the island's north-western point. There are fascinating rock formations, including one with a hole right through it.

Halifax Harbor is no longer regarded as much of an anchorage unless you anchor at the northern end of the harbor. the southern end of the harbor is blocked by an overhead wire, and also the government of Grenada has decided to use Halifax Harbor as a garbage dump. The garbage is piled down the hill side, making the anchorage less than attractive—especially when the wind is around to the south.

DRAGON BAY
(Sketch Chart 51; II B-32)

Just north of Molinière Point, Dragon Bay is fast becoming a popular anchorage. It is a place to escape the press of St. Georges Harbor without having to go all the way to Halifax. This is a confined anchorage, however, and you will have to sound your way in very carefully. Once in, you must be prepared to leave on short notice, especially in the winter, when the swell can make up in a dangerously short time. However, from June to October in settled weather, it is safe and comfortable. At night, when the wind dies down, you may swing around unpredictably, so a Bahamian moor will be required.

Grenada offers many anchorages whose possibilities have barely been discovered. For this reason, it is an inviting alternative to the popular anchorages on the islands farther north. The Grenadines are becoming a virtual thoroughfare, and in years to come, perhaps, boats will be seen rafted a dozen across in formerly deserted places such as the Tobago Cays. This catastrophe is not foreseeable along the Grenada coastline, however, where you can spend a week or two in relative seclusion visiting the anchorages I have discussed, or exploring the unexplored.

ST. GEORGES HARBOUR AND LAGOON
(Chart 41; II B-3, B-32)

Much has happened in the last five years in St. Georges, completely changing what has been said in Page 148 column 2 and 149 columns 1 and 2.

St. George's Harbour has been recently rebuilt and the Old Schooner Basin Filled for container storage. The Schooner pier has been moved along to an east west direction by the Grenada Yacht Club. The channel has been dredged to 11 feet and buoyed in a rather confusing fashion.

A warehouse has been built right smack in front of Grenada Yacht Club ruining the clubs view out to the west. However, there is talk of building a second storey to the yacht club so that you will be able to sit in the club, with drink in hand, and look out to see the "green flash".

The Grenada Yacht Club is still one of the friendliest yacht clubs in the world. It now has a small marina which provides fuel, water and electricity. There are showers available at the club and monthly membership is available to visiting yachtsmen.

The old hand powered slip is no more—a great loss to the cruising yachtsmen who was looking for an inexpensive haul.

Entering the lagoon—do not be confused access to the channel is still roughly 150° magnetic. But you will find a series of red buoys leading over to the schooner basin alongside the new dock. Favour the starboard side of the channel and head on to the lagoon. At about the first red buoy there should be a mid-channel mark—but there isn't. Again a booby trap to catch the unwary mariner. Leave the red buoy to PORT to enter the lagoon.

NOTES

On the eastern side of the lagoon one can find a number of businesses—Ace Hardware; Glean & McIntyre's Garages; .Bryden Minors Store that does photocopying, books and many other things.

Outfitters—who can order parts from anywhere in the world—is also on the eastern side of the lagoon and also have stores in St. Thomas, St. Martins, Antigua, Trinidad. What they do not have in stock they can arranged to have shipped from any of the other stores on the other islands.

Island Water World of St. Martins is scheduled to open a store in the lagoon in early 2001.

Budget Marine is in Grenada with a store at St. Davids in Grenada Marine yard St. David's.

Thus the marine supply situation for the mariner should be pretty well solved.

Many things have changed in Grenada but Basil St. Johns, who lives across the street from GYS still repairs yacht refridgeration systems and Lincoln Ross still has his iron workshop, machine shop—a little rough and ready but it is amazing the repair work he has done.

Within the lagoon the old Grenada Yacht Services now the Lagoon Marina, can only be said to be derelict. Allegedly it is said "Smart people who are heavy, and who walk down to Lagoon Marina dock, do not do so unless they are wearing snow shoes or skis—because of the danger of falling through the dock.

However, all is not lost as for medium size yachts, the Grenada Yacht Club now has a very nice marina with good security, fuel, diesel and gasoline being available alongside, as is water and electricity. With the ever hospitable Grenada Yacht Club at the head of the dock.

On the southside of the lagoon there is a dock to tie up dinghies and just a walk across the street to Foodland. Better access for the yachtman then going to Foodfare in town—bring a stern anchor to keep your boat from banging up against the dock.

HOG ISLAND

The anchorage to the west of Hog Island has now become crowded with boats semi-permanently anchored there. Ashore on Hog Island the locals have set up a mini bar and restaurant which produces good and popular bar-b-ques for the local "yachties"

At various times the Grenadian Government has decided too many yachts are in Hog Island moored there permanently or semi-permanently and has moved them out. What the situation will be when you arrive ??

Further, Hog Island supposedly has as of mid summer 2000 - been sold and by the time you read this you may discover a hotel either in the process of being built or built.

However, the story of development on Hog Island comes and goes and for the last ten years periodically reports have circulated of the island being sold and developments starting only to have the whole affair die. Thus, it is possible that when you arrive instead of finding a hotel you will still find semi-inhabited Hog Island - not inhabited by permanent residents but inhabited during the day by yachties and locals catering to the needs of yachties.

CLARKES COURT BAY
(Chart 44; II B-32)

Clarks Court Bay at the head of the Bay is Seaview Bar and Restaurant catering for the yachtsman. They provide a dock where you can leave your dinghy. The dock also serves as a base for Water Taxis that run to Hog Island and Calivigny Island. They take picnickers out to both of these islands.

Regarding the channel between Petit Calivigny and Calivigny Island - summer 2000 reportedly this channel has filled in. Before a boat try using this channel dinghy ahead to check this out.

9

Trinidad and Tobago

(Imray-Iolaire Charts 1, B, B-4, D-1, D-11; DMA 24400, 24402, 24403, 24404; BA 483, 493, 505, 508)

Trinidad and Tobago together form an independent state within the British Commonwealth that was discovered by the Spanish on Columbus's third voyage. At the head of a small fleet, Columbus entered the Golfo de Paria through the Bocas del Dragon and anchored. A minor volcanic eruption evidently caused a tidal wave or bore to sweep through the gulf, inflicting considerable damage to his fleet. He then moved north across the gulf and anchored under the south coast of the Peninsula de

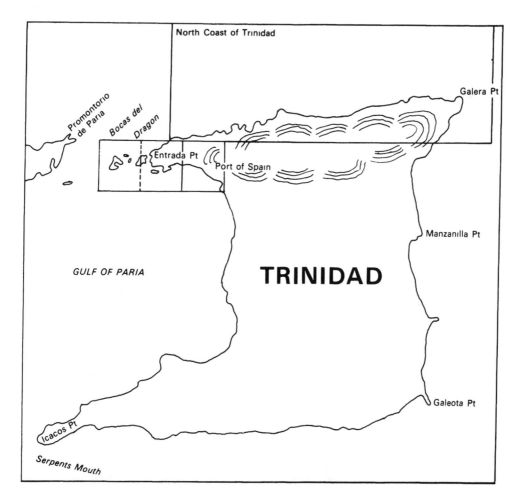

Paria. This was the first stop by a European on the South American mainland. The actual anchorage most likely was at Ensenada Cariaquita, as Dr. Daniel Camejo of *Sargasso* has maintained, although this view is disputed by Admiral Samuel Eliot Morison's biography of Columbus. Columbus all but ignored the island of Trinidad; the first settlement was not made on the island until much later, in 1552.

Trinidad

Unlike most of the South American colonies, Trinidad did not prosper. By 1780, the population was a scant 300 people. In that year, the colony was opened to settlement by all nations, and by 1797, when the island surrendered to the British without a fight, the population had grown to 18,000. The island remained in British hands for almost two centuries, administered by a governor appointed by the Crown. In 1962, a few years after the British tried unsuccessfully to set up a West Indies Federation, Trinidad and Tobago were granted independence.

In 1970, there was a rebellion by the Trinidad and Tobago Army Regiment that briefly disturbed the peace. The matter was handled judiciously by the government, the leaders being given jail sentences and subsequently freed on appeal. This was a far less bloody solution than that which befell the rebellion in 1837 by the black recruits in the West Indian regiment. The leader, Donald Stewart, was tortured and put to death, along with a number of other rebels.

Unfortunately, in 1990, Trinidad again had a blow-up, this time a coup attempt by a group of Black Muslim fanatics. They broke into the Parliament Building (the Red House) in downtown Port of Spain and took the prime minister captive. At the same time, in another part of town, they blew up the beautiful old police headquarters and headed toward the TV station, hoping to garner the support of all Trinidadians who were dissatisfied with their lot. The group that attempted the coup did not get the backing needed for success, but some of the more violent elements of Trinidad society saw a chance to run amok and get away with it. As a result, there was extensive rioting in downtown Port of Spain, and large sections of the city were looted and burned.

The police department and the army remained loyal to the government, and law and order were reestablished, but not without a three-week dawn-to-dusk curfew. Now Trinidad seems to have emerged from its difficulties, and by 1991, when yachtsmen visited the island for the annual pre-Lenten Carnival, they returned with glowing reports of wonderful experiences.

Trinidad's Carnival is without doubt the best Carnival in the Eastern Caribbean. It is a massive five-day party that is very well organized—so much so that within a week after the festivities end, the bands and troops are already preparing for the next year. I have no idea how many visiting yachts arrive in Trinidad for Carnival, but reports I have heard range from a low of 100 to a high of 300.

The Trinidadians are among the friendliest and most helpful people in the Eastern Caribbean; they will go to amazing extremes to help newcomers and convince them that their island is the best one in the entire region. Certainly yachtsmen visiting Trinidad will have a wonderful time as long as they stay on the beaten track, especially at night in Port of Spain. If you stray off the beaten track, you will discover that this is not a land for the timid; the Trinidadians are hard-living people, and their land is noted for high fences, big dogs, and grillwork on houses. You will run into bars where the bartender stands behind a wire cage, you pass your money through a small hole, and he passes out the drink. In other establishments, there is a big wire grating suspended above the bar like a guillotine with a trip lever. If a fight breaks out, the trip lever can be hit and the guillotine shoots down. Woe betide the person who happens to have an arm on the bar.

Not surprisingly, the police force in Trinidad was the first in the former British colonies to be armed with pistols—sticks were not enough to control out-of-control Trinidadians. So just heed my warnings and you will have a wonderful time in Trinidad.

Each island has its own accent: Trinidad's is a particularly pleasing one. The language has its own peculiarities, too. For instance, a Trinidadian's boat has an outhaul rather than a haulout. (I always ask whether the morning after is cursed by an overhang.) Trinidad's population is made up of a far-flung blend of English, Chinese, Spanish, East Indians, and Africans—a combination that has produced some of the most beautiful women in the world. They may not be as beautifully dressed or as chic as the women of Martinique, but if you visit Trinidad during Carnival, I am sure you will agree with me.

Trinidad is the main transshipment port for the Lesser Antilles. The commercial congestion in the harbor used to be quite beyond belief, second only to the inefficiency that it produced. It took a month

Trinidad and Tobago

or more to have goods transferred through Port of Spain to points north, so if I had important gear being shipped to me through Port of Spain, I would usually sail down and pick it up myself. Now I understand that the combination of worldwide recession and the very bad local recession spurred by falling oil prices has made Port of Spain and its docks far less crowded than in the past. As a result, less cargo gets lost, there are fewer delays, and Customs and Immigration officials are not overworked clearing freighters and cargo. Now they have time to deal with yachts, and they do so with an efficiency and courtesy that didn't exist in the past.

Trinidad's weather, for the most part, is governed by the easterly trades. When the island cools off at night, there usually is a calm in the Golfo de Paria. An easterly breeze springs up in the morning, building to anywhere from 10 to 20 knots by the afternoon and dying down at sunset. From time to time, during periods of light winds and very hot days, the island will heat up and a column of warm air rising over the land will draw in a wind from the west. The resulting southerly or southwesterly breeze is cause for great confusion among the weekend racers.

Approaching Trinidad from the north, there are no offlying hazards. The mountainous north coast gives ample warning of approach to land. Both Trinidad and Tobago are well lighted and may be approached at night, although the actual entry into harbors should be made in daylight.

As you approach Trinidad from seaward, bear in mind that the main light on Chacachacare Island is visible for more than 26 miles. It is four and a half miles to leeward of the easternmost *boca* (mouth). Do not head directly for it, as the current will most likely be setting you strongly to the west. If you do not take careful bearings, you will end up well to leeward, leaving you a rough beat eastward against wind and current.

If you happen to be approaching Trinidad from the southeast, do not enter the Golfo de Paria through the Bocas del Dragon ("mouths of the serpent"). This would put you hard on the wind for 35 miles up to Port of Spain, and the first part of this trip would be complicated by the many offshore oil rigs. I advise rounding the island to windward and entering from the north. The distance may be greater, but the effort will be far less.

You can enter the Golfo de Paria through any of four northern openings, or *bocas*. From west to east, they are Boca Grande, Boca de Navios, Boca de Huevos, and Boca del Monos (which is

recommended). The normal flow of current is from the Golfo de Paria into the Caribbean, with the current running strongest during the ebb and less fast, though in the same direction, during the flood. You should plan on using your engine through the *bocas*, no matter what the current. If you have no engine, Navios and Grande are easier to sail through—but then, of course, you are farther to leeward of Port of Spain.

Once through the *bocas*, the best move is to head for Chaguaramus Bay, north of the old Chaguaramus bauxite operation. Go to the south side of the cove opposite Trinity Yacht Yard (see Chart 52), tie up alongside the new Customs dock (11 feet at the end of the dock at low tide), and clear. Then you will be free either to stay in Chaguaramas Bay off the yacht yard or to move around to the eastern part of Chaguaramas to lie at the Trinidad Yachting Association. To do the latter, you must first visit the yachting association—within walking distance of the yacht yard—to meet the manager and obtain an invitation. Or telephone the Trinidad Yacht Club in Cumana Bay and obtain a berth there. All three of these facilities are connected to town via an excellent bus service.

In years gone by, Trinidad did not allow any Rhodesians or South Africans ashore. If by chance they did go ashore, they were promptly put in jail until their boat was ready to leave. This led to a light moment before the 1977 Trinidad—Grenada Race. We had sailed down for the race and were in the process of entering when the officer noticed that my secretary, who was traveling on a British passport, was born in Umtali, Rhodesia (now Zimbabwe). He said she was Rhodesian and could not go ashore. I protested that since she had a British passport, she was British. "No," he insisted, "she was born in Rhodesia and therefore must be Rhodesian." This went on for a while, and then I said, "Wait a minute. If a cat has kittens in the oven, does that mean they are biscuits?" Roaring with laughter, he stamped her passport and said, "You've got me there, skipper. Have a good time."

Another time, after there had been a fire in the Customs building, Customs and Immigration officials were spread from one end of Port of Spain to the other. I staggered into the Customs office, hot, tired, and thirsty, and picked up my final piece of paper for clearance. Then I asked, "Where is the nearest bar so I can buy a cold beer?" The Customs officer looked at me and said, sadly, "I'm afraid it's about a mile away from here, sir." "I don't think I'll make it," I replied, and he said, "You're in luck. In my little refrigerator here I have two cold

174   *Street's Cruising Guide to the Eastern Caribbean—Martinique to Trinidad*

Heinekens. How about we sit down and have an afternoon drink?" Customs officers in Trinidad aren't all bad!

Everything in the world is a compromise; if you keep a yacht in Trinidad, you must pick and choose what you feel is most important. Trinity Yacht Yard is doing everything possible to cater to the needs of yachtsmen—they provide a hauling facility, dinghy landing, bar, restaurant, showers, telephone, fax, etc.—but Trinity is not a marina. There are only three berths, although there is a good sheltered anchorage off the facility.

The Trinity people know what is available in Trinidad and undoubtedly can get practically anything required for a yacht repair, as Trinidad has a large commercial operation supporting the oil rigs in the Golfo de Paria.

The hauling facilities at Trinity are good—a 50-ton Tami lift and plenty of space to store boats while they are being worked on or laid up long-term during the hurricane season. You can haul there and do your own work or haul and have them do your work—or a combination of both. Rates are very competitive. The manager is Donald Stollmeyer, and the mailing address is P.O. Box 3163, the Carenage, Port of Spain, Trinidad (telephone: 809-634-4303; FAX: 809-627-0391).

Trinidadians are experienced at building small fiberglass boats, and Dougie Myer (owner of *Legacy,* a Soveril 43) actually built two Soveril 43s of fiberglass—*Legacy* and *Sea Moss.* Aluminum and stainless-steel fabrication and welding are available, and there are excellent propeller-repair facilities.

Trinidad Yachting Association (TYA) is one of the most hospitable yacht clubs in the Eastern Caribbean, but its anchorage is exposed. In the afternoon, the southwest wind builds up and a large chop results; you can even get seasick at the mooring.

The TYA (telephone: 809-634-4376) has a 15-ton Travelift, clubhouse, showers, bar, restaurant, launch service, and a few dockside berths—all free to visiting yachtsmen as long as they behave themselves. If they get out of line, however, they will be invited to leave—not in 24 or 48 hours, but IMMEDIATELY. Access to the TYA is by invitation only. Go there, convince them you are a proper yachtsman, and you are all set—that is, if you don't get seasick with the afternoon chop.

The Trinidad Yacht Club (telephone: 809-637-4260 or 7945; manager: Mr. Dopwell) bought some old barges, sank them to form a breakwater, then established a nice marina just east of Point Cumana. Berths usually are available for visiting yachts. For boats drawing more than nine feet, I suggest sending a dinghy in ahead to double-check the depth before entering. The basin has been expanded, and there are now 60 berths available for visiting yachts. It has been dredged to 12 feet, but of course will be subject to shoaling. Remember that the tide within the Golfo de Paria is considerably greater than in the rest of the Eastern Caribbean. Rise and fall at neaps is 1.9 feet; at springs, it is 3.2 feet.

If you can't fit inside the marina at the yacht club, you can anchor off. Be forewarned, however, that a southwest wind usually builds up during the day; come sunset, you will be bouncing up and down so badly that you will have difficulty getting on and off the boat, and you probably will be seasick. By nine or ten at night, it should be flat calm. Because of this situation, I advise anchoring off Trinity Yacht Yard if you can't fit inside the yacht club marina. Off the Trinidad Yachting Association, you will find the same afternoon-chop problem as at the yacht club.

Under the influence of the Trinidad Yachting Association, yachting has grown tremendously in Trinidad over the last dozen or so years. Marine supplies are now available for boats up to 50 feet from Peak and Company, 177 Western Main Road, St. James, Port of Spain. This is near Westmall. They stock Imray-Iolaire charts and Street guides.

Imray-Iolaire charts are also available from Landry and Company, Brenton Hall, Stanmoor Avenue, Port of Spain (Box 615). Landry and Company caters to the commercial ship market, so this is one of the few places in the Eastern Caribbean where you can buy charts for Europe, the Panama Canal, and the Pacific.

Marine supplies are also available at C. Lloyd Trestrail & Company, 6–8 Broadway, Port of Spain (telephone: 809-623-6109). Marine Consultants, 43 Charles Street, Port of Spain (telephone: 809-625-1308; FAX 809-625-2270), acts as the agent for Pains-Wessek-Schmurley distress rockets; does life-raft testing and recertification; handles sextant repairs, resilvering of mirrors, and compass adjustments; and stocks Imray-Iolaire charts and Street guides.

Fuel is available at the Trinidad Yacht Club, at the Texaco facility (but not the Trinidad Yachting Association), at Island Home (near the old Swan Hunter boatyard in Chaguaramas Bay), and at Trinity Yacht Yard.

In the spring of 1985, prices in Trinidad had gone sky-high, but one old standby Chinese restaurant, Shey Shey Chien, was still reasonable. The portions are huge; the best plan is to gather about 15 people, go to the restaurant (any taxi driver can take you there), set up a big table, order 15 quarter-portions of different items, put them in the center of the table, and dig right in. Now, of course, with the devaluation of the Trinidadian currency, meals should be cheap in Trinidad.

For those with wooden boats, Dougie Myer—who can be contacted easily through the Trinidad Yachting Association or the Port of Spain pilot station—reports that Trinidad now has an excellent supply of timber.

Regarding sailmakers, Dougie says that the whole situation is in such a state of flux that if you are in need of sail repair, you should go to the Trinidad Yachting Association and find him. He will explain the existing situation and send you off in the right direction.

PORT OF SPAIN

(Charts 52, 53; II D-1, D-11)

It is possible to go into Port of Spain and lie alongside the Customs dock, but this is something I would not want to do for more than a short while. (Besides, you don't need to—you can tie up at the new Customs facility in Chaguaramus Bay.) Go in, clear, and move out to either the Trinidad Yachting Association or the Trinidad Yacht Club. Port of Spain is crowded, rough, and filthy.

In 1985, the harbor in Port of Spain was littered with sunken wrecks and numerous derelict ships that obviously were not long from joining the sunken vessels. Thus, I advised NOT sailing up to Port of Spain at night, as I had grave doubts about how well marked these wrecks were. Now I have received reliable information that all of the wrecks have been removed, but I still advise against entering strange harbors at night. Plus, with the establishment of the Trinity Yacht Yard and the expansion of the Trinidad Yacht Club marina, there really is no reason to stay in Port of Spain Harbor.

Also, dozens of small freighters in various states of repair and disrepair are anchored at the eastern corner of the harbor. They are manned by crews of all nationalities whose honesty leaves a lot to be desired. Thievery in this area is absolutely rife. In fact, there has been at least one murder of a yachtsman, and possibly more. The harbor police absolutely cannot guarantee your safety, yet they insist on impounding not only your firearms but also your flare pistol. And they don't tell you how to defend yourself against marauders. With the amount of thieving in Port of Spain Harbor, and

considering the amount of illegal arms on the loose in Trinidad, I think it's a mistake for the authorities to remove the firearms from yachts.

Back in 1968, Customs officials in Trinidad handled it differently. They placed our automatic in an accessible locker, sealed it with a light wire, and said, "If someone comes aboard and you need the gun, break the seal and use it, then report to us immediately. If we later find the seal broken and you haven't reported to us, you will be in serious trouble. By the way, if you have to use the gun, please shoot straight. And have a good time in Trinidad."

Nowadays, if you have to spend the night in the eastern part of the harbor, I advise you to keep an all-night anchor watch. If it's Carnival and you want to stay downtown to be near the action and watch the fun, the best maneuver is to raft six or seven boats together, keep all dinghies alongside, and take turns standing anchor watch. Also, make sure to display an anchor light, because the police sometimes decide to enforce the anchor-light rule during Carnival, and this has cost some yachts a bit of money in the past.

Across the street from Customs and Immigration is the Seamen's Mission, which has all sorts of facilities: bank, swimming pool, showers, etc. Unhappily, the last I heard was that they have stopped letting yachtsmen use the mission. Only those with seamen's cards were allowed in. It's worth a try to see if the policy has changed again.

CUMANA BAY

(Chart 53; II D-11)

Here you'll find the Trinidad Yacht Club, about two miles west of downtown Port of Spain. It's an open, bouncy anchorage, but the yacht club has sunk a couple of wrecks to make a breakwater, so the marina inside provides excellent shelter against the afternoon breeze and bobble. Depth inside the breakwater is supposed to be eight feet, but silting may have made it less. If you have a deep hull, send in the dinghy first to take some soundings.

Contact the yacht club on channel 68. Fuel, ice, and water are available. Outdoor showers used to be available too, but the showers were in full view of the dining room, and some French sailors in town for Carnival took showers stripped to the buff, so the water was disconnected. Now, a proper shower room has been built, so yachtsmen staying at the yacht club can take showers without disturbing members dining in the restaurant.

176   *Street's Cruising Guide to the Eastern Caribbean—Martinique to Trinidad*

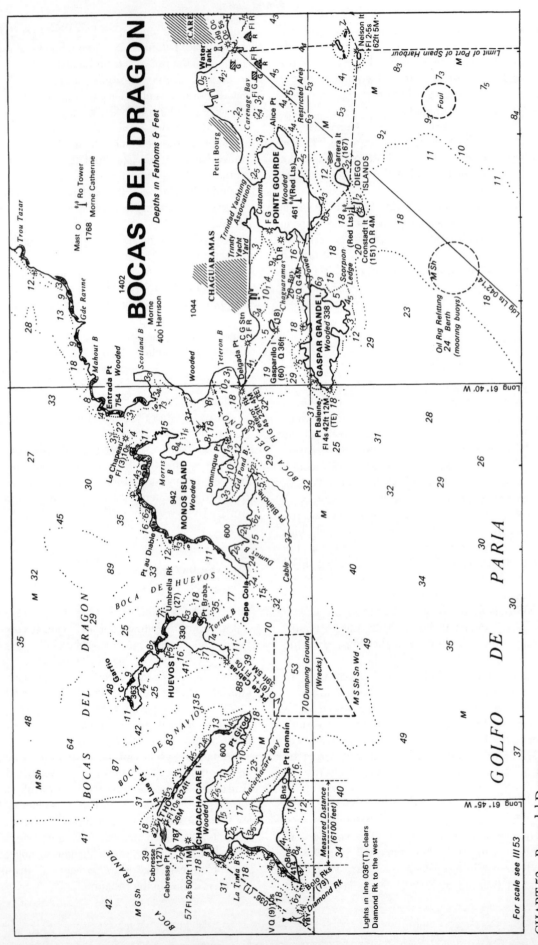

CHART 52   Bocas del Dragon

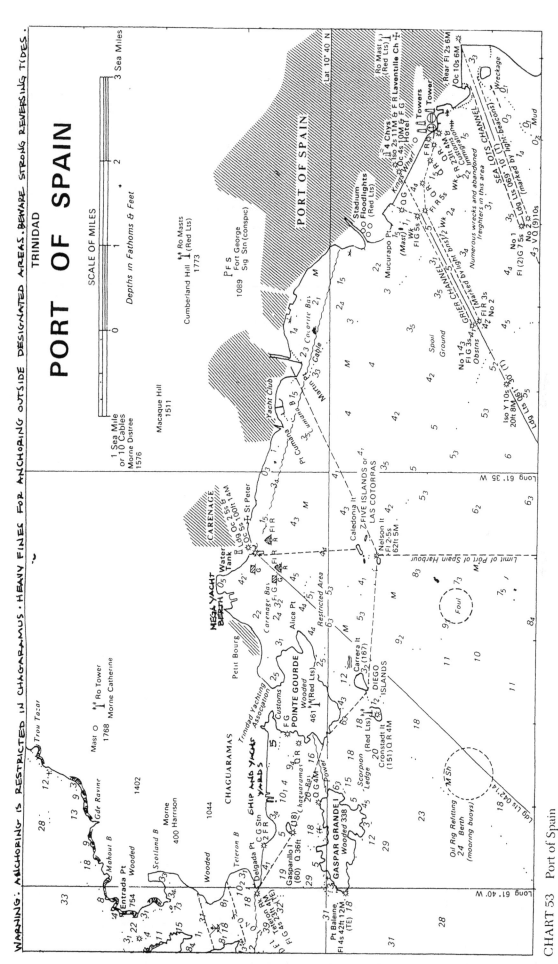

CHART 53 Port of Spain
SOUNDINGS IN FATHOMS AND FEET

178 *Street's Cruising Guide to the Eastern Caribbean—Martinique to Trinidad*

If you want to lie alongside to have work done on the boat, you must, of course, make arrangements with the club. Contact the manager, Mr. Dopwell (telephone: 809-637-4260 or 7945).

By law, the Trinidad Yacht Club is not allowed to sell drinks except to club members, so visiting yachtsmen must take out temporary memberships. Incidentally, if visiting yachtsmen do not receive red-carpet treatment here, it is completely understandable, because foreign yachtsmen descend on Trinidad each year for Carnival, and their behavior has been known to be less than proper. One year, they tore apart the Trinidad Yacht Club with overenthusiastic parties; another year, the club found itself stuck with $1,000 worth of bills for overseas phone calls made by visitors. As I have said elsewhere, quotation marks often must be put around the word *yachtsman*.

In 1990, many yachts based themselves at the yacht club—either in the basin or at anchor off it—and the club evidently was well enough organized so they were not taken to the cleaners by the visitors. As a result, in 1991, the club was inundated with some 90 boats in slips at the club, plus another 75 anchored outside. Those numbers seem rather unbelievable, but if that many boats were there, it must have been one hell of a party. I just hope the profits at the bar/restaurant helped defray some of the expenses.

CARENAGE BAY

(Chart 53; II D-11)

The Trinidad Yachting Association (TYA) is here, on the western side of Carenage Bay, just west of the former navy seaplane hangar, now used by the Trinidad government for storage and helicopter landings.

The TYA has excellent facilities, showers, launch service, ice, water, and electricity, but no fuel.

The anchorage isn't too good, since the afternoon breeze picks up in the Golfo de Paria and in turn kicks up a lot of bumpy water. Getting in and out of the launch or a dinghy can be tricky. The TYA has been hoping to obtain a couple of old freighters and sink them across the mouth of the cove to form a breakwater, as the Trinidad Yacht Club did.

The association has an extensive sailing and racing program. The racing season lasts from November through May; in the summer, they cruise up to the Grenadines, train racing crews, and work on their boats. An excellent junior program is run in

the summer by two Canadians, who also teach adults.

Their fleet ranges from tiddlers to red-hot IOR, high-tech boats such as Dougie Myer's *Legacy*. The cruising class includes *Iolaire*'s old rival, *Rosemary V*, and a former Eight-Meter, *Lara*.

The association is devoted strictly to sailing. No motorboats are allowed. Only sailboat owners can vote in the association's meetings—it doesn't matter if it's a sailboard or a 60-footer, but you have to own a sailboat. That's how they ensure that any proposals for tennis courts, swimming pools, or fancy restaurants invariably get voted down.

Otherwise, there is very little to recommend the Golfo de Paria. It is shallow, muddy, and, during summertime, full of jellyfish. No yachtsman wants to linger in this area unless he has business to conduct or friends ashore. There are, however, a few good anchorages scattered through the area. The cove on the south side of Gaspar Grande Island is attractive and well sheltered. On Monos Island are two good all-weather anchorages—Morris Bay and Grand Pond (or Dehert) Bay. On the eastern side of Boca del Monos is Scotland Bay, which is listed as restricted but nonetheless is used by local yachtsmen without any objections.

Relatively little cruising is done in the Golfo de Paria, even though there are some excellent anchorages on Venezuela's Peninsula de Paria. But Venezuela requires clearance at Güiria, which is time-consuming and out of the way to the west. Besides, the port captain can be downright hostile to yachtsmen. Most Trinidadians prefer the Grenadines and points north for their cruising grounds. Trinidad's east coast is not suitable for overnight cruising—it is a lee shore with no viable anchorages.

North Coast

This area is seldom visited by yachts, as it is completely exposed to the northerly ground swells during the winter months, from late October through April. It is visited by fishermen, who tuck themselves in behind various headlands for some respite from the wind and the sea.

During June and July, though, there are certainly some spots on Trinidad's north coast where you could find shelter while working your way east to Tobago. One problem, however, is that there are no detailed charts of this coast. DMA 24404 goes as far as Chupara Point, 20 miles east of Boca del Monos; DMA 24400 picks up 10 miles or so east of that, but it shows almost no detail. The BA chart is helpful but has little detail. The best advice is to get topo maps in Trinidad at the Ministry of Agriculture, Lands, and Survey (corner of Richmond and Queen streets, Port of Spain). Without a topo map, it's pretty hard to figure out where you are on this relatively featureless coast.

If you are going from Trinidad to Tobago, I suggest you use the easternmost *boca,* Boca del Monos, just as the tide begins to fall, then work your way eastward along the coast. For two or three hours, there should be an easterly-going current. The obvious course is to short-tack as close to shore as you dare; the coast is rather steep-to, with a few offlying rocks, which are shown best on the topo maps.

One problem in navigating this coast is that the Trinidadians have one name for a bay or an island, the American chart has another name, and the topo map has yet another. For example, 10 miles east of Boca del Monos is Saut d'Eau Island (see Chart 54), also called Maravaca Island and referred to locally as Sadau Island. Do not try to pass between this island and the mainland. A bow-and-stern anchorage can be had in calm weather behind Medine Point, and there's good diving in the area, plus all sorts of caves at water level. The island is a protected area, so it's a bird-watcher's dream.

MARACAS BAY

During June and July, this provides good shelter and a good beach. The best anchorage, of course, is in the southeastern corner referred to on the topo map as Tyrico Bay. With the high land to the east, the wind will come from all directions. The shore is quite steep-to; moor bow-and-stern. The south side of the bay has a great, long white-sand beach produced by the winter ground swells.

LA CUEVAS BAY

This bay is easily spotted from offshore by its long white-sand beach with two white houses, which are life-guard huts; this is a very popular surfing bay during the winter, and obviously not a winter anchorage. In summer, though, you should be able to find good shelter from the sea behind Abercromby Point. Ease your way in with the aid of a leadline or depth sounder and anchor bow-and-stern because of the variable wind.

CHUPARA BAY

This bay should provide shelter in summer. Again, it's a bow-and-stern anchorage, with a very small beach that should be partially sheltered by a reef that extends west from Chupara Point for half a mile. Be sure to give the point a wide berth if you are sailing into the bay or short-tacking up the beach.

East of Chupara Point, there is no place to stop before Matelot, a possible anchorage 14 miles away. Watch out for Machapure Rock, half a mile off the eastern entrance to Blanchisseuse, which is spotted by the village of the same name.

MATELOT BAY

According to the *British Admiralty Pilot,* L'Islette is joined to the coast by a small causeway or low sandspit and provides a sheltered anchorage for small craft to the west of the island off the town of Matelot. This anchorage is not shown on the Admiralty or DMA charts and can be found only with the aid of the topo maps.

GRANDE RIVIERE BAY

With the wind south of east in the summer, an anchorage should be possible off the village of Grande Rivière, six miles east of Matelot. It's the next-to-last anchorage before you go off to Tobago.

TOCO

Seven miles east of Grande Rivière Bay, Toco is the easternmost village in Trinidad. It has a small jetty, and before the roads were built, it was connected to civilization by a coastal freighter, which anchored off and put supplies ashore, winter and summer. I am told that the boatmen, all from Carriacou, were the finest surf seamen in the world. In summer, there might be a half-decent anchorage off the town of Toco; it is a case of feeling your way in, as there are no charts.

Remember that you can use the whole north coast only from late April to October, and even then only when the wind is south of east. You should be prepared to up anchor and get out if the wind goes north of east, and it can go all the way around to the north, even in the summer months.

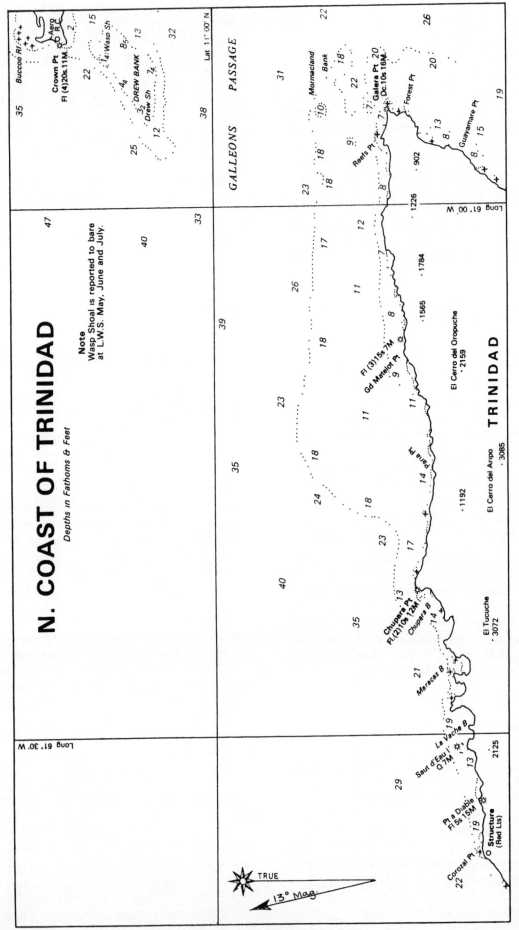

CHART 54 Trinidad—North Coast

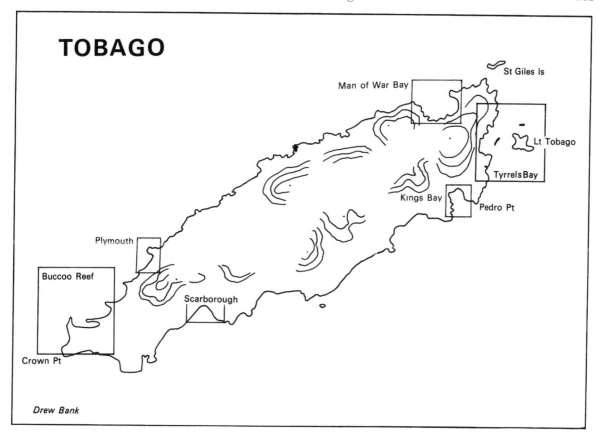

Tobago

Discovered in 1498 and settled in 1639, Tobago was neither zealously colonized nor jealously held; the island changed hands roughly 30 times before the British ultimately established control in 1814. In 1962, along with Trinidad, Tobago became independent. Lacking good deepwater harbors, it has never prospered commercially.

In 1963, the year after independence, a hurricane went through Tobago, knocked everything flat, and completely destroyed the agricultural economy that existed at the time. Relatively few of the planters tried to reestablish their farms, which they figured were going to die with independence anyway, since the Trinidad government looked to the oil industry as the salvation of Trinidad and Tobago. They dreamed of building an industrial nation with the profits from the oil industry.

In the years of high oil prices, this dream had a chance of coming true, but now, with the decline in prices, Tobago's salvation seems to be in the field of tourism. The island is well suited for this, with its beautiful beaches, a fair number of hotels, and superb scenery. It also has more birds than any other island in the Eastern Caribbean; the island was never plagued with poisonous snakes and thus escaped mongoose infestation. Mongooses were imported to other islands to eliminate the snakes; when the mongooses finished that assignment, they started on the birds—hence the relatively low bird population in most of the Caribbean islands.

One of our nicest outings in recent years was in Tobago, where we rented a van and drove around the island. Well, almost: The road from Bloody Bay to within a few miles of Charlotteville and Man of War Bay is unpaved, and just before Man of War Bay, the road was blocked by a fallen tree and a small washout. This was discouraging, because the tree had been down for four months, and the road still had not been cleared. It would have taken only a jeepload of road workers no more than a day to clear the whole road.

Tobago is very seldom visited by cruising yachtsmen because it is so difficult for most cruisers to reach. A transatlantic yachtsman who has made a landfall in Barbados, on the other hand, is all set: It's an easy, broad reach of about 140 miles to Tobago. However, you have to do your navigation very carefully as you approach Tobago, since the current runs northwest at two to three knots; if you don't make allowance for the current, you will find yourself west of Tobago and may even miss the island altogether.

This northwesterly current flow is true not only around Tobago; it also extends up the eastern side of the lower end of the Lesser Antilles. In March 1985, when we were heading from Martinique to Tobago, we were doing seven-plus knots through the water, but with the current on the nose, we were making only five knots over the bottom. It was not one of *Iolaire*'s fastest passages.

If you are in the Lesser Antilles and are trying to get to Tobago, head north or south to Martinique, go around to Sainte Anne, then take off from there on a course of about 175° magnetic, if you can average seven knots, or more to the east if you are slower.

If you are sailing from Trinidad to Tobago, you will have a long, tough haul. Even the sportfishermen think it is a rough run. For many years, the sail from Trinidad to Tobago was seldom attempted. The Lazzari brothers of *Draconius* were among the few Trinidadian yachtsmen who had made the trip successfully. With the advent of the modern IOR-type cruising boat, yachtsmen have fought their way up to Tobago more regularly; in fact, for years they have had a Spring Regatta in Tobago, although some yachtsmen have objected that it was too hard to get there.

Despite this problem, since 1985 the Trinidadian yachtsmen have fought their way eastward for Trinidad and Tobago Race Week, sponsored by Trinidad's Angostura rum distillers. Each year, approximately 30 sailboats take part in the regatta, usually held the second week in May. There are both racing and cruising divisions. The shoal-draft boats anchor up behind Buccoo Reef; the deep-draft boats anchor in Store Bay, east of Crown Point. It is a week of good, hard racing with some memorable parties. As mentioned earlier, the Trinidadians are a wonderful, enjoyable lot who are good sailors and fantastic partymakers.

If the wind is in the southeast, it is possible to stop along the north coast of Trinidad, especially from the end of March through mid-October, when the northerly ground swells are seldom encountered. (See the preceding discussion of the north coast of Trinidad.)

When heading for Tobago from Galera Point on Trinidad, it is imperative to avoid Drew Bank and Wasp Shoal. I am told by Jim Young and other divers who have dived extensively on both shoals that they are considerably shallower than the charts indicate. Jim claims that at low-water springs in May, June, and July (when the water is lower than

in the winter), the coral heads on Wasp Shoal actually break water. Yet the British Admiralty and DMA charts show a minimum depth over them of 12 feet. During the winter, when the wind is blowing hard, the entire area can be a seething mass of breakers. Under no circumstances should you allow yourself to get onto Drew Bank or Wasp Shoal; pass to windward or leeward of them, but do not cross them.

At this point, a discussion of the Tobago charts is in order. The new metric editions, 14 and 15, of DMA chart 24402, and the 14th edition of 24403, are definitely not nearly as accurate or useful as the charts they replaced. The soundings were switched from fathoms and feet to metric, many soundings were deleted, and the large-scale insert of Tyrrel's Bay was eliminated. Scrutiny of the new charts makes one wonder what is happening in Washington, as these latest charts supposedly were compiled from information in the earlier editions, yet they are full of discrepancies. How new editions of charts can be less accurate than old ones is beyond me. Both the British and American hydrographic offices insist continually that their charts are done by computers and that the chart information is exactly the same. However, in a couple of cases, we have taken two charts (one new and one old) and placed them on top of each other on a light table and have noted the discrepancies—which, I might add, often have been considerable.

In many instances, the conversion from fathoms to meters—which is still going on in both the British Admiralty and the American NOAA and DMA offices—has been a step backward, especially for the newest editions of charts for Antigua and Tobago.

In years gone by, as a yachtsman I complained bitterly about this problem, but I no longer do so—it just creates more demand for the Imray-Iolaire charts, which are accepted as the most accurate charts available for the Eastern Caribbean.

We have compiled Imray-Iolaire Chart B-4 (Tobago) from all sources available and have produced an edition that we believe to be completely accurate. And apparently it is, as none of my Trinidadian yachting friends have pointed out any inaccuracies in it.

The American and British charts are basically drawn from the British Admiralty surveys of 1864 and 1865, plus colonial surveys of 1920 and 1955; as such, they must be viewed cautiously. The Imray-Iolaire chart also is based on this information, but it has been updated with more recent observations and data.

The only point of entry is Scarborough, and foreign yachts must go into Scarborough even if they are coming from Trinidad.

SCARBOROUGH

(Chart 55; II B-4)

When approaching Scarborough, be very careful of the shoals in Rockly Bay to the west of Scarborough Harbor, which now has been well buoyed because of the ferry. (Bulldog Shoal can be particularly treacherous.)

When *Iolaire* visited Tobago in 1985, we had to anchor off Scarborough, which was not a particularly good anchorage, to say the least, as it was rocky and rolly. We had to tuck up in the corner, anchoring too close to other boats, in order to be out of the way of the ferry.

Now, however, the harbor has been rebuilt, and you no longer have to anchor outside the harbor. In the southeast corner of the harbor is a small basin for visiting yachts—a far cry from the old days when yachts were considered a pain in the neck. There is a berth here reserved strictly for yachts that are entering and clearing.

When entering the harbor, proceed with caution. Allegedly you'll find 10 feet of water in the yacht basin, but note that tides are more than two feet at springs in Tobago.

Once ashore, leave the dockyard and turn left; 600 to 800 yards to the west, just across the small river, you will find the Immigration office; you have to go back to town to clear Customs. I must say that in March 1985, the Customs officers were less than friendly. They insisted that we bring in our flare pistol from the boat and lock it up in the police armory. (What were we supposed to do if we had a problem and needed to fire a distress flare?) They also announced that we were allowed to go only to Milford Bay and Man of War Bay; we could not visit the other bays on the north side of the island because the authorities could not guarantee our safety. Very puzzling for an island whose chief salvation is tourism.

Scarborough is not one of the most scenic towns in the Eastern Caribbean. You can do your shopping in one of the three small supermarkets in the village, or go to a new, big Hi-Lo at the western end of the village, where you'll also find an ice plant (cube ice only, no blocks). There is an excellent open-air market in the same area. Water is free—when you can get alongside the dock after the ferry leaves. Fuel is strictly a case of jerry cans.

Scarborough is a town to visit, enter, and then depart as soon as possible. You'll have to return, though, to clear—another nuisance arranged by the island's officialdom! Often your yacht will be anchored off Crown Point (see below), just a short walk from the airport—where there are Customs and Immigration officials. However, they will not clear you. They will insist that you sail the boat back to Scarborough (a three-hour sail against wind and current) and anchor. Then the same officers you saw at the airport will drive to Scarborough and clear you! In my opinion, Tobago holds the Caribbean record for petty, obstructionist Customs and Immigration people.

The yacht *Phoenix* came through Tobago in December 1991 and reported that the attitude of the Customs and Immigration people had not changed. The crew ran into this same situation and said, "The hell with it!" They picked up their anchor and left without clearing.

In light of the above, I am reminded of the riddle, "Who are the three most dangerous people you could meet at an airport?" The answer? A Los Angeles mafia-type with an Uzi, a terrorist with Simex explosives, and a West Indian customs officer with a little bit of authority.

South Coast

Numerous small coves on Tobago's south coast can be visited by a small yacht drawing four or five feet and piloted by a good reef navigator. Like Anguilla, Tobago lies on a northeast-southwest axis, so that if the wind is in the southeast, most of the harbors on the south coast are uncomfortable or untenable, whereas those on the north coast are all right—and vice versa. This means, generally, that in the winter months, when the wind is from the north and the ground swell is prevalent, you should visit the south coast; in spring and summer, spend your time primarily on the north coast.

Interestingly, the original harbor and settlement on Tobago was at Pinfold Bay, behind Smith's Island on the south coast.

The anchorage behind Richmond Point, inside Richmond Island, might be worthwhile to visit to see the old Strong estate. Water for the estate's waterwheel was provided by an aqueduct more than a mile and a half long. It led back into the hills to various pools that were dammed up to provide water during the dry season.

184 Street's Cruising Guide to the Eastern Caribbean—Martinique to Trinidad

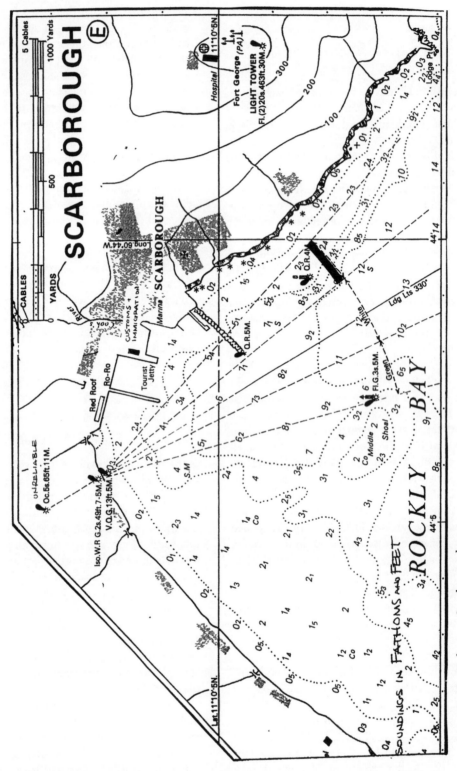

CHART 55 Tobago—Scarborough

Trinidad and Tobago

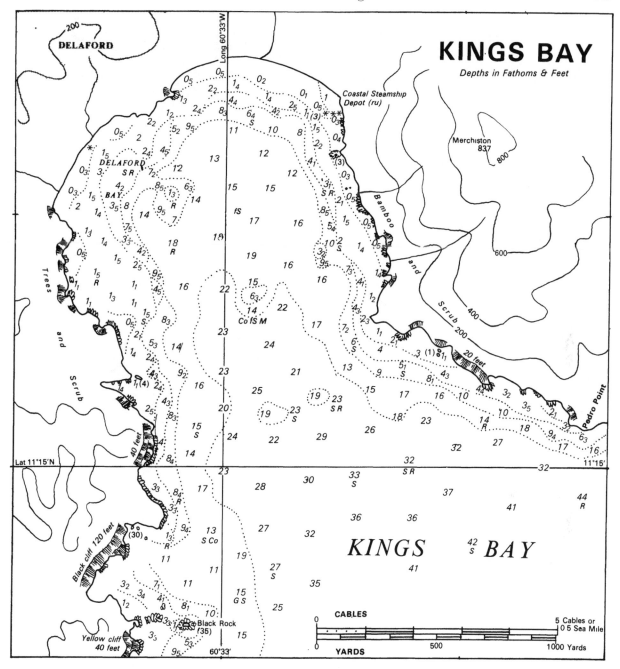

CHART 56 Kings Bay   Continuing harbor works in progress. Harbor will not Supply details, June 1992

KINGS BAY

(Chart 56; II B-4)

This is the first real anchorage on the southeast coast. It is described in the *British Admiralty Pilot* as the most secure anchorage in all of Tobago; the wind would have to go all the way to the south and blow hard to make it uncomfortable. The one problem is that the bay is very deep, so I strongly advise a bow anchor on the beach and a stern anchor holding you off.

The tourism industry in Tobago has a long way to go, and the hotels could use some upgrading, but the island has at least one outstanding feature from the yachtsman's standpoint: On every beach we visited along the coast of Tobago, we found little kiosks with bathrooms and showers. Kings Bay has

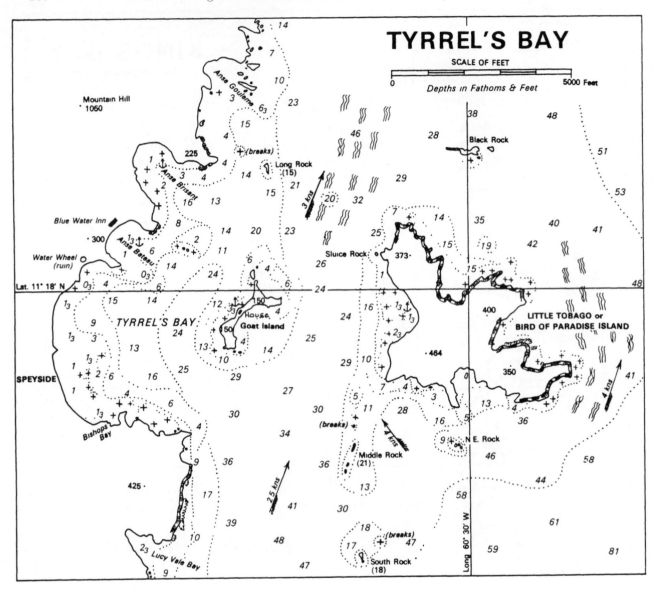

CHART 57   Tyrrel's Bay

such beach facilities, and also, after a short walk up the river, a lovely waterfall, which is featured on almost all Trinidad and Tobago postcards.

The south equatorial current that pours up against Tobago at the rate of three to four knots splits offshore of Pedro Point. One leg bends northward around Cape Gracias-a-Dios and in between Little Tobago Island and the mainland. The other branch swings west by Queens Island, then southwest along Richmond Island and down the south coast of Tobago. Note that in heavy weather, Great River Shoal off Goldsborough Bay is covered with breakers; give the shoal a very wide berth.

TYRREL'S BAY

(Chart 57; II B-4)

This area is extremely interesting, but you must be prepared for the very strong current that runs northward inside Little Tobago Island at a solid four knots and causes heavy tide rips and overfalls off the north end of Little Tobago. The best approach is from the south, between Middle Rock and the mainland, where you probably have a two-knot current under you. At this point, you have three anchorages from which to choose: in Anse Bateau off the Blue Water Inn; under the lee of Goat Island in Tyrrel's Bay; or, if you draw six feet or less and are a good reef navigator and conditions are perfect, inside the reef out of the tide in the small cove on the west side of Little Tobago.

Anse Bateau off the Blue Water Inn is easy to enter. Bear off and sail under Goat Island. Study the coastline with binoculars and you will spot a large waterwheel north of Speyside; sail north to the Blue Water Inn, then run downwind into the cove. This is strictly eyeball navigation; round up and anchor in 12 feet of water, completely out of the current.

Jim Young, who owns the Dive Shop down in Pigeon Point on the southwestern coast of Tobago, has a boat permanently stationed here and operates dive trips out of the Blue Water Inn. You can contact him via the hotel if you wish to make arrangements.

If you are anchored in Anse Bateau, northwest of Goat Island, it is worth taking a walk over to the next bay to see the ruins of a huge old undershot waterwheel. (Perhaps a hydraulic engineer can explain to me why one builds an undershot rather than an overshot wheel.) This is a magnificent piece of machinery built by W.A. Smith and Company, Glasgow, in 1871. Obviously, the plantation economy was still going strong long after the end of slavery in 1839; otherwise, who would have spent a huge amount of money to build canals, aqueducts, and a very expensive waterwheel to grind sugar? Historians who claim that sugar became unprofitable immediately after the slaves were freed apparently don't know that there is old sugar-making equipment scattered throughout the islands with dates showing that the equipment was installed from the 1870s through the 1890s.

GOAT ISLAND
(Chart 57; II B-4)

Under the lee of Goat Island, an anchorage can be had right off the large white house. It is very deep water and the beach is steep-to; you will have to drop a stern anchor, power on into the beach, and literally jump from the bow of the boat onto the sand and bury your anchor. Most of the time, the house is unoccupied, and I am told that the owners do not object to yachtsmen mooring bow-on to this beach. If yachtsmen behave themselves here, we probably will continue to be welcome; let's hope a few don't ruin it for everyone else.

LITTLE TOBAGO (BIRD OF PARADISE) ISLAND
(Chart 57; II B-4)

Little Tobago Island has long been of great interest to ornithologists because it used to be the only home in the Western Hemisphere of birds of paradise, which had been imported from an island off the coast of Borneo in the early twentieth century. The chap who imported them also installed a couple of caretakers on the island to protect the birds.

After the owner's death, the island was sold and resold, and now it is in the hands of the Trinidad and Tobago government. Apparently the birds of paradise on the island have died out completely. I am told that the last bird-watcher who came here looking for them spent six months on the island and never saw one. However, it is still a beautiful island and very much worth exploring.

When passing north of Tyrrel's Bay, favor the Long Rock side of the channel to avoid the heavy tide rip from overfalls off the northwest tip of Little Tobago. If you are heading north, I strongly advise passing outside of St. Giles (Melville) and Marble islands. Do not pass between those offlying islands and the mainland.

If by any chance you are approaching Tyrrel's Bay from the north (which I do not advise), remember that you will be bucking a four-knot current if you go south between Goat Island and the mainland. I strongly suggest that you not try it unless you have an engine, as well as a boat capable of doing six knots over the bottom. We did succeed in getting through with *Iolaire,* but the experience put more than a few gray hairs in my beard. I urge that you pass fairly close to Long Rock to avoid the above-mentioned tide rip, and then run between Goat Island and the rocks to the west. Run in and anchor off the Blue Water Inn.

Coming from the north and trying to anchor behind Little Tobago Island is almost impossible under sail because the island throws a considerable wind shadow. If you have an engine, hug the Little Tobago shore, use eyeball navigation, and pass between the north end of the reef and the shore; feel your way south behind the reef to the anchorage. This should be attempted only by very good reef navigators with boats drawing six feet or less under ideal light conditions.

West and North Coasts

When heading west from Scarborough, pass south of Bulldog Shoal off Rockly Bay, now well buoyed. You'll encounter a strong west-flowing current, but off Crown Point, close inshore, there is a strong east-going eddy. Swing well clear of Crown Point and anchor at the south end of the beach between Pigeon Point and Sandy Point. Off the north end of the beach, you will see signs for the cable that carries power to Tobago from Trinidad.

Anchor fairly far offshore here, as the fishermen shoot their nets early in the morning. Incidentally, any time you are anchored in the vicinity of fishermen shooting their nets, do not use a Herreshoff anchor, as the fluke sticking out of the bottom is bound to catch a net. Instead, anchor with a Danforth, Bruce, or plow anchor; then the net can drag across the top of your anchor and anchor line with a fair chance of not fouling.

In Milford Bay, anchor bow-and-stern; otherwise, when the wind dies, the current will swing you beam-to-wind and you will rock and roll all night. Milford Bay is open to the ground swell, which you can encounter anytime from October to mid-March, and occasionally through mid-April or early May.

Ashore, you will find the beach crowded on the weekends. Glass-bottomed excursion boats anchored off the beach will take you for a tour of Buccoo Reef. Roadside shops sell beer, *roti*, hamburgers, and so on. Three large hotels cater to various budgets. There are cars for rent, and it's a good idea to hire one and do a tour of the island, as we did; we put a big icebox in the back, loaded it with beer and wine and sandwich fixings, and drove off.

At the north end of the beach is Jim Young's Dive Shop. Jim is an experienced diver with an interesting heritage—he is part Chinese, part Carib Indian. He will be most happy to take you down near Buccoo Reef or anywhere else along the north coast of Tobago. Your diving area, of course, will be determined by your experience.

BUCCOO REEF

(Chart 58; II B-4)

Despite what is shown on the 14th edition of the DMA chart, Buccoo Reef forms an excellent harbor. You can enter through the northernmost of the two entrances. Twenty feet of water can be carried well inside the reefs, where it shoals rather rapidly to about eight feet. How far east you go to anchor depends on the time of year and your draft. When messing around in the Buccoo Reef area, remember that at spring tides there is roughly a three-foot rise and fall of tide.

Once inside the reef, if you head approximately 150° magnetic, you will reach halfway to Sheerbird Point; then eyeball and zigzag until you get to the

point, where you can anchor bow-and-stern off a white-sand beach. With care at high water, seven or eight feet can be carried all the way in to the inner lagoon. Once off Sheerbird Point or in the lagoon, you'll have approximately 20 feet of water. When threading your way through the shoals inside Buccoo Reef, you will see white flags staked out on various reefs—a privately maintained buoyage system.

On the east side of the bay inside Buccoo Reef is Nylon Pool. I don't know where it got its name, but its fame comes from the fact that it is about four feet deep and the water gets so heated up by the sun that this is just about the warmest water in the Caribbean.

Needless to say, the Buccoo Reef area provides extremely good snorkeling inside the reef for the inexperienced; outside, the reef drops off suddenly and provides good snorkeling and diving for the more experienced.

Behind Pigeon Point there is an "almost marina." I use this phrase because it seems that before independence in 1962, the swamp area was dredged out to build a large marina; then, just before they broke through, the newly independent government of Trinidad and Tobago decided that there should not be a marina in Tobago. This certainly hurt tourism severely. It is interesting to think about what would have happened had a large marina been built in Tobago in the early 1960s.

BUCCOO BAY

(Chart 58; II B-4)

Buccoo Bay has miles of white-sand beach, but it is strictly a May-to-October anchorage; the ground swell from the north makes it completely untenable in the winter. Basically, this is true for all of the bays on Tobago, except possibly Man of War Bay, on the north coast. When entering Buccoo Bay, favor the Buccoo Reef side of the bay. Using eyeball navigation, head south along the reef, then swing east in behind the shoals that extend west from Booby Point and anchor wherever you want.

MOUNT IRVINE BAY

(II B-4)

Anchorage is available in behind Rocky Point. This is an excellent, steep-to beach, with nothing much ashore; use eyeball navigation and anchor bow-and-stern.

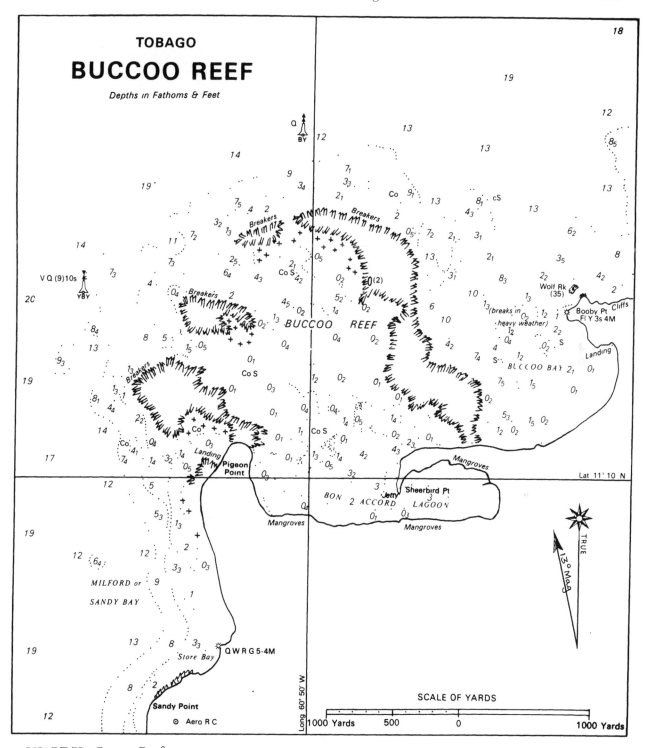

CHART 58   Buccoo Reef

PLYMOUTH
(Chart 59; II B-4)

Plymouth is reputedly Tobago's second largest town, but it looks more like a village. A small gun battery sited on Courland Point hardly fits its description as a fort, but it provides a good view of the harbor. The best anchorages are in the northeast part of the harbor. Watch out for the shoals extending southwest from Courland Point. The nice

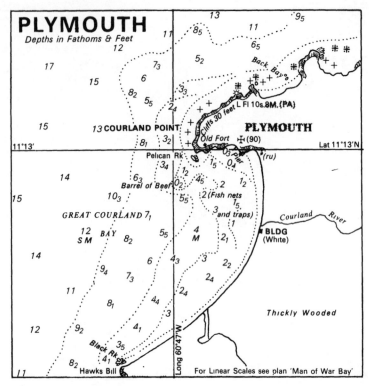

CHART 59   Plymouth

white-sand beach has a hotel on it. West of Hawks Bill there is possibly a small daytime anchorage in calm weather, right under the Trinidad and Tobago golf course, which has an excellent reputation.

CASTARA BAY

(II B-4)

This is a summer-only, bow-and-stern anchorage off the beach. Check immediately upon anchoring as to where the fishermen are likely to be shooting their nets. Shower and bathing facilities are ashore; there is a small village, but no charter boats.

ENGLISHMAN'S BAY

(II B-4)

Three streams run into Englishman's Bay. If you walk along the middle stream for about 10 minutes, you will come to a very nice waterfall that is great for showers and bathing. As with other bays along this coast, check with the fishermen upon anchoring to make sure you will not foul up their fishing.

PARLATUVIER BAY

(II B-4)

Because of the scale of the chart, it is impossible to show the very small shelf in this bay, where adventurous yachtsmen might anchor (bow-and-stern) in ideal conditions. Be wary of the reef on the north side of the bay. There's a beautiful white-sand beach, very little civilization, and excellent diving on both sides of the bay.

BLOODY BAY

(II B-4)

This bay is distinctive in that there is a white-sand beach in the northeast corner of the bay and a black-sand beach on the south side. We were told that during the wars between the British and the French in the late eighteenth and early nineteenth centuries, there was a naval battle off Bloody Bay. The bodies of those killed ended up on the beach of what they call Dead Mans Bay on the western side of the harbor; somehow or other, due to the current, all the blood got washed over to what is now called Bloody Bay. The chart shows a rather

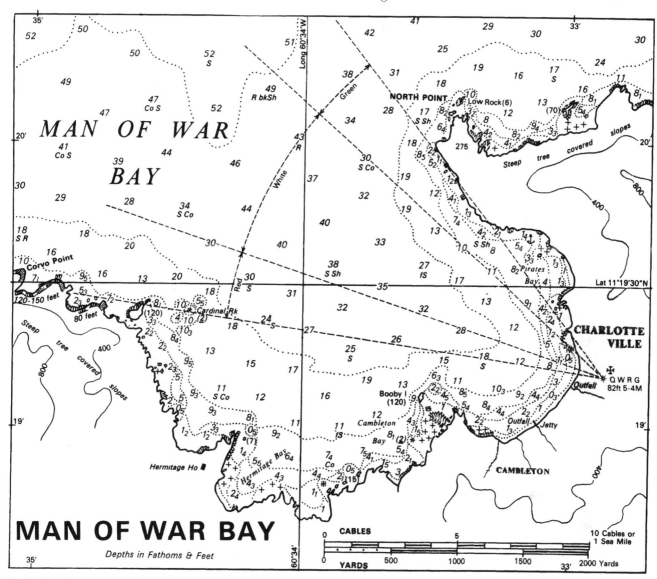

CHART 60   Man of War Bay

large river, but it was a mere trickle when we saw it in the dry season.

When sailing east from Bloody Bay to Man of War Bay, stay well clear of The Brothers and The Sisters, as both hazards appear to be improperly charted.

MAN OF WAR BAY

(Chart 60; II B-4)

This was a favorite stopping place for British ships in the West Indian fleet before World War II. Life was more relaxed then, and whenever a ship came in, parties would be organized by the various estate owners for the officers and crew. One of the high points of the pre-World War II social scene was the arrival of HMS *Hood*, later sunk by the *Bismarck* in a famous naval battle.

Today, Man of War Bay is a big, empty harbor with plenty of fishermen. The best anchorage is up in the northeast corner, tucked in under North Point, an area referred to locally as Pirates Bay. This is a bow-and-stern anchorage. Charlotteville is a small village with shops that carry the most essential supplies. You'll also find Jane Boyle, a scuba diver who runs a diving establishment from Turpin Cottages on the western side of the bay; she is easily spotted riding around on her small motorbike.

If you are going east from Man of War Bay, do

Street's Cruising Guide to the Eastern Caribbean—Martinique to Trinidad

not try to pass between St. Giles (Melville) Island and the mainland; go north of Marble Island to avoid the worst of the westward-setting currents.

In sum, Tobago is well worth a visit, especially during the summer months, when the winds are

TRINIDAD
(Chart XXXXX)

Chaguaramus marine development is happening so fast that even as I write today in the fall of 2000 things will be completely out of date by the time you arrive. Until 1992 there were virtually no facilities for anything larger than the high speed Pirogues so loved by the local Trinidadians. But in 1992, Donald Stollmeyer installed a travelift and started a yachting expansion that is incredible. It was ground zero in 1992; hurricane season in 1999 an estimated 2500 boats were in the Chaguaramus area hauled on long term storage, or shoe-horned into the various marinas and anchored into the very restricted anchoring area.

In the anchoring area, you should make sure you are inside the designated anchoring area, or you will be hit with a heavy fine. Anchoring within the designated anchoring area is difficult as the water is deep, approximately 30 feet, holding is not good—soft mud—and there is a strong reversing current. The facilities vary from very simple inexpensive dockage to Crews Inn, which is very upmarket for the wealthy yachtsman.

Any size yacht can be hauled. The largest at the commercial shipyards, medium sized yachts by the 100 ton travelifts at Peaks and Crews Inn, while most of the yards have 30 to 60 ton travelifts.

Anything the yachtsman needs can be found in Trinidad via Peaks Marine Supply or Budget Marine. If they don't have it in their extensive stocks, they can order it from the States and have it brought in Duty Free in relatively short order. However, it must be remembered that bring in anything into Trinidad Duty Free requires more than a bit of hassle.

There are a couple of riggers, the best known of which is Billy Wray who is also a recognized Marine Surveyor whose surveys are accepted by Lloyds.

There are a number of sail makers, and numerous shops who will make awnings, cushion covers and upholstery work.

There is a propeller shop that is incredible. To the point that even if you don't need your propeller repaired it is worth while going down and looking at the work they do. I have seen them take a propeller that looked like an old cauliflower and make it into a completely rebuilt, balanced propeller.

Mechanics, electronic specialists, machinists—you name it, Trinidad has it and can make it.

The one trouble is with the rapidly expanding yachting establishment there are some really fantastic workers, that can produce anything at a reasonable price. But, there are also a number of cowboys who claim to be able to produce the goods. But one discovers to your horror that it is all talk and no production.

lighter, the danger of northerly ground swells minimized, and the danger of hurricanes almost nonexistent. (There have been only two hurricanes there in recorded history.) Customs officials may be difficult, but the people are extremely friendly.

The YSATT (Yachting Services Association of Trinidad & Tobago) puts out a yearly directory which you should pick up immediately upon your arrival. This will give you a complete outline of all the services available.

One recommendation I would make would be that you do not undertake any business in Trinidad with people offering services who are not members of YSATT. If they are a member of YSATT they are likely to be good, and also if there should be a problem settling your bill or what ever, YSATT is very good at arbitrating between owners and the YSATT members. If the person you do business with is not a YSATT member it is extremely difficult to get a successful arbitration of a difficult bill.

In the Chaguaramus area one can find just about anything the mariner needs, there is not much reason to venture out of Chaguaramus unless to go to the next cove, to the Trinidad Tobago Yachting Association. A most friendly and hospitable club that runs yacht racing in Trinidad.

The town of the Port of Spain is interesting but I cannot deny the fact that, although the average Trinidadian is without doubt one of the nicest, most helpful, most accommodating persons in the world, there are a bunch of hooligans in Trinidad that create a crime problem that is one of the worst in the eastern Caribbean. Discuss any trips to town with people familiar with the area before undertaking it. Especially in the late afternoon or evening.

Carnival has been described in so many publications that I will not bother to describe it here. But, a tremendous number of yachties go to Trinidad for five days of happy madness. If so inclined go to Trinidad and enjoy the fun. The yachties organize all sorts of groups. Certainly if you stick with a group your chances of having problems during carnival are minimal.

Customs & Immigration are at Chaguaramus and it is a relatively simple procedure. Enter only during working hours as out of working hours as of the year 2000 the overtime fees were astronomical. If you arrive out of working hours, then check in when the office opens, you will still be charged over time because you arrived out of working hours - despite the fact that no one checked you in, you are still charged over time fees!!! A situation unique in Trinidad. Hopefully by the time you read this the situation will be changed, but I doubt it.

In Trinidad after the evening news on TV6 at 1900 Eric Mackey comes on—usually between 1930 and 1955 and gives a weather report which covers not only the lower end of the Eastern Caribbean but more important it covers Trinidad. This weather report is excellent as Eric is a Trinidad yachtsman who interprets the weather for Trinidad backed up with his own local knowledge. His average on accuracy is very high.

Gem Radio on 93.5 FM has a local forecast every morning at 07:30 with a yachting news bulletin on Wednesdays.

Epilogue

Nautical Publications has come out with a new set of Caribbean Charts about which I will make no comments other than as listed below:

Imray-Iolaire charts are not the cheapest Caribbean charts but they are the best value for money.

They are the ONLY charts that are a guide and chart in one as they have on the back sailing and harbour directions compiled by D.M. Street Jr. as a result of his 43 years cruising, exploring and writing about the eastern Caribbean.

1. They are the ONLY waterproof charts that can be used on deck and that can be folded and unfolded ad infinitum to any size you desire.

1. They are the ONLY charts that have been compiled by a mariner who knows the entire area intimately.

1. They are the ONLY charts that have ranges/transits to avoid rocks and shoals.

1. They are the ONLY charts that are regarded so much as standard that they are used by virtually all the bare boat companies and by the U.S. Coast Guard.

1. They are the ONLY charts that have the Way Points carefully placed clear of all navigational dangers.

1. They are available electronically in raster form from: Laser Plot and Live Chart.
   and in vector form from: CMAP & EURONAV.

1. They are the only charts for which you can obtain updates every six months. If every six months you order your updates you can keep your charts up to date for ever.

It is my fond hope that in the year 2101 that this guide will still be available with updates periodically added to the books to keep them current.

I have done the best I possibly could to update this guide to the beginning of the year 2001. For the year 2003 contact Imray and a supplement will be available. It is planned that a supplement will be issued for this guide every two years. Always available from Imray. The costs of these supplements will depend on how much work the author has to put in and how much the current costs are to Imray to produce and mail the supplements.

Bibliography

Cruising Guides

Buzby, V. M. *Virgin Island Sailing Directions.* 1952. Privately printed by the Coast Guard Auxiliary in the early 1950s.

Carey, Charles, and E. A. Raiwhold. *Virgin Anchoraging.* A superb collection of aerial photographs.

Chubb, Percy, III. *Cruising Guide to the Windward and Leeward Islands of the Eastern Caribbean.* 1961. Privately printed.

Eggleston, George Teeple. *Virgin Islands.* 1959; reprinted, Huntington, N.Y.: Krieger, 1974. Available at Palm Passage Bookstore, St. Thomas.

Eiman, William J. *St. Maarten/St. Martin Area Plus St. Kitts and Nevis Cruising Guide.* Copyright 1983 by Virgin Island Plus Yacht Charters, Inc. Also covers Anguilla, St. Barts, Saba, and Statia.

Forbes, Al. *Virgin Islands Cruising Guide.* Hollywood, Fla.: Dukane Press, 1970.

Kelly, Tom, and Jack Van Ost. *Yachtsman's Guide to the Virgin Islands.* 1968. Now Van Ost, John R., and Harry Kline. *Yachtsman's Guide to the Greater Antilles.* Coral Gables, Fla.: Tropic Isle, 1979.

Mitchell, Carleton. *Islands to Windward.* New York: Van Nostrand, 1948. Now out of print, this classic yarn of Mitchell's cruise from Trinidad to Nassau on board the *Carib* in 1946 is the first cruising guide written for the area.

Street, D. M., Jr. *Cruising Guide to the Virgin Islands.* 1963. Privately printed. No longer available.

———. *Yachting Guide to the Grenadines.* Hollywood, Fla.: Dukane Press, 1970.

———. *A Cruising Guide to the Lesser Antilles.* New York: Norton, 1964, 1974.

Stevens Yachts of Annapolis, *A Crusing Guide to the Windward Islands,* Annapolis, Md.: 1979. A picture and text guide.

Wilensky, Julius M. *Yachtsman's Guide to the Windward Islands.* 2nd ed. Stamford, Conn.: Wescott Cove, 1978.

General

Fenger, Frederic A. *The Cruise of the Diablesse.* New York: Yachting, Inc., [1926]. A description of cruising through the islands in 1915. Possibly back in print. If not, try the library. A truly great book on the Lesser Antilles.

———. *Alone in the Caribbean.* Belmont, Mass.: Wilmington Books, 1958. A description of cruising through the Islands in a decked canoe in 1911. Another great book on the Lesser Antilles.

Mitchell, Carleton. *Islands to Windward.* Washington, D.C.: National Geographic Society, 1967. A description of the author's second cruise through the islands in 1965 aboard the *Finisterre.*

Robinson, William. *Where the Tradewinds Blow.* New York: Charles Scribner's Sons, [1963]. A collection of stories about various cruises by the editor of *Yachting.*

History

Kay, Francis. *This—Is Grenada.* St. George's, Grenada: Carenage Press, [1971]. An excellent description of Grenada and a must for anyone who loves it.

Lewisjohn, Florence. *Divers Information on the Romantic History of St. Croix.* Hollywood, Fla.: Dukane Press, [1963?].

———. *Tales of Tortola and the British Virgin Islands.* Hollywood, Fla.: Dukane Press, 1966.

———. *St. Croix under Seven Flags.* Hollywood, Fla.: Dukane Press, 1970.

Mann, Zane B. *Fair Winds and Far Places*. Minneapolis: Dillon Press, 1978. Excellent account of a successful executive who chucks it all and runs away to the Lesser Antilles. An honest appraisal of the joys and sorrows involved. Required reading for anyone thinking of doing the same.

Morison, Samuel Eliot. *Admiral of the Ocean Sea*. Boston: Little, Brown, 1942. Superb biography of Columbus with vivid descriptions of the men, ships, islands, and sailing. Voluminous and interesting footnotes.

————. *Christopher Columbus, Mariner*. Boston: Little, Brown, 1955. A condensed version of *Admiral of the Ocean Sea*, and infinitely more readable.

O'Neill, Edward A. *Rape of the American Virgins*. New York: Praeger, 1972. A must for anyone who wishes to understand the problems of the U.S. Virgin Islands.

Thomas, G. C. H. *Ruler in Hiroona*. [Port of Spain], Trinidad, [1972]. Novel of a mythical island, but an all-too-apt description of the typical West Indian situation.

Waugh, Alec. *Island in the Sun*. New York: Farrar, Straus and Cudahy, [c. 1955].

Westlake, Donald E. *Under an English Heaven*. New York: Simon & Schuster, 1972. Provides valuable historical insight into island governments throughout the Lesser Antilles. A must for anyone who wants to understand the islands.

Humor

Wibberley, Leonard. *The Mouse That Roared*. Boston: Little, Brown. Side-splitting description of the invasion of Anguilla, with local island characters very thinly disguised.

Wouk, Herman. *Don't Stop the Carnival*. New York: Doubleday, 1965. A perfect description of St. Thomas in the late 1950s.

Flora and Fauna

Chaplin, C. G. *Fish Watching Guide*. New York: World.

Collins, James Bond. *Birds of the West Indies*. 2nd ed. Boston: Houghton-Mifflin, 1971.

Devas, Father Raymond. *Birds of Grenada, St. Vincent and the Grenadines*. Grenada: Carenage Press.

Groome, J. R. *A Natural History of the Island of Grenada*. Privately printed. Available at Sea Change Book Stores, St. George's, Grenada.

Hargreaves, Dorothy, and Bob Hargreaves. *Tropical Blossoms of the Caribbean*. Kailua, Hawaii: Hargreaves, 1960.

Mognotte, Sony. *Shelling and Beachcombing in the Southern Caribbean Waters*.

Murray, Dea. *Birds of the Virgin Islands*.

Randall, John E. *Caribbean Reef Fishes*. Neptune, N.J.: T.F.H., 1978.

Among the most readable books for those wishing to know about the Eastern Caribbean's colorful past are the novels and nonfiction works of Dudley Pope. His knowledge and research are impeccable. The following are highly recommended.

Dudley Pope: Nonfiction

The Black Ship. Philadelphia: Lippincott, 1964. The story of the worst single-ship mutiny in the Royal Navy. On board the *Hermione*, in 1797, between Hispaniola and Venezuela, the captain and all the officers were murdered.

The Buccaneer King. New York: Dodd, Mead, 1978. The first third of this biography of Sir Henry Morgan gives a wide-ranging introduction to the early days of the Eastern Caribbean.

Dudley Pope: Novels

Governor Ramage, R.N. New York: Simon & Schuster, 1973. Covers the U.S. Virgins and Culebra.

Ramage and the Freebooters. London: Weidenfeld & Nicolson, [1969]. (In the United States, *The Triton Brig*. New York: Pocket Books, 1978.) Covers Grenada and St. Lucia.

Ramage and the Rebels. Describes how the island of Curacao was handed over to the British—and captured by them when the Dutch changed their mind.

Ramage's Diamond. London: Fontana, 1977. Describes the capture by the British of Diamond Rock, off Fort-de-France, Martinique.

Ramage's Mutiny. London: Secker & Warburg, 1977. Set in English Harbour, Antigua, and then in Venezuela.

Ramage's Prize. New York: Simon & Schuster, 1975. Covers the Lesser and Greater Antilles.

Index

Abercromby Point, 179
Adam Island, 157, 158
Admiralty Bay, 4, 13, 14, 67, 88, 89–94
Anse à L'Ane, 27–28
Anse aux Epines (Prickly Bay), 7, 8, 141, 146,
    153–55
Anse Bateau, 186
Anse Bonaventure, 75
Anse Cayenne, 75
Anse Chastanet, 59
Anse Chaudière, 30
Anse Cochon, 59
Anse Coco, 40
Anse de Chemin, 94
Anse des Canaries, 59
Anse des Pitons, 61–62
Anse des Trois Rivières, 31
Anse du Ceron, 31
Anse du Four, 28, 30
Anse du Sans Souci, 35
Anse Goyeau (Guyac), L', 103–4
Anse la Raye, 59
Anse Mitan, 19, 21, 22, 24, 25–26, 27, 28, 47
Anse Noire, 28
Anse Rafale, 63
Anthony (Black) Rock, 10
Antigua, 7
Ashton, 120, 121
Aves Island, 7

Bacaye Harbour, 159
Baie de Fort de France, 23–28, 27
Baie de Mulets, 37
Baie de Saintpée, 42
Baie des Tourelles, 25
Baie du Carenage, 25
Baie du Trésor (Cul-de-Sac Tartane), 15, 34,
    42–44
Baliceaux, 4, 99
Baline Rocks, 4, 13, 114
Banc de la Rose, 42

Banc des Trois Cayes, 31
Banc du Fort St. Louis, 25
Banc du Gros Ilet, 15
Banc du Mileu, 31
Banc du Singe, 31
Banc Guillotine, 42
Banc Mitan, 44
Baradal, 4, 11, 110, 112, 113
Barbados, 68, 78–83, 120
Barrel of Beef, 164–65
Basseterre, 28
Battery Point, 63
Battowia, 67, 99
Bay à L'Eau (Watering Bay), 6, 11, 134
Bedford Point, 10, 165
Belmont Peak, 128
Belmont Shoal, 90
Bequia, 3, 4, 13–14, 67, 87, 88–97, 99, 101, 114
Bequia Channel, 4, 14
Bird of Paradise (Little Tobago) Island, 13, 186, 187
Black Bay, 7, 165
Black (Anthony) Rock, 10
Blanchisseuse, 179
Bloody Bay, 190–91
Blue Lagoon, 67, 72
Boca de Huevos, 173
Boca del Monos, 173, 179
Boca de Navios, 173
Boca Grande, 173
Bocas del Dragon, 7, 173
Bonaparte Rocks, 137
Booby Point, 188
Break Rock, 4, 11
Bridgetown Harbour (Carlisle Bay), 80–83
Buccament Bay, 75
Buccoo Reef, 182, 188

Calivigny Harbour, 158–59
Calivigny Island, 8, 157, 158
Calivigny Point, 7
Calliaqua, 67, 71–72

195

196 *Index*

Canouan Island, 4, 11, 13–14, 68, 101–6, 103, 109, 114
  East Coast, 104–6
  North Coast, 106
  South Coast, 104
Cape Gracias-a-Dios, 186
Cap Ferré, 34, 35, 44
Cap Salomon, 3, 14, 15, 23, 27, 28
Carlisle Bay (Bridgetown Harbour), 80–83
Carriacou, 6–7, 9–13, 109, 114, 119, 124, 127–39, 161
Case Pilote, 47
Castara Bay, 190
Castries, 3, 14, 49, 50, 52–53, 58, 63, 72, 80
Catholic Island, 4, 6, 11, 13, 117
Caye Brigantine, 40
Caye des Couillons (Idiots' Reef), 25
Caye Pinsonnelle, 41
Caye Rone, 40
Caye Sante-Luce, 31
Cayes du Sans Souci, 37
Cayes du Vauclin, 37
Chacachacare Light, 7
Chaguaramus Bay, 173
Channel Rocks, 4, 11, 13
Chapeau Carré Mountain, 132
Charlestown, Nevis, 28
Charlestown Bay, Canouan, 101, 103, 104
Charlotteville, 191
Chateaubelair, 68, 74–76
Chatham Bay, 121–23
Cheltenham, 97
Chemin Bay, 158
Chupara Bay, 179
Chupara Point, 179
Cistern Point, 10, 132, 161
Clarkes Court Bay, 156, 157
Clifton Harbour, 120–21, 124
Clinton Harbor, 121
Cohe du Lamentin, 27
Corbec Bay, 103
Corn Store Bay, 137
Cor Point, 104
Courland Point, 189
Craigston Point, 134
Crazy Corrigan's Crooked Channel, 123
Cross Hill, 63
Crown Point, 182
Cuevas Bay, La, 179
Cul-de-Sac des Anglais, 34, 35–36
Cul-de-Sac Ferré, 35, 37
Cul-de-Sac Frégate, 34, 35, 38
Cul-de-Sac Grenade, 35, 37
Cul-de-Sac Maci-Maci, 37
Cul-de-Sac Marin, 19, 27, 31–32, 33, 47
Cul-de-Sac Paquemar, 37
Cul-de-Sac Roseaux, 40
Cul-de-Sac Tartane (Baie du Trésor), 15, 34, 42–44

Cumana Bay, 173, 175–78
Cumberland Bay, 72–74

Dathan Shoal, 149
David Point (Tangle Angle), 6–7, 161, 165
Dead Mans Bay, 190
Deep-Water Harbour, 79, 80
Devil's Table, 14, 90
Diamond Island (Kick 'em Jenny), 6, 9, 139
Diamond Rock (Rocher du Diamant), 3, 14
Dominica, 15, 47, 49, 66
Dorsetshire Hill, 67
Dove Cay (L'Islot), 104
Dragon Bay, 169
Drew Bank, 182
Duvernette Island, 14, 67, 71

Egmont/Calivigny Harbour, 10
Englishman's Bay, 190
Esterre Bay, L', 129, 132

Fond Blanc, 15
Fort Charlotte, 67
Fort de France, 3, 14, 15, 19, 23–25, 26, 28, 30, 44–45, 47
Fort Hill, 121
Fort Jeudy Point, 10, 158
Fort Point (Point Peter), 14, 90
Fort St. Louis (Royal), 23, 25, 27
Fota, 4, 6, 11, 13, 126, 134
François, Le, 34, 38
Friendship Bay, 95
Friendship Hill, 11, 13, 104
Friendship Point, 104
Frigate Island, 4, 6, 10, 11, 119, 121, 137

Galera Point, 182
Gary Island, 158
Gellicaux Bay, 99
Glossy (Glass) Hill, 4, 6, 11, 13, 101
Glover Island, 8, 10, 153
Goat Island, 186–87
Goldsborough Bay, 186
Golfo de Paria, 7, 173
gommier races, 22, 23
Government House, St. Georges, 9
Grampuses (The Porpoises), 7, 8, 10, 155
Grand Anse, 8, 149
Grand Baleine Bay, 75, 76
Grand Bay, 6, 97, 99
Grand Col Point, 13, 115
Grand Cul-de-Sac Bay, 56–57
Grand de Coi, 4, 6, 11, 13, 87, 114, 119
Grande Anse d'Arlets, 28–30
Grande Anse Macabou, 35
Grande Caille Point, 50, 59
Grande Passe du Simon, 38
Grande Rivière, 179
Grande Rivière Bay, 179

Index

197

Great Bacolet Bay, 162
Great Bacolet Point, 164
Great River Shoal, 186
Green (Thompson) Island, 10, 121, 165
Grenada, 6–7, 8, 9–10, 80, 120, 140–69
    South Coast, 150–59
    Southeast Coast, 159–69
Grenadines, 3, 68, 87–139
    Northern Grenadines, 87–106
    Southern Grenadines, 109–39
Grenville, 10, 146, 163–65
Gros Islet, 53, 56
Gros Piton, 62
Guadeloupe,15
Gun (Rapid) Point, 6, 11, 13, 134

Halifax Harbor, 165–69
Hardy Bay, 8, 10, 153
Harvey Vale (Tyrell) Bay, 6, 9, 10, 127–29
Havre du Robert, 41
Hawks Bill, 190
Hermitage Point, 6
High North (Mount St. Louis), 4, 6, 11, 13, 113, 114
Hillsborough, 4, 10, 11, 129–34
Hog Island, 7, 156, 157
Horseshoe Reef, 110

Idiots' Reef (Caye des Couillons), 25
Ile de Caille, 10, 137
Ile de Ronde, 6, 9, 137–39
Iles de la Petite Terre, 15
Ilet à l'Eau, 41
Ilet Anonyme (Aubert), 38
Ilet à Ramiers, 28
Ilet Bouchard, 40
Ilet Cabrit, 34, 35, 80
Ilet de la Grotte, 41
Ilet de la Rose, 41
Ilet de Ramville, 34, 41
Ilet de Ronde, 87
Ilet des Chardons, 41
Ilet Hardy, 35
Ilet Lézards, 35
Ilet Long, 38, 40
Ilet St. Aubin, 44, 46
Ilet Tartane, 44
Ilet Thiery, 38, 40
Ilet Toisroux, 37
Ilet Vigne, 40
Isla Pirata, 63
Isle Quatre, 13, 95
Islette, L', 179
Islot, L' (Dove Cay), 104

Jack a Dan, 4, 6, 10, 11, 134
Jamesby, 4, 11
Jew Bay, 134
Johnson Point, 67, 75
Jondell Cays, 117

Kendeance Point, 134
Kick 'em Jenny (Diamond Island), 6, 9, 139
Kings Bay, 185–86
Kingstown, 4, 14, 66, 67, 68, 71

Laborie, 62–63
Large Island, 137
Lascar Cove, 161
Layou Bay, 75
Levera Island (Sugar Loaf), 9, 10, 165
Little Bay, 104
Little Carenage Bay, 11
Little Mushroom Island, 137
Little Requin River, 162
Little Tobago (Bird of Paradise) Island, 13, 186, 187
Lobster Point, 159
London Bridge, 139
Long (Quarantine) Point, 8, 9, 150
Long Point Shoal, 7, 9
Long Rock, 187
Lookout Point, 10
Loriston Point, 132
Loup Bordelais, 34
Loup Garou, 41
Lower Bay, 94
Luffing Channel, 165

Mabouya Island, 10, 132
Mace (True Blue) Point, 153
Machapure Rock, 179
McIntosh Point, 132
Maho Bay, 106
Manchioneel Bay, 137
Man of War Bay, 188, 191–92
Maracas Bay, 179
Maravaca (Saut d'Eau) Island, 179
Marble Island, 187, 192
Maria Island, 63
Marigot Bay, 50, 52, 53
Marigot du Diamant, 31
Marigot Harbour, 58–59
Marin, 32
Marina du Pointe du Bout, 19, 21, 24, 26–27
Marquis Island, 162
Marquis Point, 10, 159, 161
Martinique, 3, 7, 14–15, 19–49, 53, 54, 59, 80, 104,
    110, 120, 182
    East coast, 33–44
    North coast, 44–46
    South coast, 30–33
    Southwest coast, 28–30
    West coast, 46–47
Matelot Bay, 179
Mayreau, 4, 6, 11, 13, 110, 113, 115–17
Medicine Point, 179
Melville (St. Giles) Island, 187, 192
Menere Point, 10, 162
Middle Hill, 4
Middle Rock, 186

198 *Index*

Milford Bay, 188
Molinière Point, 7, 169
Mona Island, 47
Montezuma Shoal, 4, 87, 97, 99, 114
Mont Pelée, 20
Moorings, The, 10
Mopion, 4, 6, 11, 13, 119, 123
Morne Belle Vue, 63
Morne Ronde, 75
Morne Rouge Bay, 8, 150
Mouillage de Sainte Anne, 32–33
Mouillage des Flamands, 23
Mouillage du François, 40
Mount D'Or, 132
Mount Hartman Bay (Secret Harbour), 7, 10, 141, 155–57, 161
Mount Irvine Bay, 188
Mount St. Louis (High North), 4, 6, 11, 13, 113, 114
Mount Taboi, 4, 11, 121
Mustique, 4, 97–99, 100, 101, 115, 119

Necker Island Passage, 7
Needham Point, 79, 80
Nens Bay, 103
Nevis, 28, 53
North Piton, 61
North Point, 191
Nylon Pool, 188

One Tree Rock, 9, 129, 137

Paget Farm, 88, 94, 99
Palm (Prune) Island, 4, 6, 11, 13, 109, 113, 114, 115, 117–20, 121, 124
Parlatuvier Bay, 190
Passe de Caye Mitan, 40
Passe du Sans Souci, 37, 38
Passe du Vauclin, 34, 35
Passe Sud du Vauclin, 34
Pedro Point, 186
Petit Bateau, 4, 11, 13, 110, 112, 113, 114
Petit Bordel, 75
Petit Calivigny, 157
Petit Canouan, 100, 101
Petit Carenage Bay, 134
Petite Anse d'Arlets, 30, 31
Petite Anse du Diamant, 30
Petite Caye, 40
Petite Grenade, 37
Petit Martinique, 4, 6, 11, 41, 109, 123, 124, 126, 134
Petit Mustique, 100
Petit Nevis, 13, 95
Petit Piton, 60
Petit Rameau, 4, 11, 13, 110, 112, 113, 114
Petit St. Vincent, 4–6, 11, 13, 99, 109, 114, 115, 117, 119, 120, 123, 124–26, 127, 134
Petit Tabac, 4, 11, 110
Petit Tobago, 4, 6, 11, 126

Petit Trou, 161
Pigeon Island, 13, 14, 53–56, 95
Pigeon Point, 187, 188
Pinese, 4, 6, 11, 13, 119, 123
Pinfold Bay, 183
Pinnacle, 4, 11, 121, 126
Pirates Bay, 191
Pitons, 3, 4, 50, 61, 63
Plymouth, 189–90
Pointe Baham, 37
Pointe Borgnesse, 31
Pointe Caracoli, 34, 42, 44
Pointe Cerisier, 38
Pointe d'Alet, 28
Pointe de la Rose, 40, 41–42
Pointe de l'Etang, 44
Pointe des Nègres, 26, 47
Pointe des Salines, 34
Pointe du Diamant, 3, 31
Pointe du Marigot, 31
Pointe du Marin, 31, 32
Pointe Dunkerque, 35
Pointe du Petit Trou, 161
Pointe du Sable Blanc, 42
Pointe Fort, 41
Point Egmont, 158
Pointe Hyacinthe, 42
Pointe Royale, 42
Pointe Simon, 22
Pointe Ste. Marthe, 47
Pointe Zombi, 40
Point Peter (Fort Point), 14, 90
Point Sable Bay, 63
Point Salines, 7, 8, 9, 10, 141, 150, 153, 157, 161
Porpoises, The (Grampuses), 7, 8, 10, 155
Port Elizabeth, 14, 95
Port of Spain, 7, 173, 175
Presqu'île de la Caravelle, 15, 34, 44
Prickly Bay (Anse aux Epines), 7, 8, 141, 146, 153–55
Prickly Point, 8, 9, 156, 158
Princess Margaret (Tony Gibbon) Beach, 94
Prune Island, *see* Palm Island

Quarantine (Long) Point, 8, 9, 150
Queens Island, 186
Questelles Bay, 75

Rachette Point, 60, 61
Rade de St. Pierre, 47
Rameau Bay, 103, 104
Rapid (Gun) Point, 6, 11, 13, 134
Red Island, 4, 6, 11, 13, 120, 121
Requin Bay, 161–62
Richmond Island, 183, 186
Richmond Peak, 67
Richmond Point, 183
River Madame, 20–21, 22, 24
Rivière Pilote, 31

Index

Robert, Le, 34, 37
Rocher de la Grotte, 41
Rocher du Diamant (Diamond Rock), 3, 14
Rocky Point, 157, 188
Rodney Bay, 50, 52, 53–56
Ross Point, 149, 150

Saga Cove, 157
Sagesse, La, 10, 159–61
Sail Rock, 4, 6, 11, 134
Sainte Anne, 30, 32, 34–35, 182
Saline Bay, 4, 11, 13, 115
Saline Island, 9, 128, 134
Salt Whistle Bay, 115
Sandy Island, 10, 129, 132, 165
Sandy Point, 188
Saut d'Eau (Maravaca) Island, 179
Sauteurs, 9
Savane, 19, 23, 24, 25, 27, 28, 47
Savan Island, 100
Scarborough, 183
Scotts Head, 15
Secret Harbour (Mount Hartman Bay), 7, 10, 141, 155–57, 161
Shark Bay, 99
Sheerbirds Point, 188
Sion Hill, 67
Sisters, The, 9, 139
Smith's Island, 183
Soufrière, 50, 52, 60–61, 62
South Glossy (Glassy) Bay, 103, 104
Speyside, 187
Spice Island, 153–55
St. Croix, 7
St. Croix Roads, 53
St. David's Harbour, 159
St. David's Point, 159
St. Georges, 7, 9–10, 141, 144, 145, 146–49, 150, 153, 162, 165, 169
St. Giles (Melville) Island, 187, 192
St. Kitts, 28
St. Lucia, 3–4, 7, 14–15, 34, 49–64, 66, 67, 72, 80, 120
St. Pierre, 19, 47–48
St. Thomas, 7, 8
St. Vincent, 3–6, 14, 49, 59, 63, 66–76, 78, 87, 90, 101, 109, 114
    West coast, 72–74
Stevens Beach, 157
Store Bay, 182
Sugar Loaf (Levera Island), 9, 10, 156

Table au Diable, 44
Taffia Hill, 4, 11, 13, 101, 103, 104
Tangle Angle (David Point), 6–7, 161, 165
Tante Bay, La, 162
Tantes, Les, 139
Tara Island, 155–56
Tartane, 44
Telescope Point, 10, 164
Thompson (Green) Island, 10, 121, 165
Tobago, 171–72, 173, 179, 181–92
    South Coast, 183–87
    West and North Coasts, 187–92
Tobago Cays, 4, 11, 13, 87, 109–15, 120, 169
Toco, 179
Tony Gibbon (Princess Margaret) Beach, 94
Tortola, 55, 56
Trinidad, 7, 140, 171–80, 181, 182
    North Coast, 178–79
Trinité, La, 19, 34, 41, 44–46
Trois Ilets, 26, 27
True Blue Bay, 153
True Blue (Mace) Point, 153
Tyrell (Harvey Vale) Bay, 6, 9, 10, 127–29
Tyrico Bay, 179
Tyrrel's Bay, 182, 186–87

Union Island, 4, 6, 10–11, 13, 87, 104, 115, 117, 119, 120, 121, 124
Union Island Harbor, 115

Vauclin, 34, 37
Vieux Fort, 49, 50
Vieux Fort Bay, 63
Vigie Cove, 52
Vigie Point, 50
Village Cay Marina, 55

Wallibou, 75
Wallilabou Bay, 68, 74
Wash Rocks, 14, 90
Wasp Shoal, 182
Watering Bay (Bay à L'Eau), 6, 11, 134
West Cay, 4, 13, 90
Westerhall Bay, 159
Westerhall Point, 10, 157, 158, 159
Whale Bay, 137
White Island, 128, 134–37
Windward Side, Carriacou, 4, 6, 11
Worlds End Reef, 4, 11, 110

Young Island, 4, 14, 67, 70–71, 72

NOTES

AUTHORS GUILD BACKINPRINT.COM EDITIONS are fiction and nonfiction works that were originally brought to the reading public by established United States publishers but have fallen out of print. The economics of traditional publishing methods force tens of thousands of works out of print each year, eventually claiming many, if not most, award-winning and one-time best-selling titles. With improvements in print-on-demand technology, authors and their estates, in cooperation with the Authors Guild, are making some of these works available again to readers in quality paperback editions. Authors Guild Backinprint.com Editions may be found at nearly all online bookstores and are also available from traditional booksellers. For further information or to purchase any Backinprint.com title please visit www.backinprint.com.

Except as noted on their copyright pages, Authors Guild Backinprint.com Editions are presented in their original form. Some authors have chosen to revise or update their works with new information. The Authors Guild is not the editor or publisher of these works and is not responsible for any of the content of these editions.

THE AUTHORS GUILD is the nation's largest society of published book authors. Since 1912 it has been the leading writers' advocate for fair compensation, effective copyright protection, and free expression. Further information is available at www.authorsguild.org.

Please direct inquiries about the Authors Guild and Backinprint.com Editions to the Authors Guild offices in New York City, or e-mail staff@backinprint.com.

Printed in Great Britain
by Amazon.co.uk, Ltd.,
Marston Gate.